# American Metropolis

Mexico City was America's largest city in the seventeenth century – a genuine metropolis. In this deeply researched book, Tatiana Seijas reveals a rich tapestry of stories about essential workers who remade and transformed the city during this period. Her narrative style carries readers to a unique place and time with residents from around the world who sold food, facilitated transportation, provided care, and valued the city's silver. Free and enslaved people from Africa and Asia, immigrants, and Native Americans pursued opportunities in a wealthy, yet deeply unequal environment, where working people claimed parts of the city for themselves. They carved out spaces to create new businesses and protect their livelihoods, altering the cityscape itself in the process. *American Metropolis* brings Mexico City to life from the perspective of the working people who transformed this early modern metropolis.

Tatiana Seijas is Associate Professor of History at Rutgers University. She is the author of *Asian Slaves in Colonial Mexico: From Chinos to Indians* and coeditor of *As If She Were Free: A Collective Biography of Women and Emancipation in the Americas.*

# American Metropolis

## The Making of Mexico City

**TATIANA SEIJAS**

*Rutgers University*

CAMBRIDGE
UNIVERSITY PRESS

CAMBRIDGE
UNIVERSITY PRESS

Shaftesbury Road, Cambridge CB2 8EA, United Kingdom

One Liberty Plaza, 20th Floor, New York, NY 10006, USA

477 Williamstown Road, Port Melbourne, VIC 3207, Australia

314–321, 3rd Floor, Plot 3, Splendor Forum, Jasola District Centre, New Delhi – 110025, India

103 Penang Road, #05–06/07, Visioncrest Commercial, Singapore 238467

Cambridge University Press is part of Cambridge University Press & Assessment, a department of the University of Cambridge.

We share the University's mission to contribute to society through the pursuit of education, learning and research at the highest international levels of excellence.

www.cambridge.org
Information on this title: www.cambridge.org/9781009692779

DOI: 10.1017/9781009692809

First published 2026

A catalogue record for this publication is available from the British Library

A Cataloging-in-Publication data record for this book is available from the Library of Congress

ISBN 978-1-009-69277-9 Hardback

Cambridge University Press & Assessment has no responsibility for the persistence or accuracy of URLs for external or third-party internet websites referred to in this publication and does not guarantee that any content on such websites is, or will remain, accurate or appropriate.

For EU product safety concerns, contact us at Calle de José Abascal, 56, 1°, 28003 Madrid, Spain, or email eugpsr@cambridge.org

*Para mi mamá, María del Pilar Alicia Parra Cabrera.*

# Contents

# Contents

*The plates will be found between pages 97 and 98.*

# Color Plates and Figures

## COLOR PLATES

## FIGURES

# Acknowledgments

Books have histories. This one involved people who helped me think, research, write, research, rewrite, and rewrite again. Thank you.

*American Metropolis* began as an idea in Spring 2016 when I was at the National Humanities Center. A fellow asked for book recommendations on the history of Mexico City, and I shared my favorite. I began a bibliography.

Fast forward to Fall 2018 when I was at the Newberry Library, which, like the Humanities Center, gifted me with time and sources. I had been writing another book for years, and it was time for a change; I paused the writing, if not the researching, and reoriented my attention to a familiar place and time. I wrote the introduction to a book framed as a global history of Mexico City. Keelin Burke and Brad Hunt organized a workshop with fellows, and they all gave me feedback, including Jodi Bilinkoff, pushing me to define my terms, explain the periodization, distinguish my historiographical contributions, assert my claim about the significance of showing what was possible in a diverse city, and "write with joy" – I wrote that down in my notes. Thank you.

I continued writing, and in Spring 2019, Steve Pincus at the University of Chicago invited me to share a work in progress. Once again, I had the privilege of sharing my ideas with scholars who encouraged me and confirmed that readers would be interested in reading about my wondrous city. I can close my eyes and see everyone who was in the room. Thank you for being there, for joining me in conversations and inspiring me to be Braudelian in my reconstruction of space, and to pay attention to upward and downward mobility, think comparatively, and, most importantly, to keep writing. Thank you.

Months passed, and friends and colleagues read drafts and gave me written feedback, including Gary L. Dunbar, Toby Green, Robert Lockhart, and Camila Townsend. Conversations with Atzin Bahena Pérez, Gibran Bautista y Lugo, Amber Brian, Rachel Devlin, Roquinaldo Ferreira, Kris Lane, Mark Lentz, Matthew Restall, Stuart M. McManus, Stuart B. Schwartz (my forever advisor), Pablo Miguel Sierra Silva, and Amara Solari helped me think about what type of book I wanted to write. I am grateful.

Edward Alex Killough has shared ideas, heartened me, and read drafts since this early stage. Cheers.

Attendees of the What is a legal archive? workshop (part of the American Society of Legal Historians conference in November 2019) encouraged me to embrace a narrative style. Thank you Julia Stephens for saying that there is a place for stories in legal history.

Participants in the conference "Archival Lives," organized by Adriana Chira at Emory University in December 2019, helped me clarify my arguments about coachmen operating in a context that afforded economic possibilities.

I was writing when the COVID pandemic hit my home city – New York City. The streets emptied; everyone was scared. I was awed by hospital workers and so very grateful for the people who sold me food at the supermarkets and kept the subway running. Neighbors in Brooklyn put up signs thanking nurses and doctors. What would I do, I wondered, without all these people? I was obviously not the only one; the term essential workers appeared in *The New York Times*. In retrospect, I see that this experience formalized what I intended to do: to write the history of people who did this hard work in the past.

At this point, I had the privilege of being a fellow at the William P. Clements Center for Southwest Studies at Southern Methodist University. I moved to Dallas for the 2020–2021 academic year, where Ruth Ann Elmore, Neil Foley, and Andrew R. Graybill welcomed me and encouraged my work. It was a joy to be at SMU. I had an office with a view and access to one of the best and underutilized university libraries for Mexican history in the United States. Librarians from the Bridwell, DeGolyer, Fondren, and Hamon collections helped me continue researching my other monograph on New Mexico and write this one. Adam Jasienski gave me fellowship, shared my enthusiasm for the seventeenth century, and read and commented on the first draft of the manuscript. Martin A. Nesvig read that draft as well as subsequent iterations – thank you.

Linda Arnold, my archival guru, answered endless questions. Thank you for helping me find historical actors in the archives of Mexico City.

Colleagues and friends read chapters and gave me feedback that helped me ask different questions and make new arguments.

Attendees of the New York City Latin American History Workshop in November 2020 read the chapter on provisions and raised insightful questions about free trade in the context of market regulations and the role of consumers in shaping market dynamics, among other topics. Thank you for encouraging me to find the answers.

Attendees of the Atlantic History Workshop at NYU in January 2022 read the chapter on money and gave me invaluable suggestions, including centering my analysis of value vis-à-vis human beings, underlining the endurance of the Nahua monetized economy, and considering counterfeiting. Seth Koven generously read this chapter as well, offering comments that helped me center my historical actors.

Attendees of the Global Philippine Studies Forum hosted by NYU in February 2022 read the chapter on barbers; thank you Erica Field, Leo Garofalo, Kristie Flannery, and Marcella McGee Hayes for giving me written comments.

Attendees of the Seminar on the History of Early America at Providence College in October 2022 read a revised introduction, and we agreed that it is the most important section of any book. Thank you to Edward E. Andrews, Elise Bartosik-Vélez, Patrick H. Breen, and David Orique for giving me written feedback that helped me rewrite it again.

In January 2023, I decided to ignore the first draft of the book and write the chapters from scratch. The first draft read like a thesis, and I wanted to articulate a different history, so I set it aside. The same thing happened while writing my first monograph, and I am now grateful for that decision. I wrote this new manuscript at the Vartan Gregorian Center for Research in the Humanities at the New York Public Library. My thanks for the space and to the librarians. I am proud to be among the authors of Books Made at the NYPL.

James Woodard and Marc A. Hertzman read the introduction in February 2023, and their thoughtful feedback encouraged me to continue writing a new book.

Attendees of the *Slavery, Racialization, and Gender Dialogue*, part of the Sawyer Seminar: Global Slaveries, Fugitivity, and the Afterlives of Unfreedom at Indiana University, organized by Olimpia E. Rosenthal and Pedro Machado, in October 2023, helped me think through Chapter 2. Thank you Amrita Chakrbarti Myers for the written comments.

That same October, I shared the book as a lecture at the John Carter Brown Library, one of my favorite places, and questions from the audience pressed me to articulate some of my historical claims more forcefully. Thank you José Montelongo and Karin Wulf for the invitation.

In the summer of 2024, I walked across Mexico City, some five hours a day for two weeks. The streets are longer and the squares larger than they appear on the maps that helped me locate historical actors. It takes ten minutes to walk around the Main Square, the *Plaza de la Constitución*. I met working people who are doing the same tasks as their predecessors. Barbers from Haiti have stands on *Avenida México-Tenochtitlán*. Carters pushing dollies stacked with boxes sprint down *Calle Mesones*. I bought fresh fruit juice from vendors at street corners. I remembered stories about their counterparts narrated in the following chapters, who, like today, are the hum and drive of the city.

My publisher Cecelia A. Cancellaro came to my rescue in October 2024. Thank you for being kind and expressing interest in my work. My thanks to David Greenberg for helping me at this juncture as well.

Five generous scholars wrote reader reports. Thank you for your time and suggestions.

In January 2025, I asked Christopher Heaney, Andrew Konove, Jacqueline Ly, Stuart B. Schwartz, and Max J. Pfeffer to read the introduction, the umpteenth version, and I am thankful for their suggestions. Konove – thank you for commenting on Chapter 4 as well, and for years of sharing documents and understanding my fascination with Mexico City. Ayesha Ramachandran and Louise Walker have been my dear friends and intellectual interlocutors since graduate school. I am indebted for the last push and comments on the introduction and conclusion.

Attendees of the Global History Seminar at Yale University joined this final stretch. Thank you Marcela Echeverri for inviting me. Lauren Benton confirmed my centering of work by articulating the idea that this book is about labor's metropolis. Thank you Marc Eagle, Valerie Hansen, and Oren Okhovat for the written feedback. Hansen has guided and helped me write more clearly since graduate school.

That is the end of this history – the book is done. But I have more thank-yous and recognitions.

I have had the privilege of being on the faculty of two great history departments while writing this book. A subvention award from the Rutgers University Research Council supported its publication. I am grateful for my colleagues at Pennsylvania State University and Rutgers, among them Matthew Restall and Camila Townsend, who have encouraged me for many years.

Thank you Jacqueline Ly for indexing this book.

I love seeing history. Thank you Matilde Grimaldi for the maps and renderings. The following individuals went out of their way to help me acquire images for publication: Lizzeth Armenta (Museo Vizcaínas); Mathias Böhm (Österreichische Nationalbibliothek); Felipa Díaz (Museo Arqueológico Nacional de España); Kim Nusco, Donna Dorvick, and Pedro Germano Leal (John Carter Brown Library); Ana María Palacio (Museo de América); and Tania Vargas (Museo Franz Mayer).

My family is the center of my world. My parents María del Pilar Alicia Parra Cabrera and Max J. Pfeffer sustain and inspire me, so do my brothers Ángel Allende Parra and Daniel Fermín Pfeffer, and my aunt Elvira Parra Cabrera. Tías, tíos, primas, primos, sobrinas, sobrinos: los quiero mucho.

I am a very fortunate person.

# Note on Orthography and Measures

*American Metropolis* draws from sources in various languages, but mainly Spanish – the lingua franca in Mexico City. It was the language of the royal government and spoken by most residents. Nahua residents used their own language for their own government affairs, yet they too understood Spanish to varying degrees, especially as the century wore on. Residents from other nations had to adopt Spanish as well. Writing this rendering of their history in English required orthographical choices in terms of place names, people's names, and untranslatable words.

All place names are in English. But the Spanish names are in the notes at first mention to orient readers familiar with the locations. Silversmiths had their shops along Saint Francis Street rather than *Calle de San Francisco*, for example. There are places, however, that have no true equivalent, such as the city's public park, the *Alameda* – a name that means park, so it reads Alameda in the text.

Residents' first and last names follow the modern spelling for consistency, including diacritical marks. The Spanish last name García, for example, was not accented in the seventeenth century and had various spellings, including Garçia; it is spelled here according to modern conventions. The same is true for Portuguese and other European language last names. The spellings also vary in the documentation in terms of pronouns and prepositions. For example, people used the preposition from (*de*) in their names, such as Joseph de Tobar, in some instances but excluded it on other occasions. Someone might say their name was María de la Cruz, and the scribes would render it Maria Crus – a practice that requires careful investigation to ascertain if documents are related to the same person. Due to this variance and for clarity, the preposition is omitted in the text, rendering their names José Tovar and María Cruz. The original orthography is sometimes noted for archival identification. African, Asian, and Indigenous names and ethnonyms are in the original. Scribes noted the first and last names of free residents; enslaved people, however, often appear under their first names only. Slaveowners gave them these names; their family names are lost in the historical record unless noted in the text. Narrating the experiences of historical actors requires referencing them repeatedly, done here by last name after the first mention, unless the person appeared in the records with one name only.

# Introduction

Bartolomé Dias was living in Mexico City in March 1629.[1] He sold fine *sinabafa* cotton in the Main Square from an assigned spot where he stacked bolts of cloth on a wooden box. Dias called out to passersby. "Touch this material," he would say, "see how soft it is, and I will give you a good price, at whatever length you need." He would point to his ruler and hold up the scissors. The plausible scene matches the observations of a Genoese merchant, who noted the cloth's popularity. Sinabafa was "white and easy to wash," good for bedding and clothing, and relatively inexpensive, some three feet sold for about two *reals*.[2] Nahua men purchased it to use as a cape tied with a knot over one shoulder.[3] Dias was from the Philippines; the cloth was from China; his customers included Native Americans who paid with silver coins or cacao beans. Thinking about these particulars – the origin of its residents, the availability of imported goods, and the persistence of commerce on Indigenous land – suggests that Mexico City was a unique place during the seventeenth century. It was America's first colonial metropolis: a seat of commercial and political power with global ties. Once Tenochtitlan, capital of the Mexica empire, the city was now capital of the Viceroyalty of New Spain, a jewel in the Hapsburg Crown.[4]

To get there, Dias followed maritime and terrestrial routes that linked the Spanish empire. He endured a months-long journey from Manila to Acapulco on board a ship of the Manila Galleon, a royal fleet. Sinabafa cloth made the transpacific crossing in tightly packed crates on the same ships. From the port, Dias headed northward, walking some 235 miles to Mexico City, which was like the hub of a wheel with routes as spokes reaching in all directions.[5] Another road ran eastward for a similar distance over mountainous terrain to reach Veracruz, the gateway to the Atlantic's commercial world.[6] Dias's travels mirrored the circulation of people and goods across the far-reaching networks that connected the city to the world.

Now imagine his everyday interactions.[7] Early in the morning, Dias stopped for breakfast at the stand of an African woman selling warm drinks and bread. He chatted with Nahua carters who delivered goods to the square. He went to see a barber for a shave and companionship after closing his stand. And when he got home, he counted silver coins kept hidden in a box; coins were the city's most precious commodity, valued by silversmiths. Dias relied on the work that occupied his neighbors all day, to eat, to transport his goods, to care for his body, and to secure his livelihood. All the people he met were equally interdependent, as they needed each other to provide essential services that enabled them to do their own work.

Perhaps it seems obvious that resourceful people sustained Mexico City, but how and why did they do so? What do their stories reveal about the experience of living in early modern cities? His experience shows where local trade and global commerce met: at a stand on the Main Square where Dias resold Chinese cloth purchased in Asia with silver coins minted in Mexico City.[8] The invitation here is to observe the local: to follow people such as Dias across the city as they pursued opportunities in a wealthy, yet deeply unequal city. For it was through these efforts, their daily work, that residents made the city.[9]

## I.I  A TOUR OF THE CITY

The city in 1629, when Bartolomé Dias was selling cloth in the Main Square, looked a lot like a plan drafted a year earlier by the architect Juan Gómez de Trasmonte (Color Plate 1, Figure I.1).[10] The two men may have crossed paths. Trasmonte gained intimate knowledge of the city's topography by surveying public works, which he used to good effect in composing this work.[11] The plan, one of the few that survive from the seventeenth century, presents a stunning vista.[12] It is a visual expression of the characterization of the city's size and unique location made by a contemporary visitor from England: "Mexico is one of the greatest cities in the world in extension," meaning its size.[13] The cityscape spanned 2.1 miles east-to-west and 1.3 miles north-to-south in the late 1630s.[14] Dias must have been similarly impressed when he first approached its environs. Everyone who moved there or visited

FIGURE 1.1 Mexico City in 1628

Source: "Mexico City aus der Vogelperspektive" by Johannes Vingboons (1660), from *Atlas Blaeu – Van der Hem*. Based on "Forma y levantado de la ciudad de México" by Juan Gómez de Trasmonte (1628). Sign. E 34.414-C. Courtesy of the Österreichische Nationalbibliothek.

A black and white version of this figure will appear in some formats. For the color version, please refer to the plate section.

throughout the century seemed to remark that the built environment "in the middle of a lake" was a site to behold.[15]

Mexico City was crisscrossed by streets and canals, surrounded by water, and connected to overland routes by great causeways. It was an aquatic and terrestrial space. Trasmonte's plan depicts this reality. The city grew on an island located in the fresh and saltwater lakes complex that once existed in the Valley of Mexico.[16] It retained an island character, even as residents reclaimed more land from the water over the course of the century. The plan is a bird's eye view, flying in from the west; the sun rises in the east on the top.[17] The mounds and peaks on the plan's upper register represent the mountain ranges and volcanoes that surround the valley and embrace the city.[18] The salty water of Lake Texcoco stretches below this mountainous scape, while the city's agricultural hinterland extends in the plan's lower register.

Trasmonte offers a guide to this landscape, yet the city's residents are absent. A metropolis is both. The Nahuatl word *altepetl* for city refers to the community of people who live there and contains the elements for water (*atl*) and hill (*tepetl*). Similarly, the Latin word *urbs* for city refers to its people as well as its buildings and streets. Residents' stories provide a worm's eye view, revealing what it would have been like to be part of this political community and live in this place.

Maps in the chapters based on a graphic rendering of the plan zoom in and out of the vista (Figure I.2). They locate the spaces where residents worked and experienced community, say at the city's public park, the *Alameda*, G on the map. Pictorial works and narrative accounts from printed materials contribute to this imagining of space. So do descriptions drawn from court cases and property records, which are the main sources for this new telling of Mexico City's history. The aim is to have readers visualize the city from the perspective of the historical actors who sustained it over the course of the century.

The cityscape extended outward from the Main Square, a main stage for historical actors, as shown in a graphic rendering of Trasmonte's map (Figure I.3). They worked in a space long claimed by Native Americans, as well as newcomers such as Bartolomé Dias. His rented quarters were in a building next to the Convent of Jesus Mary, a short walk away. In the mornings, he headed to Coin Street, where he took a left, passing the House of Coins, to enter the square on the corner of the Viceroyal Palace, A on the map.[19] He was feet away from where the Mexica's Great Temple stood more than a century earlier.[20] From his stand, Dias watched as the space filled with vendors who opened the doors of their

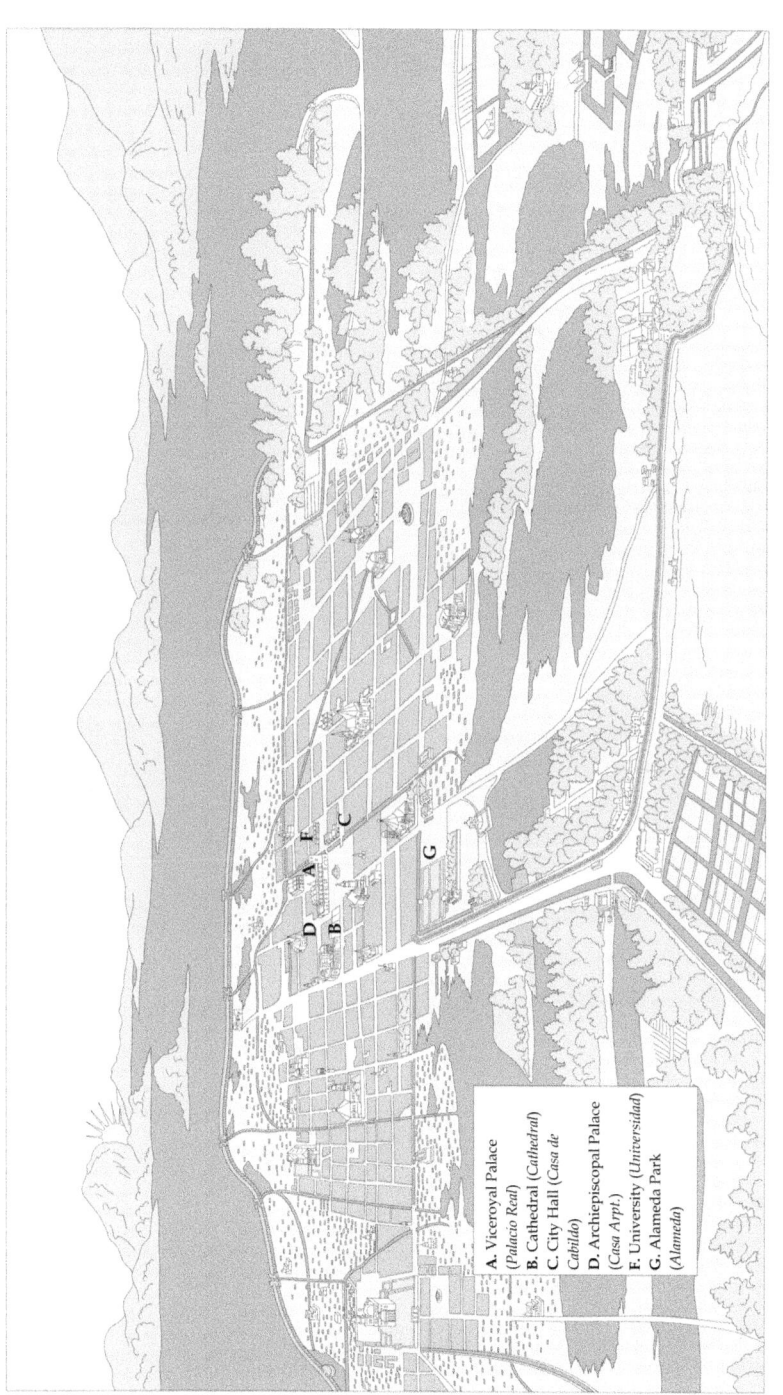

A. Viceroyal Palace
(*Palacio Real*)
B. Cathedral (*Cathedral*)
C. City Hall (*Casa de Cabildo*)
D. Archiepiscopal Palace
(*Casa Arzpt.*)
F. University (*Universidad*)
G. Alameda Park
(*Alameda*)

FIGURE 1.2   The cityscape

Source: Graphic rendering of "Mexico City aus der Vogelperspektive" by Johannes Vingboons (1660), from *Atlas Blaeu – Van der Hem*. Based on "Forma y levantado de la ciudad de México" by Juan Gómez de Trasmonte (1628). Sign. E 34.413-C. Courtesy of the Österreichische Nationalbibliothek. Image by Matilde Grimaldi.

The rendering crops Trasmonte's map on the bottom and right sides. It includes the original legend names and lettered places in the same location, with the exception of F, the University of Mexico, which is repositioned to its actual location.

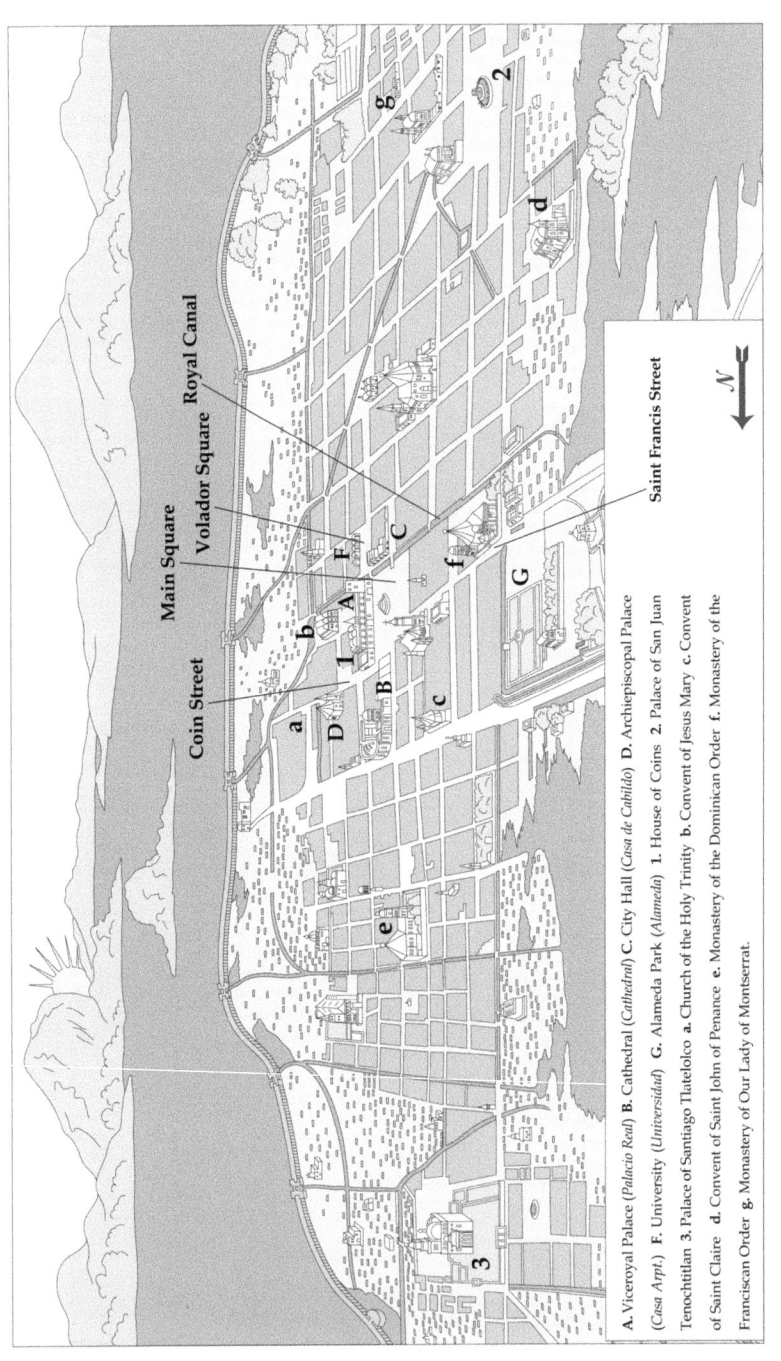

Coin Street

Main Square

Volador Square

Royal Canal

Saint Francis Street

*N*

A. Viceroyal Palace (*Palacio Real*) B. Cathedral (*Cathedral*) C. City Hall (*Casa de Cabildo*) D. Archiepiscopal Palace
(*Casa Arpt.*) F. University (*Universidad*) G. Alameda Park (*Alameda*) 1. House of Coins 2. Palace of San Juan
Tenochtitlan 3. Palace of Santiago Tlatelolco a. Church of the Holy Trinity b. Convent of Jesus Mary c. Convent
of Saint Claire d. Convent of Saint John of Penance e. Monastery of the Dominican Order f. Monastery of the
Franciscan Order g. Monastery of Our Lady of Montserrat.

FIGURE I.3  The residents' city

Source: Graphic rendering of a detail of "Mexico City aus der Vogelperspektive" by Johannes Vingboons (1660), from *Atlas
Blaeu – Van der Hem*. Based on "Forma y levantado de la ciudad de México" by Juan Gómez de Trasmonte (1628). Sign. E
34.413–C. Courtesy of the Österreichische Nationalbibliothek. Image by Matilde Grimaldi.
The rendering has locations mentioned in the Introduction.

6

wooden stalls, including barbers. The viceroy's coachmen approached the palace from streets laid out as a chessboard. Silversmiths headed to their shops on Saint Francis Street, which began on the square's western side. Their stories unfold in the chapters, each dedicated to showing how residents in these professions transformed the city.

## I.2 CHAPTERS

Short chapter titles name the economic activities of residents who fed, transported, and cared for their neighbors and helped them value their possessions. This activity had working people feeding, transporting, caring, and valuing the city's silver. *American Metropolis* reconstructs their history for the first time.[21]

Tomato sellers arrived at the Main Square on canoes with their produce and set up their stands along the Royal Canal. Poultry vendors arranged their cages in preparation for their first customers at Volador Square. The smells of fresh and cooked food wafted through the air. *Feeding the City* is about the previously untold history of the rise of the central market food complex over the course of the century.[22] Nahua market women fiercely defended their privilege as Indigenous vassals to sell what they called "fruits of the earth." Residents conceived of privileges as advantages or concessions accorded by the crown, often in relation to their rights.[23] Recent migrants secured a space for their wooden-stall eateries by paying rent at city hall. Market women from Upper Guinea obtained trading licenses at the Viceroyal Palace and negotiated credit arrangements with purveyors at their warehouses. They all came together to create a food complex that straddled Main and Volador Squares. A reconstruction of their political actions shows that they convinced officials to support their efforts by reminding them that they had a royal mandate to secure provisions as part of their governing responsibilities. As the crown told one viceroy, the city had to have "an abundance of all necessary foods," for without it "people would not able to sustain themselves."[24] Food vendors used these very same words.

The carters who dropped off wine barrels at the food court in the market complex were part of a transportation network that enabled movement within the city and connected residents to the hinterland and further afield. *Transporting the City* articulates a new history of motion based on the lives of residents who pushed carts over small bridges and steered horses and mules across the city's streets.[25] A detailed description of the city's byways locates this movement. Carters gained concessions from city officials by creating new businesses that supported government efforts to maintain public order, defined at the time as building and maintaining the city's infrastructure. Coachmen created safe havens across the city in response to officials' attempts to regulate the movement of enslaved and formerly enslaved people at night. During their daily traversals, they made contacts and gathered information about the latest happenings to earn money on the side. The possibility of making such deals enabled enslaved coachmen to purchase their freedom, which was unique in comparison to people who lived in other imperial settings where self-purchase was nearly impossible. Their history shows that residents took over the city's streets to sustain themselves, and in doing so, facilitated commercial activity.

Like food vendors, barbers claimed the Main Square for themselves, setting up stands, sometimes simply a stool, to cater to people who streamed in and out of this space. They also worked at shops across the city. *Caring for the City* recovers the previously unknown history of men from the Philippines who opened new businesses called blade-and-scissors shops to separate themselves from traditional barber surgeons.[26] They forged their own path by challenging members of the established professional association, the Barbers and Surgeons Guild, who tried to shut down their competitors for decades. The history of public health provides context for their economic achievements because they had to deal with officials and doctors who regulated caregivers. They hid that they offered an alternative wellness experience in their shops and suggested instead that residents only patronized their businesses for grooming, which did not concern doctors.

The Main Square stood between Saint Francis Street and the House of Coins. Silversmiths stopped at a food stall or visited a barber as part of their daily routine, which took them from their shops to that building to have officials hallmark their objects. *Valuing the City* demonstrates for the first time that silversmiths served as the arbiters of value in Mexico City. They persuaded officials to trust them, to allow them to govern their affairs, by preserving the silver standard. It was their way of protecting the crown's money, reals minted at the House of Coins that served as a global currency during the seventeenth century.[27] Examining the lives of silversmiths shows how residents used silver locally in an economy that operated on credit and with cash, which was not the case in other early modern cities. A food vendor rented a wooden stall on the square; when he sold his business in 1617, the buyer paid him "400 pesos in reals," in coins, for the equipment and inventory.[28] Silversmiths made objects that had intrinsic and monetary value, so residents relied on them for investment advice and to understand the crown's complicated fiscal policy. Their experience closes the history of working people, for they were the ones with the closest tie to the one thing – silver – that everyone else worked to have, to buy things and to save it in the form of silver coins or wrought silver.

## I.3 RESIDENTS' ECONOMY

A silversmith described his friend's inheritance as "the means to seek out his life"; he said it was "capital for trade and commerce."[29] He meant that having money would enable his friend to pursue opportunities and make more money. His friend was fortunate; other residents had to earn it by working. What do I need to do to secure a livelihood? The silversmith may have asked himself this question when he was a young man. He was clearly able to pick his profession, not true for everyone, which made it possible for him "to seek out his life." The silversmith was talking and thinking about his friend's and his own economy.

At the time, contemporary writers discussed the economy in terms of the responsibilities people had to one another, and the actions they took to meet them. Economy was what people did to have resources and how they managed them, be they a king or a silversmith. The king needed "to write down with his hand the intake and outlay of imperial rents"; he managed (accounted for, budgeted, and spent) money from taxes to sustain the empire.[30] Individuals bore the same responsibilities; they had to acquire money and manage it to be able to buy a sack of maize for the people with whom they shared their meals. They also earned and saved it for themselves, say to buy a pair of silver earrings.

*American Metropolis* recovers people's actions and choices to examine their economic lives.[31] Working meant "doing useful things" for the "self and the republic."[32] Residents worked to support themselves and their families, but the contemporary understanding was that they also worked to be useful for the republic. This dual understanding relates to residents' political achievements. They got officials to protect their businesses precisely because they did useful things that sustained the city.

Working involved a range of economic activities. Market women traded, described as the "buying and selling of merchandise."[33] They did the hard labor evoked by the untranslatable word *trafago*, which was the sound made when "moving goods from one place to another" to sell them.[34] Silversmiths "made" things.[35] They fashioned objects, wrought silver, a term that conjures the physical energy, the heating, bending, and polishing, that these men spent on their work. Coachmen reined mules and horses to convey passengers from place to place; barbers wielded combs to coif their customers' hair. People in these occupations assisted other people, doing something for them that they could or would not do for themselves. All these individuals did "useful things."[36]

They would not have used the phrase working people. Residents did not refer to themselves as workers, and they certainly did not say they were laborers or plebs.[37] Instead, they specified their profession. They said they were food vendors, carters, and silversmiths. They made it clear that what they did was distinct and that they had different, often opposing, interests than residents in other occupations.

The experiences of residents such as Bartolomé Dias reveal that they exerted economic agency. Beyond securing food and shelter, they acted to achieve financial goals in the face of considerable obstacles. Their motivations were as varied as they were: a desire to change their legal status; a longing for comfort; an easier tomorrow. As people noted in their wills and testaments, they aspired to leave something for their families, even if it was just enough "for them to be able to eat all the days of their lives."[38]

## I.4  RESIDENTS' POLITICAL WORK

A return to Trasmonte's map situates where residents exerted political agency (Figure I.3). Working people entered buildings with legislative and judicial requests. They asked officials to change local ordinances, to grant them licenses, and to demand justice. These appeals to government were part of their work, in the sense that making a living often required the involvement of officials, or at least their implicit support. Working people were thus political, which meant being litigious. This form of political activism was characteristic of vassals of the Hapsburg empire, known for its responsiveness, immense bureaucracy, and devotion to the law and legal practice.[39] The crown charged the viceroy with the "administration of justice equally to all royal subjects and vassals."[40] Residents took that directive to heart; they interpreted the law in creative ways to serve their purposes. They petitioned the viceroy directly, as well as the judges and officials of the city's myriad tribunals and councils, including at the Viceroyal Palace, the palaces of the Indigenous polities, city hall, and the archbishopric palace.[41]

Bartolomé Dias navigated these political bodies to protect his interests. By this point, he had arranged to become part of the polity of San Juan

Tenochtitlan, which, along with Santiago Tlatelolco, governed the affairs of Indigenous residents.[42] Dias would have gone to the government palace in the district of San Juan Moyotlan "to matriculate" and be added to the "tribute rolls" to pay his taxes, which secured him the rights and privileges of an Indigenous vassal, number 2 on the map (Figure I.3).[43]

One such privilege was direct recourse to the viceroy. In 1631, a newly appointed tax collector attempted to solicit sales tax from vendors at the Main Square.[44] To fight this person, Dias and five others appealed to Viceroy Villena (residents referred to viceroys with shortened names).[45] He acted "on behalf of all natives of the city of Manila in the Philippines who are traders in Mexico City."[46] As Indigenous people, they had access to the General Indian Court, headed by the viceroy (the physical representative of the monarch), which met at the Viceroyal Palace, at letter A on the map (Figure I.3).[47] The litigants knew about "a royal decree from 1592" that exempted Indigenous people from this tax, so they asked for confirmation and that it apply directly to them.[48] They succeeded. The viceroy agreed and ordered officials to protect them "from inconveniences and disturbances."[49] Dias was a political and economic actor when he secured vassalage and organized efforts to prevent taxation. He exemplifies working people named in the chapters who mobilized to protect their finances.

Residents also went to the Viceroyal Palace to secure privileges from the judges of the High Court of Mexico, who were the most powerful statesmen in the land after the viceroy.[50] They served as a court of appeals, but the judges also governed the city because they had judicial, legislative, and executive powers.[51] The judges took interest in provisions, transportation, public health, and especially silver, so historical actors turned to them, for example, to override city ordinances that hindered their ability to do their work.

City hall was perhaps the most frequented location, letter C on the map (Figure I.3).[52] The head of city hall and members of the city council were the primary actors charged with municipal affairs.[53] Carters lobbied councilmen, for example, to award them sanitation contracts. Silversmiths had them confirm guild ordinances that secured their position as the artisans who assessed value. The crown conferred on the city the title "Very Noble, Distinguished, and Loyal City of Mexico" in 1548, which recognized the privilege of residents (colonists from Spain and their descendants) to govern.[54] Philip IV articulated this vision of municipal government when he ascended the throne in 1621 and wrote directly to city hall – his "council, justices, gentlemen … officials and good men of my city of Mexico" – to remind them of their responsibility to uphold "good government," a common phrase for the crown's responsibilities, on his behalf.[55]

The city's eminence and governing independence were enacted ceremonially when incoming viceroys accepted keys to the city upon taking an "oath to keep the liberties of the city."[56] Residents gathered in August 1640 to welcome Viceroy Villena at the corner of the Dominican monastery (letter E), next to temporary decorative gates, where he swore to guard the city's "rights," "privileges," and "liberties" (Figure I.3).[57] But whose rights exactly? City hall council members governed for the sake of "Spaniards," especially rich ones like themselves. Their decisions, however, show that working people persuaded them to serve their interests as well. Residents, including formerly enslaved people and Native Americans, insisted that they govern for them. Their stories show that essential workers compelled municipal officials to govern in a more representative manner than they may have otherwise preferred.

The archbishopric palace (letter D) was the site of ecclesiastical government and royal patronage (Figure I.3).[58] Enslaved residents went there to have judges confirm rights accorded by canon law. The right to marry, for example, meant that people could try to prevent slaveowners from sending them away from their families. Residents also relied on churchmen who oversaw the execution of wills and testaments, which for a food vendor, for example, might have meant having the surety that her daughter would inherit the pots and utensils they used to prepare meals for sale at the central market complex.

The brief mention of buildings and governing bodies explains how and why residents acted as members of a political community.[59] They met their obligations as vassals, mainly the payment of taxes, which was supposed to guarantee their rights and privileges.[60] But they had to seek them out actively. Working people did so by organizing by profession or occupation. They came together to define what they did and determine what they needed and wanted. Then, they related it to the public good, say transportation, to have officials facilitate their work and protect their profession. Dias and his fellow petitioners banded together "as traders" to secure a tax exemption.[61]

The chapters follow residents who identified by profession to articulate this history of political and economic activism. "I am a carter," a man would respond when asked who he was. His response at the turn of the century meant that he was one of the carters who understood street ordinances and acted on them to reconfigure a section of the city for their occupation. They changed the neighborhood.

## I.5 THE PEOPLE

The metropolis had a large and diverse population for the time. Some 60,000 residents lived in Mexico City in the late 1620s and 85,000 by the end of the seventeenth century.[62] Making demographic comparisons to other capital cities and commercial centers is challenging but useful for scale.[63] Lima had some 37,000 residents by century's end.[64] Amsterdam's population, by contrast, more than doubled over the seventeenth century from around 100,000 in the 1620s, while Beijing's population remained at approximately one million during the same period.[65] Mexico City's residents inhabited a place teeming with people like urbanites elsewhere, but they had the less common experience of having neighbors from all over the world.

Dias married Mariana San Juan in 1605. She was a woman of African descent and she was enslaved.[66] Dias was once enslaved as well. Indeed, their presence shows that Mexico City was at the crossroads of slaving networks that stretched around the globe, especially during the first half of the seventeenth century. Slave traders, mainly Portuguese but also Spanish and Genoese merchants, employed captains and agents who forced Africans to board ships, suffer the Middle Passage, disembark in Veracruz, travel inland, and stand on temporary stands erected on the Main Square to sell people.[67] San Juan bore this experience or heard stories about the terror from a parent or kin. Her people used ethnonyms to denote their culture or region of origin, such as Biafra or Mozambique.[68] So did people from Southeast and South Asia. Going back to the beginning, Dias boarded a ship of the Manila Galleon, which served as the conduit for the transpacific slave trade until it ended in the 1670s.[69] Asians who migrated to the city freely had to contend with people assuming they were enslaved. And those who managed to gain their freedom, like Dias did, repeatedly noted that they were "free from captivity" to clarify their legal status.[70]

The city's demography reflected the persistence of trafficking and slavery, as well as the displacement of Indigenous people and the ongoing arrival of newcomers.[71] By the beginning of the century, enslaved and free people from Africa and Asia and their descendants were the second majority after Native Americans. Contemporaries separated residents into these groups, categorizing people by origin and legal status.[72] In the early 1610s, a visitor estimated that 50,000 African-descended people, 80,000 Native Americans, and 15,000 "Spaniards" lived in Mexico City.[73] The numbers are overly high in terms of the population overall, but the breakdown was accurate.[74] Moving forward into the 1670s, contemporary estimates consistently recorded the minority status of Europeans.[75] These residents were largely born in Mexico City who called themselves Spaniards, claiming descendance from original colonists, as well as immigrants from Spain.

The city also had a perhaps surprising number of migrants from other European states. Hapsburg policy dictated that traveling to its overseas territories was a privilege reserved for Spanish subjects. The licensing system meant to uphold the restriction, however, did not work as intended.[76] Philip III wrote to Viceroy Guadalcázar in 1615 expressing concern about the "Italians and those from Greece" and other "foreigners" who "resided in New Spain."[77] Yet, people moved to Mexico from cities such as Emden in Lower Saxony, and certain individuals gained official residency like in other parts of the empire.[78] A silk maker "from the kingdom of Scotland" migrated in the 1620s and soon listed two enslaved people in a property inventory.[79] His choice to invest in slavery exemplifies a reality of the labor market and the monetary aspirations of certain working people, who earned money to become slaveowners.

Native Americans remained in the majority at least through the 1640s, despite the catastrophic population losses of the previous century.[80] Most were Nahuas, with ancestors from Tenochtitlan and Tlatelolco, original inhabitants of the islands, and surrounding city-states who maintained distinct ethnic identities.[81] Mixtecs and Purépechas were among the other Native people who joined them.[82] They were all free, Indigenous vassals, except for a few individuals from frontier areas such as New Mexico.[83] Their numbers overall diminished over the century, with estimates down to 10,000 Indigenous people by the 1680s.[84]

People with diverse backgrounds lived side by side and formed families together. Native Americans continued to concentrate in the city's Indigenous neighborhoods (associated with the two polities), but these areas were also home to non-Native people.[85] In 1600, Catalina, a Nahua woman, owned a home located in the vicinity of the monastery of Our Lady of Montserrat; it was next to the house of Domingo Davilos, a trader of African descent.[86] This proximity concerned officials who endeavored to keep residents in distinct categories and separate from one another. Spanish colonists and city planners in the first half of the sixteenth century sought to institute physical segregation, with themselves at the city center and Indigenous residents in the outskirts. This ideal remained unrealized but emerged again as a desired solution to perceived

ethnic conflicts after the 1692 bread riots, when it failed once again.[87]
Catalina and Davilos made decisions about housing based on proximity to family or workplace, property values, and the cost of rent, rather
than abiding by officials' expectations of where they were supposed to
live. In addition, Native Americans, migrants from overseas, colonists,
and enslaved people married one another. Bartolomé Dias witnessed the
marriage of Salvador Aviles, an enslaved African-descended man, and
Juana Avila, a free woman with mixed Native American and European
heritage.[88] The notary categorized them in the records; the categories did
not divide residents on a personal level.

Where people were born and their ancestry tended to correlate with
their legal status; residents were either free or enslaved, a vassal of the
Hapsburg Crown or not. It is evident in the sources. Archival documentation contains words that reference people's physiognomy and place of
origin. Scribes identified enslaved people from sub-Saharan Africa by the
color of their skin; they noted variations in shade. The word for enslaved
people from South and Southeast Asia referenced China. Slaveowners
employed these color and place names in an offensive manner to transform people into commodities – human chattel.

Color classifiers remained with people who gained their freedom, so
that the only change in documents with their names was the word free to
replace slave.[89] Once manumitted, they were vassals of the crown with
fiscal responsibilities, but the stigma of slavery remained. Their descendants contended with color descriptors in the same fashion. If a person
looked like they might be from sub-Saharan Africa, scribes always noted
if they were enslaved or free. By contrast, scribes did not include categories related to color or legal status in documentation about people who
looked like they were from Europe. This absence, unlike the documentation related to Africans and Asians and their descendants, confirms the
privilege and assumption of free status for people with no visible ties to
slave trafficking.

What people looked like and where they came from had an impact
on their lives. The use of geographic identifiers acknowledges this
reality: Native American, African and African-descended, Asian and
Asian-descended, and European and European-descended. Residents
identified their place of birth, they named their town or region, not a
continent. Francisca, an enslaved person who lived in a silversmith's
house, said she was from Angola.[90] Bartolomé Dias said he was from
Manila. People also noted their "nation."[91] When evident, their stories
recognize this self-identification. The primary identifier of historical

actors, however, is their names, which is part of a methodological commitment to reconstructing the experiences of individuals.

## 1.6 PERIODIZATION AND METHODOLOGY

*American Metropolis* begins and ends with people and rests on hundreds of moments that are meaningful because they explain changes in
people's lives. They capture the reality that working people were oper-
atives of change. They transformed parts of the city, changed government oversight, created new businesses, and claimed privileges enjoyed
by subsequent generations. These changes emerge in all chapters, as
seen and experienced by working people during the seventeenth century. The long arc of time – more than a century – serves to chart these
changes on the ground.

The reigning years of three Habsburg monarchs, Philip III, Philip IV,
and Charles II, coincide with the book's periodization (1598–1700).
The historian Chimalpahin, writing in Nahuatl, noted in February
1599 (3 Reed year in the Nahua calendar) that Philip II had died four
months earlier. The "pealing of bells" filled the air, and residents put
on "mourning clothes."[92] His son Philip III had inherited the charge "to
govern the universal *altepetl*."[93] Following Chimalpahin, this history
notes changes in imperial governance in passing – the death of a king,
the arrival of a new viceroy. The everyday lives of the residents who put
on mourning clothes in Chimalpahin's telling did not change with the
king's passing, neither did those of residents who prayed for Charles II
100 years later.

Residents valued the peaceful succession of royal power in so far as
it ensured political stability. Yes, there were several riots; failures of
government related to food shortages elicited fierce demonstrations.[94]
People who experienced insufferable exploitation challenged their sub-
ordination, sometimes in violent ways. Viceroys and other high officials
regularly heard rumors that enslaved people were plotting revolts, evincing a fear of reprisal expressed by slaveowners throughout America.[95]
An overemphasis on outbreaks of public violence, however, obscures the
reality that these were rare events; working people safeguarded the city's
peace because it was good for their economies.

Mexico City was undeniably different in 1700 than a hundred years
earlier, starting with the landscape. Constant flooding transformed the
city. Chimalpahin gave an eyewitness account in 1604: "It kept raining
for a week, night and day … and in many places the houses collapsed

and crumbled ... and the roads everywhere disappeared ... and all the canals were entirely full of water."⁹⁶ "Great fear" gripped residents who asked, "what is happening to us in Mexico?"⁹⁷ Bartolomé Dias must have wondered the same in June 1629, when the city experienced the worst flood of the century, as told in the chapters. Thousands of residents perished and tens of thousands left the city. He may have departed as well, but Dias was back by 1631, selling cloth at the Main Square and organizing to have officials protect his livelihood. He would have heard about the hydraulics project aimed at preventing the floods, which began in 1607 and progressed in fits and starts, gaining traction in years of deluging rains, and continued beyond the seventeenth century.⁹⁸ The flooding never ended.

Dias also experienced reoccurring earthquakes. "The earth here in the city of Mexico actually moved" in August 1611, wrote Chimalpahin. It jolted people from their beds around three in the morning. He remembered the "frightful slapping sound" of water that "flew, boiled and splashed against the cistern walls."⁹⁹ The soundscape of the city added to the drama. The diarist Antonio de Robles wrote that the earth shook with a force that made "dogs howl" in August 1696.¹⁰⁰ Buildings had to be strong "but not high" because tremors "endangered houses if they were above three stories high."¹⁰¹ Local volcanic stone of various shades of gray and red decorated building exteriors, and its lightness and porous quality served the valuable function of not adding extra weight to trembling buildings.¹⁰²

There is no comparable plan for the end of the seventeenth century to compare these physical transformations vis-à-vis Trasmonte's vision from 1628. Yet new buildings testified to the passage of time. The new cathedral was the most impressive.¹⁰³ Trasmonte became the chief architect of the cathedral in 1632 but did not live to see its dedication in 1667.¹⁰⁴ That year, however, a mason could have described his own decades-long contribution to the reconstruction of the cathedral. Seeing the building go up through this mason's eyes is more in line with an approach that names the historical actors, the working people, who kept rebuilding and remaking the city. Walking to work in the morning, tending to customers, and closing shop in the evening: these were the everyday activities of residents who made Mexico City.

This history is an archival reconstruction of city life. The methodological choice is to employ the experiences and observations of historical actors extracted from surviving documentation as evidence for historical arguments. Readers will find quoted phrases throughout the book, all from archival documentations and printed sources from the period. This practice, of inserting words and using phrases from documents, is a constant reminder that the people speaking are historical actors. To say that people's stories evince the past and that their actions carry arguments is an empirical claim. The essay on sources explains in more detail the evidentiary basis of their history.

\* \* \*

Seventeenth-century Mexico City – a "famed city" – was alive with the movement of "muleteers, officials, traders ... soldiers, merchants ... men and women of varied colors and professions" who spoke in "different languages" as they walked along its "wide streets" and around its many canals.[105] The poet Bernardo de Balbuena wrote this description at the turn of the seventeenth century in an extended homage to "Mexico's greatness." He stopped at the stands of market women, rode in carriages, and owned silverware. He did not name the individuals in these occupations, but he certainly relied on them.

Balbuena also celebrated that the city received the "best of the world," evoking the draw of its consumer market.[106] Merchants sent commodities from "China, Italy, and Japan" in return for "fine silver."[107] Like Bartolomé Dias's story, Balbuena's poem inspires reflection on commerce – how it worked and who it benefited. A Nahua tailor counted a "sack of cacao beans from Guatemala" and "a chamber pot from China" among his possessions.[108] Residents valued his work, they paid the tailor, and he used that money for his own investments and comfort.

People transformed Mexico City by working. Individuals changed the course of their lives by working. They made this modern American Metropolis work. Here are their stories.

# 1

# Feeding the City

Isabel and Luisa were part of a grassroots movement that built a central market food complex during the seventeenth century.[1] Isabel specialized in root vegetables. Her stand in the Main Square had neat stacks of orange, purple, and yellow sweet potatoes.[2] She also had jicamas, a Mesoamerican white crunchy root. Luisa sold tomatoes, the fruit of another locally domesticated plant. Thomas Gage, an Englishman who visited the city in 1625, might well have stopped at their stands; they were some of the "women selling all manner of food and herbs," he described.[3] Like the cloth seller in the Introduction, Isabel and Luisa arrived in the Main Square early each morning and piled their produce for the day's sales. The area accommodated wide-ranging commercial exchange, filled with vendors selling all kinds of goods and services, but these market women were part of a distinct trajectory. Isabel and Luisa were among the vendors who centralized the sale of food over many decades by staking a claim to the combined space of the Main Square and adjoining Volador Square. They transformed it into a central market complex by taking political action and following economic strategies that demonstrate the persistence of working people who sustained Mexico City. This chapter recovers their experiences.

A detail from a painting offers a glimpse of the people who built the complex (Figure 1.1). The painter, who remains anonymous, rendered the image on a folded screen, which depicts the Viceroyal Palace and the everyday activity that surrounded it, as well as the Alameda (Color Plate 2).[4]

A graphic rendering captures the market exchanges (Figure 1.2). Indigenous market women are selling produce beneath canopies

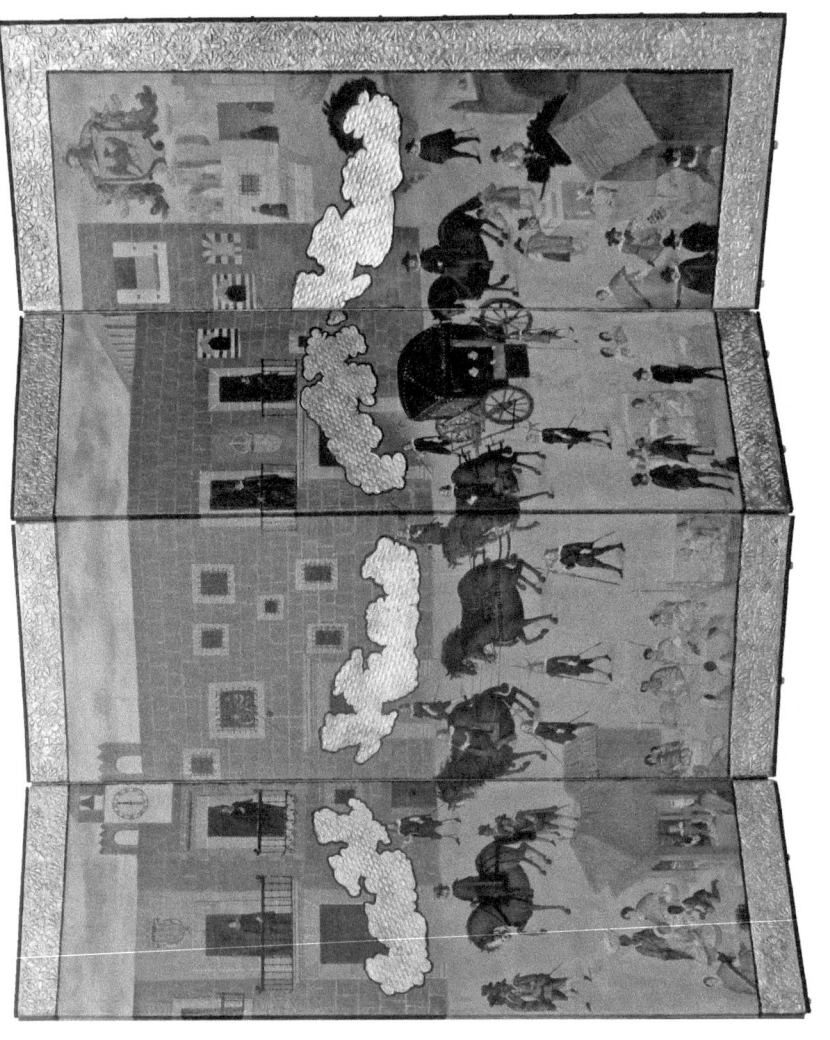

FIGURE 1.1  Food vendors in the forefront

Source: Detail from "Biombo del Palacio de los Virreyes de México" (c. 1675). Courtesy of the Museo de América. The market scene is visible on the lower register of the folding screen, over four panels on the right. Food vendors are facing away from the Viceroyal Palace.

FIGURE 1.2  Food vendors in the central market complex

Source: Graphic rendering of a detail of "Biombo del Palacio de los Virreyes de México" (c. 1675). Image by Matilde Grimaldi. The detail shows the variety of stands found at the food complex, where people piled produce in baskets or woven mats on the ground, set up canopies, and operated out of wooden stalls.

for shade. Such women proclaimed their Native identity by wearing traditional garb, embroidered cotton dresses. Their clothing denoted that they were vassals who had obtained "fruits of the earth" selling privileges, fought for by people discussed in this chapter. The man with the flared white lapels poses inside a wooden kiosk; he represents the vendors at the food court. The round blocks, possibly cheese wheels, stacked on a ledge advertise his goods. An African-descended market seller kneels beside a customer.[5] All of them typify vendors who identified this area as the best place to make a living by feeding the city.[6]

The term central market complex serves to indicate the achievement: working people selling food carved out a space consisting of different parts – a complex – at the commercial heart of the city. A multiplicity of businesses operated in the open air. Indigenous market women sold fruits and vegetables, African-descended men hawked poultry, and families ran outdoor restaurants. Residents purchased food throughout the city, in grocery stores, taverns, and butcher shops, and at small weekly markets run by Indigenous governors.[7] These neighborhood food outlets offered quick convenience, while the central complex presented an endless selection of produce. One day, a resident might purchase olives, lemons, and pomegranates for a Mediterranean-style feast, and the next day, they might buy maize, squash, and lake fowl for a locally inspired meal.

The food vendors who made and maintained the complex were part of a herculean endeavor: the work of provisioning Mexico City. They sold produce from the city's immediate hinterland, in the same fashion as during the height of the Mexica empire.[8] In the surrounding towns, farmers grew all manner of produce, while fishermen had the lakes as their aquatic grounds.[9] Vendors also acquired food from further afield, such as bananas from the Gulf Coast, pine nuts from New Mexico, and spices from across the Pacific Ocean.[10] Their history shows how they inserted themselves into short- and long-distance supply networks to profit from the sale of food.

The rise of the complex also involved city officials charged with food security, an idea that royal decrees defined as the need to ensure ample supplies of food to sustain the populace.[11] The government made a promise to city residents: There will be food in the markets and stores. To fulfill it, officials had to rely on market sellers, who galvanized to take advantage of this dependence on their hard work. They secured concessions from the High Court, obtained trading licenses from viceroys, and negotiated with officials at city hall about taxes, prices, and rents to secure spaces for their businesses. All these actions represent the political agency of food vendors, working people who sustained the city by way of provisions. Their history is about individuals' efforts to claim the city center as recompense for feeding the city.

### 1.1 VISUALIZING MARKET SPACES

Two chroniclers, writing at the bookends of the seventeenth century, noted the transformation of the city's markets. Juan de Torquemada described the city's markets in the early 1610s. He witnessed the beginnings of the food complex, describing its reach across the "connected" space of the Main Square and Volador Square.[12] In doing so, he also commented on the history of the city's markets and fairs. The greatest and "universal" fair during the Mexica empire was held in Tlatelolco, which remained the Indigenous market of the Santiago Tlatelolco polity.[13] But, as Torquemada noted, much of "this trade had passed" decades earlier to the Saint John Market, which was held on a square "of enormous size" across from the Palace of San Juan Tenochtitlan.[14] In the 1610s, Native Americans and "Spaniards" sold provisions at Saint John every day, except for Wednesdays and Thursdays.[15] On those two days, food vendors met at Saint Hippolytus Market next to the Alameda.[16] A Nahuatl source from Xochimilco notes that it opened in 1545, revealing its significance for Indigenous farmers who traveled to the city on market days.[17] In the 1610s, "a great number of people from the surrounding towns," as well as "far away and remote lands," continued to travel to Saint Hippolytus on market days.[18] Torquemada's description offers a glimpse of the changes that were taking place. The large fairs of the sixteenth century were becoming small neighborhood markets, leaving an opening for a new central marketplace.

Agustín de Vetancurt described the energy of the central complex in the 1690s. Vendors selling "provisions and food" gathered in the combined space so that "commerce never ceased."[19] He could still remember, however, the activity that had once energized the Saint John Market, "where there was continuous trade."[20] Following Torquemada, Vetancurt also noted that Saint Hippolytus had been a "great gathering place for people who sold provisions."[21] All of that had changed. By his time, the sale of food was concentrated in the Main-Volador-Squares area. Working people, food vendors, were responsible for this transformation; they had occupied the space decade after decade despite efforts to dislodge them. Vetancurt explained that officials had ordered vendors to "repopulate" the other markets and return to doing business as before, "but it had proved difficult to achieve."[22] He confirmed what working people had done by the end of the seventeenth century. They had created and maintained a market with the highest density of food vendors operating daily in the city.

The color of fruits at the stands of the central market changed with the seasons. Vendors presented a rotation of hues and flavors. Vetancurt wrote that customers "at any one time" could find "twenty to thirty different fruits in the squares"; this astounding variety "was one of the marvels the city enjoyed, unique in the whole orb."[23] The fertility and climate of the Central Valley allowed for the domestication of tree species such as the Mexican hawthorn, whose fruit, *tecojotes*, added shades of orange-yellows to stands starting in late October. Giovanni Gemelli Careri, a world traveler, loved avocados: "It grows on a tree like the walnut, it is sometimes long like a pear and sometimes round, the color without is green, and green and white within, with a large kernel in the middle; it is of the most exquisite taste."[24] By the early 1610s, trees, vines, and shrubs domesticated across the world grew within miles of the city. Carters delivered fruit straight from local orchards to market stands.[25] They sold purple figs from northern India, pears from China, and apricots and apples from Central Asia.[26] The colors of tropical fruits entered the city via mule trains carrying papayas and mangos from groves on the Pacific Coast. Sapotes were among "the most valued of all" the native fruits that grew "in hot country" to the south.[27] The black sapote variety was a special treat needing delicate handling, "with a thin skin and a black creamy inside, a delicious fruit."[28] All these fruits and more, plus countless vegetables and herbs, could be found in the central complex.

Cartographer Johannes Vingboons's orthogonal map of Mexico City conjures the market spaces occupied by historical actors named in this chapter (Color Plate 3; Figure 1.3).[29] Based on Juan Gómez de Trasmonte's plan discussed in the Introduction, it presents an orderly rendition of the central complex, located in the middle, and the markets discussed by Torquemada and Vetancurt. Visible too are the canals and causeways that facilitated the delivery of provisions sold in those spaces. Antonio Vázquez de Espinosa, a Spaniard who visited the city in 1612, remarked on the volume of traffic he witnessed each day, including "more than a thousand canoes loaded with provisions" and "more than three thousand mules carrying wheat, sugar, and other things."[30] It seemed to him from visiting the markets that the city "was one of the most abundant places in the world."[31]

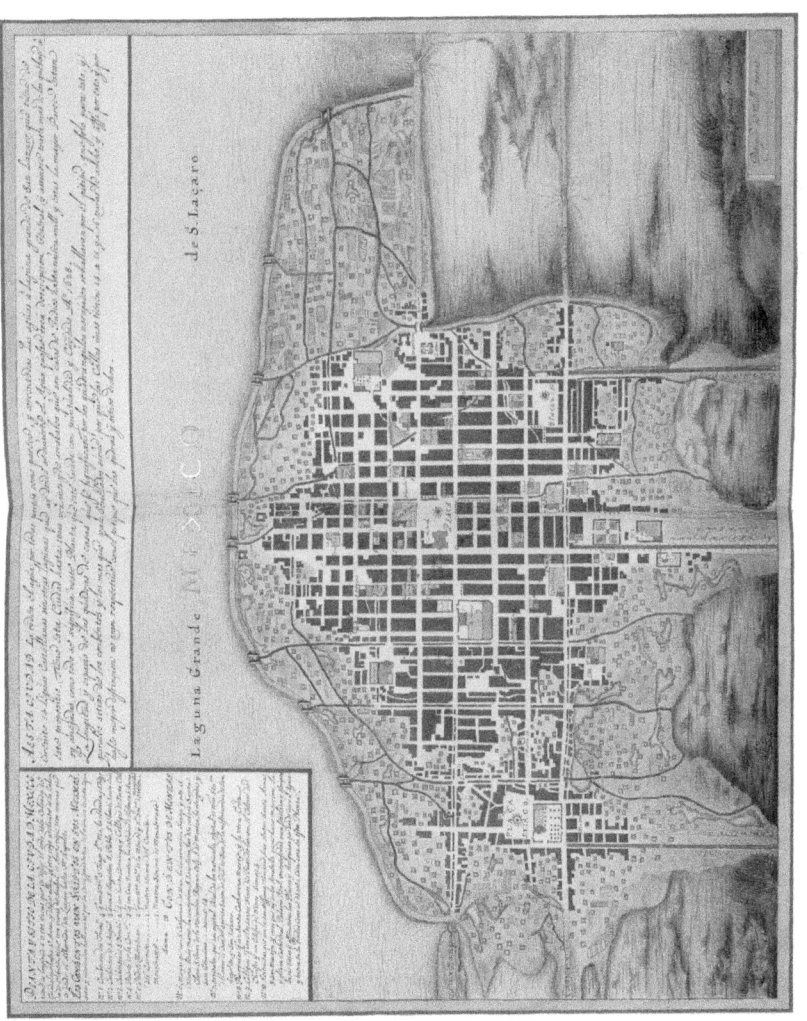

FIGURE 1.3  Mexico City's footprint

Source: "Plan von Mexico City" by Johannes Vingboons (1660) from *Atlas Blaeu – Van der Hem*. Based on "Forma y levantado de la ciudad de México" by Juan Gómez de Trasmonte (1628). Sign. E 34.413-C. Courtesy of the Österreichische Nationalbibliothek. A black and white version of this figure will appear in some formats. For the color version of this figure will appear in some formats. For the color version of this figure, please refer to the plate section.

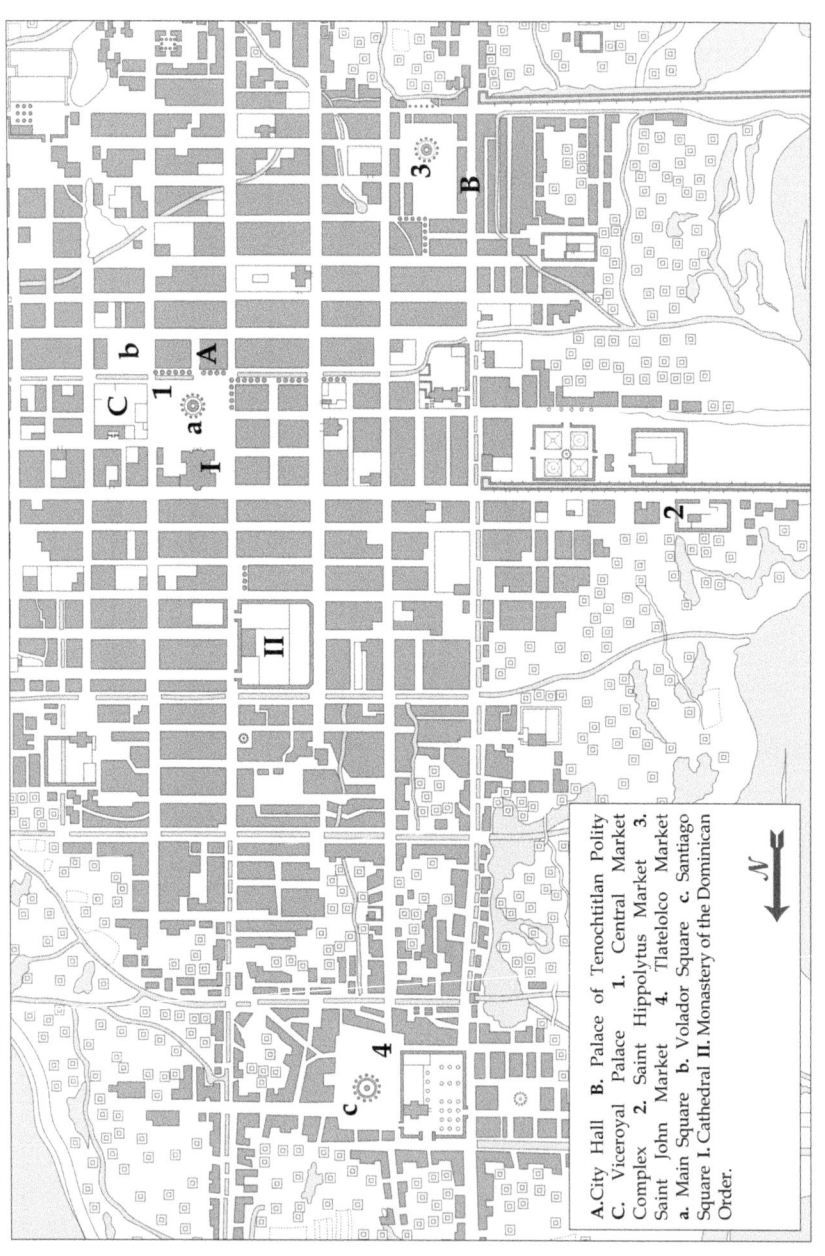

FIGURE 1.4 The city's markets

Source: Graphic rendering of a detail of "Plan von Mexico City" by Johannes Vingboons (1660), from *Atlas Blaeu – Van der Hem*. Based on "Forma y levantado de la ciudad de México" by Juan Gómez de Trasmonte (1628). Sign. E 34.413-C. Courtesy of the Österreichische Nationalbibliothek. Image by Matilde Grimaldi.

The map's legend lists the markets and other places mentioned in the chapter.

**A.** City Hall **B.** Palace of Tenochtitlan Polity **C.** Viceroyal Palace **1.** Central Market Complex **2.** Saint Hippolytus Market **3.** Saint John Market **4.** Tlatelolco Market **a.** Main Square **b.** Volador Square **c.** Santiago Square **I.** Cathedral **II.** Monastery of the Dominican Order.

A detail from Vingboons's map, rendered graphically, visualizes the open area of the central complex in relation to the other markets (Figure 1.4). Market sellers congregated in the Main Square and at Volador Square.[32] The number 1 designates the location of the complex, which spread across the two squares. Vendors used the fountain depicted as a circle, which was built in the early 1620s to deliver fresh water from the aqueduct.[33] The Saint John Market stood less than a mile away, a twenty-minute walk, from the Main Square to the southwest; Saint Hippolytus Market was equidistant to the west.[34] The Tlatelolco Market was located on the northern part of the city.[35]

## 1.2 SIXTEENTH-CENTURY PRECEDENTS: HOW NATIVE AMERICANS GAINED FRUITS OF THE EARTH PRIVILEGES

Juan García traveled to the viceroyal retreat in Chapultepec Forest in December 1600 to request an audience. Viceroy Monterrey received vassals even while on holiday.[36] García crafted his proposition to elicit the viceroy's interest in the city's food supply. To "sustain" his family, García "intended to go to towns more than five leagues away from the city to buy hens and other food supplies for the provision of the city."[37] With this phrasing, García reminded the viceroy that he would be providing a service. He would travel to places more than thirteen miles away, at a cost to himself, to get provisions. To do so, García needed the viceroy "to grant him a license so that no one would impede him."[38] The viceroy agreed, with a caveat. García had to purchase the produce and animals in the towns' public markets and bring them straight back to the city. He could not sell them anywhere else on his way back because they were meant "for the provision of the city."[39] To ensure easy delivery and sale, the license forbid "officials from embargoing" his goods.[40] The viceroy's designation of where García was allowed to make his purchases, the reference to embargoes, and the phrase about having "to guard the ordinances on this matter" point to why he needed a license.[41]

García aimed to circumvent restrictions imposed by a series of ordinances issued over the past twenty-some years regarding food provisions. His petition to the viceroy addressed a city ordinance from 1583 that prohibited vendors who were not Native Americans, such as himself, from buying "maize, hens, rabbits, fresh fish, fruits, legumes, vegetables, or other provisions" within the noted radius of thirteen miles to sell in the city.[42] Why would officials seek to regulate where non-Native vendors acquired provisions and where they sold food?

The 1583 ordinance and similar ones discussed in this section relate to a struggle dating to the mid sixteenth century, when Indigenous residents and farmers from the surrounding towns appealed to the Hapsburg Crown to mitigate the heavy burdens officials placed on them to deliver provisions to the city's markets. This legal history is critical for understanding the strategies deployed by Native Americans and people such as García to profit from the produce business during the seventeenth century. They had to show officials that providing residents with food required the participation of different people, rather than forcing one group to bear the responsibility. The work was hard and precarious, market people jostled with competitors to buy and sell the best produce, but it was a way to make a living.

Back in the early 1550s, governors of Indigenous towns located within twenty-six miles of the city had described the extraordinary demands made on farmers by the viceroy and High Court of Mexico in an appeal to the crown. Every Saturday, officials in Mexico City expected the delivery of 100 turkeys, 400 "hens from Castile," and 2,800 eggs from every town.[43] Men left their homes before dawn carrying crates and bundles to the city, where officials recorded their cargo and directed their subsequent sale. They set prices at a quarter below market value: an egg for two cacao beans, for example, rather than eight beans as sold in their own towns. Apart from turkeys, hens, and eggs, farmers had to deliver other provisions and sell them for prices "so low" that profiting from their labor was impossible. Worse still, the judges of the High Court had shut down markets in Indigenous towns to force farmers to bring their produce to the city.

The king took notice in March 1552.[44] Existing decrees protecting the right of Indigenous people to "dispose of their fruits" and "sell freely" were plainly being ignored.[45] As the petitioners explained, "there was no justice" in having to sell produce "without benefit."[46] From the crown's perspective, farmers would ideally want to bring their produce to the city and compete for customers by lowering their prices, which "made things cheaper" and assured "abundance in the markets."[47] The goal, after all, was for "the city to be well provisioned with food." At the same time, the king acknowledged that farmers might indeed have "to be compelled" to sell their produce in the city to "sustain" its residents.[48] The practice of forced provisioning remained in place because the crown prioritized the needs of Spanish settlers over Indigenous vassals.

The crown, however, agreed to reopen markets in the surrounding towns. Indigenous farmers had a right to "sustain themselves" by selling what they cultivated in markets held in the squares of their own towns, and not risk "dying along the roads" to Mexico City.[49] The reference to this peril reveals another concern. Ongoing epidemics were devastating the Native population in the wider region, and officials in Spain feared there would be no farmers left to provision the capital. Indigenous governors thus succeeded in reopening their towns' markets. It was a momentous gain that Indigenous people in other regions of the empire used as precedent. A royal decree soon confirmed the allowance and was later codified in the Laws of the Indies.[50] This law employed the Nahuatl-derived word *tianguis* (*tianquiztli*) for market used by the supplicants, a language reference that memorialized the Indigenous people from the Basin of Mexico who appealed to royal justice.

In the mid 1560s, Indigenous officials once again appealed for a respite. Mexico City officials continued to levy forced deliveries with the "pretext" that Indigenous farmers had a duty to ensure that residents have provisions.[51] But what of their "wives and children"?[52] How were they to sustain their own families? Farmers needed to sell produce in the city on their own account, freely, apart from the forced provisions. City officials, however, refused "to let them trade" and "sometimes confiscated their fruits and provisions."[53] Based on this report, the crown recognized the injustice and ordered the judges of the High Court not "to impede" their "commerce."[54] The decree, however, needed enforcement, so Indigenous governors lobbied city officials to abide by it, suggesting that Indigenous farmers would help them manage food prices.

Middlemen "used force and violence" to prevent them from profiting from their own labor.[55] They "pressured" Indigenous farmers "to lower their prices"; then, back in the city, middlemen sold their produce at a higher price than what they would charge.[56] These "hagglers," using a derisive term, were the reason residents complained about food prices. So why not protect Indigenous farmers and vendors who wanted to provision the city? To do so, officials simply had to ban middlemen from the produce business. Viceroy Enríquez agreed with the logic in 1579 and encouraged people "carrying fruits, chiles, tomatoes, and other produce" on canoes to "go straight to the markets" and "sell their goods freely."[57] They were not to "disembark anywhere else" or sell to "hagglers."[58] The viceroy supported Indigenous market people because he expected that they, unlike middlemen, would sell their produce at a fair price.

Indigenous farmers and vendors won additional support against competitors in the following decade. In 1583, the judges of the High Court banned non-Natives from buying produce in the city or within thirteen miles to resell it.[59] This prohibition made an ethnic differentiation. It identified vendors of African and mixed descent as hagglers, suggesting that they were the ones who sold food at inflated prices. The racialized accusation served the interests of producers in that it enabled Indigenous officials to press for another intervention. Despite the ordinances, non-Native market sellers had continued to stop farmers on their way into the city and force them to sell their goods at "low prices."[60] Indigenous officials reminded Viceroy Villamanrique that produce was the reserve of Native people; they were "things that truly belonged to them, their harvest."[61] They wanted to provision the city, but middlemen "tormented them."[62] The only solution was an outright prohibition against non-Natives who sold at the "retail" level.[63] The viceroy agreed; he prohibited "Spaniards" and Africans "free or enslaved" in 1587 from selling "fruits and vegetables of any type, chiles, tomatoes" in the city's markets.[64] Such goods were the reserve of Indigenous vendors.

Spanish-descended officials enforced this prohibition selectively, targeting food vendors who were of African descent. Gonzalo Gómez de Cervantes articulated their prejudice. Writing in the late 1590s, he described African and African-descended food vendors as "untrustworthy"; they "resold provisions" and "made excessive profits."[65] Gómez waxed about times past when Indigenous farmers brought "great quantities of vegetables and legumes … beans, pumpkin seeds, garbanzos, lentils … all things necessary for our sustenance."[66] He used the adjective our to refer to settlers from Spain and their descendants, such as himself. They were the residents who mattered and deserved to have low food prices. To his chagrin, Indigenous farmers were no longer the only people at the markets, which now had "more than 300" African-descended women who had "too much liberty."[67] Gómez suggested they had purposely driven out Native vendors and commandeered the sale of food, with the added derision for acting freely when they were supposed to act submissively.

Reading beyond the racist diatribe, Gómez's writings provide an eye-witness account of the first generation of African-descended food vendors who established their "businesses" at the central complex.[68] Their presence in the market shows that officials were not enforcing the 1587 prohibition. Most of these market sellers were free, he wrote, but "others" were enslaved. These vendors worked under the daily-fee arrangement, by which enslaved people paid slaveowners part of their daily earnings and kept the rest to sustain themselves.[69] This practice explains why the prohibition went against the economic interests of slaveowners: it cut off a source of income. Officials who were slaveowners had little incentive to enforce ordinances against so-called hagglers.

Enslaved market sellers, at the same time, embraced the daily-fee arrangement because it gave them a degree of independence in terms of their daily activities. Spanish law, based on Roman jurisprudence, allowed enslaved people to save part of their earnings to self-purchase.[70] Some of the historical actors who built the central complex in the seventeenth century started working as food vendors while enslaved and used their money to pay for manumission. They ignored the prohibitions and sold produce at the market to access capital. The ordinances on "hagglers" were too broad to be enforceable. They referred to anyone who "bought and sold things to eat and drink."[71] There was only so much that city officials could do to restrict their activities.

Indigenous residents, for their part, insisted that they had a right to sell produce they did not grow. In 1590, food vendors with stands in the Main Square made this point, arguing that it was illegal for officials to prevent them from selling produce.[72] The ordinances on hagglers had aimed to protect Indigenous farmers by prohibiting the sale of produce by nonproducers. But the ban could not apply to Indigenous vendors. They had to make this crucial distinction because Viceroy Enríquez's earlier ordinance had noted that Indigenous people who were "hagglers" could only sell their produce "after three in the afternoon and not before."[73] Officials at that point had tried to make a distinction between Indigenous farmers and retail vendors, but this separation went against their interests. Markets such as Saint John had food vendors who were farmers and others who simply sold their produce. City hall officials, they insisted, were in no position to distinguish between them, or to regulate their sales by applying haggler ordinances meant for non-Native people. Indigenous vassals had the right to sell produce in all the city's markets.

Indigenous officials focused on two other matters during the last three decades of the sixteenth century that relate to the history of food vendors and the rise of the central market food complex in the seventeenth century: taxation and prices. During the 1580s, Native Americans gained a tax concession regarding the sale of produce, which they called "fruits of the earth" to distinguish them from other comestibles. Fruits of the earth were all fruits and vegetables, as well as animal fodder and firewood. Indigenous food vendors insisted that they were exempt from paying sales tax on fruits of the earth based on knowing the instructions given when it was first instituted. Announced by the viceroy in 1574, sales tax was levied on almost everything sold or exchanged in Mexico

City, including "all fruits, green and dry, and things to eat," except from grains.[74] He dictated, however, that Native Americans "would not pay sales tax" on anything, so long as what they sold was theirs or belonged to other Native Americans.

Tax collectors in the subsequent years, however, abused their office. These men did not believe Indigenous vendors when they "swore, when asked, that their goods belonged to them" and charged them regardless.[75] Indigenous officials had to appeal to the High Court to demand the full implementation of the viceroy's original concession. In 1588, the judges resolved that Native American vendors were indeed exempt from paying sales tax on "goods of the earth, or their harvests."[76] The caveat, however, was that they did owe sales tax on "goods from Castile," a vague phrase that Native Americans would later challenge.[77] For the moment, Indigenous vendors insisted that tax collectors had to provide them with receipts for the taxes they paid on goods that were not fruits of the earth to stop overcharges. Native American food vendors with stands in the food complex claimed the sales-tax exemption on produce throughout the seventeenth century. It was a legal strategy that allowed them to compete with non-Native vendors who did pay sales tax on produce.

Native residents of Mexico City employed similar tactics in the early seventeenth century to gain exemptions from maximum-set rates or prices.[78] City hall officials established maximum rates almost from its inception, focusing first on the price of meat in 1524 and wine two years later.[79] The crown gave them this charge: "to set just prices for vendors who sold things to eat and drink," with the understanding that they had to be able to make "moderate gains" or profits.[80] Organizing these efforts, however, took time and deliberation. Council members at city hall debated the practice in 1553. Vendors were not supposed to sell provisions at a higher price than the maximum rates, but these rates had to allow for some profit. Working people needed "to be able to gain" from the sale of food, echoing royal decrees.[81] Prices, at the same time, could not raise too high because it "endangered and was a detriment to the republic," meaning the city's residents.[82] The maximum rates were supposed to keep food prices affordable, while allowing vendors to make a living. They could buy and sell so long as they priced their goods below the maximum rates. The discussion at city hall in the mid sixteenth century concerned non-Native market sellers, tavern keepers, butchers, and other people selling food. In the early 1600s, Native market sellers fought this practice when officials threatened to impose maximum rates on them.

During the sixteenth century, officials in city hall, viceroys, and the judges of the High Court expressed an ideal about the provisioning of produce: it was the responsibility of Native Americans. Farmers in the surrounding towns were supposed to sell their produce in the city's markets directly to consumers at low prices. So were residents who grew food in gardens and small plots. The dependence on Native American producers, however, was unsustainable amid decimating epidemics. The Indigenous population of Mexico City diminished from approximately 22,000 in 1563 to 8,000 in 1610, according to eyewitnesses.[83] Officials in the seventeenth century acknowledged the devastating reality as it pertained to them. They could no longer rely on Indigenous farmers and vendors. To secure provisions, they would have to depend on non-Indigenous market sellers and their supply networks.

Juan García got a trading license in 1600 precisely because officials conceded that they could not ban food vendors for being "hagglers." They needed market people to do this work. The rise of the central market food complex in the seventeenth century began with the efforts of vendors such as Juan García.

## 1.3 THE RISE OF THE CENTRAL MARKET COMPLEX

The rise of the central market food complex began at the turn of the seventeenth century, when residents who sold food embraced the opportunities of congregating at the heart of the city (Figure 1.4). Market women who sold fruit moved their stands from street corners to Volador Square at the urging of Viceroy Monterrey in 1600.[84] His predecessor had called on them to move fifteen years earlier, but relocating to markets would have restricted the number of days and times to do business, so they demurred.[85] The call in 1600, by contrast, acknowledged that they needed to work every day. Officials had also eased the restrictions on hagglers, which meant that vendors were no longer having to evade constables who seized their goods. Indeed, they were more likely to be left alone in Volador Square than at street corners. So, when street criers reminded vendors that "fruit" belonged in Volador in 1602, vendors organized to get a spot in that square.[86] Residents selling poultry gravitated toward Volador Square as well, such as Juan García, who obtained a license at this time to buy birds in surrounding towns to resell at market. Women selling vegetables lined up along the Royal Canal on the Main Square.[87] Residents who made prepared meals chose another side of the Main Square. Food vendors thus slowly positioned themselves across the squares, carving out spaces according to their specializations.

This history narrates the experiences of Indigenous market sellers, poulterers, and prepared-food vendors separately because each group faced different challenges and pursued distinct strategies. Nahua women fought to maintain their "fruits of the earth" privileges to compete with non-Native market sellers. African-descended poulters had to manage licenses. Having a stand at the food court required securing services that produce vendors did not need. All food vendors, at the same time, had to deal with city officials who tried to control and organize their space. A quick overview of their response to these interventions shows that their collective actions enabled all of them to remain in the market complex.

Vendors interacted personally with officials from city hall. Fernando Oñate, head of city hall in 1605, would walk through the squares, stopping at stands to inspect produce and the other food offerings. He "took care to check that the food was good and fresh."[88] Vendors showed Oñate their goods, perhaps handing him a ripe fruit to impress him. There had to be "plenty of provisions," so they assured him that they had plenty to sell.[89] These visits showed residents that he took seriously the charge of overseeing food provisions. As per local mandates, "the head of city hall had to guard food supplies very carefully," so he made periodic rounds to publicize his attentiveness.[90] By contrast, vendors maintained regular contact with the members of the city's Faithful Enforcement Tribunal, a division of city hall that enforced food ordinances discussed later in the chapter.[91]

There was also the Leasing Office, which collected rents from buildings owned by the city.[92] Food vendors began meeting with these officials after councilmen decided to turn their growing presence in the squares into a source of revenue. In 1609, Viceroy Velasco II approved their proposal to charge rent to "people with tables," stalls, and stands at the two squares.[93] He wanted leasing officials to organize vendors in the Main Square into rows and generally manage the "disorder" he observed from his balcony at the palace. Food vendors and residents who sold other goods appealed to the High Court to prevent this imposition. They implored the judges to understand that a yearly rent would be calamitous to their finances, but the magistrates sided with city hall and had the crown confirm the ruling.[94] Only Indigenous vendors, as discussed later, were able to avoid the rents. Faced with a new fiscal reality, non-Native food vendors negotiated with officials in the subsequent decades to secure assigned spots for them to do business. Paying rent confirmed their right to be there.

Luis Solaga lobbied council members in June 1620. The Royal Canal had a wooden bridge at the corner of both squares (Figure 1.4). No one had yet claimed it, and he had a plan. Solaga explained that he wanted to set up a permanent fruit stand, more like a kiosk, on that bridge; he was willing to pay a "just" rent for this privilege.[95] The construction superintendent who worked for the Leasing Office visited the site and reported that the "city would be served at no one's detriment" to have him pay rent like the other food vendors.[96] Regrettably, the councilors disagreed and nixed the proposal. They said that having a fruit stand next to the Viceroyal Palace would be "indecent," plus they worried that the stand would encumber the passage of residents who used the bridge. Solaga would have to wait for a designated space to become available. This interaction exemplifies the political strategies pursued by other historical actors named in the following pages. Vendors got spaces and thus created a central market food complex because officials charged with provisioning the city needed them. At the same time, vendors had to keep reminding officials of their services because men in city hall and the Viceroyal Palace repeatedly failed to consider the consequences of new initiatives. Their ability to negotiate with different governing bodies proved useful in the decades to come.

In September 1625, councilmen considered a plan to have all food vendors move to the Main Square. Residents who "brought provisions of all kinds, fruits and things tended to sell at Volador and other squares."[97] But what about the Main Square? Vendors paid rent for spots there, but there was plenty more space left to contain everyone who sold provisions. It would be better, they said, for "good government" to have all food vendors – "Spaniards," Indigenous people, and African-descended people – congregate in this one area.[98] There was no explanation for why this relocation would serve a civic purpose. The idea passed. Vendors at Volador had no intention of leaving their spots. Notably, efforts to move food vendors from one square to the other resurfaced intermittently over the course of the seventeenth century, and there were years when officials forced them to do so. Generations of food vendors weathered it all and remained in the combined space of the two squares, the central complex.

Food vendors paid to stay. Rents varied by the size of the space, location, and structure. Market women who sold produce under a thatch lean-to paid less than residents who had kiosks at the food court.[99] A listing of city hall revenue from 1646 included: 7,000 pesos from vendors with wooden stalls; 500 pesos for "tables and stands"; and 275 pesos for lean-tos.[100] There were 124 stalls and an untold number of tables and lean-tos, which gives a sense of the scales at which they operated and their corresponding rent. A fruit seller who piled her goods on a straw mat would have paid a real a month, an almost negligible amount for a registered space. The graphic rendering from the chapter's introduction conjures the people who secured their businesses in this manner.

Vendors at the Main Square faced a grave challenge in November 1658, when a fire damaged their structures. Viceroy Albuquerque decided to clear the area.[101] Individuals who ran their businesses from wooden kiosks at the food court suffered the greatest setback. They had "to abandon" their places and "hand over their keys" to the Leasing Office at city hall by the end of the year.[102] Vendors hesitated. Where were they supposed to go when every space in Volador was already assigned? In early January, officials swept through and forced "bakers, fruiterers, sausage-makers, and the rest" to move.[103] It was a chaotic situation; vendors at Volador resented having to make space for the newcomers. Faced with their resistance, the viceroy realized that food vendors would have to remain in the Main Square, but he tried to delimit their location. The head of city hall hired men to disassemble the kiosks and sell the wood. Then, they led "yoked-oxen till the ground to break up the foundations and smooth the ground" along the Royal Canal.[104] Leasing officials divided the space once again and "distributed them to vendors who wanted to set up their stands in this space."[105] Food vendors returned to the Main Square because the whole of the complex was their domain.

## 1.4  THE ORDINANCES THAT RECOGNIZED FOOD VENDORS' WORK

In early 1601, Viceroy Monterrey allowed all fruit vendors to sell at prices of their own "volition."[106] Indigenous market women heard street criers make the announcement and swiftly raised their prices, just by a few cacao beans (the money used in the central market complex, as discussed in the Conclusion). When officials challenged them, these women replied that "they were at liberty to sell as they wanted."[107] They added that they rejected the jurisdiction of the Faithful Enforcement Tribunal; "no justice could limit their prices."[108] This declaration shows that Indigenous women had a civic understanding of government workings. A viceroyal command superseded the power of city hall to enforce regulations regarding provisions, so city constables had to abide by his declaration on prices. City officials lamented their political and economic savviness. Fruit vendors "knew that buyers, out of necessity, pay whatever price is asked."[109] Their obvious awareness that prices correlated with supply and demand was, in the words of councilors, a "great inconvenience" to the city's "principal people." It was, on the other hand, convenient to Indigenous market women. They used the viceroy's temporary injunction to declare their right to sell fruits of the earth at their own prices.

Maximum rates returned in the coming years, but not for Native Americans. In 1617, Indigenous traders from the nearby town of Saint Matthew Churubusco appealed to Viceroy Guadalcázar for a license that would protect their right to sell their produce at their own prices.[110] City officials had tried to make them sell food at the established rates, and they would not abide by such interference. This claim to free price setting exemplifies the agency of vendors who reacted to food ordinances and remembered old ones. Indeed, their strategies appeared in a subsequent compilation. Viceroy Guadalcázar may have remembered the petitioners when he prepared the Ordinances for Provisions in 1619, which finally confirmed the concession they secured: Indigenous market people were not bound by price regulations.[111]

This corpus, in twelve clauses or chapters, regulated the sale of food. It incorporated dictates from the previous four decades and added new ones, and became the standard set of local laws on the subject because subsequent viceroys endorsed them. The Ordinances for Provisions concerned all residents who sold "things to eat and provisions," including market sellers named in this chapter. They acknowledged that food vendors were building a food complex at the center of the city. "People who traded in produce" congregated at the "large market" that stretched across Volador and the Main Square.[112]

Indigenous food vendors formulated the third clause of the 1619 ordinances by means of legal appeals. It summarized the concessions they had won over the last forty years: Native Americans "who bring fruit and other provisions to this city can sell them in market squares or elsewhere freely, wherever they want, without abiding by maximum-rates, and at any hour, to residents and all people without any limitation, so long as they sell what is theirs."[113] The phrasing about the location and hours of sales dated back to gains made since the 1560s. The clause reflected the political activism of Native American food vendors.

Non-native food vendors, by contrast, had to abide by the practice of setting maximum rates. The 1619 Ordinances mention this measure in five of the twelve clauses – a repetition that points to their significance. As noted, food was sold at fluctuating prices in markets and stores according to supply and demand, but they could not exceed the rates. Government officials had to balance the need to encourage people who provisioned the city with the need to make food affordable for all residents. The flexibility in prices below the maximum allowed food vendors to make some profit. The maximum capped prices aimed to make food affordable.

Vendors who sold produce followed the guidelines outlined in the ordinances, which differed according to scale and location. Wholesalers who brought "loads on mules or canoes" declared their cargo to a clerk who informed them of the rates confirmed daily by the head of city hall.[114] The maximum rates for grocers were higher than for suppliers. As per the ordinance, it was "just to allow them moderate profit considering their occupation, work, and risk, especially in fruit and other goods that perish."[115] The allowance for grocers to markup their prices is notable given that officials disdained middlemen (defined as vendors who sold food they did not produce). By contrast, city officials deemed that market sellers at the central complex were less worthy of profits than grocers. They did the same "work" (resold produce purchased from farmers or suppliers) and took on the same "risk" (the possibility of food spoiling before they could sell it). Yet, they had to abide by the same maximum rates as wholesalers, which reduced their profit margins. Grocers evidently had more influence on officials than market sellers. The maximum rates were public, listed on two placards, one outside of city hall and the other next to the Viceroyal Palace at the corner of Volador Square.[116] Vendors at the central complex, except for Indigenous people, were thus obliged to sell produce at relatively low prices. Their customers could simply point to the placards and bargain them down.

The Ordinances for Provisions forced non-Native market sellers to contend with remnants of the sixteenth-century "haggler" ordinances. Officials continued to insist that vendors acquire their goods outside the city because that activity – the effort of securing and transporting the provisions – justified the allowance to charge higher prices than farmers. Back in 1600, Juan García obtained a license to sell provisions he purchased at least thirteen miles away from the city.[117] A clause in the new ordinances doubled the requirement; "fruit sellers," which stood in for everyone who sold produce, had to purchase it in towns that were at least twenty-six miles away.[118] Officials from the Faithful Enforcement Tribunal enforced the distance condition by demanding paperwork from "justices at the place where they purchased" that testified to their source.[119]

Market sellers built the central complex with documentation. The 1619 ordinances required them to show proof of provenance, and they obliged. They got purchase receipts when they traveled for their goods, or credit receipts from wholesalers. They got receipts from clerks at city hall who collected the rent they paid for their allotted spots. They got receipts from the tax collectors who collected sales tax. Safe in a box or wrapped with cloth, market sellers kept their paperwork close, ready to show officials that they belonged in the central complex.

Juan Xiraldo, "a native of the city of Emden in Lower Saxony," grew wheat at his farm in Tepeaca, about 100 miles southeast of the city, which he regularly sold at the grain exchange.[120] Though unrelated to the work of produce vendors at the central complex, some mention of the grain exchange is useful for understanding officials' attitude toward provisions. Xiraldo was subject to a different set of ordinances.[121] He went to city hall to do business, which housed the exchange.[122] There, he interacted with an overseer who accounted for all the shipments of wheat, maize, barley, and other cereals that growers sent from the hinterlands. After paying a light fee, Xiraldo joined other farmers and wholesalers who sold their grain from assigned spaces at the exchange.[123] He followed the procedure outlined in the Ordinances for the Grain Exchange for Mexico City, which became the model for grain exchanges in other American cities.[124] The measures reflected the idea that "well-governed republics" required "well-provisioned grain exchanges" filled with "maize, grains, and seeds."[125] This civic commitment drew from Mesoamerican and Mediterranean legacies of governments prioritizing grain as the most necessary of foods and the main sustenance of the poor.[126] Officials from the Faithful Enforcement Tribunal enforced the grain ordinances. They monitored supply and demand and regularly intervened to retain reserves, acquire stocks, and stabilize prices by purchasing grain on the government's account. Despite these mechanisms, there were years when such measures failed to prevent prices from skyrocketing, usually due to weather-related lapses in supply.[127] The worst crisis led to the century's major bread riot in June 1692, discussed at the end of the chapter.

Over the course of the seventeenth century, food vendors confirmed the Ordinances for Provisions of 1619 by drawing on them to confirm their rights and to challenge new regulations that negatively impacted their businesses. Future viceroys endorsed them as well. Their incorporation into the Compilation of Mandates and Ordinances for Government collected for Viceroy Payo Enríquez in 1677 confirmed that they remained relevant and useful for market sellers and regulators.[128]

Anyone could sell fresh produce so long as they paid sales tax and other levies, and sold at prices that abided by the maximum rates. Indigenous residents were exempt.

## 1.5 NATIVE AMERICANS AT THE CENTRAL COMPLEX

Indigenous market women, as noted, were part of the complex from its beginning. And they remained because they found it lucrative, more so than selling their fruit in other locations such as Saint John, Saint Hippolytus, or Tlatelolco. These markets largely remained Native American spaces during the first four decades of the seventeenth century because they were under the purview of Indigenous governors. Custodians allocated places in the markets, arbitrated conflicts between sellers and buyers in Nahuatl, and oversaw daily operations.[129] Their responsibilities mirrored those of officials at the Faithful Enforcement Tribunal and the Leasing Office, who regulated sales at the Main and Volador Squares. As that market complex grew, however, Indigenous officials struggled to keep vendors at the old markets. The city's ongoing problems with seasonal flooding contributed to their decline.

Floods forced the markets to close and pushed market women to move to the central complex. Some closures were only temporary, while others lasted considerably longer, which led to their long-term reduction in scale. The city experienced devastating floods in July and August 1607. As the historian Chimalpahin recorded, rain pounded from the sky and water from the lakes "spilled over and swelled," coursing through the streets and canals and rushing into people's homes.[130] The Saint Hippolytus Market space filled with water so that "commerce no longer went on there." Half of Saint John lay under water, forcing market sellers to crowd into the "little bit that was left."[131] Vendors who usually alternated days between these two markets remained in Saint John for months, while others moved permanently to the city's center. The market at Tlatelolco was spared in 1607, so Indigenous officials raised the possibility of having vendors from Hippolytus and Saint John relocate to that space. The Indigenous government of the Tlatelolco polity, however, fought to preserve their market space for their own residents. Market sellers of Tenochtitlan also questioned the viability of this move. The waters would soon subside, they hoped, so that they could return to their spaces in Saint Hippolytus and reoccupy the whole of Saint John Square.

The three markets were back in full operation within a few years. The chronicler Antonio Vázquez de Espinosa visited them in 1612, confirming

Torquemada's account that Saint Hippolytus retained its Wednesday-Thursday schedule, while also noting the growth of new markets. The neighborhood market of Tonatlan on the eastern edge of the city had a "food fair every day."[132] Some Indigenous food vendors followed the rhythm of market days at the different locations, while others opened their businesses in the same place daily, including at the rising central complex.

The floods returned in 1629, the worst inundation of the century.[133] All the markets closed. As one official reported, "no place was spared" and the "floodwaters remained stagnant for four years, causing such great ruin to buildings and other property that it was impossible to enumerate the damages."[134] Saint Hippolytus and Saint John never recovered. Instead, as the city slowly rebuilt, Indigenous food vendors returned to the city's center and continued to take over that space.

Indigenous vendors spent the next thirty years fighting the efforts of one viceroy after another to move them. They were all convinced that Saint John and Saint Hippolytus had to be resurrected. In October 1635, officials from city hall stopped by their stands to tell vendors that they belonged elsewhere. They had "to return" to the two markets.[135] Food vendors ignored them. Reconstruction had focused on the center, postponing work at the city's other squares. Vendors who previously attended the named markets identified this problem: the lack of infrastructure. Where were they to set up their stands when those market spaces remained abandoned? They refused to go back until officials turned their attention to reconstructing those spaces.

Meanwhile, Indigenous market women at the central complex guarded their spots. Officials from the Leasing Office periodically tried to expel them, possibly to rent their spaces to residents who would pay more for their choice locations. To fight them, market women turned to the highest powers in the land to confirm their privileges.[136] The Ordinances for Provisions assured Indigenous vendors that they could sell produce "in market squares or elsewhere freely, wherever they want."[137]

Isabel Francisca had "an assigned place" in the Main Square where she sold cacao-based drinks.[138] She told Viceroy Cadreita that she had no plans of going elsewhere.[139] When market inspectors tried to dislodge her in January 1639, she marched into the Viceroyal Palace for protection and came out with a constable of the General Indian Court who confirmed that she had every right to keep her stand where it stood.[140] Francisca Cruz took the same political action two years later; she got a personalized viceregal license that confirmed her privilege to sell fruit, produce, and eggs from her stand in the Main Square.[141] In doing so, both women confirmed the strategy Indigenous vendors used throughout the seventeenth century: they turned to the viceroy to challenge abusive officials from city hall.

Viceroy Cadreita's concern with provisions encouraged him to support market women's claim to the central complex, but he also pushed for the reopening of Saint John and Saint Hippolytus. City criers made their rounds in April 1640, announcing that these market spaces were ready for repopulation. Workers had removed the silt that remained after the floods and elevated the ground with sand and new stones. Cadreita wanted food vendors to return to the renovated areas on market days "as customary" before the flood.[142] The past four decades, however, had already shown that Indigenous food vendors changed their practices in response to changing circumstances. María Francisca and Antonio Santiago made their appeal within weeks of Cadreita's call. They did not want to move their business to Saint John or Saint Hippolytus markets, so they convinced him to approve a writ of protection to remain at the Main Square.[143] A certain flexibility had to prevail for Indigenous vassals who opposed a move to reinstitute a customary practice that was no longer useful, or that had never been their custom.

The diarist Gregorio de Guijo noted in January 1659 that Indigenous market women "were beginning" to do business at Saint John, but only late in the day.[144] Viceroy Cuellar had been encouraging people "to sell fruit" there to revive the market.[145] Vendors resisted a permanent move because the 1629-closure remained a vivid memory thirty years later. As Guijo explained, there was little activity at Saint John since "the general flood."[146] This market and Saint Hippolytus, once so critical to the city's provisions, were a shadow of the past. In the decades that followed, more and more market women chose to work at the central complex.

Francisca Monica, her daughters Nicolasa Francisca and María Ángeles, and daughter-in-law María Nicolasa built a business together on the Main Square in the early 1680s. They were all from the polity of Tlatelolco, so they crossed the city every morning to set up their stand. They could have done business at the Tlatelolco market for convenience, but these market sellers preferred to be in the city's center, which was "their right as tributaries of His Majesty."[147] They sold "vegetables" and other "fruits of the earth" to "sustain themselves" and pay their taxes.[148] In Summer 1685, "certain people had started to bother them," saying that they "could not sell their produce at their stand."[149] Worse still, these "people," meaning constables from city hall, were "demanding that they give them" food.[150] It had to stop. So, in August 1685, they petitioned Viceroy Paredes to intervene. They wanted him to send a palace official "to notify" the offenders that it was illegal "to disturb them" and "prevent them from trading."[151] Paredes agreed. It "was customary" for Indigenous women "to have stands in the Main Square." Francisca Monica and her daughters got his protection, continuing a tradition of Indigenous women's activism.[152] They could sell food wherever they wanted.

Market women from the polity of Tenochtitlan similarly chose the complex. Governor Joseph de la Cruz of Tenochtitlan still expected in 1692 that "Indigenous market women" attend the neighborhood markets.[153] Some did, others remained at their spots on the Main Square.

## 1.6 SELLING PRODUCE

The central market complex was a key theater for non-Native food vendors who gained a foothold in the produce business. People from Africa, Asia, and their descendants formalized their involvement by claiming the same space as Indigenous vendors.[154] Isabel and Luisa, the market women who began this chapter, were among these individuals. The scribe that wrote the document that testifies to their working lives categorized Isabel as an African-descended person and Luisa as a person of mixed Indigenous and European descent. He also noted that Isabel was "free," while making no reference to Luisa's legal status.[155] Luisa lived with the privilege of having fellow residents assume that she was not enslaved by virtue of what she looked like. Calling attention to these modifiers underlines the reality that officials, in the same manner of scribes, categorized people when they enforced food ordinances in a selective manner.

Obtaining trading licenses from the viceroy was a key tactic during the first decade of the seventeenth century. Food vendors flooded him with petitions for protection from city officials who stopped them at the city's entrances and embargoed their goods. The haggler ordinance from the late sixteenth century remained applicable, which banned vendors who were not farmers, or who did not buy their produce at a considerable distance from the city. The penalties, moreover, incentivized city hall constables to enforce them: they kept part of the confiscated produce and a share of the fines. Food vendors needed viceroyal licenses to get past them.

The licenses given to non-Native vendors confirmed viceroys' growing recognition that residents who provisioned the city deserved allowances. They were not hagglers because they journeyed to far-away towns to acquire their produce. The time spent and cost of transportation gained them the right to charge higher prices in the city. In just four months in 1606, at least eight residents convinced Viceroy Montesclaros to acknowledge this work and grant them licenses to sell their produce "without impediments" – that was the repeating refrain.[156]

Manuel Sánchez made his case in July 1606. He "provisioned the city" by buying and selling fruit, tobacco, and legumes.[157] Sánchez "knew about the ordinances": residents had to trek to towns that were at least ten miles away from Mexico City and buy goods "without aggrieving" Native Americans.[158] He abided by these mandates to make a living. As of late, however, "certain justices had impeded him," preventing him from going about his business. Montesclaros heard Sánchez's story and granted the license.

Manuel López, a "free man" of African descent, pursued the same course in October.[159] He described his work, obtained a license, and walked out of the Viceroyal Palace with a document that confirmed his service to the city. Subsequently, when officials bothered him, López took out the piece of paper, showed it, and turned his attention back to customers.

These two petitioners represent the food vendors who demanded a clarification. Market sellers such as them were not hagglers, needlessly raising prices as proclaimed by alarmists such as the writer Gómez discussed earlier. Sánchez and López spent years traveling through towns, building relationships with farmers who sold them fresh produce. They carried it back to the city. All this work gave them the right to set up their stands in the central complex.

Over the following decades, vendors of African and Asian descent continued to turn to the viceroy when officials from city hall threated their businesses. Francisco Camacho and his son Juan ran a fruit stand in the central complex. In August 1644, constables paid them a visit, questioning their papers. Had they paid rent for their spot? Did they have a trading license? Camacho tried to explain that they did not need one. He showed them receipts that proved they had bought their goods in towns that were at least twenty-six miles away, as dictated in the 1619 Ordinances.[160] But the officials kept threatening them. The Camachos knew that the best response to this aggravation was to obtain more paperwork. So, they closed their stand for the day and went to the palace to wait their turn for an audience with the most powerful man in the city: Viceroy Salvatierra.[161] They succeeded. He signed a license confirming their right "to sell fruit in the square."[162] No official dared to challenge the viceroy's declaration. By confirming their place of business, the Camachos joined the tradition of food vendors who challenged being associated with hagglers by demonstrating that their work sustained the city.

While the Camachos sold local produce, they knew vendors who worked with wholesalers to acquire fruit from regions beyond the Central Valley of Mexico. Salvador Martín maintained networks in the 1640s that gave him access to fruits that grew in warmer areas to the east and south of the city.[163] He worked with a mule train operator based in the town of Tepoztlán to buy crates of whatever happened to be in season, such as pink pitayas, the fruit of a cacti. Martín gave him fifty pesos in reals in July 1644, and the freighter promised to return to the city in two months' time with the merchandise. That same summer, Martín purchased pineapples from a farmer in Veracruz.[164] Vendors went to Martín's warehouse because he carried a wide variety of fresh fruits that would have been difficult for any one of them to source on their own.

An incident from a few years later hints at the antagonism experienced by African-descended food vendors precisely because some residents associated them with slavery. The need to get viceroyal licenses already showed a pattern of harassment by low-level officials, but vendors also contended with threats of violence and the destruction of their property. On March 29, 1648, Guijo wrote down in his diary that a crime had occurred while the city slept. Market women of African descent had wooden stands "along the Royal Canal" (Figure 1.4).[165] They "were set on fire overnight."[166] It could have been an accident, but as Guijo wrote, he had already heard people whispering about the incident, "suspecting that someone had done this damage."[167] It was intentional. The names of the victims are unknown, or what they did in the aftermath. The market women may have reported the loss to leasing officials at city hall. To stay in business, they surely went back to the spaces they rented, cleared the debris, and arranged their produce for the day's sales. Refusing to leave, claiming their spaces at the complex – these were the tactics they shared with the other food vendors who built the central complex.

## 1.7 CARVING A PLACE FOR SELLING BIRDS

Poulterers raised their voices over squawking birds. Brown, blue, and yellow feathers floated in the air. The poultry section at the central food complex was a noisy and colorful place, where residents bought eggs, meat, and live birds from vendors who identified as *gallineros*, whose "trade was the buying and selling of chickens."[168] The name stood in for all fowl, including domesticated birds from the Old World ("hens from

Castile") and America (turkeys called "hens of the land" and Muscovy ducks). A customer could select her next meal from a crate and have the poulterer kill and skin the bird, while someone else got precut meat.

The poultry section grew from the incentive of vendors who knew that officials expressed a particular concern for this food. They considered chicken to be especially nutritious and the prescribed diet for ailing people. In November 1600, the administrator of a hospital visited Viceroy Monterrey to explain a crisis. The latest fleet had anchored in Veracruz with "many sick people" who traveled to the city and were now in their care.[169] These "poor people" needed "hens from Castile" to recover their strength.[170] He meant to send someone from the kitchen staff to nearby towns to purchase "hens to provision the hospital."[171] The administrator's insistence shows the contemporary mindset: only chicken would do.

The people who organized this niche business obtained trading licenses at the turn of the century, in the same manner as residents who sold fruits and vegetables.[172] Diego Bañon secured a license in December 1603 to "provision the republic," meaning the residents of Mexico City.[173] He traveled to towns with empty cages and crates to buy "chickens, chicks, and eggs" in nearby town.[174] When Bañon returned, he sold them at the space poulterers were beginning to claim in Volador Square. Congregating together abided with an ordinance dictating that poultry had to be sold in open markets.[175] They also assembled to share the work of keeping their section clean. Joining forces at this juncture fostered a legacy of poulterers supporting one another in subsequent decades.

As more residents entered the business, there was a shift toward working with wholesalers. Some vendors continued to venture to farms in surrounding towns seeking lower prices. In 1614, Andrés Cuenca "paid Indigenous farmers for hens, roosters, and eggs" for his stand at the complex.[176] Think of the physical effort of carrying cages and holding baskets close to avoid cracked eggshells during the journey back to the city. Women poulterers found it challenging to transport fowl. So, they established working relations with suppliers who kept coops in the city. These wholesalers, moreover, were willing to extend credit, which made it possible for newcomers to get started.

María Cruz had a poultry stand in the central complex in the mid 1630s. It was a remarkable achievement given her trajectory. In her own words, she was "from the land of Biafada," denoting her culture and place of birth in the Upper Guinea region of West Africa.[177] Years earlier, slavers forced Cruz to travel down to the coast and embark on a slaving ship. She survived the Middle Passage and the journey to Mexico City. When she started in the poultry business, she gave part of her daily earnings to a slaveowner and kept the rest, saving for self-purchase. Cruz referenced this past when a scribe asked for her name during a financial transaction. She was trustworthy and able to meet her credit obligations. Cruz's poultry business represented years of effort aimed at living freely.

Building on this experience, Cruz became the patron of enslaved people from Africa seeking to have their own stand in the complex. In August 1636, she helped fellow poulterers buy "hens from Castile" and "hens of the earth" from her supplier.[178] Cruz went with them "to the house of Esteban Iturbide," who raised fowl for wholesale, where they selected "twenty-two turkeys" and "twelve hens."[179] Knowing that the wholesaler required half-payment to release the animals, Cruz brought silver real coins for the deposit. She then promised Iturbide that she would "collect the remaining amount" from the other parties and return to pay him in full. The poulterers would pay her directly in installments, which was a considerable risk. What if the animals died? What if they failed to pay her? Cruz would nonetheless have to pay for the hens and turkeys they took with them that day. She swore to do so. And the supplier agreed to the arrangement because Cruz had been a good customer in the past, paying her debts in a timely manner to build up credit that she subsequently used to assist others.

Vendors got started in the poultry business by selling eggs because residents valued the eggs of "hens from Castile" more highly than those of turkeys. Hens, however, sold for less than turkeys, which were valued for their meat. The wholesaler Iturbide sold hens for five-and-a-half reals each in comparison to toms for eight-and-a-half reals.[180] The price of hens ranged from four to six reals throughout the seventeenth century, so the initial investment remained relatively low.[181] A vendor could thus begin with one hen and subsequently invest in more birds for a small brood. Hens are omnivores and do well with food scraps, so the maintenance costs were relatively low. They kept the hens for their eggs.

Cruz needed to help newcomers because the price of one hen was still beyond the reach of working people. Ana Gutiérrez lost her father when she was only twelve years old. He had purchased his freedom and hers, but now there was no one to support her.[182] Facing destitution, she was forced into a personal service agreement with a resident, "a Spaniard," who pledged to provide food and lodging and pay her a salary of "two pesos a month."[183] The conditions were comparable to other service agreements signed in 1636, when Cruz arranged the purchase of birds from Iturbide. Two pesos equaled sixteen silver reals, meaning that the girl would have had to work for over a week to buy a hen valued at five-and-a-half reals. An enslaved person working in this same man's household would obviously not get a salary. Cruz's credit assistance was critical if such a person was ever to start selling eggs.

People in the poultry business relied on forerunners who supported them. Apart from investing her own money, Cruz guided them on how to set up a formal stand at the complex. They had to obtain a trading license and then secure a spot in the poultry area from the Leasing Office. Perhaps she accompanied them to advise them on the paperwork.

Cruz was part of a community of poulterers in the 1630s who purchased their freedom. Gracia claimed her legal status when she identified as a "free woman" and a "poulterer at the square."[184] Andres Francisco "sold hens in the square."[185] Their stands were next to one another in the loudest section of Volador Square, hens clucking all day long. In the evenings, they swept the floor and cleaned their cages. Having carved out degrees of financial security, they showed others how to do the same.

Francisco Tavares followed in this tradition. His stand in the poultry section was remarkably profitable given the money he had on hand to support other people in the business. Juana Cruz needed a loan in January 1646. She planned to expand her business from a "stand in the square" to "trading" at a larger scale and becoming a wholesaler.[186] To do so, Cruz needed to build a large coop and an open pen to raise turkeys, so Cruz asked Tavares for a loan. "As a good deed," Tavares handed her 120 pesos in real coins.[187] And she agreed to return the amount in cash in six months' time, with no additional cost.[188] Tavares, however, required a signatory, someone who shared the liability for the debt "*in solidum*," which would enable him to sue both parties for payment if necessary.[189]

Tavares, born in the Philippines, had once been enslaved. Juana Cruz had Native American and European ancestry. Poulterers who worked in the central complex fostered ties based on their occupation rather than simply on commonalities related to their legal trajectory, birthplace, or ancestry. Their daily interactions fostered community, which helped individuals cope with the harassment they experienced when officials targeted vendors based on the color of their skin.

Poulterers at the market suffered grave losses in September 1653. Officials from city hall seized the "hens" of African-descended vendors.[190] Viceroy Albuquerque was new to the city, and like his predecessors, one of his first charges was to review the city's ordinances. He read the Ordinances for Provisions from 1619 with racial prejudices that harked back to the sixteenth century, when officials derided market sellers from Africa for "haggling" and rising food prices. Albuquerque prohibited "women and men" of African descent from selling poultry, "publicly or secretly."[191] He used the clause on "hagglers" who sold "birds and eggs" to attack certain people at the poultry section.[192] Imagine the frustration. Constables walked away with their crates and cages, leaving them without anything to sell. The punishments Viceroy Albuquerque prescribed were outrageous: "lashes" if they dared engage in this commerce.[193] The next months were extremely difficult. The targeted individuals dared not return to their tables. They asked their fellow poulterers to sell their birds. Residents complained about higher prices and fewer choices at the market, so Albuquerque was forced to step back and allow business to go on as usual. African-descended poulterers went back to the stands they leased from city hall and showed the viceroy that they played a critical part in feeding the city.

Wealthy residents had coops and pens in the courtyards of their houses. Keepers counted the number of birds daily, always suspecting that they would be stolen. And hungry people did. Late in the evening, Blas Loya tried stuffing a hen into his pants, but the watchman saw the bulge and pulled out the poor animal.[194] His story is in Chapter 2. Residents such as Loya, working people who struggled with food security, turned to poulterers at the complex, where they could at least buy eggs for their meals.

## 1.8 SELLING CONVENIENCE AT THE FOOD COURT

The food court was busy at all hours of the day, "be it at six in the afternoon or nine in the morning."[195] Customers gathered before women who "beat chocolate" to make frothy drinks, and "cooks who sold dishes for every taste and appetite."[196] The writer Agustín de Vetancurt, who wrote this description in the 1690s, captured the actions of working people who carved out a space for themselves in the central market food complex over the course of the century. Some vendors simply had a table, while others had elaborate wood stalls. Customers sat on woven-palm mats and ate with tortillas. They perched on stools in larger establishments that had wrap-around counters.

A drawing from 1596 locates the food court when it first formed (Color Plate 4, Figure 1.5). Drawn with sepia ink, it depicts the Main Square in the middle register and Volador on the upper left. Residents who sold meals claimed the space in front of the buildings on the western side of the Main Square, which was lined with storefronts under a

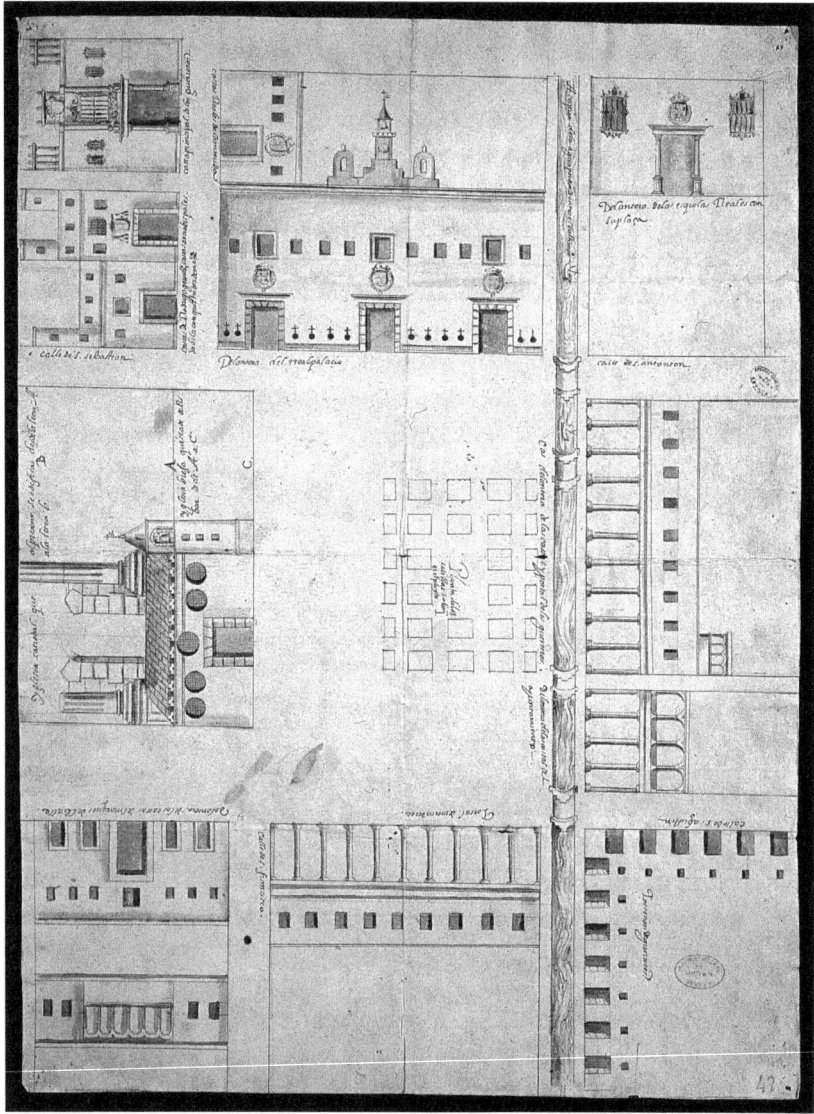

FIGURE 1.5  The central market complex on the Main Square and Volador
Square
Source: "Plaza Mayor de la ciudad de México" (1596), AGI MP-México 47.
Courtesy of the Archivo General de Indias.
The drawing accompanied a report sent to the Council of the Indies opposing
Viceroy Velasco's plan to build permanent stores on the Main Square, depicted
here as squares on the middle register. Officials rejected it, in part, because the
structures would have displaced the food vendors who already occupied this
area and changed its open character.
A black and white version of this figure will appear in some formats. For the
color version, please refer to the plate section.

porticoed passageway. They called it the "place of the food stands"[197] Like the other food vendors named previously, residents who sold meals interacted with officials at city hall and at the palace. Vendors who worked at the food court selected this space for themselves and made it a destination for hungry residents throughout the day.

A popular snack for mornings or early evenings was *atole* and sweet fritters, a unique local combination of a Mesoamerican beverage and Mediterranean bread.[198] The women who ran these stands made atole by boiling finely ground maize and lime. "Mixed with cacao" and a little sugar was a favorite, while others preferred it more bitter.[199] They would set up shop each day, arriving with "large earthenware jars" that kept the beverage warm and small charcoal grills for frying the dough.[200] Their regulars loved getting the warm, nourishing drink and crunchy treat.

Women with atole-and-fritter stands claimed their space at the food court from its earliest incarnation. Back in 1585, a viceroyal ordinance encouraged them to move from their street corner locations to the Main Square.[201] And, like the fruit sellers at Volador Square at this time, they took to the place because it promised more foot traffic. Indigenous women had been selling atole for centuries and continued to do so. The maize drink and wheat flour fritter combination, however, was a more recent culinary habit that lent itself to the food court model, which had customers getting their meals in one place.

The midday meal was a substantial affair, offered by food stands that approximated an outdoor restaurant. Beatriz Acosta and her daughter Isabel ran one of these businesses at the food court in the 1610s.[202] They received a steady revenue from customers who enjoyed well-cooked meals served with imported wine. Their supply networks linked their stand to Atlantic commerce. The Acostas purchased Spanish wine from a former naval officer based in Veracruz, who acted as a broker for merchants who sent pipes of wine on ships that disembarked at that port.[203] In mid November 1615, they purchased four of these containers (some 500 gallons) for 720 pesos. Each glass served at their eatery was priced to profit from the investment. Beatriz Acosta, like the poulterer María Cruz, had impeccable credit, which enabled her to get a loan for the pipes. The creditor paid the broker and gave her two and a half months to repay him along with the usual costs. Their stand must have been extremely popular to give them the confidence to assume this considerable debt. Notably, the credit agreement explicitly refers to the Laws of Toro, which protected the property rights of women in the Iberian empire.[204] Beatriz was married, but she owned her business and the loan was her responsibility. The Acosta's story exemplifies the financial independence women achieved by working at the central market complex, which would have been much more difficult in legal contexts where women did not control their property.

In the afternoons, customers stopped at stands that sold drinks and lighter fare. Ventura Lorenzana served food inspired by the ingredients of his childhood in the Philippines.[205] He partnered with Juan Amor, a baker, who made pasties.[206] In the words of a contemporary, these hand-held pies, filled with meat and seasoned vegetables, were "the refuge of those who cannot cook" – a quick bite.[207] The dish was a Spanish tradition that spread across the empire. Lorenzana would have preferred rice flour like the ones made back in Manila, but the baker used wheat. His customers enjoyed the variety of flavors and textures that emerged from having diverse people combine their culinary knowledge to create unique food offerings.

Lorenzana had his business partner, the baker, cosign a fifty-peso loan in 1635. Perhaps he intended to invest in a wooden kiosk rather than selling pasties from a table and basket. Lorenzana's status as a formerly enslaved person may have given pause to the creditor who required a promise from Amor that he would pay the debt "as his own" if necessary.[208] The condition is an example of the challenges formerly enslaved people encountered in making financial transactions. In this case, Lorenzana made the arrangement with the surety that sales from the pasties stand would allow for full payment in three months' time, and Amor supported him.

The unnamed women who made atole and fritters, the Acostas, and Lorenzana represent the range of foods and setups at the food court. Selling prepared food to residents who streamed into the Main Square was part of a larger effort by which working people fed the city. They too interacted with officials who regulated provisions. The Acostas visited city hall to rent their spot at the food court. Amor relied on officials who oversaw the granary and inspected the butchery where he secured key ingredients for Lorenzana's pasties. Zooming into the food court reveals that residents who sold prepared meals made business choices that paralleled the actions of the other vendors who gave rise to the central market complex.

## 1.9 RECLAIMING SPACES AFTER THE FIRE

The fire that ravaged the Main Square during the bread riot of June 8, 1692, destroyed at least 280 out of 320-plus businesses.[209] Food vendors scarcely had time to gather some of their goods and flee to their homes, where they remained in the days that followed. Supplies ran low as residents consumed what they had in store. "No one entered the city" for nearly two weeks, preventing the delivery of the "fruits, vegetables, fowl, and everything else carried into the city each day for the sustenance of residents."[210] Food vendors prepared their return to the central market complex while they waited for officials to open the roads for their suppliers. Once traffic resumed, they filled the market from one day to the next, arranging their stands in rows as they had stood previously. Vendors came back with new wooded tables and crates, while others arrived with woven-palm mats to unroll on the ground. "Poles and cloth hangings" provided shade and shelter from the rain.[211] Residents streamed into the food market, eager to restock their pantries and enjoy fresh produce after so many days of shortages.

Indigenous market women took special initiative at this point to preserve their spaces. They remained at the complex even as Indigenous officials worked to maintain a market schedule that had vendors going once a week to the four Indigenous districts, as noted previously. Viceroy Galve agreed that the "custom of the tianguis should be preserved," but he noted that market women were not "to be obligated" to sell at the other markets; they had a right to stay at the Main Square if that was what they wanted to do.[212] So in August 1692, market women organized their stands "in rows" and grouped themselves according to what they sold. Fruit sellers in one area; those selling aquatic animals in another. They imposed order to counter the viceroy's fear of disorder, which is what he expressed in mandates after the riot.

At the same time, these market women had to cope with the viceroy's plan to force Indigenous residents living in the center to leave and move to the city's outskirts. The effort ultimately failed, but it caused considerable heartache and confusion while residents organized to prevent the loss of property they would have had to endure.[213] Market women's claim on the central complex was part of the fight against the dislocation. They were there to remind Viceroy Galve that provisioning the city required the presence of Native Americans at its very center.

City officials debated over the next few years about who should be allowed to run businesses in the combined space of the Main and Volador Squares. The discussion was partly about removing vendors with wooden kiosks, which had been tinder and fuel for the fire back in June 1692. The other part related to an ongoing effort to clamp down on illicit trade. Officials suspected residents who sold used clothing, for example, of dealing in stolen goods, which they hoped would be "eradicated" by shutting down their stands.[214] The presence of food vendors, however, was never part of the conversation. Working people had succeeded in building a centralized food complex that officials deemed vital. In August 1693, the head of city hall acknowledged the need for "the fruit stands" to remain in their space and for "market women who sold vegetables and seeds" to continue their work.[215]

The viceroy confirmed the decision not to disrupt the central food complex three years later with an ordinance posted around the squares in March 1696.[216] Officials walked up and down the area to notify vendors who did not sell food that they had to leave the area, warning that they would otherwise "lose all their goods and merchandise and have their tables publicly burned."[217] "All stands were gone" by dawn of the next day, except for vendors "who sold comestibles."[218] They had been assured that "all people selling fruits and other food" would keep their "places in the Main Square."[219] The area around the fountain was to be kept clear, just as Viceroy Galve had wanted as part of his orderly rows-market vision. And, "to avoid confusion," the head of city hall confirmed "their spaces," noting the exact location where each market seller belonged.[220]

City officials sanctioned the practice that had emerged over the course of the century. Individuals who sold food in the complex claimed their spaces by registering their businesses with city hall. Having assigned spots facilitated their interactions with officials and prevented conflicts with competing vendors. Everyone had their own space. The 1696 ordinance thus confirmed one of the long-standing strategies that enabled residents to build and be part of the food complex, which was to secure the sanction of city hall.

The vendors of cooked food also retained their place in the central market complex in the aftermath of the June 1692 fire. They returned to their location by July and rebuilt the food court by setting up stands that had woven palm roofs and sides held up by sugarcane poles. The 1696 ordinance, however, ordered them to move from the Main Square to the Volador section of the food complex. They were supposed to set up their businesses in a more "open manner" than before and to use "a cloth covering for shade" instead of keeping their palm-and-cane structures, which officials deemed a fire hazard.[221] The accommodation made for food court vendors confirms that working people had successfully shown officials that they provided a critical service, feeding the city, which entitled them to stay in the center.

Construction began in 1693 in the Main Square for a building with interior courtyards that came to be known as the Parian. Completed ten

FIGURE 1.6 The central market complex at the end of the century
Source: Cristóbal de Villalpando, "View of the Plaza Mayor" (c.1697).
Courtesy of Corsham Court, Wiltshire, England. Bridgeman Images.
A black and white version of this figure will appear in some formats. For the
color version, please refer to the plate section.

years later, the edifice, which took over the southwest corner, had stores
that sold all manner of merchandise, from textiles to fancy paper. The
Parian, however, did not lessen the importance of the central food market complex, or displace the working people who remained there.

Cristóbal de Villalpando bought food at the central complex. A resident of Mexico City for most of his life, Villalpando painted a view of
the Main Square that captures the resiliency of food vendors (Color Plate
5, Figure 1.6).[222] The painting, commissioned by Viceroy Galve, illustrates the accord reached between food vendors and the city's officials:
they belonged at the heart of the city.[223] Market women sit behind piles
of green fruit at their stands with palm-thatched roofs. Their businesses
appear as neat rows organized around the fountain. The Viceroyal Palace
in the upper register is under reconstruction from the fire damage of the
1692 bread riot. Canoers pass along its southern façade laden with vegetables as they maneuver down the Royal Canal, depicted at a slight

angle on the right side of the painting. The depiction of Volador Square hints at the presence of the food court in its new location. The Parian in the foreground appears fully built. The organization of the businesses – food vendors on one side of the square, vendors of other goods in the Parian on the other side – is what the viceroy hoped to achieve when he signed the March 1696 ordinance earlier noted. These details suggest that Villalpando completed the painting later than its catalogue date. More to the point, Villalpando presents what food vendors wanted: to remain in the central market complex.

### 1.10 CONCLUSION

Isabel and Luisa worked at the central complex in 1625 selling produce. María de la Cruz worked in the poultry section ten years later. Francisco Camacho and his son Juan worked at their fruit stand a decade after that. Gregorio Guijo described the complex in his diary in the mid 1650s. Antonio de Robles wrote about food vendors ten years later. A folded screen from the mid 1670s captures their work (Figure 1.1). Francisca Monica, Nicolasa Francisca, María Ángeles, and María Nicolasa, Indigenous market women from Tlatelolco, fought to stay at their space in 1685. Villalpando painted the food complex in the mid 1690s (Figure 1.6). Naming these historical actors, all a decade apart, charts the passage of time. For those who worked at the complex, their experiences reveal the sustained solidarity that enabled them to take political action to preserve their livelihoods.

Market sellers arrived at the food complex knowing they would have a steady stream of customers who relied on them for sustenance. There were food vendors whose ancestors had once lived in Tenochtitlan, while others were born in Africa, Asia, Europe, and other parts of America. All these individuals and their descendants identified the complex as the most profitable location for their line of business. Indigenous residents had to fight to keep their fruits of the earth privileges, while enslaved and formerly enslaved people had to challenge food ordinances that excluded them.

Over the course of the seventeenth century, food vendors negotiated with governing bodies to protect their businesses in the central market complex. Historical actors showed officials at the palace and city hall that provisioning the city required them to be flexible when it came to enforcing food ordinances. They had to be accommodating because market people fed the city.

When viceroys were drafting letters to the crown, they could look out from the palace and confirm that they were doing their part to ensure that the city was amply provisioned. They supported working people in that space. Council members at city hall acknowledged the same. They were pleased that the food stands on the Main Square were a source of revenue, as well as a convenience for their clerks who frequented those businesses for quick meals on workdays. Food vendors knew that they were the ones who did the hard work and demanded recognition from these same officials. They empowered themselves by selling a necessity, by sustaining Mexico City.

# 2

# Transporting the City

Diego Escovedo returned home in 1640, disembarking at the port of Veracruz in June after two months at sea.[1] It had been a long journey, from Mexico to Spain and back again, and years spent as an enslaved person. Now free, the brand on his body testified to that experience. Diego's wife Josefa Hernández traveled with him, crossing the Atlantic on one of the ships that carried the family and staff of newly appointed Viceroy Villena.[2] Escovedo was one of three coachmen who accompanied him. The ship's mariners cried, "land, land," when mountain peaks appeared in the distance.[3] The couple knew they would have to cross a mountain range and skirt around the volcanoes of the Trans-Mexican Volcanic Belt to reach their destination: Mexico City.[4] They had made the outward journey years earlier. The group moved slowly, stopping at cities and towns that celebrated the viceroy's arrival and "going from inn to inn."[5] Mules, agile and extremely strong animals, carried their possessions on their back and pulled wagons and carts. Having traversed the mountains, Escovedo drove the viceroy's carriages along the road's "rough terrain" to Puebla, City of Angels, Hernández's birthplace, where the couple reunited with her family.[6] The retinue pressed forward. Meanwhile, the coachman of exiting Viceroy Cadreita drove him from Mexico City to the town of Otumba to meet Villena. Nearing each other, Escovedo coordinated with the other coachman so that the two carriages stood "side by side," allowing the viceroys to step down in front of each other for the welcoming.[7]

A few days later, Escovedo guided the carriage into the viceroyal retreat in Chapultepec, at the city's outskirts, which had "a large patio" at the front that led to the "stables and carriage house."[8] The inland trip had lasted nearly two months. At the palace, the viceroy drank from "Venetian glasses," admired "Chinese screens," slept on a "curious bed from the Philippines, plated with gold," stepped on "rugs from Cairo" and prayed before an "ebony crucifix."[9] Muleteers and wagoners had transported these imported luxuries from the ports to the palace in years past, bringing together furnishings that represented the greatest artisanship in the world.

In the days that followed, coachmen drove carriage owners to greet the viceroy so that the "road to Mexico swarmed with people and coaches."[10] Then, it was time to move to the Viceroyal Palace on the Main Square. Coachmen guided the viceroyal entry, moving slowly along the Tacuba Causeway. Escovedo drove the viceroy's "richly embroidered carriage,"[11] witnessing enslaved women "dancing gayly," who took the celebration as an opportunity to claim the streets. This chapter picks up Escovedo's story metaphorically as it played out inside the city, where he joined coachmen and carters who kept the city in motion.

A painting from the 1670s shows the city on the move (Color Plate 2, Figure 2.1). The painter covered an eight-panel folding screen with a panorama that joined the Main Square, on the right, and the Alameda, the city's public park, on the left. Coachmen and carters, like the figures in the painting, daily traversed the city's stone-cobbled streets. These individuals sustained the city by enabling the movement of residents and their goods across the metropolitan space.

A graphic rendering of the scene before the Viceroyal Palace focuses on historical actors who worked as coachmen and related occupations throughout the seventeenth century (Figure 2.2). An entourage of men on horseback, mules, and the rest on foot accompany the carriage of a high official, passing in front of the palace. Contemporaries used carriage and coach interchangeability, though the latter implied that the vehicle was less ornate than the first. The privilege of riding within the city in a carriage drawn by four or more horses or mules was supposed to be the reserve of high-ranking people, such as viceroys and archbishops, but residents flaunted their wealth and power by owning such vehicles.[12] In the rendering, two postilions guide the carriage and walking drivers lead at front.[13] The painter used darker colors for their skin than other people in the ensemble, identifying them as men of African descent. They stand in for the individuals named in this chapter: coachmen who used this occupation to claim certain freedoms and pursue prospects in Mexico City.[14] Coachmen turned carriage houses and stables into community spaces that protected African- and Asian-descended residents from government efforts to control their movements.

FIGURE 2.1  On the move: Scenes from the Alameda Park and Main Square

Source: "Biombo del Palacio de los Virreyes de México" (c.1675). Courtesy of the Museo de América.

The folding screen, examined in Chapter 1, has a gold border that connects the scene in front the Viceroyal Palace with the one at the Alameda. Coachmen drove along the carriage lanes that crossed the park. The painter imagined the spaces next to each other, even though the palace and the Alameda are located three quarters of a mile apart.

A black and white version of this figure will appear in some formats. For the color version, please refer to the plate section.

FIGURE 2.2 The city's coachmen

Source: Graphic rendering of detail from "Biombo del Palacio de los Virreyes de México" (c.1675). Courtesy of the Museo de América. Image by Matilde Grimaldi.

The detail is from the middle register of the four panels on the right of the folding screen. Walking drivers lead the way, part of an ensemble of men charged with heightening the pageantry of the carriage owner's movements.

A graphic rendering of the scene by the fountain of the Main Square draws attention to local transporters, residents who used carts, mules, and donkeys to transport the city (Figure 2.3). The figures gather by the water. The man at the top is pushing a small one-wheeled cart.[15] Other carters guided pack animals who pulled two- and four-wheeled carts

FIGURE 2.3 The city's carters
Source: Graphic rendering of detail from "Biombo del Palacio de los Virreyes de México" (c.1675). Courtesy of the Museo de América. Image by Matilde Grimaldi.
The detail is from the lower register of the fifth panel from the left. The pack animal on the left is eating fodder. Muleteers are readjusting barrels to balance the weight on the animals' backs. At the top, a young man lifts the handles to push a one-wheel cart laden with four containers.

for heavy and bulky loads. The sound of wheels on stone – of carts "grating along" the streets – was the background hum of city life.[16] These figures represent carters identified in this chapter who created new businesses in response to city ordinances that restricted the passage of large wagons and heavy carts to protect the cobbled streets. Carters, as did coachmen, occupied spaces in the city that served as bases for political and commercial action.

Water carriers are filling their barrels and placing them on mules (Figure 2.3).[17] In the 1610s, Juan de Torquemada wrote that a hundred years earlier, canoers used to deliver fresh water to residents' homes, filling their water tanks. They continued to do so in Torquemada's time, but were now joined by water carriers, mainly Native Americans, who used mules "to deliver water in barrels."[18] The rendering of the man holding a barrel under a stream of water wears clothes preferred by Indigenous residents: a cape and short, loose-fitting pants. This "mode of transporting water," Torquemada added, was now as common as via canoes.[19] The painting, from the 1670s, confirms that this transition from water to land transport continued in the subsequent decades, which was part of a trend shown in the following pages. Mexico City became more terrestrial over the course of the seventeenth century, due in part to carters and coachmen who claimed the city's streets, lanes, and causeways.

The water carriers in the rendering represent the small-scale local counterpart to the muleteers who worked for large mule train outfits that transported goods from Mexico City to the ports and as far north as New Mexico and south as Guatemala.[20] Carters worked with these long-distance transporters, taking over at the city's limits to deliver goods within the city. The verb to carry in Spanish derived from the vehicles used for this work, including carts and carriages.[21] The root signaled that carters and coachmen were involved in the same endeavor. To carry also implied trade, discussed in the Introduction as a word that captures the work done by people who sustained commerce.[22] This chapter examines the lives of residents who maneuvered these vehicles, who facilitated trade, and who kept the city in motion.

## 2.1 VISUALIZING TRANSPORTERS' TERRESTRIAL BYWAYS

Juan de Torquemada chronicled the activities of transport workers and described the city's transportation infrastructure in the 1610s, just as he did for the historical actors and markets of Chapter 1. People entered the city via three main causeways built under Mexica rule that ran high and wide over the lakes. Three large wagons crossed easily side by side, or ten horses trotting in line.[23] These "principle causeways" from centuries past remained the "most transited" during the seventeenth century.[24] The streets, by contrast, had changed. As Torquemada explained, they used to be narrower in the time of the Mexica because residents walked or traveled by canoe. The Indigenous neighborhoods still had these lanes, but the widened streets in the city center now allowed residents to ride in carriages and on horseback. Carters with small vehicles took advantage of the narrow lanes and streets. They waved at canoers on the canals and maneuvered their vehicles to get out of the way of coachmen who yelled at them to cede the way.

Writing in the 1690s, Agustín de Vetancurt, like Torquemada, remarked on the "three causeways from antiquity" that connected his city to the world.[25] By his time, there were six causeways, pointing to the rise of new transportation infrastructure that facilitated the shift from aquatic to terrestrial transportation that occurred during the seventeenth century. He commented too on the interior arteries. "Most streets" in the center "were stone paved" and wide, while the Indigenous neighborhoods in the city's outskirts still had narrow lanes alongside canals, confirming Native American residents' usage of canoes.[26] Their "adobe houses," according to another resident, were alongside "their canals" in the "appearance and form" of antiquity.[27] This contrasting infrastructure – wide streets in the center and narrow lanes and canals at the edges – indicates that Indigenous residents maintained their ancestral configuration of space for local transport.

Such was the traffic of carriages in the city's center that "pavers never ceased in their repairs."[28] Vetancurt's statement about the constant repairs captured the challenges and expense of keeping the city in motion. Mexico City's transportation infrastructure – its streets, causeways, embankments, bridges, gates, and canals – facilitated the easy movement of people and merchandise, but required officials' constant attention, as explained in the following pages.[29]

A graphic rendering of Johannes Vingboons's orthogonal map of Mexico City (Color Plate 3), discussed in Chapter 1, identifies the spaces traversed by historical actors named in this chapter (Figure 2.4). The tour begins in the center. The streets are perpendicular and parallel lines that extend from the Main Square. The rendering shows what visitors described in their recollections. During his visit in 1612, Antonio Vázquez de Espinosa was taken by the "straight, wide, and spacious streets," which had "wide and deep-water canals" running along their side and "bridges

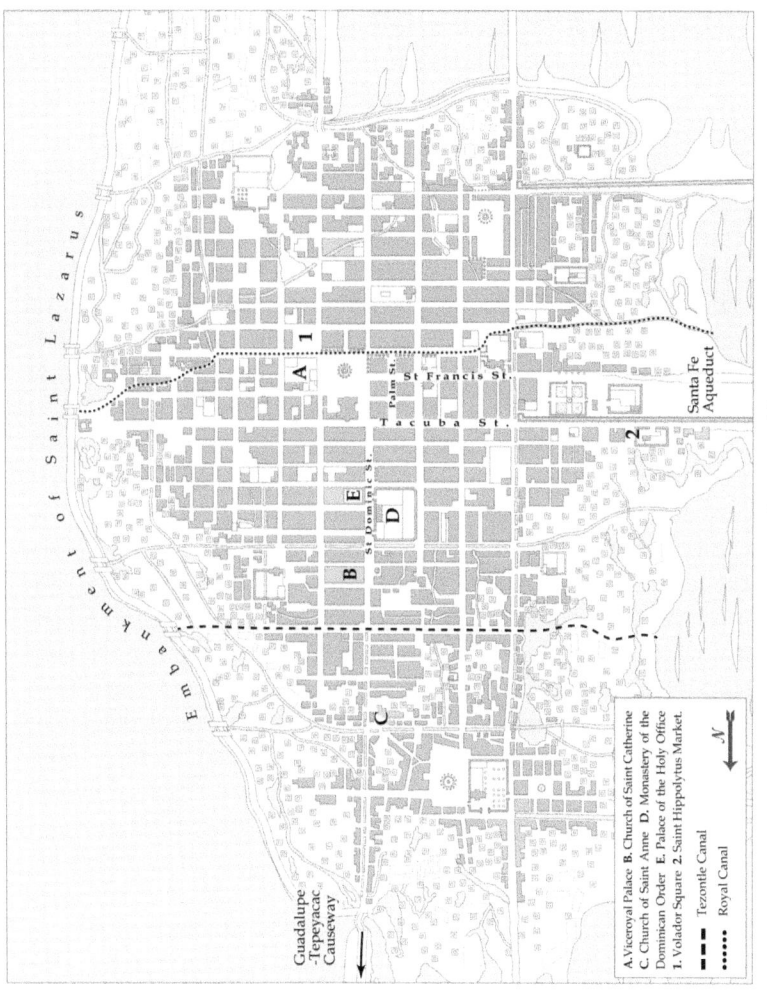

FIGURE 2.4 Places and byways

Source: Graphic rendering of a detail of "Plan Von Mexico City" by Johannes Vingboons (1660), from *Atlas Blaeu – Van der Hem*. Based on "Forma y levantado de la ciudad de México" by Juan Gómez de Trasmonte (1628). Sign. E 34.413-C. Courtesy of the Österreichische Nationalbibliothek. Image by Matilde Grimaldi.
The map's legend lists byways and places mentioned in the chapter.

to pass from one side to the other."[30] When chronicler Giovanni Gemelli Careri visited eighty-five years later, he too remarked on the "long, wide, and well paved streets, lying north and south, east and west," which made the city "look like a curious chessboard."[31] Coachmen and carters knew the street names, which changed in segments to reference the buildings that faced them.

The rendering signals the city's aquatic byways (Figure 2.4). It shows that some of the city's major canals ended at floodgates at the embankment of Saint Lazarus.[32] This massive barrier or levee, some seventeen-feet wide and nearly five miles long, buffered the city from the "pounding force" of Lake Texcoco.[33] The gates of the embankment's seven flood-gates opened in the morning, when the lake's water level fell, "to evacuate rainwater"; and it was through these gates that canoers "transported supplies into the city."[34] They traversed new and centuries-old canals that followed natural channels.[35] The Royal Canal passed by the central market complex, as noted in Chapter 1. The Tezontle Canal similarly bisected the city from east to west. Coachmen and carters went over stone bridges where the canals intersected with streets.

The city's infrastructure made it viable for people to use either water or terrestrial transport to move goods based on weight, distance, and other considerations. The reality of seasonal flooding encouraged flexibility, so that a resident who kept a carriage might also own a canoe. During the floods of 1607, "one could not move" around the city "if it were not for canoes."[36] Hernando Castro owned three canoes, mules, and a carriage.[37] He held different fiscal positions, including accounting magistrate for the nearby lakeside city of Xochimilco to the south. When it flooded, he traveled there via canoe, taking one of the canals near his home.[38] The rest of the time, Castro traversed the city on his carriage, which was "a little old" but presentable. An enslaved person was his coachman.

Extending outward from the gridded center, another rendering locates the great earthen and stone causeways, raised roads over the lakes that served as the city's terrestrial entry and exit points, as noted by Torquemada and Vetancurt (Figure 2.5). On the left side is the Guadalupe-Tepeyacac Causeway, and below it the Teneyuca Causeway, which ran northward, both turning into roads beyond the lakeshore. Wagoners and muleteers traveling from Zacatecas, "the celebrated and famous city that swelled and filled the world with silver," arrived via these causeways.[39] Residents regularly reminded officials of the economic importance of keeping them in good repair.[40] The Saint

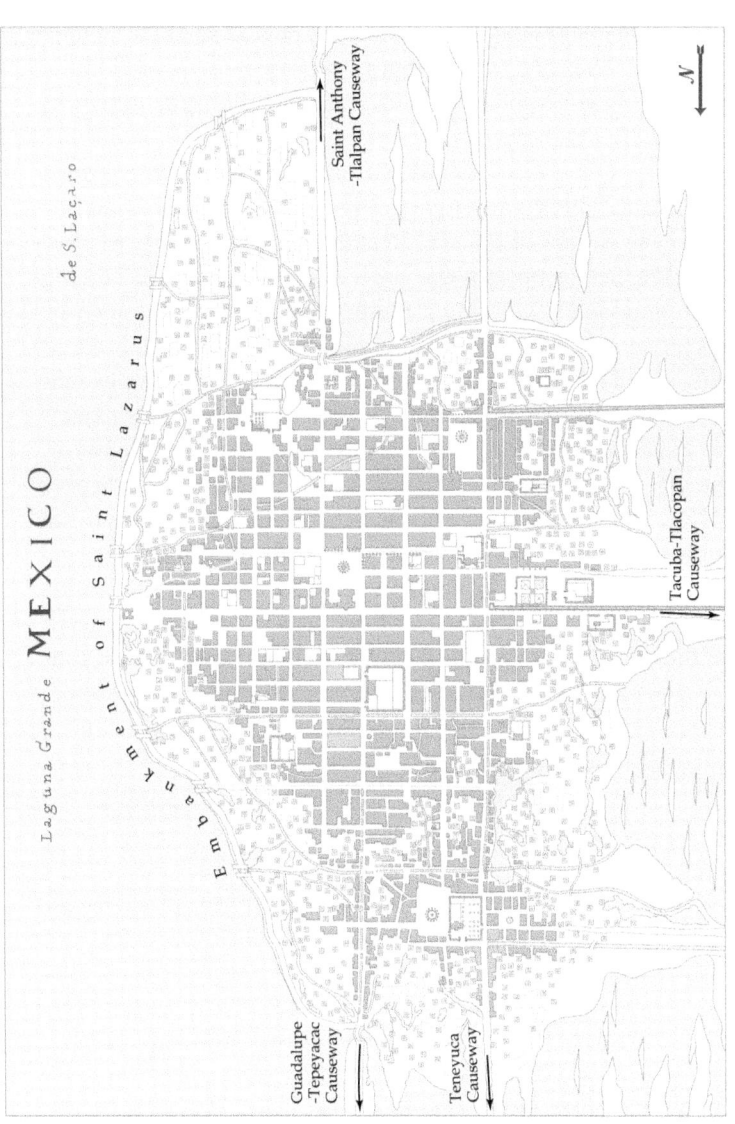

FIGURE 2.5 Streets and causeways

Source: Graphic rendering of a detail of "Plan Von Mexico City" by Johannes Vingboons (1660), from *Atlas Blaeu – Van der Hem*. Based on "Forma y levantado de la ciudad de México" by Juan Gómez de Trasmonte (1628). Sign. E 34.413-C. Courtesy of the Österreichische Nationalbibliothek. Image by Matilde Grimaldi.

The rendering shows the causeways mentioned in the chapter, extending outward to roads that connected the capital to trade and migration networks overland and overseas.

Anthony-Tlalpan Causeway going southward is visible on the right. The
Tacuba-Tlacopan Causeway, "one of the longest and broadest," began
its course westward as a street from the Main Square and continued
alongside the Santa Fe Aqueduct (Figure 2.5).[41] Upon exiting the city,
Tacuba was identified as a "royal road for wagons" as early as the mid
sixteenth century.[42] As noted, the causeway was Mexica infrastructure,
which Hapsburg officials appropriated to maintain the trade networks
that had long enriched the capital.

The city's location on a lake required a transport system that operated
over water and land, which was a logistically challenging and expensive
endeavor. Over the course of the seventeenth century, officials worked
out different strategies to upkeep the city's streets and canals. Bearing
the cost of building and maintaining these works was supposed to be
a shared enterprise. According to royal dictates, the "construction and
repair of bridges and roads had to be borne by those who receive benefit
from them."[43] Officials interpreted this royal dictate in the most expansive manner. Everyone, they argued, who used the city's thoroughfares
ought to be liable in some way for the expense of keeping them in working order. How this cost-sharing played out varied depending on the
administration; officials used funds from city hall, the royal treasury,
and the mandatory donations from property owners in varying ratios
to pay for the stone-paved streets.[44] Carters kept track and sought to
benefit from these initiatives, creating new businesses, as told next, that
purported to preserve the streets to secure profits from the transport
enterprise.

## 2.2 SIXTEENTH-CENTURY PRECEDENTS: PROTECTING AND CLEANING THE CITY'S STREETS

Domingo González petitioned Viceroy Monterrey for an exemption on
September 1, 1600. A carter, he did business with farmers in the hinterland, transporting their grain to Mexico City. His large, oxen-pulled
wagons carried heavy loads. The grain exchange was low on reserves,
and residents, González reminded the viceroy, "needed" provisions.[45]
He linked his appeal to the city's food supply in the same manner as
vendor Juan García, discussed in Chapter 1. González needed a license
to take his grain-loaded wagons all the way to the grain exchange,
visible from the second floor of the Viceroyal Palace. The viceroy
agreed that the delivery served the public good and granted the license,
with restrictions. González's wagons were "to enter slowly, and in

intervals," letting "half an hour pass" before one followed the other.[46] Plus, it was "for this one time only."[47] If González did it again, the head of the city had the power to embargo the goods or fine him, which were the decreed penalties for entering the city center with such vehicles. The delivery addressed the temporary need for grain supplies, but the license could not set a precedent. The permission prescribed the speed of González's wagons and timed their entry because reducing the strain of the wagons' weight on the city's cobbled streets was an official priority.

González obtained this license in response to a recent rise in the enforcement of ordinances related to the circulation of heavy vehicles and the city's transportation infrastructure. A 1585 ordinance prohibited carters and wagoners who used "carts with iron-rimmed wheels and wagons" from advancing into the city's center beyond established points.[48] Transporters entering from Tacuba Causeway, for example, could only go as far as Saint Hippolytus Market (Figure 2.4). Recurring discussions at city hall revealed the reasons behind these restrictions. Nearly two decades earlier, residents had petitioned the banning of mule- and ox-driven wagons because they "destroyed the streets' stone-paving" and damaged unpaved streets, making it impossible "to drive through the city."[49] The weight of the wagons, moreover, posed a risk to the city's water pipes, which cracked from the pressure. The proposal back in 1568 was for wagoners "to unload" at docks on the lakes and "have canoes bring their contents into the city."[50] Canoes at that time, as noted, continued to be the primary form of transportation. The recommendation to transfer goods to curtail wagon traffic proved unenforceable because the shift toward terrestrial transport was already underway. By 1585, the increased volume of terrestrial traffic and corollary damages forced the viceroy to ban iron-wheeled wagons and large carts, imposing a fifty-peso fine for deterrence.[51] González appealed to the viceroy in 1600 to avoid this very fine.

The 1585 ordinance hints at the rise of small-scale carters. Under the new plan, once the "merchandise and things" were unloaded from incoming wagons, carters took over.[52] Men working with wheelbarrows and carts that had simple wooden wheels were to deliver them to "stores and residents' homes."[53] The ordinance encouraged "residents to avail themselves" of these transporters; it did not mention canoers, indicating that local carters were available to take their place.[54] In the subsequent decades, small-scale carters took advantage of the entry restrictions to grow local carting businesses.

At the same time, during the 1580s and 1590s, residents who invested in long-distance transport increased terrestrial traffic to Mexico City. They purchased wagons, large carts, and pack animals (especially mules) to cater to people such as the wheat farmer who hired González because he needed to move heavy, bulky goods. They ignored the 1585 ban or simply paid the fines to reach their destinations directly. Within years of the ordinance, councilmen were again complaining of the "damages done to streets and stone pavement by the wagons that entered the city."[55] They insisted that transporters had to change vehicles at the city's outskirts and bring their goods "in lightweight carts" that did not have "iron-rimmed wheels."[56] In response, the owners of large-scale outfits pointed to a lack of infrastructure to excuse their actions.[57] The city had only built two new dockyards, which were overcome with traffic.[58] Long-distance operators wanted direct access. Stopping to move goods from large vehicles to canoes at the dockyards or to carts on the causeways was costly and increased the time it took to make deliveries.

So, long-distance operators continued to lobby the city to build and maintain thoroughfares that could withstand the weight of their vehicles. They pressed for greater investment in terrestrial infrastructure, while finding ways to circumvent government efforts to protect the existing streets. As explained later, entry restrictions changed their connection to local carters. These men instigated a new business – parking corrals – that facilitated the change in vehicles. Carters' innovation enabled operators with heavy wagons to stop at these service centers to unload, and thus abide by the bans on iron-rimmed wheels to avoid the fines.

Carters mobilized as well to respond to related discussions at city hall regarding the city's streets: how to keep them clean. Council members identified the need to organize street cleaning as early as 1527.[59] Directed efforts to regularize sanitation services, however, did not begin for another sixty years, at around the same time as the growing concern about wagons damaging the stone pavement. Keeping the streets clean, the water pipes in good condition, and repairing the causeways and streets were all connected.[60]

Viceroy Moya had been in the city for fifteen years prior to his appointment, and it seemed to him that the streets were getting progressively dirtier.[61] It had already been dictated that residents were supposed to keep the immediate area of their property clean. They could otherwise expect to have a bailiff forcibly enter their household to embargo valued goods (such as garments) and keep them until they removed the "filth" from their streets.[62] The threat was not working. So, newly empowered,

Moya issued a reminder in July 1585: "All residents have the obligation to sweep and keep clean the streets facing their property."[63] A crier made the announcement up and down the streets, shouting out the threat of a four-peso fine. Enforcement, once again, proved difficult.[64] Neither exhorting residents to comply with the ordinances as a civic duty nor threatening them with fines was sufficient to the task.

At this point, city hall shifted the focus away from street cleaning being residents' sole responsibility to more coordinated efforts. In July 1586, a councilman entreated his colleagues "to come up with a solution" to the "cleanliness problem."[65] It was about streets and garbage. Fellow councilors thus recommended that the head of the city ask the viceroy to assign 200 Indigenous residents "to clear the garbage piles," which would take fifteen days; "it could not be done without them."[66] The request evinced an oppressive reality.

Officials at the Viceroyal Palace, the High Court, and city hall dictated that Native American residents and from the surrounding towns had to provide labor for public works, which included the construction and maintenance of the city's streets, causeways, and canals.[67] This labor draft secured Indigenous men on a rotating basis (by community) who were paid approximately forty percent less than workers with wages, which varied by profession and skills.[68] Indigenous governors coordinated with residents enrolled in tribute rolls to work on designated projects, such as the cleaning of canals. Back in 1583, for example, historian Chimalpahin wrote: "All the canals here in Mexico were cleaned and cleared out, from everywhere the people of the [various] altepetl came."[69] He chronicled in Nahuatl the contribution of Indigenous men to the city's canal – to their ancestral transportation infrastructure. In the years that followed, Indigenous governors continued to lead the cleaning of canals annually.[70]

Streets were different. City hall council members wanted the cleaning of streets to be added to the list of projects charged to Indigenous governors on a recurring basis. In December 1586, they once again asked the viceroy to assign Indigenous men "every week" to "go around with carts" and "do this work."[71] The governors objected.

Officials at city hall slowly realized that they would have to manage street cleaning directly, and that it had to be part of a greater effort to provide sanitation services. Residents needed official garbage dumps and regular garbage collection. They complained about the smell.[72] "Vapors" emanating from "piles of garbage" were to blame for the "many diseases" that struck their loved ones.[73] Manure and garbage filled empty lots throughout the city and impeded traffic. City hall thus designated "six places, marking them with tall poles" and criers informed residents "to throw their garbage in those places."[74] This initiative addressed the household trash problem, but what of the streets? Here is where carters stepped in.

Local carters encouraged high governing officials to institute sanitation services and charge them with the business. Councilmen discussed it for several years and decided to contract out the work.[75] In October 1589, they released city funds to have wainwrights "make carts" and "to purchase mules" for this endeavor.[76] Gaspar Pérez, who organized carting for construction, won the first one-year contract, which promised to pay him 1,000 pesos and the use of the city's carts and mules.[77] The carters he worked with asked for direction for what seemed like an overwhelming task: were they supposed to clean all streets?; shovel all the garbage piles?; and where were they "to dispose of the garbage they collected"?[78] The carters needed logistical guidance, so Pérez asked the city to appoint a councilman "to order what needed to be done."[79] This request became the grounds for a new position – Deputy of Sanitation Carts – held by council members on a rotating basis starting in November 1590 and throughout the seventeenth century. Carters' demand for logistical oversight thus pushed the council to take direct responsibility for sanitation and street cleaning, which follows a pattern revealed in other chapters of working people encouraging government interventions that enabled them to create new businesses.

The first deputy reminded residents that they were responsible for cleaning their immediate property, their sidewalks, and taking their garbage to the new city dumps. The city's refuse carts were meant to support their efforts by clearing garbage piles from the squares and stone-paved streets. In the months that followed, local carters using twelve carts and twenty-four mules began to regularize street cleaning.[80] When their experiences on the streets confirmed that they needed more equipment, Pérez arranged for additional vehicles.[81]

The city's sanitation carting services began with small carting outfits owned by carters who prescribed the parameters of the contracts. By the turn of the sixteenth century, the contracted person "was obligated to clear manure and garbage from the streets and squares of the whole city of Mexico, and to clear all the garbage dumps."[82] Councilmen wanted them to clean the city "all day" and "without taking on any other jobs," but contractors took liberties in how they fulfilled their obligations and organized workers to make it more profitable.

The first sanitation contractors were able to hire Indigenous residents to supplement their workforce. They arranged with the city to have men assigned to their crews to work alongside their full-time carters, shoveling, sweeping, and moving garbage. As noted, city hall had previously asked the viceroy to appoint Native American residents to clear garbage dumps, but that had been on a one-time basis. The contractors wanted a permanent arrangement.

Indigenous governors, in turn, soon organized to refuse the assignment and their resistance gained traction in early 1597. As Chimalpahin described, an "epidemic raged very terribly" and "there was a great deal of death" at that time.[83] Native leaders decried the burden of the labor drafts when so many of their people were dangerously sick, and they successfully evaded the demands for men to work in street cleaning. In March 1597, Agustín Reina, the second sanitation contractor, complained at a city hall meeting that "it had been more than three months" since he was assigned workers due to the epidemic.[84] Faced with the labor shortage, Reina had to pay additional carters to keep the refuse carts "rolling."[85]

Contractors tried to keep the draft labor allowance because it ensured that they would have workers and saved them money (draft workers, as noted, got paid less than salaried carters). Indigenous governors, however, continued to challenge the assignments and gained two concessions. The 1598 sanitation contract award specified that only twenty-four individuals from the labor draft would work with the sanitation carts, and contractors had to provide them with meals.[86] The number of assigned people was smaller than what contractors had hired previously. The food provision, moreover, was notable because grain was scarce and prices high at this time due to drought and bad harvests. The requirement made it possible for Indigenous men to reduce the burden on their families' food supply during their labor assignments.[87]

In the years to come, Indigenous governors periodically organized one-time street-cleaning projects with hundreds of tributaries, but these were unrelated to the sanitation contracts. In July 1600, Jerónimo López, governor of the polity of Tenochtitlan, arranged for 100 men to clean Tacuba Street, off the Causeway, for four days, and then supervised as the head of public works paid each of them two silver reales "in cash" for their work.[88] The governor's direct involvement in the direct payment of salaries in coins demonstrates a shift, by which Indigenous residents demanded silver money to align their wages with non-Indigenous workers.

Indigenous leaders used the establishment of regular sanitation services to prevent city hall from relying on draft labor. During the seventeenth century, they organized the cleaning and repair of the canals because they remained the main transit ways for Native American residents, not the streets. Regular street cleaning and refuse collection had to be the responsibility of contractors. Sanitation contractor Francisco Hidalgo complained in 1600, the same year Governor López led the Tacuba Street project. He was not getting assigned draft laborers and "was unable to find" Indigenous workers "to clean the city's streets."[89] Raising the salary he offered carters would have helped in recruitment, but Hidalgo refused.[90] Subsequently, men who won the contracts relied on the labor of enslaved people. The sanitation business remained exploitative.

During the seventeenth century, carters continued to create businesses that provided services and supported the city's transportation infrastructure. Someone had to clean the streets. Someone had to ensure the free passage of vehicles through the streets. Someone had to manage the delivery of goods across the city. What follows are the stories of carters who did this work, and how they came to be associated with public order.

## 2.3 SUSTAINING PUBLIC ORDER

The Ordinances for Public Order, executed by Viceroy Guerra in 1612, reveal that carters gained concessions for new businesses by showing officials that they provided essential public services.[91] These ordinances reflected dictates issued during previous administrations, in the same way as the Ordinances for Provisions discussed in Chapter 1. The concept of public order was related to good government, which meant having officials charged with overseeing sanitation and public infrastructure, as well as security and law enforcement.[92] The 1612 ordinances only addressed the first two matters and focused on streets. First sanitation: maintaining public order meant keeping them clean. This understanding of public order, as the linguist Covarrubias explained, derived from the Greco-Roman tradition of *politeia*, defined as "governing the things of the city, its ornament, and cleanliness."[93] He included an example that city carters would have embraced because it referenced their work: in "places with public order, people go out with their bins when the refuse carts pass by to empty them."[94] Clauses 5 to 9 formalized what carters had managed to achieve: the establishment of sanitation contracts.

Members of the newly created Public Order Board were responsible for supervising the contractors, who, according to the ornament and orderliness principle, contributed to public order.[95]

The Ordinances for Public Order included mandates that contractors used for their own advantage. The prohibition on throwing garbage or waste on the streets, for example, was meant to help them by reducing the amount of refuse carters were required to clear.[96] Residents, moreover, had to take their own waste to the garbage dumps, located around the city for their convenience. This requirement opened an opportunity. Realizing residents might pay to have this done, the contractors organized household collection services. They convinced residents to have them cart their garbage away. The Ordinances for Public Order thus formalized the city's dependence on sanitation contractors for street cleaning, which in turn, empowered them to manage the work for their own best interests, which included using city property, carts, to engage in side businesses.

Andres Pérez Mariñas convinced the Public Order Board to grant him the sanitation contract and kept it for two years despite repeated complaints. In October 1635, councilmen refused to pay him because he had not fulfilled the contract requirements. Pérez "had an obligation to report every day at seven in the morning to the house" of the designated board member to receive orders on "what had to be done," and he was failing to do so.[97] Nonetheless, Pérez received 500 pesos, a third of the annual payment. He was reprimanded again six and ten months later for failing to comply with the terms.[98] By the time the contract ended, it had already provided Pérez with income and connections, which he mobilized to run a business that provided sanitation services privately.

Gonzalo Cruz had been working for hours, loading a cart with refuse, when he asked three men passing by "to help him."[99] His assignment that day was to remove the garbage from a house on Saint Francis Street (Figure 2.4). They were visiting the city from their hometown in Michoacan, 150 miles away, a trip that had taken days and exhausted them. Cruz could not understand why the men refused. They spoke P'urhépecha – a language he could not comprehend.[100] Frustrated and angry, Cruz looked at Sebatián Avellanedo, the only one who knew a little Spanish, swiped his hat off, dragged him to the carriage house, and took his money. Avellado tried "to resist," explaining that the ten silver coins wrapped in a handkerchief were all that they had brought "to buy things" for their community. Cruz ignored him and raised a knife to his chest, promising to kill Avellanedo and "bury him in the carriage house," right where they stood, if he told anyone.[101] His friends later explained that they simply watched, too afraid of "getting beaten" to interfere.[102] Instead, they headed directly to the Viceroyal Palace to denounce Cruz; he ended up in jail, and they recovered their money.

This violent incident locates the work of carters who were enslaved and exposes the conditions that led to desperate acts. They went to residents' homes and carted away their garbage and "filth," which included dung from their stables. Slaveowners in the sanitation business, in this case Andres Pérez Mariñas, charged them with this dirty work.[103] In September 1643, when the crime took place, Pérez had Cruz and other enslaved men in his crew doing residential pick-ups. They had started out clearing the city's streets and dumps when Pérez had the sanitation contract.

The matter of funding the contracts was a problem that plagued city hall throughout the century. Members of the Public Order Board repeatedly pressured council members to pay the sanitation contractors, who refused to provide their services for free. Councilors claimed they lacked the funds and refused to pay, so the streets got dirtier, which pressured viceroys to make the payments. Viceroy Mancera, for example, contributed money from the royal treasury in 1669 for this purpose.[104] He agreed to transfer 700 pesos "for the refuse carters who clean the streets and squares."[105] Governing officials recognized carters' role in supporting public order decade after decade. Yet, they complained about individual contractors who used the city's carts to work for residents, instead of clearing the city' street. It proved a cycle, contractors exacted payment, and councilmen demanded clean streets. When Giovanni Gemelli Careri visited the city at the end of the century, he complained that the streets were "always fetid and muddy" and recommended "wearing boots."[106] It depended on the season. Wont to exaggeration, his words nonetheless reflect the constant challenge of street cleaning. The practice of contracting sanitation services remained largely unchanged throughout the century because contractors convinced officials that there was no other way to maintain this aspect of public order. Who else would organize the refuge carts? Officials failed to devise alternatives.

Carters were also involved in the second element of public order: building and maintaining transportation infrastructure. In the words of Covarrubias, "stone-paving the streets and causeways was an important matter and part of public order."[107] The Ordinances for Public Order from 1612 mandated that the city's causeways and streets had to be paved and in good condition.[108] As per the ordinances, residents on "foot, horseback, or carriage" needed to be able to move "easily" across the city's streets and "exit and enter" by way of the causeways.[109] The question was how to organize the labor required to do so, and how to pay for it. Indigenous governors, as noted, secured dispensations from street cleaning, but they could not do so for street building or maintenance. City officials continued to burden them with organizing labor for this purpose. Indigenous carters and canoers, for example, delivered silt, sand, and gravel from the rivers that emptied into the lakes to elevate the streets. They conveyed the stones that formed the pavement. Though required to do this work, officials still had to pay them, but with what funds?

Council members decided to have property owners bear part of the cost of paving and maintaining the city's streets because it served their interests. They all owned carriages, and carriage wheels loosened the stones of the cobbled streets, which meant that the streets needed constant repairs. When Thomas Gage visited Mexico City in 1625, he "judged" that "half the city" kept coaches; he wrote that "it was a most credible report ... that there were above fifteen thousand coaches" in circulation.[110] Gage's number is an exaggeration; their cost was prohibitive for the majority of people. New carriages were expensive, valued in the 1620s at 800 pesos or more, though individuals with less disposable wealth purchased used carriages that sold for less.[111] Residents who called themselves Spaniards thought that having a carriage was very important, so anyone who could afford one, did. Gage's estimate is therefore evocative of their ubiquitous presence. An official estimated 2,000 carriages a year later.[112] This figure means that one in ten "Spanish families" had a carriage in the mid 1620s.[113] Hundreds of carriages left the city after the 1629 flood, but they were back congesting the city's streets within a matter of years.

The 1612 ordinances specified that property owners had to contribute two-thirds of the cost of maintaining stone-paved streets.[114] The financing for paving streets was worked out in segments. The Public Order Board's accountant drew up budgets and then negotiated with residents who owned property facing the street in question to share the cost. For example, the Convent of San Bernard paid a little over ninety-eight pesos in 1636 as its share of the cost of repaving a one-block segment of an adjoining street.[115] Residents who owned houses on the same street would have paid their shares as well. Council members floated other possibilities over the century to subsidize paving, such as collecting fees from carriage owners, but the fiscal responsibility mainly remained with property owners and the city's budget, with intermittent subsidies from the royal treasury.[116]

The 1612 Ordinances for Public Order, which centered carters' work and facilitated the use of carriages, remained in place throughout the century.[117] Public order, according to the ordinances, depended on work done by carters. Carters in the local carting businesses, in turn, built businesses based on officials' mandate to maintain the streets. Residents depended on carters, and these working people showed once again that they could mobilize the need for their labor to get government concessions that improved their own economies.

## 2.4 CREATING A PARKING DISTRICT DURING THE 1600S–1630S: HOW CARTERS LINKED LONG-DISTANCE AND LOCAL TRANSPORT TO DELIVER GOODS ACROSS THE CITY

Transporters who entered the city from the north on the Guadalupe-Tepeyacac Causeway followed its inward extension, becoming Saint Dominic Street and ending at the Main Square (Figure 2.4).[118] In July 1592, Viceroy Velasco II reissued the ordinance restricting the entry of wagons with special mention of this busy thoroughfare, reiterating city hall's ongoing concern that it seemed to require new stone paving every year.[119] What could be done to protect it? A carter proposed a solution.

The Dominican Order owned a large lot on this thoroughfare close to the causeway (Figure 2.4).[120] It had a small house and two corrals. Anton Gómez, a local carter, located this spot for his business and rented it from the Dominican Order. He planned to create a space where wagoners would unload their goods while he arranged to deliver their merchandise. The lot was located right at the entry limit imposed in 1585 for iron-wheeled vehicles, so Gómez did not expect constables to object.[121] When they did, he convinced the treasurer of the order to secure a license from the viceroy that allowed vehicles "to enter freely" up to his rented property.[122] The appeal acknowledged officials' concern that wagons damaged pipes, so he explained that the property abutted a segment of the street that did not have them, so the water infrastructure was safe. This clarification gave Viceroy Monterrey confidence to make the allowance in September 1600. Without knowing it, Gómez established a precedent. He reconfigured the use of space near the thoroughfare, which made it possible for local carters with simple wooden vehicles to work directly with the owners of long-distance transportation outfits. Gómez created a new business: parking corrals.[123]

Within months, Gómez's neighbors followed suit. Juan García went to the Viceroyal Palace in November. A carpenter, he had recently started making small carts for local carters who started frequenting this part of the city to pick up delivery jobs. Seeing the need for more parking space, he invested "many pesos" to outfit his property as a corral, located near the Chapel of Saint Anne (Figure 2.4).[124] A constable soon after threatened to fine him for permitting "wagons to unload" at his place, revealing that his new venture took off quickly.[125] García responded with a typical political action: he appealed to the viceroy. He knew about the license Gómez had obtained for his business, which was only "two blocks way," and thus asked for the same privilege. García wanted an allowance for "wagons to enter his corral" to unload, which would thwart the potential damage to the stone paving. García left the palace with a license in hand, proving the soundness of the argument used to get it.

These enterprising carters – Gómez and García – inspired Cristobal Cotan to establish his own corral. He wanted to do business with the long-distance transporters who "came from Veracruz and Zacatecas," so he rented a parcel of land in the same neighborhood of Saint Anne.[126] In February 1601, Cotan asked that his license specify he would be able "to receive mule trains" and store wagons that arrived from the port and the northern silver mines.[127] His place attracted so many customers that yet another carter, Diego Luna, "adapted his property to house wagons from abroad."[128] Indeed, the same Juan García sent wagons Luna's way when his corral was full.[129] Wagoners were obviously directing their vehicles to this part of the city, creating a demand for more parking corrals.

It was like a cascade.[130] Lots that had once had gardens were cleared and enclosed for corrals. In this way, carters placed themselves at the center of local and long-distance transport networks. They gave themselves business by opening corrals that facilitated the transfer of goods required by the entry ordinances of years past. Rather than working with canoers at landing docks, wagoners could now cross the Guadalupe Causeway and drive straight to their parking corrals. Carters such as Gómez, García, and Luna took over from there.

The parking-corral pioneers had to overcome attempts by the owners of large transport outfits to take over their business. These individuals owned hundreds of mules, oxen, and wagons housed at large estates outside the city for long-distance transport. They soon recognized that the corrals presented an opportunity to invest in local transport. Juan Castillo, for instance, purchased a house with a stable along the Tezontle

Canal near Anton Gómez's parking corral in 1601. Then, he appealed to
Viceroy Monterrey for "the same permission as the carters" – to drive
into the city as far as they were allowed.[131] Castillo wanted to park his
wagons on his own property rather than paying carters for corral space.
Other residents in long-distance transport moved into the area in the following decades, but they did not displace carters with parking corrals.
They continued to cater to individual wagoners and the owners of small-
scale outfits, who could not afford to rent property in the city. These
transporters came and went from the establishments run by Gómez and
the other innovators.

What started as a response to entry regulations became a distinct
business that provided long-distance transporters a variety of services.
Apart from parking spaces, the new establishments had enclosed stables
for pack animals, fenced-in open areas, and storage for goods. They
were filled with working people who unloaded and transferred goods
from wagons to carts, washed and repaired the vehicles, took care of
the animals, and maintained the wooden enclosures and stables. Long-
distance transporters could thus simply arrive and hand over the reins.

In the early 1600s, Blas Hernández had a corral on the street extension of the Guadalupe Causeway, near the Church of Saint Catherine
(Figure 2.4).[132] It needed some repairs, "a door was falling over," but he
was slowly building his business to improve the facility.[133] Hernández
allowed fellow carters to keep their vehicles and animals in his space
as tenants for additional income, and he passed them carting jobs.
Francisco, though "slight in stature," had a handcart and took on light
loads.[134] Wagoners that unloaded at Hernández's business thus had
access to prompt distribution services; if his vehicles were occupied, the
tenant carters made the deliveries.

Hernández also made agreements with nearby businesses. His customers needed lodging, so he made an arrangement with his neighbor
Martín Gómez, who had an inn.[135] Hernández offered to recommend
the inn to wagoners who parked with him in exchange for Gómez referring his lodgers to his corral. Gómez agreed because he had opened the
inn in the neighborhood for this purpose – to take advantage of the
convergence of visitors. He knew that wagoners and muleteers needed
a convenient place to stay after long days on the road. He had spent his
childhood in the Triana neighborhood of Seville, known for its docks
and shipping services.[136] When Gómez moved to Mexico City, he realized that the parking-corral neighborhood was Triana's counterpart.
A transporter from the city of Puebla always parked at Hernández's

corral and lodged at Gómez's inn when he came to the city.[137] The convenience of staying next to their parked vehicles and animals encouraged transporters to return, so the arrangement benefited both men.

Carters transformed the neighborhoods bordering the street extending inward from the Guadalupe Causeway into a critical terrestrial gateway. By the early 1610s, corral keepers stopped requesting licenses. Constables no longer monitored that section of the city, which had become the zone of the corrals. This claiming of space changed ownership patterns.

The area carved out by local carters was part of the Indigenous districts of San Sebastián Atzaqualco and Santa María Cuepopan. Residents who identified as Mexica Atzaqualca and Mexica Cuepopan witnessed the transformation of their neighborhoods into a commercial hub, which raised property values.[138] Newcomers sought proximity to the causeway, so they increased their bids to convince Indigenous property owners to sell their land. Property records document that it worked. A carter who ran "a corral for wagons" had purchased the plot from Indigenous residents.[139] Such sales intimate a wider pattern, by which neighborhoods that were predominantly inhabited by Indigenous residents in the 1590s shifted demographically to include residents who were not. The creation of new businesses contributed to the diversification of the city's Indigenous districts.

The corral business allowed carters to go into long-distance transport for themselves. Francisco Martín moved into the neighborhood in 1606 and obtained a license like the others to receive wagons at his property.[140] By 1620 he had wagons of his own and specialized in the delivery of fruit.[141] Martín sent wagoners to farms in the hinterland to pick up produce, which they unloaded and stored at his facility, located eight blocks from the Main Square. Vendors at the central market complex got their fruit from Martín because his carters delivered it straight to their stands. He provided a service that shows working people relying on one another for their own enterprises.

Local carters also worked as intermediaries between long-distance transporters and merchants. In the early 1620s, Marcos Vilches carted goods around the city from his base next to the Church of Saint Anne (Figure 2.4).[142] He welcomed wagoners, such as Luis Reina, who traveled with his vehicles and mules to wherever customers sent him with deliveries. Away for months at a time, Reina trusted Vilches to take care of some business in his absence. Reina knew other carters, counting them as friends, but Vilches inspired greater trust.[143] This ability gained him a network of customers who trusted that he carted their goods across the city without stealing from them. When Reina arrived with goods from the hinterland, he knew that Vilches would make room in his corral and help him with the unloading. He also appreciated that Vilches had jobs waiting for him; the corral keeper handled requests from traders who needed to transport their merchandise out of the city and passed business his way. Vilches and Reina had a personal and business relationship that reveals how transporters worked together to maintain the city's long-distance networks.

Their story is also about the ways small-scale transporters created side opportunities. Vilches' contacts with local merchants and store owners allowed both men to do some trading of their own. In February 1621, Vilches convinced a customer, a merchant with dealings that usually involved tens of thousands, to let them sell goods valued at 250 pesos.[144] As a favor, the merchant allowed the carter and wagoner to take a small amount of indigo dye and a bolt of cloth from his reserves. Vilches and Reina planned to sell the goods at a higher price than the merchant's evaluation to make a profit in time to pay him back. Vilches planned to sell the cloth in measured segments to his acquaintances, while Reina took the dye to towns in the north, far from indigo-producing regions to the south. The merchant thus enabled them to make money without needing to front the capital for the initial purchase. Transporters such as Reina and Vilches embedded themselves in wealthy merchants' networks to carry out small-scale trading of their own. The merchants, in turn, supported local carters' initiatives to foster relations with workers who helped them move their goods across the city.

Carters also relied on credit from merchants to pay the costs of sustaining their businesses, including the purchase of pack animals and vehicles. Carting mules in the mid 1620s sold for sixty pesos each.[145] Alonso Palacios's cart was falling apart. In 1625, he inquired about prices at the shops of several wainwrights and the kind he wanted cost eighty pesos; he would have to borrow that amount. Palacios turned to merchant Lorenzo Caraballo for a loan because he had made deliveries for him in the past and knew him to be a creditor.[146] Paying Caraballo back in the agreed-upon time proved impossible. Palacios thus offered to provide carting services at reduced rates to make up for part of the payment. Merchants extended credit to carters because they knew they would get their money back, if not in coins, then in cheap labor.

Local carters faced challenges posed by large outfits who tried to move into their corner of the transport business. By the late 1610s, local carters specialized in the goods they carried. There were carters, for example, who transported wine barrels in carts pulled by mules. They moved the barrels one-by-one to the city's "warehouses and taverns."[147] This method abided by the vehicle and weight restrictions on streets. Luis Nieto got a hearing at city hall in October 1619. His family had a business that distributed wine from wine-growing regions in Mexico and imported from Spain, and he wanted a concession to take over local wine transportation. Nieto told council members that he would dedicate twelve carts for wine deliveries, "or more if needed."[148] In return for prohibiting local carters from transporting wine, Nieto would pay city hall a "rent" of 500 pesos annually for ten years.[149] He would have a monopoly on this service. To strengthen the proposal, Nieto appealed to the councilors' ongoing concern for stone pavement worn from haphazard driving. He offered to limit his carts to "designated streets" and to contribute an additional 100 pesos to city funds for "street repairs"; the plan would "benefit the whole republic."[150] Nieto calculated that providing this service would yield him significant profit, more money than the 600 pesos he promised city hall on an annual basis. Council members considered the proposal.

Their response, two weeks later, confirms that officials recognized the commercial importance of local carters. A resident operating with a sole wheelbarrow provided a key service, so did the owner of a parking corral. "The republic" needed to support carters and "allow everyone who wanted to be in this trade to do so."[151] Nieto's proposal was declined. Councilmen reasoned that if they allowed Nieto to monopolize wine delivery, others might consider controlling the carting of other goods. They would raise carting prices, which did not serve the city's interests. Carters needed to be able to negotiate their fees to make a living. Residents benefitted from working with local carters of their own choosing. At the same time, councilors appreciated Nieto's suggested contribution to the upkeep of the streets. Heavy loads were an ongoing problem. Would it hinder commerce if the city issued "a moderate levy" on local carters?[152] The funds would be used "to repair bridges, causeways, and streets." They posed the question as a proposal for another day.

Councilmen returned to the matter in 1626. Residents complained about having to pay for the upkeep of streets fronting their property. Would it be easier to place that burden on the carters and carriage owners who used them? Members of the Public Order Board disagreed. Collecting a fee or "pension" from carters to fund stone paving would be an unfair imposition and a "danger to the republic."[153] All residents benefitted from carters' work; they cleaned the streets and moved goods with small carts to protect the streets. City hall needed to encourage rather than penalize the city's carters. As carriage owners, these officials would also be liable for the proposed fees. The councilors agreed and conveniently shelved the funding proposal once again.

The corral zone was devastated by the "general inundation" of 1629.[154] That year, "no place was spared" and the "floodwaters remained stagnant for four years, causing such great ruin to buildings and other property that it was impossible to enumerate the damages."[155] Markets closed as told in Chapter 1. Bernabé Cobo, a Jesuit from Spain, reported in 1630 that "all the streets were flooded," so that everyone "went about in canoes instead of coaches."[156] The causeways were damaged.

As the city rebuilt, local transporters slowly went back to business in certain parts of the city. In 1635, however, the Saint Anne neighborhood in the corral zone remained "largely depopulated" and terrestrial transportation was "inconvenient."[157] Corral keepers and carters struggled to rebuild their businesses. The economic importance of long-distance transport, however, required that city hall invest in terrestrial infrastructure. How else, argued local and long-distance transporters, was Mexico City to regain its status as a commercial hub? The street from the Guadalupe Causeway to the previously established entry limit had to be repaved.[158] Councilmen conceded it was a necessary investment that would encourage carters to return to the area. They were, after all, central players in the network that joined long-distance transporters to the city's consumer market. The corral district around Saint Anne Chapel remained a center for local transporters for the rest of the seventeenth century (Figure 2.4).

Bernardo Cruz worked as the coachman of a cloth merchant in the 1640s.[159] While driving him around the city, Cruz interacted with other local and long-distance transporters who enabled the merchant to run his business. Cruz took the merchant to the parking-corral zone, where wagoners handed him bills of lading that listed the bolts of imported cloth they carried from the ports. He saw workers at these businesses open the merchant's crates to show him the textiles and then repackage the bolts to load them on carts. Cruz drove the merchant back to this house and greeted the carters who delivered the merchandise hours later. Through these interactions, Cruz helped orchestrate the movement that made it possible for residents to purchase goods such as Chinese silk and Dutch lace.

The experiences of coachmen demonstrate their own role in keeping the city in motion. Like carters, coachmen witnessed the city's transformation into an increasingly terrestrial place. They took advantage of residents' dependence on their work to pursue financial opportunities related to long-distance and local transportation. The Ordinances for Public Order's emphasis on stone paving facilitated their transit through the city's streets. These men, however, faced different challenges than historical actors named so far because most coachmen were enslaved and free people of African and Asian descent. They experienced racism, defined as the attempt to categorize people with the purpose of denigrating them. Coachmen lived with the constraints imposed by laws that upheld slavery. Their history, told next, shows that coachmen came together in political action to claim freedoms that other residents took for granted.

## 2.5 CLAIMING SPACES: HOW COACHMEN CREATED NETWORKS FOR COMMUNITY, ECONOMY, AND POLITICAL ENGAGEMENT

Sebastián arrived in Mexico City in 1616 from Acapulco, where he disembarked from a ship of the Manila Galleon. A slaveowner had sent an agent to the port to purchase "one of the enslaved people who came from the Philippines" to work as his coachman.[160] The grid layout of the streets helped Sebastián orient himself, and he was soon driving the slaveowner's carriage across the city. He met other coachmen and learned that they were part of a community that included enslaved and free men who claimed the freedom of movement that characterized their profession. They seemed to know everyone involved in transportation and shared their contacts. It took Sebastián a little over a year to gather information and make plans to leave the city. He meant to free himself from the slaveowner. Sebastián spoke with people who worked in long-distance transport to figure out a destination and decided to travel to Veracruz. He was living there in 1619 when the slaveowner located his whereabouts. Sebastián was working for a baker who had taken him in when he appeared at his door "beset with hunger."[161] The phrase hints at the challenges enslaved people faced after they fled, but it also indicates that they found work and managed to remain free, at least for a time. The slaveowner explained to officials that he had "been forced to pay a free man six pesos a month plus meals" to work as his coachman. This cost drove him to track down Sebastián, who was forced to return to Mexico City. Enslaved coachmen lived with the reality that property laws circumscribed their freedom of movement; they could not leave the city. Ordinances related to people who self-freed prescribed horrifying punishments if caught.[162] These mandates did not deter people from taking the chance to do so, but they inspired caution.

Coachmen needed safe spaces within the city to protect themselves from laws that upheld slavery. For enslaved coachmen, they were an escape from slaveowners' vigilance. For free coachmen, they offered opportunities to trade goods, learn about side jobs, and find better employers. Enslaved and free men created sanctuaries in carriage houses and stables across Mexico City to sustain themselves. They were social spaces for men who resisted the efforts of slave-owning "Spaniards" to control and treat them as property.

Slaveowners associated coachmen and their vehicles. Hernán Altamirano, a lawyer, did not even refer to the coachman by name; he was simply the coachman.[163] And having this person drive him around the city was a way for Altamirano to display his wealth. Thomas Gage noted the connection during his visit in 1625, writing that "the pride of some" carriage owners led them to "spare no silver … to enrich them."[164] That year, a resident paid handsomely to decorate his carriage: green waxed-cotton cloth for the enclosure, red wool for the interior seats, and twisted-silk thread fringe for the curtains.[165] "Gentlemen" had coachmen "waiting on them" who wore "gallant liveries," referring to their uniforms.[166] Carriage owners' vanity, Gage suggested, compelled them to have enslaved coachmen drive their fancy cars.

The location of carriage houses and stables in the city's buildings, usually behind the main patio, reflected the attitude that coachmen were an extension of their carriages. Slaveowners got off before coachmen led the animals away and parked the vehicles in the back. Their quarters were in the same area. Enslaved coachmen used this spatial separation to their advantage. Carriage houses were private areas, where they rested, socialized, and hosted fellow coachmen who were free.

African- and Asian-descended men, stigmatized by slavery even if they were free, claimed the profession to make a living. A barber surgeon working at a hospital, by way of comparison, received a salary of a little more than eight pesos per month.[167] A coachman's salary, around six pesos a month, was less than that, but still a relatively good wage.[168] They could also lodge with their employers to avoid the cost of housing. Carriage houses were thus home to free and enslaved coachmen. Cohabitation and conviviality strengthened relations between individuals that transcended legal status and ethnic differences. They depended on that solidarity to face the restrictions officials imposed on the movement of people associated with slavery.

Coachmen responded to discrimination by creating a network of community bases across the city. Officials passed ordinances prohibiting enslaved and free residents of African descent from gathering in groups since the mid sixteenth century, following royal decrees for Hapsburg territories.[169] The curtailment on the size of gatherings in Mexico City imposed in 1589 limited them to four people.[170] It was reduced further two decades later in response to a supposed plot. An ordinance from April 2, 1612, stated that African-descended people could not "gather in groups greater than three in public or private places, by day or night" on pain of 200 lashes.[171] Two weeks later, additional ordinances specified that only four individuals could gather for funerals and prohibited enslaved people from being outside between eight in the evening and five in the morning, among other proscriptions.[172] They also banned them from carrying weapons but made exceptions within months because "ministers" insisted that enslaved people accompany them "with swords" for their protection and to convey their status.[173] Criers took to the streets with the announcements. The prohibitions expressed officials' hysteria regarding alleged revolts.[174] As Chimalpahin recorded a day before the ordinances, people of African descent "were accused … that they were declaring war, that they were going to rebel."[175] In the coming days, he added, "Spaniards who live in Mexico became very agitated and fearful."[176] Soldiers guarded the streets and causeways. Judges of the High Court ordered terrifying punishments for the alleged conspirators, hanging thirty-five people. A coachman, unnamed in the documentation, was one of the accused.[177]

The community of coachmen lost one of their own. Like other residents of African descent, they fell under suspicion and feared for their lives for months to come while the apparent crisis subsided. Then, residents slowly began to ignore the prohibitions. Men obtained licenses to bear swords, they carried knives, people gathered to bury their dead, and enslaved people visited family and friends across the city late into the night. They asserted their freedom by purposely going against the 1612 ordinances and those from previous decades. Residents, however, had to be careful, especially about holding large gatherings at night when it was not a feast day, when all residents had sizeable reunions. Coachmen avoided drawing the attention of constables tempted to collect the fines outlined in the ordinances by gathering in private places. Carriage houses and stables were their sanctuaries.

Antonio Perea lived in Seville for over a decade, where he met fellow coachmen Francisco Rodríguez and Sebastián Mondragon, who became his lifelong friends.[178] Perea, originally from Sanlúcar, and Rodríguez from the Canary Islands, moved to Seville, the headquarters for Spain's Indies trade, to find work. Once there, they considered the possibility of migrating to America. They seized the opportunity when Mondragon, who was enslaved, told them that he was moving because the slaveowner had been appointed to the High Court of Mexico City.[179] He encouraged them to join him, and the three mates made the journey on the same ship in 1631. On arrival, coachmen welcomed them and helped Perea and Rodríguez find employment. The three newcomers joined a community that accepted and helped them find their paths in a city that had residents who considered themselves superior to working men of African descent.

The experiences of coachmen who were not African descended stand in contrast to those who contended with racism. Miguel Rivas worked as the coachman of a marquess in the mid 1630s.[180] He crossed Perea and his friends on the streets. Rivas received a salary, but his main source of income came from lending money to clients who turned to him for quick cash. When Catalina Daza needed thirty pesos in real coins, she went to his house and trusted him with a bolt of purple damask, left as collateral until she repaid the loan. Rivas stored it in a locked desk filled with accounting receipts. Rivas grew this side business in a matter of years, having arrived in Mexico City in 1621 when he was 24, thin, and with a slight beard, which made him look younger. Born in a village in northern Spain, Rivas moved to Seville because he had "wanted to go to the Indies to the province of New Spain."[181] He signed on as the "servant" of a judge appointed to the High Court who paid the passage. Riva's patron died suddenly within a year, threatening his livelihood, but Rivas quickly found a position in the household of the marquess.[182] Then, he used his employer's connections to meet people and gain their trust.

Rivas's trajectory from poor migrant to moneylender would have been difficult if he was not the son of "old Christians."[183] This phrasing in official documentation meant that he looked like he was a free, European-descended person. City-born residents who called themselves "Spaniards" rarely worked in the profession because they did not want residents to associate them with slavery. Coachmen such as Rivas were conflicted by this connotation. What they looked like, however, mattered. Their physiognomy protected them from the prejudice of residents who were in a position help them.

Diego Escovedo, from the beginning of the chapter, had African ancestry and was once enslaved. Like Rivas and Mondragon, he moved to Mexico City with a high official, Viceroy Villena, alongside fellow coachman Juan Núñes, who had blond hair.[184] Both entered the Viceroyal Palace through a stone-arch entrance that led to a large patio surrounded by rooms on two floors.[185] They stabled the animals and parked the carriages on the lower level. They waited until they received orders to pick up a resident invited to the palace; they drove members of the court to the Alameda. That was their work, but what of their social network?

Escovedo joined a community of African-descended coachmen that was partly based on people's need to seek shelter from discriminatory legislation. Núñes was exempt; he carried arms and gathered with as many people as he wanted without fearing punishment. The way he looked enabled him to follow a different trajectory, like Rivas, who lent money to garner sufficient funds to change his profession. Núñez and Rivas wanted to socialize in the rooms of property owners rather than in their employers' carriage houses, which African-descended coachmen appropriated for themselves.

Jacinto and Diego fostered their community of coachmen in the early 1640s with nightly card games. After long days of work, they would clear their room and welcome their friends and guests for the evening's entertainment. The hosts, enslaved men, lived in the large house of the slaveowner, a wealthy merchant, with a stable and carriage house. Jacinto knew his fellow coachmen "from the streets"; they were his social network, which he cultivated by inviting them to their get-togethers.[186] Card games encouraged relaxation after long driving days. Players used official decks of cards to avoid the fines that came with playing with hand-painted cards. Jacinto and Diego acquired theirs from a selected dealer, as per royal decree, who sold decks for six reals, wrapped in paper, tied with a string, and sealed with the crown's insignia.[187] It was an investment in socializing.

Small wagers, in coins or objects, enlivened their games and allowed talented or lucky players to make money. Coachman José Tovar won a shirt and turned it into cash by pawning it; "he needed money."[188] Jacinto and Diego, however, were careful on the betting front.[189] Allowing high bets threatened their community's cohesion. So, they fostered an environment where coachmen played for small gains, but remained watchful of the bets to prevent players from becoming overly indebted to one other.

Jacinto demonstrated his commitment to camaraderie when he followed up on suspicious games. Newcomers to the group were tempted to wager on pilfered goods. When this happened in 1645, Jacinto traced the object in question to inform the owner of its whereabouts. Then, he excluded the culprit from their group. Salaried coachmen who joined them could not afford losing the trust of those who hired them by associating with thieves. Enslaved coachmen like him needed to protect the relative freedom of movement that came with their profession. They could not afford a situation that would have an official knocking at their door. Accusations could instigate a sale – a rupture in their lives that raised the possibility of experiencing worse treatment and greater oversight in the household of the next slaveowner.[190]

Carriages and stables throughout the city had to remain safe spaces because viceroys reissued ordinances on gatherings and bearing arms. They were committed to the ongoing effort to control the movements of African- and Asian-descended people, especially those who were enslaved. New prohibitions acknowledged that people were not abiding by them and indicate that officials had difficulty enforcing them throughout the century. The draconian ordinances of 1612 were reissued within a decade.[191] Viceroy Salvatierra referenced the long history of evasion in 1645, at the same time that Jacinto and Diego were holding their card games. His predecessors, Salvatierra noted, had all "issued ordinances prohibiting" people of African, Asian, and mixed descent from gathering at night and from bearing arms.[192] Yet, there was no doubt that people gathered in large numbers and that they bore arms. The prohibitions were related because people supposedly planned armed rebellions when they socialized. Salvatierra lamented that the ordinances had not "produced the desired effect."[193] The practice of gathering and bearing arms was "widespread," which showed a lack of "respect towards Spaniards and ignored the differences between people."[194]

Undeterred by years of evasion, Viceroy Salvatierra reissued the prohibitions on gathering in threes at night or fours during the day and on bearing arms. A crier walked around the city on August 19, 1645, calling people with the sound of a trumpet to gather in squares to listen while he read the ordinances.[195] Jacinto, Diego, and the city's other coachmen heard him and spread the news. The new prohibitions recognized the freedoms African- and Asian-descended coachmen claimed for themselves: they carried arms for protection and gathered in groups in the evenings. The coachmen took notice, at the same time, of the immediate danger. They had to remain vigilant to avoid the constables and other officials "charged with the precise execution" of the new ordinances. No one wanted to be apprehended or serve as an example for the intended punishment of 200 lashes. In this context, Jacinto and Diego's room, inside a carriage house, afforded a safe enclosure to meet with their friends.

In the evenings, Blas Loya enjoyed the company of fellow coachmen in the community's bases. He frequented Jacinto and Diego's get-togethers. During the day, Loya worked as the coachman of the general receptor of the Holy Office.[196] When Loya drove him to the Palace of the Holy Office, he went down Saint Dominic Street to enter its carriage house, which was in dire need of repair (Figure 2.4).[197] He waited until it was time to drive back to the receptor's house, and in the meantime, Loya ran errands. He took his employer's animals to a farrier who tended their shoes. He walked down the street to the Main Square to pick up supplies. And he visited acquaintances. When a French carriagemaker told him that he was in the market for a horse, Loya volunteered to get one for a fair price. He knew of a horse stabled across the city that was for sale and brokered a deal in exchange for a tip. Loya's exchanges typify the ways free coachmen used their contacts in the transport business to supplement their income. They occupied the city's streets during daylight, but acted with caution after sunset.

They were free inside carriage houses. A coachman and his wife hosted a New Year's party in 1664 in their employer's carriage house, located on Palm Street (Figure 2.4).[198] Friends played the harp and guitar. There was singing and merriment. The party overflowed into the street, as the players "strummed and sang" under the stars into the evening. The wife stood at the carriage house door and waived to late arrivals, "calling them to join the others."[199] These guests came with their instruments as well, already playing as they rounded the corner to attend the party.

At that point, some neighbors, "Spaniards," complained of the noise and told them to leave the street. Their reaction revealed the racial tensions that stressed relations between some of the city's residents. The partygoers simply responded that "they did not want to go, they had to sing."[200] The surety of the response came from the strength of their numbers and a shared sense of community. They were willing to fight. One of the complaining neighbors unsheathed his sword to threaten the celebrators, but he soon retreated inside and closed his door to dodge the stones partygoers threw his way. The names of the hosts, the coachman and his wife, escaped the historical record, but not their communal initiative. In the same way as Jacinto and Diego twenty years earlier, the couple turned their home into a space where coachmen from across the city felt a sense of belonging. The gathering on New Year's Eve in 1664 was more than a party; it was a confirmation that African-descended coachmen turned carriage houses into havens.

People attended the party knowing that ordinances restricted gatherings. They felt emboldened that New Year's Eve to extend their festivities to the street. The neighbors felt empowered by the existing ordinances, so they expressed their fear and resentment by reporting them to officials within days. The guests had ignored their warnings to leave Palm Street, challenging their entitlement. A short investigation followed, which included other instances of "Spaniards" reporting people who challenged the gathering restrictions.[201] The government's response to the complaints, once again, was to reissue ordinances. But this time, in 1665, the prohibition was only on bearing arms, without mention of the size of gatherings.[202] The same ban had been reposted a few years earlier, but as noted during the investigation, "in spite of the published bans on bearing arms, they use them."[203] Parties did not threaten officials. Armed people did.

Yet, the same officials who issued the ban had carriages, and they knew that their coachmen carried daggers and knives for their protection, especially when they were driving them at night. Did they expect their coachmen to give up their arms? What of the dangers of driving after nightfall? The ordinance on arms ignored the reality on the streets, which is why officials hesitated to enforce it.

Viceroy Mancera made a notable generalization in 1673 that suggests he gained some insight during his tenure about the need for flexibility when it came to controlling people's mobility and ability to protect themselves. African-descended people, he wrote, "are naturally proud, audacious, and friends of change, so it is advisable to watch their movements and designs, but without showing distrust."[204] The viceroy needed to trust his coachmen to feel protected in the streets. They also provided logistical support for travel outside the city, so Mancera discouraged enforcement. Implementing the ordinances went against his own interests because Mancera relied on coachmen, and he hesitated to offend them.

José Romero, an African-descended man, drove Viceroy Mancera around Mexico City during his tenure and traveled with him on the way to Veracruz when it was time to return to Spain.[205] Romero made Escovedo's journey, from the beginning of the chapter, in reverse. His last duties as head coachman were to help the chief equerry organize the trip and manage the mules and horses that transported the viceroy's household.[206] In the days prior to departure, the equerry visited coachman Pedro Alvarado at the stable of the Count of Santiago with a job proposal.[207] He was gathering a team of trusted men to make the journey. Alvarado had previously worked at the Viceroyal Palace, but now earned more money and had a flexible schedule, so he declined the equerry's offer. Romero seized the moment to ask for greater responsibilities before departure.

The viceroy's party left Mexico City on April 2, 1674; they would stop to rest at towns and cities on the way to the coast. When they got to Otumba, they lodged at the Franciscan convent, where Escovedo had stayed almost thirty years earlier.[208] During this sojourn, the chief equerry learned that a prized black-maned mule named Secretariat had an injury from the cinch that secured the saddle.[209] An assistant pointed it out when they were at the watering trough. The viceroy's pages had ridden Secretariat, nicknamed "the canoe," in the city, it was supposed to carry one of them to port. The injury sidelined that plan. The party continued and Secretariat remained stabled for his recovery.

When they arrived in Tepeaca on April 21, some ninety miles beyond Otumba, the party suffered the loss of Vicereine Leonor Carreto.[210] Romero was among those who returned to Mexico City with the news. The intellectual Sor Juana Inés de la Cruz had lived at the Viceroyal Palace years earlier, at the same time as Romero. When she learned of the vicereine's passing, she composed a poem, with "the black tears of my sad pen," to commemorate the life of her friend and patron.[211]

Romero picked up Secretariat in Otumba on his way back home. Secretariat had been gifted to a resident in the viceroy's circle. The departure of a viceroy's court commonly included this kind of gift-giving, as those leaving settled their financial and social debts by giving away valued property. Romero expected to garner the patronage of a new employer when he delivered the animal. In the meantime, Romero stabled Secretariat with Diego García, who rented carriages and mules out of his parking corral. He used a service innovated by carters at the beginning of the seventeenth century, who, like coachmen, did work that supported local and long-distance transport.

When Bentura Medina sought to marry in 1694, he asked his fellow coachmen Gaspar Reyes and Diego Nicolas to testify on his behalf.[212] The Council of Trent dictated that people had to petition the local ecclesiastical court for a license to marry, which required witnesses to guarantee the petitioners' single status. The intended party gathered before a churchman, declared their intention, and their witnesses stepped forward to explain their connection to the bride and groom. The act of witnessing and later attending the ceremony confirmed the fraternal bond Medina, an enslaved man, had with Reyes and Nicolas, who were free. Coachmen regularly supported one another in this manner throughout the century, strengthening the fraternal ties they created in carriage houses.[213]

Two coachmen died tragically in Fall 1700, murdered by a resident who thought he was above the law. The diarist Antonio de Robles only identified the father, Pascual Rodríguez, a wealthy silver merchant, omitting the names of his homicidal son and the victims.[214] The first to die was an Asian-descended man on the night of October 18, shot with a blunderbuss, a short-barreled firearm, at close range. News of the incident spread across the city within hours. Was there an altercation that led to this fatal encounter? Robles did not record it, but the description of the second victim's murder reveals the assailant's state of mind. Five days later, the second coachman, who was of African descent, was driving when the assailant ordered him to stop the carriage, so as "not to splash him."[215] It had been raining and water puddled on the streets. The coachman responded with strong words. The assailant felt "disrespected" – that was his reason for attacking the driver.[216] The coachman died three weeks later from his wounds. Did officials prosecute him for the crimes? The diarist did not record it. Their deaths evince the dangers coachmen faced. They transformed carriage houses into community centers to feel safe.

Coachmen did not have a guild to govern their profession or a religious brotherhood solely for coachmen, which was common for other professions.[217] City officials who approved guilds did not allow enslaved people to form such associations, which were reserved for "Spaniards" and hence not for African- and Asian-descended coachmen who were free. They nonetheless supported one another in similar ways. Guilds, as explained in Chapters 3 and 4, for example, supervised training through apprenticeships. Coachmen did so informally. They imparted skills that helped young men, free or enslaved, enter their profession. Religious brotherhoods linked to guilds fostered unity and mutual help during meetings at chapels. Coachmen secured their fraternal bonds in carriage houses.[218]

## 2.6 CONCLUSION

An anonymous painter created a vista of Mexico City on a ten-panel folding screen around 1690 that locates the byways crossed and the spaces

FIGURE 2.6 The streets of working people

Source: "La Mui Noble y Leal Ciudad de México" (c.1690). Courtesy of the Museo Franz Mayer.
The painting's perspective is from Chapultepec, similar to Trasmonte's plan, with the Main Square in the middle of the upper register. The legend on the lower left identifies seventy places, including the Church of Saint Anne in the corral district created by carters. The wagons painted in nearby buildings testify to their work.
A black and white version of this figure will appear in some formats. For the color version, please refer to the plate section.

claimed by historical actors discussed in this chapter (Color Plate 6, Figure 2.6).[219] Carters and coachmen had a street-level view. They sustained the city by keeping residents and goods in motion and connecting them to long-distance networks.

Though this chapter focuses on terrestrial movement, the painting is a reminder that Mexico City was also an aquatic space. Indigenous canoers traversed the city's waterways, such as the Royal Canal, shown in the center of the painting running alongside the Main Square. Indigenous governors organized regular canal cleanings to support Native American residents who used these water byways for their own transport and trade.

Carters traversed the streets that stretch across the painting. Muleteers and wagoners entered the city from the northeast via the Guadalupe-Tepeyacac Causeway, visible on the painting's top left. They stopped at transport facilities in the parking-corral district, where carters unloaded their vehicles and pack animals. Carters carved out this space in the city's outskirts when they created the corral business at the beginning of the seventeenth century to link their work to long-distance commerce. Goods reached residents' homes, shops, and open markets thanks to them.

Carters in sanitation walked through the streets to clear the refuse that otherwise obstructed wheeled passage, and they offered residents private garbage removal services. City hall formalized carters' contributions in 1611 with the Ordinances for Public Order, when they defined public order as the "ornament" of the city, specifying the need to have clean, orderly stone-paved streets and to maintain the causeways. Viceroy Alba explained the economic underpinning in a letter to Philip IV in 1653: "public order" facilitated "commerce."[220] The head of the city made the same connection in 1681: failure to upkeep the city's infrastructure was a threat "to commerce."[221] The highest officials of Mexico City thus recognized over and over again that trade required the easy movement of goods across the city, and that carters facilitated commerce by clearing the streets and transporting goods with vehicles that did not damage them.

Coachmen drove residents across those same streets, keeping the city in motion. But what of their own mobility? Legislation sought to curtail the gathering and movements of African- and Asian-descended people at night, especially at certain times during the century when slaveowners panicked on hearing rumors of rebellion. In response, coachmen organized a collective resistance; they gathered in the evenings in carriage houses and stables, turning them into centers for community and fraternity. Armed rebellion against slaveowners was suicidal – the community did well to remember the events of 1612 – but there were other ways of taking political action. Claiming safe havens at night was one them, as was simply greeting one another on the streets.

This chapter zoomed in from the coasts to the causeways and streets of Mexico City to reconstruct the lives and underline the contributions of workers who transported Mexico City. Coachmen and carters, in turn, relied on the food vendors named in Chapter 1 and on healers who helped them keep their strength. The story of these essential workers comes next.

PLATE 1  Mexico City in 1628

PLATE 2 Everyday life on the Main Square and the Alameda

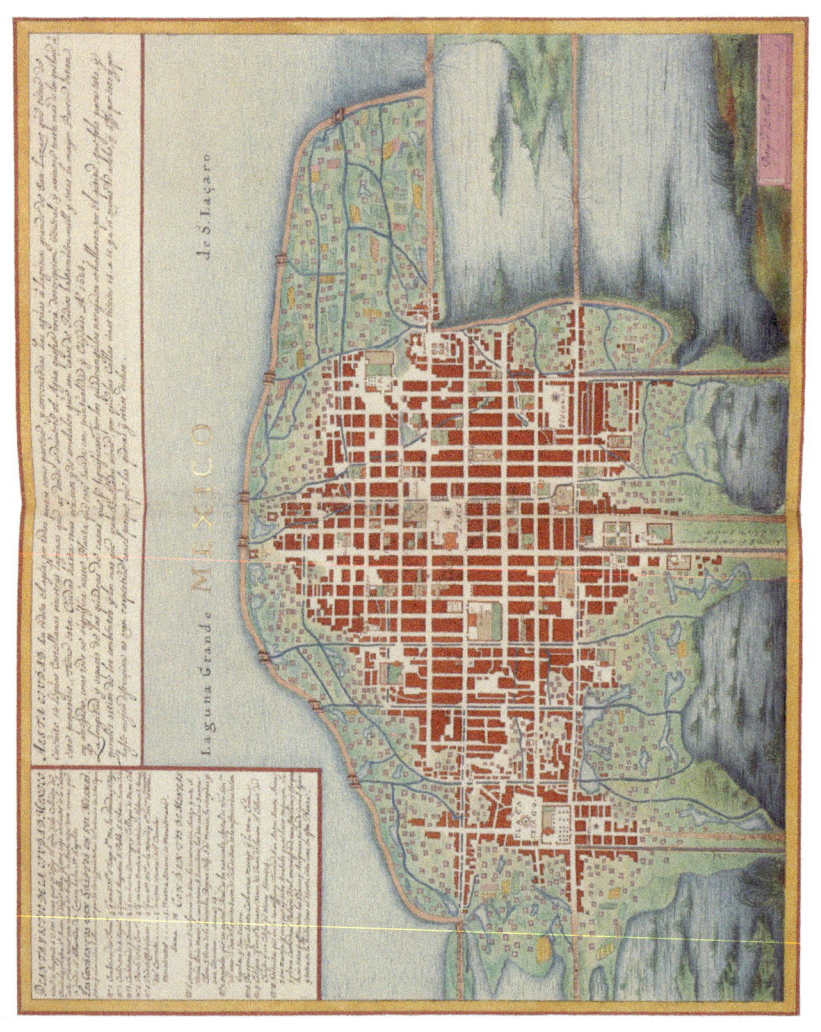

PLATE 3  Mexico City's byways

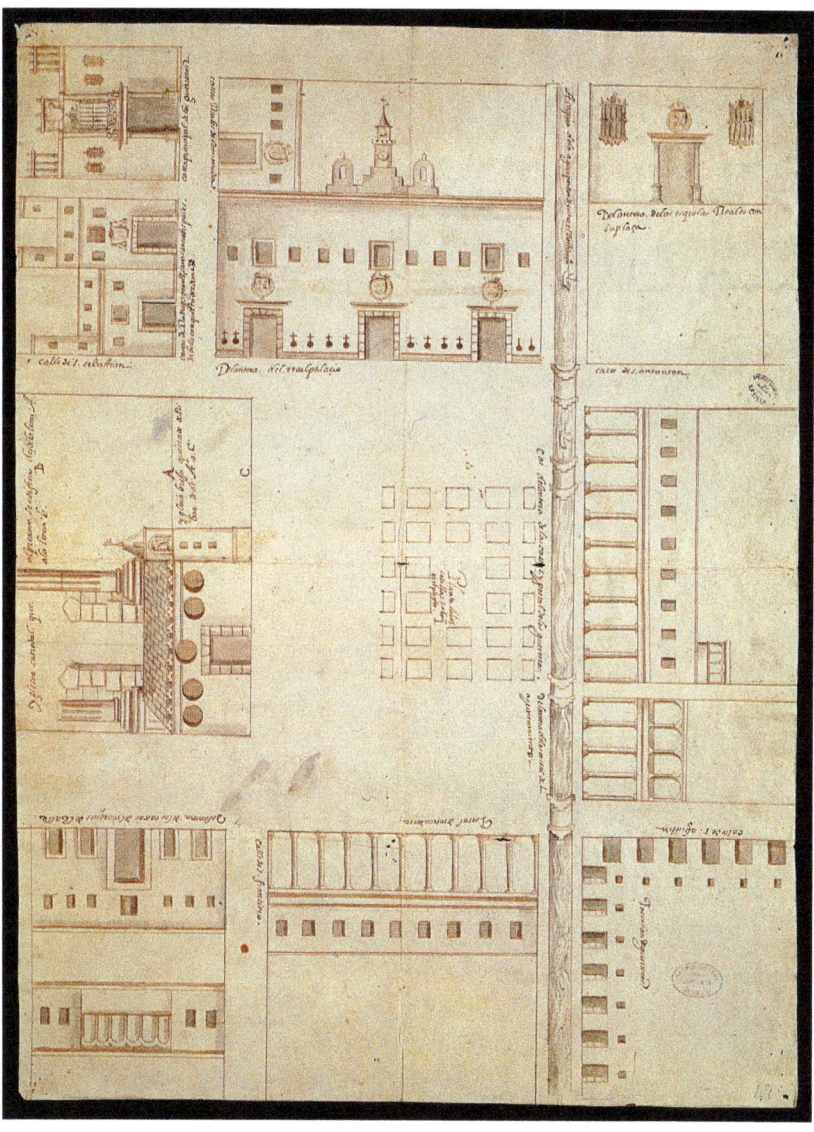

PLATE 4  The Main Square and Volador Square

PLATE 5  The city's center

PLATE 6 A view of the city at century's end

PLATE 7 Commemorating Maundy Thursday

PLATE 8  Silver coin

PLATE 9  Candlesticks fashioned by Diego Mota

# 3

## Caring for the City

Alonso Cortés Siles was a "young man" when he sailed away from his birthplace on Cebu Island to Manila, and from there to Acapulco, arriving in late January 1684.[1] He made his way to the mining town of Taxco, where he heard about a unique business in Mexico City. Men from the Philippines had pioneered a distinct barbering practice seventy years earlier, which remained in the hands of a close-knit community that welcomed newcomers from the islands, free migrants now that the trade of enslaved people from Asia had ended.[2] Seizing the opportunity, Cortés got a recommendation for a "master barber" in the capital who could train him.[3] Knowing no one else, Cortés must have been grateful to live with this hair barber while he learned the trade like other apprentices. Cortés's first language was Cebuano, but he was fluent and literate in Spanish and easily conversed with customers at the master's shop. These establishments existed because a founding generation of enslaved men created a niche in the barbering trade by taking legal action and following economic strategies that enabled them to gain a degree of economic security. This chapter charts their experiences to foreground the history of migrants who helped their fellow residents look and feel better.

A detail from the painting mentioned in Chapters 1 and 2 hints at the services provided by the city's hair barbers (Color Plate 2). Though absent from the scene, the painter depicted their work on men's faces. A graphic rendering captures the animation (Figure 3.1). The two guards have stylized facial hair. The man on the left had his barber trim and wax his whiskers to accentuate the upward curve. His fellow guardsman asked the barber to wash his beard. They have shoulder-length haircuts. These figures represent the customers who frequented blade-and-scissors

FIGURE 3.1  Styling hair
Source: Graphic rendering of detail from "Biombo del Palacio de los
Virreyes de México" (c.1675). Courtesy of the Museo de América. Image
by Matilde Grimaldi.
The detail is from the middle register of the larger work, on the third panel
from the right. The figures represent men in the retinue of a wealthy carriage
owner, who would have known the coachmen discussed in Chapter 2.
They are holding tridents to mark their status as guards.

shops, where barbers took care with their appearance, listened to their
stories, and promoted well-being. The term hair barber does not capture
these services – those oriented toward caring and healing people – but it
is useful for distinguishing them from other types of barbers.

Hair barbers redefined what constituted care and grooming in Mexico
City. They provided services based on an understanding of preventive
treatment that differed from the reactive procedures favored by traditional barbers and doctors. Phlebotomy, or bloodletting, from their
perspective, did not necessarily promote health and could indeed be dangerous. Instead, they served fortifying drinks and offered services such as
massages and the application of compresses to soothe bodily aches. Hair
barbers stressed cleanliness and style in a way that helped residents associate the feeling of wellness with their outward appearance. These men,

however, had to mask their work as healers. So, they called their establishments blade-and-scissors shops to suggest that all they did was hair.

The creation of this business involved an epic decades-long struggle against self-identified "Spanish barbers and surgeons" who did everything in their power to shut them down.[4] These men performed surgical and medical procedures such as phlebotomy, but they gave shaves and haircuts as well. Indeed, grooming services were the mainstay of their own business. They attacked barbers from the Philippines because they could not bear the thought that formerly enslaved men drew customers away from their barbershops and threatened them economically. The experience of traditional barbers is thus part of the history of the rise of blade-and-scissors shops and the working men who healed and styled the city.

### 3.1  VISUALIZING HEALING SPACES

By the time Agustín de Vetancurt was writing in the early 1690s, barbers divided themselves into three groups: barber phlebotomists; barber surgeons; and hair barbers.[5] Vetancurt referenced the first two in his book. These men belonged to the Barbers and Surgeons Guild and the Confraternity or Brotherhood of Holy Christ.[6] He identified barber phlebotomists and barber surgeons as healers and aligned their work with the city's doctors. In the heat of April and May, Vetancurt noted, children endured outbreaks of "measles and smallpox."[7] During these months, the city's "many physicians and barbers rushed to care for the sick" and ease the hearts of worried parents.[8] These afflictions seemed to pass with the arrival of the rainy season, only to be replaced with eruptions of typhus, followed by the flu in cold-weather months. Dysentery was among the "most distressing" – a "general affliction" present year-round to vex even those with the hardiest constitutions.[9] Guild members, Vetancurt suggested, alleviated these maladies. They visited residents in their homes and worked at the city's nine hospitals, where they "acted charitably towards the sick."[10] Vetancurt did not mention hair barbers. They provided care, but the writer shared the perspective of guild members who excluded them from their ranks and ignored their contributions to public health.

Vetancurt's understanding of who healed the city's residents and where it happened reflected the perspective of the Chief Medical Tribunal (*Protomedicato*), which was responsible for overseeing public health in Mexico City.[11] The crown employed this very term in reference to the government's responsibility to provide for the sick and prevent the spread of disease.[12] Public health policy under the Hapsburgs focused on building hospitals, the education of physicians, and the regulation of other healers. Doctors (Latinists) oversaw barber phlebotomists and barber surgeons (also called surgeon empiricists and surgeon romanticists) because officials agreed with the sentiment that learning acquired at the university was superior to learning from experience. The linguist Sebastián Covarrubias captured this distinction in the example he included in his dictionary entry for the word experience. "Experience is knowledge ... learned from using, trying, and experimenting with something."[13] "Empiricists," he added, "treat people without having studied, only from experience," so they "tend to be very dangerous, which is why it has been mandated that they cannot treat people without first being examined by doctors in the faculty [of medicine]."[14] Covarrubias was referring to barber phlebotomists and barber surgeons – they learned from experience and hence required supervision, as dictated by the crown's public health policy. This chapter examines the rise of the Medical Tribunal as it related to the emergence of blade-and-scissors shops. Migrants from the Philippines used doctors' distrust of empiricists to create a new branch of barbering.

A graphic rendering of Johannes Vingboons's orthogonal map of Mexico City (Color Plate 3) discussed previously reveals where caring and healing took place (Figure 3.2).[15] At first glance the original map seems only to reference places where the men lauded by Vetancurt worked: the city's hospitals. Juan de Torquemada, the chronicler who described the working spaces examined in Chapters 1 and 2, wrote about them as well. In the 1610s, the Hospital of Saint John of God, he noted, had a "rotating door" where residents left "children who did not have parents."[16] Residents with mental illness found shelter at the Hospital of Saint Hippolytus.[17] The oldest and most important hospital was the Royal Hospital for Indigenous People, which, despite its name, served all residents; "everyone, universally," according to Torquemada, "was cured" in this place.[18] The doctors of the Chief Medical Tribunal taught at the University of Mexico. These buildings represented the official landscape of public health, but zooming in reveals an alternative vision.

The rendering calls attention to the places claimed by hair barbers. They opened blade-and-scissors shops near hospitals as a strategy; the location drew customers looking for different care. There was a blades-and-scissors shop, for example, next to the Hospital of Saint John (Figure 3.2).[19] Hair barbers had stands in the Main Square and Saint Dominic Square. They met at the church of the Convent of Saint Claire, where they founded their own brotherhood.[20] These individuals changed the landscape of healing in Mexico City during the seventeenth century. They formed a community to sustain themselves in the face of constant

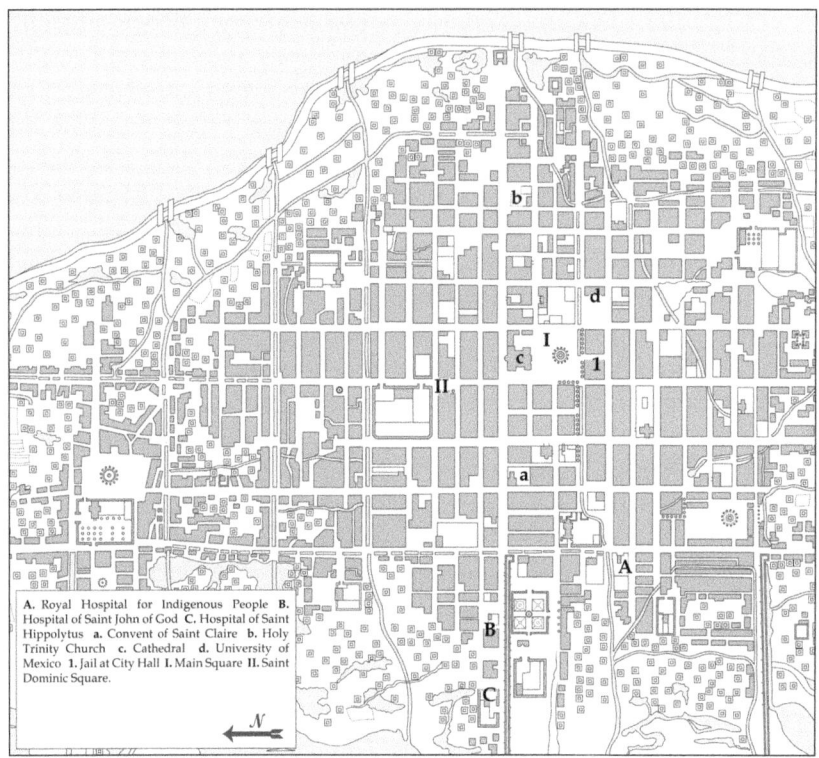

A. Royal Hospital for Indigenous People **B.** Hospital of Saint John of God **C.** Hospital of Saint Hippolytus **a.** Convent of Saint Claire **b.** Holy Trinity Church **c.** Cathedral **d.** University of Mexico **1.** Jail at City Hall **I.** Main Square **II.** Saint Dominic Square.

FIGURE 3.2 Finding care in Mexico City
Source: Graphic rendering of a detail of "Plan Von Mexico City" by Johannes Vingboons (1660), from Atlas Blaeu – Van der Hem. Based on "Forma y levantado de la ciudad de México" by Juan Gómez de Trasmonte (1628). Sign. E 34.413-C. Courtesy of the Österreichische Nationalbibliothek. Image by Matilde Grimaldi.
The map's legend lists locations frequented by historical actors named in the chapter.

antagonism from barber phlebotomists and barber surgeons. The history of the three groups is intertwined and begins, as told next, in the sixteenth century.

## 3.2 SIXTEENTH-CENTURY PRECEDENTS: CHANGES IN THE BARBERING TRADE

Alonso López Hinojosos moved to Mexico City in 1564.[21] On arrival, he sought out the help of Doctor Juan de la Fuente since they had already met back "in Spain" years earlier.[22] Like Alonso Cortés Siles a century plus later, López relied on his contacts to find a place to live and a job. Knowing the doctor was important because López needed him to certify his training and license him to work. City hall council members had appointed him Chief Doctor the year prior, with the power "to examine people who sought to practice as physicians, surgeons, and barbers."[23] The examination or certification was a prerequisite for getting a permit to open a barbershop or secure a hospital position, which López did at the Royal Hospital for Indigenous People. López also introduced himself to members of the Barbers and Surgeons Guild to join their community.[24]

Now, it used to be that elected guild masters certified the training of apprentices and licensed them to practice, which was how other tradesmen and artisans managed their affairs. When Lopéz arrived, however, guild members were in the midst of a struggle to regain that privilege, which pitted barber surgeons against doctors and placed the newcomer in a delicate political situation. During the next three decades, López sought the patronage of Chief Doctors but also remained loyal to his fellow practitioners and their quest to remain somewhat independent. Changes in the city's public health policy, however, ultimately empowered doctors over barber surgeons. This outcome, in turn, helped hair barbers free themselves from the guild in the early seventeenth century.

The move to have appointed officials oversee guild members began when Queen Isabel appointed Chief Barbers in Castile to examine practitioners and license them to work.[25] They "had to ensure that no one have a shop, make incisions or bleed, apply leeches or cups, remove teeth or molars, without first being examined."[26] The first barber surgeons from Spain who settled in Mexico City brought their "examination letters" (licenses) with them. Back home, they had "been asked questions before knowledgeable people trained in the trade," meaning master barber surgeons, "and answered them well."[27] As a "reward" for learning the "barbering trade" and "art of phlebotomy," a Chief Barber had given them "license" to "open shops" in "any city or town in the kingdoms."[28] Chief Barbers were guild members, so the certification process remained a guild matter.

Starting in 1523, however, barbers in Spain faced increased pressure to show their licenses to members of the crown's Medical Board.[29] This change was part of the crown's evolving health policy, which aimed to have doctors examine "surgeons, apothecaries, and barbers."[30] Cities were meant to have Chief Doctors or Medical Officers who did this work, and the first appointment in Mexico City happened in 1527.[31]

Members of the Barbers and Surgeons Guild subsequently tracked over-sight initiatives in Spain to estimate the impact on their local affairs.

In the early 1540s, councilmen increasingly required tradesmen and artisans to present examination letters from their guilds to obtain per-mits.[32] This requirement promised to keep certification and licensing under the purview of the Barbers and Surgeons Guild. Indeed, it became a way to control who could join them. In April 1549, guild members reminded councilors that "unexamined barbers" should not be allowed to operate barbershops.[33] Two master barbers, "honorable men of great ability" who had the appropriate "examination titles," were ready to rectify the matter.[34] They proposed to carry out examinations within two weeks to enforce the certification mandates. These examiner appoint-ments, repeated six years later, were akin to Chief Barbers in Spain.[35] They had the power to certify and hence determine who worked as a barber in the city.

The crown's policy on examinations was about public health; barbers needed to demonstrate their knowledge of phlebotomy to be "rewarded" with a license for a shop. The wording of the examination letters made this association. There was no mention of "shaving beards" and "cutting and washing hair" – the common phrasing for grooming services.[36] Did men who only did the latter need to be examined to have a barbershop? For guild members, the answer was yes. A barber was not a barber if he did not know how to perform the bloodletting procedure. They tied phlebotomy with grooming to exclude anyone who did not go through the apprentice process: no examination letter, no shop. The problem for the guild, however, was that doctors were also adamant about this proce-dure. Phlebotomy was a treatment that could only be performed at their discretion. Doctors argued that they had to be the ones who proctored examinations and licensed barber surgeons. They were more convincing than guild members. By 1560, council members regularly appointed two Chief Doctors, such as Juan de la Fuente, to license barber surgeons, which replicated "the practice in Spain."[37]

Alonso López witnessed changes in the city's public health policy that subsequently influenced hair barbers' choices. López was working at the Royal Hospital for Indigenous People when Doctor Francisco Hernández arrived in Mexico City in 1571, recently appointed Chief Doctor of the Indies. Philip II sent him to establish a Medical Board like the one in Spain that would supplant city hall's oversight of public health, including the appointment of examiners.[38] In the king's words, the "desire that our vassals enjoy a long life and remain in perfect health" prompted him to mandate that there be "physicians and masters who governed, taught, and cured" royal subjects of "their illnesses."[39] It took decades for the Medical Board initiative to succeed. Yet, it reminded the city's doctors and barber surgeons that their work was subject to royal scrutiny. Hernández was stationed at the Royal Hospital during his time in the city. López assisted the renowned doctor during autopsies, for example, and considered him a mentor and teacher.[40] Indeed, working with Hernández may have inspired López to write a book to share his own knowledge, like the doctor had done with him.

López was working as a "surgeon, caretaker, and nurse at the Royal Hospital" when he wrote the influential treatise *A sum and compilation on surgery, with a course on bleeding, and an exam for barbers*, based on his experience and information garnered from printed works.[41] First published in 1578, its popularity merited a second, much expanded edition within twenty years.[42] The first edition covered topics such as anatomy and the treatment of bone fractures and other injuries. The second edition, which doubled in length, added sections on rheumatism, childbirth, and the composition of medicines, among other topics.

The work reflects the increased distinction officials and doctors were making between the training and certification of barber phlebotomists versus barber surgeons. The subtitle of the book, "a course on bleeding," suggests that phlebotomy is a main topic, but only "Book Three on Phlebotomy" (out of eleven books) is expressly related to the "exam for barbers" (Figure 3.3).[43] López wrote this section to help barber phlebotomists pass their examination; they needed to show doctors that they had a command of the procedure.

López began the phlebotomy section with a summary of Hippocratic-Galenic humorology, which posited that sickness resulted from an excess or deficiency in the body's humors or bodily fluids (blood, phlegm, and black and yellow bile).[44] Bloodletting, he wrote, was "the opening of a vein to empty the over-abundance of humors."[45] Barber phlebotomists needed to know the difference between veins and arteries, their names, and their locations in the body to do this procedure properly. As López explained, for example, "there are two veins underneath the tongue, called leonic, which are bled in the following manner": first, the practitioner placed a ligature around the patient's neck; second, he used a wood clamp to hold the tongue to the roof of the mouth; third, he made a small incision along one of the veins and allowed the blood to flow out.[46] If too much, the patient simply "drank some water to halt the bleeding."[47] The "veins of the neck," he quickly added, "should never

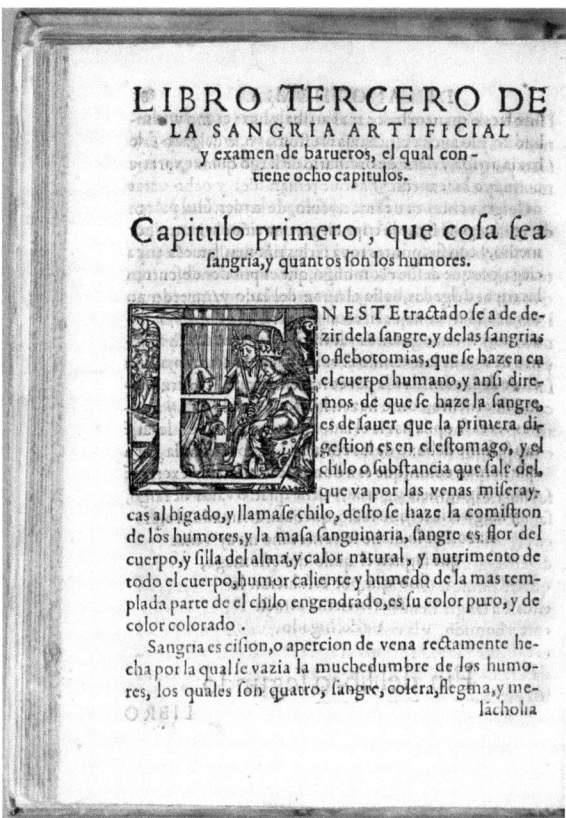

FIGURE 3.3  Preparing for the phlebotomy examination
Source: Alonso López de Hinojosos. Svmma y recopilacion de cirvgia, con vn
arte para sangrar, y examen de barberos, f.86v. México: Casa Pedro Balli,
1595. 1578. Courtesy of the John Carter Brown Library, Brown University.
"Blood," López wrote, "was the flower of the body, the seat of
the soul, natural heat, and the nutrient of the whole body." This
description from the first paragraph of the bleeding section captures the
value he placed on the substance.

be bled" because the bleeding would not stop.[48] López also described
how to apply cupping glasses, always on the back of the body, in the
parts "where doctors ordered."[49] Doctors, López implied, rather than
barbers, made treatment decisions. The repeating deference to doctors
in this section modeled the attitude barbers were supposed to have at
their oral examinations, when they assured doctors that they would
follow their instructions on the precise manner and place of the bleeding
they prescribed.[50]

López's empirical training as a barber surgeon enabled him to speak authoritatively on the material included in "Book Three on Phlebotomy."[51] The treatise, however, could not pretend to impart knowledge that replaced consultation with physicians or risk offending them, so López solicited their validation to secure the book's publication. Francisco Bravo noted in his blurb that he had "read, amended, and corrected" the work "with great care," which meant that he approved its content.[52] López's patron, Chief Doctor Juan de la Fuente, followed suit in his commendation for the second edition, confirming his credentials by writing that he had "seen Master Alonso" treat people and practice "his surgeon's trade."[53] The key point, however, was that *A sum and compilation on surgery* was supposed to be a handbook for people who lived outside of Mexico City – that is how López justified it to the city's doctors and Viceroy Enríquez.[54] He granted the publishing license in 1578 because the author told him that it would be "beneficial for people living in places that had no doctors or surgeons ... to cure their illnesses."[55] López well knew that barber surgeons in Mexico City would purchase his book, but he had to appease his patrons, "erudite" doctors, who expected residents to turn to them for treatment.[56] His tactic mirrored the efforts of his fellow guild members who deferred to doctors while seeking to regain the power to examine men trained in their shops.

As in previous decades, members of the Barbers and Surgeons Guild found it useful to refer to happenings in Spain in the 1580s to gain concessions from city hall council members. Philip II issued a pragmatic in 1588 related to the Medical Boards in cities in Spain that granted them greater power as tribunals, including jurisdiction over examinations.[57] Barbers in Castile, however, successfully lobbied for the reinstitution of the Chief Barber position to retain the responsibility of examining barber phlebotomists.[58] Guild members in Mexico City followed suit, requesting the same appointment. Councilmen agreed to do so in 1590 with the caveat that the new Chief Barber would "examine barbers along with the Chief Doctors."[59] Juan Rodríguez was the first and only guild member to hold the position, last appointed in 1594.[60] The two Chief Doctors arrangement remained in place until the city appointments ended ten years later. It was the guild's last successful attempt to be involved in the licensing of barber phlebotomists. The procedure became the service that separated them from hair barbers.

The guild lost because Chief Doctors disapproved of the temporary allowance to have a Chief Barber involved in examinations and licensing. It was not that they mistrusted guild members who plainly knew how to bleed their patients and trained their apprentices to perform the procedure. The hesitancy lay in their belief that academic doctors were superior to barber surgeons. Francisco Bravo, appointed Chief Doctor during the brief Chief Barber period, expressed this opinion in a preface to the second edition of López's *A sum and compilation on surgery* in 1595.[61] Bravo approved yet diminished it, writing that "it was well written" and would be "beneficial and useful for simple and uneducated people" and those who "could not easily turn to a physician to cure them."[62] Bravo was referring to barber surgeons such as López, who practiced "simple medicine" rather than "administering drugs," which was the reserve of doctors.[63] Bravo appreciated López's summary of humorology and instructions for bleeding, which helped barber phlebotomists prepare for their examinations, but final licensing power resided with doctors. López got his book approved for publication by applying this logic for his own ends.

The crown's public health policy reified the position of doctors over barber surgeons from its beginnings. Barber surgeons in Mexico City tried to strike a balance during the second half of the sixteenth century but, in the end, accepted that licensing was the purview of doctors. Guild members, however, retained the ability to conduct the first evaluation. Candidates received certificates, which they presented to Chief Doctors who did the final examination and granted the license. This licensing process remained in place after the creation of a Medical Board in the early seventeenth century, when guild members faced a new challenge to their authority. How were they to retain power over people who provided services that did not concern the city's Chief Doctors? Guild members needed a license to have a barbershop. The people they sought to exclude used this fact to their advantage. Barbers who did not do phlebotomy, they argued, did not require the certification of doctors, much less the approval of the Barbers and Surgeons Guild.

The Brotherhood of Holy Christ, formed by members of the Barbers and Surgeons Guild, was an avenue for exclusion.[64] They began meeting in the late 1520s at a small chapel and hospice dedicated to Saints Cosmas and Damian and Saint Amarus, funded by the Tailors Guild.[65] Given the choice of avocations, some of them were likely from Burgos, where they would have walked by the Hospital of the King, associated with Saint Amarus's cult, and the church dedicated to the other two saints.[66] Saints Cosmas and Damian, always invoked together and known as the Healing Saints, were the patrons of barbers and surgeons, so they appreciated the affiliation. By the time López attended their meetings, they had their own side chapel at Holy Trinity Church, which arose from the tailors' original structure (Figure 3.2).[67]

Upon joining the Brotherhood of Holy Christ, López received a letter or patent that outlined members' responsibilities and rewards.[68] The brotherhood subsequently became an aggregate of the Archconfraternity of the Holy Trinity, when the pope exhorted the brothers to attend mass, confess their sins, receive communion, give alms to the poor, and attend their brothers' funerals to share papal indulgences.[69] As evoked by the pope, residents joined brotherhoods to earn the promise of life after death and secure a "good death," which included receiving the last rites, being buried in consecrated ground, and having masses sung for the soul's safe journey to heaven. The archconfraternity also prioritized involvement in the procession of Maundy Thursday or Holy Thursday, when they wore a "red habit."[70] This event became a site of contention between traditional barbers and hair barbers more than a century later.

Barbers and surgeons, like the members of the Smiths Guild of Chapter 4, belonged to their trade association (guild) and their religious association (brotherhood). The first governed their trade and the second deepened members' connection to one another through religious devotion.[71] Their shared membership, however, meant that the two associations seemed to be the same. Guild members took care of business related to their trade during their brotherhood meetings at Holy Trinity Church. Like other guilds, they would have elected their guild leaders and examiners at the beginning of the year in their chapel.[72] This confluence explains why guild members acted under their religious banner for purely professional ends, as detailed later in the chapter. Excluded from the guild and brotherhood, hair barbers founded their own brotherhood to achieve their political ends.

### 3.3 THE FIRST DECADE: THE PATH TO BECOMING A BARBER

Juan Martín and Juan Delgadillo moved to Mexico City from different worlds. Martín was Nahua, born in Xilotzingo, a town some twenty-five miles to the northwest of Mexico City.[73] Delgadillo was from Seville, mountains, and an ocean away. Both wanted to become barbers, which required years of training, rising from apprentice to journeyman to master of the trade.[74] Their experience shows how this process worked at the beginning of the century, when all barbers trained as phlebotomists and blade-and-scissors shops did not yet exist. First, Martín and Delgadillo had to find a master, someone "examined in the art of barbers," meaning certified and licensed, who would take them on as an apprentice.[75] The newcomers made inquiries at barbershops and introduced themselves to masters who expressed interest in teaching them. Masters showed them where they would stay during their apprenticeship and answered their questions. If it seemed a good match, they took the next step: securing a contract.[76]

People usually began their apprenticeships, described as "entering into service," when they were around twelve years old. Parents made the arrangements and signed contracts with master tradesmen on their children's behalf. Martín and Delgadillo migrated to the city alone, so they turned to an appointed guardian who presided over the legal transaction because they were under the legal age of twenty-five.[77] The apprentices and masters met before the head of city hall and swore to the agreement. A notary wrote everything down and made copies for both parties.[78] Martín and Delgadillo needed this paperwork to protect their interests; it was a promise of food and shelter, good treatment, and an education. The master barbers required it as insurance. They could return to city hall and file a suit if the apprentices left their service. As per custom, Martín's and Delgadillo's apprenticeships started the same day of the signing. So, contracts in hand, they headed over to the masters' homes and barbershops and began their service and training.

Martín arranged a contract with Bernardino García, a master barber, in November 1604. Gathered at city hall, he had a translator confirm that the contract matched their verbal agreement because he was not fluent in Spanish. Over the next three years, García was to "teach him the trade of barber, which was to shave, bleed, and everything else."[79] The "training" to become a barber phlebotomist "had to occur within this period."[80] Martín insisted on the finite time and a one-peso-monthly salary to preclude the possibility that García would make him work without teaching him the trade. Apprentices did not get paid, so the salary provision further suggests that Martín and city officials were well aware of previous cases when masters had extracted labor from Indigenous apprentices and did not train them.

Delgadillo was eighteen when he met Gabriel Villalba. The master barber welcomed him into his home in August 1606 without the customary reference. No one knew him. Yet, Villalba took a chance, promising Delgadillo that he would "know the trade and be able to work anywhere" after this apprenticeship.[81] On completion, Villalba agreed to give Delgadillo a barber case "with all its tools" and a "full set of clothing."[82]

Delgadillo envisioned his new clothes, specifying what he wanted in unusual detail. He fancied "two shirts, a doublet [padded jacket], hose, shoes, garter, hat, jerkin [leather vest], drawers, cloak, and belt," and he would get to pick the garments' colors.[83] It was a fashionable outfit that would make a good impression once he became a journeyman.

The two masters who accepted them had once taken the same steps to secure their own training, and so it continued with each generation. The contract for Domingo Saucedo, a "Spanish boy born in Mexico City" included the phrasing related to the certification process discussed earlier: he "would be able to be examined" after four years.[84] The master, in other words, would work with the guild to assess his skills, grant him a certificate, and, as per public health policy, have a Chief Doctor test his knowledge and license him as a barber phlebotomist. Twenty years later, Saucedo went back to city hall and promised an orphan that he would "teach him the barbering trade until he became a journeyman" and give him "a barber's case with all the necessary tools" at the end.[85] The very same notary who had written Saucedo's apprentice contract in 1605 filed this one. Perhaps they remembered one another, noting their role in the cycle of working life as masters passed on their knowledge to the next generation.

Returning to Saucedo's apprentice contract, it too stipulated a barber's case: "a shaving kit with all its tools."[86] These promised cases contained some of the instruments that Martín, Delgadillo, and Saucedo learned to use during their apprenticeships.[87] Masters, "as customary" at this time, supplied basic kits, which included, with some variation, "some scissors, two blades, a comb, and a mirror" – instruments for the grooming aspect of their work.[88] Journeymen typically purchased tools needed for other services on their own.

At the beginning, the three apprentices learned by watching the masters and journeymen who worked in their respective barbershops. They swept the floor and washed the towels. They held up mirrors to show customers the barber's handiwork. They used a whetstone to sharpen scissors and blades. They listened while the barber explained how to use a lancet with a sharp point "to open a vein to bleed."[89] They held a bowl to catch the substance. Phlebotomy was a delicate procedure, so they began their hands-on training by wrapping wounds to stop the bleeding. The apprentices practiced cutting hair and trimming moustaches on their friends. They shaved themselves with a straight blade. Martín, Delgadillo, and Saucedo watched and practiced for several months until they were finally allowed to groom customers on their own.

Apprentices turned next to the tools of phlebotomy and dental work. They practiced making small incisions on their limbs. The masters who trained Martín and Saucedo likely owned Alonso Lopéz *A sum and compilation on surgery*, or at least parts of it copied by hand.[90] They would have read out loud the section on phlebotomy, discussed earlier, to prepare their apprentices for the eventual examination. The 1595 edition has three short chapters on molars and teeth covering topics such as the cause of cavities, but no detailed instructions on how to remove them.[91] Apprentices examined their teeth and molars in the mirror and learned to handle instruments used for pulling them. Then they practiced on someone with a horrific toothache, when extraction was a last resort. This aspect of their work concerned the guild, but not the doctors who licensed them, which proved crucial for hair barbers in the future who did dentistry. After a year of training, masters expected apprentices "to do all the things related to the trade as if they were journeymen," which included "shaving, bleeding, applying cupping glasses, and removing molars."[92] A customer described their work in this fashion, indicating that apprentices did the work of barber phlebotomists during their training.

The next step in becoming a barber was certification by the Barbers and Surgeons Guild. By 1608 or 1609, Martín, Delgadillo, and Saucedo were ready to demonstrate their skills to become journeymen. Masters arranged this next step by pledging that their trainees were able and proficient before the guild's appointed examiners. As noted, these individuals were gatekeepers and could prevent qualified men from being certified due to personal antagonisms. Did they allow Martín, an Indigenous person, to take their exam? Perhaps. Certification as a journeyman did not mean approval to join the guild. It was simply a confirmation of training that enabled them to obtain licenses from a Chief Doctor. Delgadillo and Saucedo, by contrast, were surely certified. Guild members promoted men such as Delgadillo, a migrant from Spain, whom they identified as one of their own. His guild sponsor may well have paid the Chief Doctor's exam-licensing fee. They wanted Delgadillo to join them one day as a master guild member.

Enslaved people followed a different path. There were no apprentice agreements, no specifications for their training. Slaveowners taught them the trade so that they could assist them in their shops. Luis worked at the barbershop of Francisco Rodríguez, located on Regina Coeli Street.[93] He learned the trade in the same way as Martín, Delgadillo, and Saucedo, but the guild would not certify him. Members who were slaveowners never expected that barbers such as Luis would become the pioneers of a different kind of barbering, as discussed later in the chapter.

The fourth step for licensed journeymen who wanted to become barber surgeons involved additional training. After 1603, following changes in Spain, barber phlebotomists were supposed to work for at least five years under the supervision of a doctor, spending some of that time at a hospital, before they could be examined and licensed as barber surgeons by a Chief Doctor.[94] Men who followed this path would have read *A sum and compilation on surgery* as part of their education. Implementation of this added layer of licensing, however, took time.

Through the 1610s, apprentices began training as surgeons if the master was a long-time practitioner. The apprentices who worked with Diego López Salazar, a master barber surgeon, accompanied him to see patients. They went to the jail at city hall, for instance, when the bailiff called López to treat prisoners who arrived with wounds or fell dangerously sick during their stay (Figure 3.2). They saw him inspect the victims of violent crimes and prepare reports to prosecute prisoners. López explained to a lawyer in 1600, for instance, that Felipe Juan had sustained a terrible blow to his head that lacerated his cheek.[95] Following *A sum and compilation on surgery*, López used his thinnest needle to suture the wound with "stitches close to one another" and cleaned it with alcohol.[96] Juan testified against the perpetrator after he healed.

Starting in 1607, López and his assistants visited the jail more regularly because council members appointed him to a newly created position.[97] "Poor people detained in the jail" were hungry and sick; they needed "a doctor, apothecary, and barber" to care for them.[98] The city bailiff pressured councilmen on this account.[99] He had collected donations to set up an infirmary at the jail with new wooden beds and linens and asked that López be appointed. He had to provide all services associated with the profession, so López relied heavily on his assistants. "Attending to people in jail," in his words, "was a lot of work," so prisoners got haircuts and shaves from apprentices, while he treated their injuries.[100] More than a decade later, upon retiring, López sought recognition for his work. He reminded council members that he had been "healing and bleeding poor people in jail" all these many years.[101] He did not mention grooming services, underlining the distinction and hierarchy that were beginning to prevail. Barber surgeons like him were different and more important than barber phlebotomists because they afforded more services.

Viceroy Montesclaros named Jéronimo de Herrera Chief Doctor in 1606.[102] As noted, council members had made the Chief Doctor appointments up to this point. The viceroy outlined Herrera's expansive responsibilities in the appointment letter: "to oversee all people who cure with medicine and surgery, or by other means."[103] "Barbers," it continued, "had to present their certifications and licenses to cure and practice their trade."[104] After reviewing this paperwork, Herrera was "to visit them to ensure they were sufficiently" trained.[105] This requirement applied to existing barbers, and he was to license them himself going forward. The phrasing is notable because this process was supposed to be in place already. Indeed, Herrera had already served as Chief Doctor. Had he ignored his responsibilities? If so, the appointment letter served to remind the busy and elderly doctor to pay due attention to barber phlebotomists and barber surgeons as per the crown's public health policy dictates.

*True Medicine and Surgery*, written by a doctor, was published the following year.[106] Herrera wrote a blurb praising its content. The book mentions bleeding over one hundred times as the preferred treatment for countless diseases and ailments. The word barber appears only once. The omission suggests that the city's doctors, including Herrera, tended to ignore the men who performed the procedure, yet they still insisted on their right to license them. Delgadillo and Saucedo, at some point, secured the Chief Doctor's attention because they needed him to proctor their phlebotomy exam. Herrera's interest grew once he began to charge higher fees.

Alonso Espinoza had a barbershop on Saint John Street, but "he dared not open" the doors in January 1615.[107] The Chief Doctor had forewarned him of the consequences of failing to submit to the examination. The cost, however, was prohibitive; the doctor charged "fifty pesos."[108] How was he to save that much money, Espinoza asked, when he could not work? So, he implored council members for permission to reopen his establishment. Sebastián Aguilera made the same appeal; he needed at least eight months to make enough money to pay the Chief Doctor for the final examination.[109] Councilors no longer appointed Chief Doctors, nor did they have any power to license barbers, but they did issue permits for shops. They granted these temporary permits to support residents who exerted their right as political subjects to make money.

Herrera was the sole Chief Doctor until 1624, when Viceroy Cerralvo finally created a genuine Medical Board, with more than one member.[110] In the twenty years since his appointment, the Barbers and Surgeons Guild had intensified their exclusionary practices, pushing to have only "Spaniards" in their professions. Members of the new Medical Board were indifferent to the guild's internal politics. Phlebotomy, on the other hand, remained a concern.

## 3.4 THE RISE OF A DISTINCT SORT OF BARBERING
### IN THE 1620S: THE FOUNDING GENERATION

Francisco ran an open-air barber stand and lived with his family in their own home. He paid a slaveowner a daily fee to have these freedoms, like the market women of Chapter 1.[111] Francisco had been providing shaving services "forever" and "no one impeded him" – until 1624.[112] That year, "ministers from the Medical Board" began to come around to explain that he had to shut down "his shop."[113] What would he do, he asked the lawyer at the Viceroyal Palace? He "had no other trade" and needed to continue working to provide for his children. Francisco went to the palace because he knew that Viceroy Gélvez had given licenses to other men "to operate barbershops."[114] They had convinced the viceroy to permit them "to offer haircuts and shaves."[115] He wanted the same allowance, to continue shaving people at his stand, and "only" that.[116] Such a license would in turn prevent members of the board from "obstructing" his work.[117] Francisco's initiative reflects the pioneering work of barbers of his generation who broke away from traditional barbering to create a new business.

In the 1610s, licensed barbers had shops where they performed all services related to their profession, including phlebotomy. While the Barbers and Surgeons Guild excluded them as members, they still certified non-Spaniards, which, as noted, enabled them to be licensed. This allowance stopped. In 1622, guild members, threatened by the competition, sued Asian barbers. They brought a case before the High Court because their rivals were a "threat to the republic."[118] Guild members identified them with a derisive word that aimed to obscure that they were from the Philippines, grouping them with enslaved people from other parts of Asia. Guild leaders claimed it was dangerous for them to have barbershops because they had assistants who were enslaved. The plaintiffs raised the specter of enslaved people wielding deadly weapons, sharp blades, which gained the judges' attention. Guild members had enslaved people working in their shops as well, so the charge was disingenuous. What they meant was that people who were not "Spaniards" were unable to control enslaved people. More to the point, they resented that formerly enslaved men had barbershops like theirs.

Men from the Philippines organized a legal defense that prevented the eradication of their businesses, but their services had to change. Perhaps they found out that the royal pragmatic of 1500 related to the certification of barbers in Spain had expressly excluded men who only "shaved with a blade or scissors"; they did not need "the license of the exam-iner."[119] Viceroy Gélves certainly knew of this exemption because he had a copy of the *Laws of Spain* compilation of 1598, which clearly spelled it out.[120] When barbers from the Philippines turned to him in 1622, the viceroy agreed to license them directly. Men "who were free" were "to have shops," but for cosmetic barbering only, with a marked prohibi-tion against bloodletting.[121] They could use a straight-edge razor to "do beards and necks," but their enslaved assistants were only "permitted" to use scissors to trim hair. The specification of tools related back to guild-members' absurd claim that enslaved people posed a danger to customers because they might at any point decide to murder slaveowners. It may well have crossed their minds, but doing so would have been suicidal.

Viceroy Gélves's decision to grant these new licenses for what became known as blade-and-scissors shops was related to the Medical Board's rising power. He would not usurp the board's authority. Indeed, he had given members the explicit charge of licensing barber phlebotomists and barber surgeons. The viceroy could, however, license working men who provided noninvasive services. Grooming and restorative conversation was not medicine, and hence outside the board's purview.

Francisco's petition from 1624 reveals that the guild tried to use the Medical Board to refute the distinction between blade-and-scissors shops and their own barbershops. The board "ministers" who stopped at Francisco's stand saw him shaving a man with a sharp blade, a service all barbers trained for. Did they suspect him of bloodletting? That was, after all, the practice that had preoccupied Chief Doctors since the six-teenth century. Given the context, guild members likely tipped them off. They claimed that Francisco was providing services that only they were licensed to do. Grooming and bloodletting went hand in hand. Men who refused to provide both services, from their perspective, did not have the right to have a barbershop.

The guild's strategy did not work. The Medical Board had no author-ity over men who simply "did beards." The blade-and-scissors shops and stands could operate with a viceroyal license. This allowance enabled hair barbers to go around the guild's refusal to certify their training. They did not need it because they did not intend to get examined by the board. Men from the Philippines and their descendants embraced the limitation as an opportunity and henceforth focused their energies on building a business based on an alternative form of barbering.

Hair barbers were shrewd and practical when they petitioned for the licenses that kept them in business. Their wording matched the requirements of the new regulations for blade-and-scissors shops. Francisco Antonio wrote out his own petition in 1625 with shaky handwriting, affirming his knowledge of the petitioning procedure, which allowed people to submit their own petition or have lawyers draft them on their behalf. He explained his situation: "I employ my trade as a barber among poor people ... I do not let blood."[122] Antonio understood the restrictions and the allowances for men like himself. There were "Spanish barbers who wanted to stop him unjustly," but he well knew that it was his right and privilege as a vassal to work. Viceroy Cerralvo, newly arrived, was not sure about the precedent, so he asked a city judge to confirm Antonio's request. Yes, the judge responded, the viceroy "could permit him to cut hair and beards," but Antonio was "not to do bloodletting or anything else related to surgery."[123] Officials at city hall, in other words, recognized that blade-and-scissors shops were a new business, unrelated to medicine, which was why a viceroyal license sufficed to secure a city permit for a shop.

Hair barbers, however, soon realized that the Medical Board could indeed sanction their work, indirectly, because it granted licenses for the production of tonics. Tomas López and Nicolas García, both "natives of the Philippine Islands," made a unique petition to the Medical Board in early June 1628.[124] They needed a license to produce and sell maguey liquor because apothecaries were supposed to be the only people who could do this work.[125] City residents imbibed this drink for its perceived medicinal properties, and, no doubt, for recreation. The two men had special skills and equipment "to extract liquor from maguey" that made it especially "beneficial and good" for treating "many illnesses, from asthma to flatulence." López and García were so confident of their product that they invited board members "to observe and examine" the process and "industry" required to make it. Promptly accepting, the doctors invited the two men "to bring their instruments and wires" and make their demonstration.

They all met the very same day at the house of doctor Jerónimo de Herrera, identified as the "oldest *protomédico*."[126] Upon arrival, López and García covered and placed a "large clay pot" filled with *pulque* (another drink made from maguey) on "a wood fire at low heat."[127] Then, they used a "vessel filled with water" and a "medium pipe made from" the stem of a plant to deliver the distilled liquid.[128] Satisfied with the exhibition, the presiding physicians sampled the liquor and opined that their extraction method was "healthier" than other distillations, which used lead. López and García got their license. It was a privilege that would enable them to grow their business and prevent anyone from "bothering them," such as meddling apothecaries jealous to keep their monopoly. Hair barbers were thus able to serve the restorative drink at their shops. Indeed, board members may have considered that having residents imbibe this maguey drink under their supervision reduced the likelihood of intoxication.[129]

Taking a sip of maguey liquor was part of the relaxing experience of going to a blade-and-scissors shop. There was also conversation and good cheer. The linguist Covarrubias derided barbershop gossip, evinced in the use of "barber bowl" to refer to "a small room where whatever happened to you was divulged to all your neighbors."[130] He missed the positive aspect of sharing and overhearing stories while having someone touch your head. Barbers patiently pulled out "white hairs" from men's beards who wanted to look "younger" than their years.[131] They trimmed and waxed whiskers to accentuate their shape. All these services were moments of respite in residents' busy lives.

Hair barbers greeted their customers with offers for preventive services, such as dental hygiene. They placed a clove between the teeth and used a brush and paste "to remove plaque," followed with a quick gurgle of wine and incense ash.[132] They also encouraged a "good regiment," as recommended by Alonso Lopéz, which involved "washing one's mouth three times a day, after waking up, after finishing the mid-day meal, and after dinner" so as to "never have a cavity."[133]

The new blade-and-scissors shops thus innovated services and also retained some of the character of traditional barbershops. They served restorative drinks and encouraged relaxation in clean spaces that did not smell of blood. They washed and styled their customers' hair to promote self-adornment and impart confidence. Business boomed.

## 3.5 THE FORMALIZATION OF THE BUSINESS

By the mid 1630s, there were blade-and-scissors shops throughout the city, run out of open-air stands, stalls, and storefronts. At the Main Square, customers sat on stools under tents made of palm-reed mats and poles that protected them from sun and rain. Or, they could step into a stall for more privacy. Hair barbers rented these wooden structures with shingled roofs from city hall, like food vendors named in Chapter 1. These varied in conditions, but an enterprising hair barber could make even a weather-beaten, aged stall more comfortable and inviting with textile hangings and other decorations. And for even greater convenience, customers went into shops in buildings.

Customers visiting storefronts were promptly greeted by "four to six" barbers.[134] Indeed, Francisco Cruz's shop became so popular that he needed extra staff to serve his growing clientele. A "Spaniard and journeyman tailor," a regular customer, noted Cruz's success in 1634.[135] Journeyman Benito Cruz, who worked for a barber surgeon during the day, stopped by in the evenings to lend a hand. He intended to set up his own blade-and-scissors shop in the future to leave an employer who mistreated him. Francisco Cruz gave him a chance to make extra money and learn how to run a shop under the new business model.

Members of the Barbers and Surgeons Guild were aghast at the change. Why were their customers abandoning them? Residents still turned to them for phlebotomy, but the real money lay in grooming. Their businesses suffered without the everyday traffic of men seeking a quick shave, or so they claimed. In June 1635, guild members asked Viceroy Cerralvo to come to their financial rescue by limiting the competition. The viceroy asked council members to review their petition.[136] It was "unfair" that customer "preferred" hair barbers when their own services were quite "satisfactory."[137] There were simply too many of them: "more than 150" men from the Philippines had blade-and-scissors shops.[138] Worse still, hair barbers "occupied the best places in the city."[139] "Spanish barbers" assumed they would get preferential treatment, but landlords preferred to sign leases with these Asian barbers because they paid higher rents.[140] Their competitors, in other words, were stealing their customers and occupying spaces that rightly belonged to them.

The "Spanish barbers" also brought it back to public health. They accused hair barbers of endangering their customers because they "were not examined."[141] It was a curious claim since the guild had already lost the right to certify hair barbers more than ten years earlier because they did not do phlebotomy. Yet that is what guild members wanted, to link grooming with bloodletting once again to make all barbers subject to the Medical Board. Now committed to their role as proxies for doctors, traditional barbers sought to claim their role as healers as a way to regain their power. They reminded council members that they had risked their lives "caring for the sick" during the recent epidemic, while hair barbers "did nothing."[142] They were licensed by the Medical Board, and that extra training and confirmation, to their mind, merited that they profit from the barbering business, rather than men who did not do phlebotomy.

The repeated use of derogatory words to describe their competitors reveals the racial antagonism that fueled their complaints. It was not

only about money. "Spanish boys" did not want to apprentice with guild
members given the "preponderance" of Asian barbers already in the
business.[143] People like them, in other words, were looking down on
their trade because people associated with slavery were providing some
of the same services.

To solve the matter, the litigating barber surgeons proposed that the
government "reduce the number of shops to twelve." These blade-and-
scissors shops would be in the "outskirts of the city," and those presently in the "Main Square and vicinity" shut down.[144] The hair barbers
who ran the twelve shops, moreover, were only to "shave ordinary people."[145] Wealthy people, "members of the republic," they claimed, "only
called upon Spanish barbers."[146] The statement belied their intent. The
restriction was meant to entice so-called commoners and everyone else
back into their own shops. Barber surgeons wanted as much grooming
business as they could get.

City officials sided with the litigating barber surgeons. In July 1635,
Viceroy Cerralvo mandated that only twelve blade-and-scissor barbershops were to remain in operation.[147] The swift legal response of hair
barbers, however, mitigated the consequences. First, they filed an appeal
with the High Court to remain open, but to no avail. The judges declared
that no one, "free or enslaved," would be allowed to have a shop except
those who received one of the twelve licenses.[148] Viceroy Cerralvo, moreover, included restrictions sought by the guild toward their own members. He prohibited "Spaniards" from taking on apprentices who were
from the Philippines, or hiring them as assistants.[149] The mandate specified a fifty-peso fine for noncompliance. Guild leaders, it seems, suspected
that some of their peers would be disinclined to change the way they ran
their barbershops. They needed the threat of a fine to stop them from
training enslaved men or hiring free journeymen from the Philippines.

Diego Ayala, a master "barber and surgeon," was among those who
dissented from the guild's actions. He had a barbershop near the cathedral and held a position at the School of Saint John Lateran, about a
fifteen-minute walk away (Figure 3.2).[150] Ayala also made house calls.
He managed to be everywhere because his barbershop was in the good
hands of a "Spanish journeyman" and three Asian barbers, who took
care of his customers.[151] His was exactly the type of establishment targeted by guild superiors – a successful one – that did not abide by the new
mandate. So, they asked Viceroy Cadreita to issue yet another execution
order in January 1636: "Spaniards could not have apprentices" who were
not Spaniards.[152] The guild's henchmen tried to scare his men and visited

the barbershop personally with a copy of the ban. Ayala ignored them. He appreciated his employees and resented intervention in his affairs.

The guild's difficulty in policing their members on this front meant that much remained unchanged in subsequent years. The idea that the city's barber surgeons would all immediately fire their assistants was simply untenable.[153] Asian barbers continued to find work with guild members. Slaveowners, moreover, were not about to stop having enslaved people work in their shops.

Hair barbers, at the same time, realized that they had to train apprentices and hire journeymen in the same way as guild members. There had to be more of them, so they started by ignoring the restrictions. When the Barbers and Surgeons Guild had the High Court confirm that only twelve of them could have a licensed shop in August 1639, hair barbers "failed to comply."[154] The ongoing pressure showed hair barbers they had to rely on the strength of their numbers, so they helped one another open more blade-and-scissors shops.

They also needed to differentiate themselves from "Spanish barbers" to erase terrifying memories. Barber surgeons branded people. Cecilia could well remember when the slaveowner "called a barber who branded her on both cheeks."[155] Given the cruelty, those who were willing performed the harrowing procedure at the home of slaveowners. The smell of burning flesh and screams would have been unbearable for their regular clientele; the fear and pain experienced by the victims unimaginable. Hair barbers who had once been branded hoped never to witness that again.

Silvestre Vicente was among the pioneers. He had gotten started back in the late 1620s, with a license from Viceroy Cerralvo, the same person who subsequently dictated in 1635 that there could only be twelve blade-and-scissors shops. Perhaps Cerralvo remembered him because Vicente received one of the new licenses and in 1642 used that allowance to keep his storefront near the Royal Hospital (Figure 3.2). Vicente was intent on training enslaved people, so he insisted that his license include a clause allowing him to have two Asian men, "free or enslaved," to "assist him."[156] He took on apprentices to impart skills that could one day serve as a pathway to freedom and helped enslaved journeymen save for manumission. Cognizant of the value of viceregal patronage, Vicente assiduously petitioned four viceroys over the years to confirm his status, which protected his business and the men who worked for him for over twenty years.[157]

The community of hair barbers grew because they invited newcomers from the Philippines to join them. Pablo Jiménez heard that Agustín

Encarnación was known for helping men from his parents' homeland.[158] So he visited Encarnación at this blade-and-scissor shop near the
Convent of Saint Augustus and asked for an apprenticeship (Figure 3.2).
Encarnación became his patron, training and subsequently providing
financial assistance when Jiménez opened his own shop.[159] Encarnacíon
did not see his fellow hair barbers as competitors, but rather as members
of an extended family. He welcomed them as neighbors even if their businesses were in his immediate vicinity.[160] His attitude stood in contrast
to members of the Barbers and Surgeons Guild, who tried to prevent
barbershops from opening on the same block as theirs.

Maintaining ties with family members back in the Philippines encouraged solidarity within the community. Francisco Domínguez, born in the
city, had a parent from Cavite in Luzon Island who told him stories that
inspired him to embark on a ship of the Manila Galleon in 1639 to visit
this place.[161] He left his blade-and-scissors shop on the Main Square in the
hands of his partner. Perhaps he encouraged family members and acquaintances to join him when he returned to Mexico City after five years. If so,
they would have followed the pattern of people moving and joining the
businesses established by previous migrants from their homeland.

In 1642, Sebastián Castillo, a "master surgeon," went to the house
of a slaveowner to treat an enslaved person, unnamed in the documentation.[162] He must have been extremely sick or injured because Castillo
returned, eventually charging twenty-five pesos for his services. He was
a firm adherent of the policies of the Barbers and Surgeons Guild.[163]
Castillo would only take on apprentices who were "Spaniards," as guild
members had agreed to do. Two "Spanish boys" went to live in his house
the same year he treated the enslaved person.[164] Their apprentice contracts specified that he would train them to become "barber phlebotomists." By using this term, rather than simply barber, he underlined
the service that set apart "Spanish barbers" from the men who had
blade-and-scissors shops.[165] They bled people; their work concerned the
Medical Board.

The specification, moreover, was related to the growing distinction
between barber phlebotomists and barber surgeons such as himself.
Castillo still managed his business in the same way as barbers in the early
seventeenth century. He spent most days in his barbershop, located along
the Royal Canal, bleeding people but also giving them haircuts.[166] A journeyman and his apprentices took over when he got called to residents'
homes. Castillo's story shows that the rise of hair-barbering influenced
the way "Spanish barbers" thought about their work. Castillo could

train apprentices to become barber phlebotomists and prepare them for the guild certification, but only a physician specialized in surgery had the power to confirm the training of a barber surgeon like himself. They aligned themselves with doctors out of necessity (the Medical Board licensed them) and by choice. The link was a way of setting themselves apart from men, who, from their perspective, did not heal people since they scorned bloodletting.

Barber phlebotomists and barber surgeons confirmed their affiliation to the Medical Board when it became a Medical Tribunal in 1646.[167] The transformation was related to curricular reforms at the University of Mexico, which emphasized the study of surgery as a medical specialization.[168] Sebastián Castillo, along with other practicing barber surgeons, presented their "titles and licenses" to Tribunal members, who checked their "legitimacy."[169] Chief Doctors had accredited barber phlebotomists in previous decades, but the requirements of the new tribunal structure gave members of Barbers and Surgeons Guild the power to grant these titles instead.

### 3.6 THE HAIR-BARBERING BUSINESS AT MID CENTURY

Antonio Cruz had a blade-and-scissors shop on Saint Dominic Street (Figure 3.2).[170] Friars from the nearby Dominican monastery stopped by his place to maintain their tonsure, which they wore as a sign of devotion.[171] Cruz shaved the top of their head in a circle and trimmed the hair around it. Other customers came in for therapeutic services, such as a tonic and a massage for an aching back. The flourishing business inspired jealousy among his competitors. Barber phlebotomists sent their apprentices to "perturb" his customers.[172] They stopped by and threatened to report him to the Medical Board. But how could they? Cruz was "was one of the twelve permitted to have a shop" – one of the twelve Asian and Asian-descended barbers who held a license for a blade-and-scissors establishment.[173] He had a city permit. Cruz, however, needed more than the license and permit to stop the intimidation. So, he went to the Viceroyal Palace in early January 1641 to request that guards come around his shop to deter the offenders.[174] And he returned eighteen months later to ask the new viceroy for the same protection.[175] In the meantime, Cruz continued his work, showing a resilience that characterized hair barbers at mid century.

Hair barbers were determined to succeed in the business they pioneered in the 1620s. They trained men to follow their path, celebrated milestones, lent each other money, and formed a brotherhood to strengthen their ties to one another as a "nation."[176] Unable to form a guild, they found other ways to govern their profession and strengthen their ties as a community. They appropriated the titles master and journeymen. From the perspective of the Barbers and Surgeons Guild, these designations were not official because they had long banned Asian men from their guild. Hair barbers ignored them. They were part of a different entity, which had its own training guidelines and ways of certifying individuals who learned the trade. Jacinto Cruz self-identified as a "master barber," an honorific that acknowledged his stature in the community, literacy, and expertise.[177] Cristóbal Catanga, "master barber," said the same when he signed his name.[178] His business was at the corner of Saint Francis Street and Tacuba Street. Both were masters with blade-and-scissors shops because they had passed the examination of their peers.

Barbers expressed their solidarity toward each other through credit. The most common financial arrangement was a "friendly loan" between known parties that represented goodwill but also protected the lenders, who held a promissory note or acknowledgment of debt.[179] These were usually short-term loans and involved a guarantor depending on the amount. Jacinto Cruz, once enslaved, had a blade-and-scissors shop near the Hospital of Saint John (Figure 3.2).[180] A journeyman had worked for him for several years when he asked to borrow 100 pesos. For scale, Cruz would have paid five to six pesos per month to rent a small room in a building downtown.[181] It was a lot of money. Cruz agreed based on the knowledge that the journeyman could work off the loan if payment did not materialize, which did indeed happen.[182]

Cruz had the journeyman imprisoned in 1652 to instigate a judicial resolution. In debt disputes, judges had the power to hand debtors over to their creditors, by force if necessary, to work off their loans.[183] The district judge at city hall handled most debt disputes, but judges from the High Court periodically visited the city jail to review the inmates' paperwork and resolve such minor civil cases. In Cruz's case, the judge ordered his debtor to "serve in his shop as a journeyman and hand over half of his salary each month" until the debt was paid.[184] Commonalities based on their profession and legal trajectory from slavery to freedom invited trust, but hair barbers needed to protect their interests, so they insisted on formal credit arrangements. They ensured that the city's courts would uphold their cause if debtors failed them. Cruz was intent on survival, which required securing credit instruments to his best advantage.

It worked, within a decade he moved to a large storefront in the same neighborhood, where Cruz employed more hair barbers than before.[185]

Credit took on special poignancy when it enabled enslaved men to buy their freedom. Juan Alvarado owed his liberty to fellow barbers who helped him self-purchase. Antonio Cívicos and Juan Gómez Veloz had modest blade-and-scissors stands, yet they gladly signed their names as guarantors for their friend Alvarado, who borrowed 100 pesos "to finish paying for his liberty" in 1648.[186] Creditors regularly went after guarantors, so this loan agreement reflected a very serious commitment on the part of three men – that they would, together and somehow, raise the needed amount within four months to meet their obligation. It was a pledge to the value of liberty.

During this time, the hair-barbering community formed a religious brotherhood that similarly expressed a commitment to manumission. Juan Cruz, an enslaved person, was one of the founders of the Brotherhood of the Holy Cross and Maundy, established at the church of the Convent of Saint Claire (Figure 3.2).[187] He was "more than seventy years old," the eldest member, when his brothers paid for his freedom.[188] The brotherhood's leaders handed the slaveowner 250 pesos. Cruz, in their words, "belonged to their nation," and they wanted to "free him from all captivity, servitude and subjugation."[189] Nationhood was tied to liberty, which is why they facilitated their brother's self-manumission. Men from the Philippines who had, or their parents, arrived in Mexico City through the transpacific slave trade asserted their liberty. Their trajectory distinguished them from "other nations."[190] In 1647, the brothers insisted that residents who belonged to "different nations," including African-descended people, could not participate in their penitential processions on Maundy Thursdays.[191] Hair barbers who belonged to the Brotherhood of the Holy Cross and Maundy identified as members of a nation and a community of caregivers. In the decades to come, this organization played a key role in the ongoing struggle with "Spanish barbers," members of the Brotherhood of Holy Christ at Holy Trinity Church, who similarly organized by ethnicity and occupation.

In the 1640s, at least ten hair barbers had stands at the Main Square, and they claimed spaces in squares throughout the city.[192] Officials made no concerted efforts to keep track of their number, which angered members of the Barbers and Surgeons Guild. They asked judges at the High Court to confirm the twelve-license restriction in November 1643, but hair barbers, as before, "failed to comply."[193] For them, it was not a matter of complying. Twelve of them did operate with licenses for blade-and-scissors shops; others used a different legal claim to secure their businesses.

Juan Agustín and Pedro Asqueta rented stalls in the Main Square, drawn by the bustle of its commercial activity.[194] The stalls, however, were only part of their business. They also provided services out of their homes, so they went back and forth between both locations to supervise the journeymen who helped them manage the workload. Agustín and Asqueta convinced two viceroys to grant them a license for this dual-location in 1648.[195] Having a blade-and-scissors business in two locations enabled them to train and give jobs to members of their community.

Neither of them based their appeals on being one of the twelve hair barbers with the blade-and-scissors storefront concession. Their confreres Antonio Cruz and Jacinto Cruz already held those licenses. Instead, Agustín and Asqueta treated the matter as the right of Indigenous vassals. Enslaved people from the Philippines who gained their freedom became members of one of the city's Indigenous polities and classified as Native Americans under tax regulations.[196] Francisco Vélez, a "blade-and-scissors barber," followed the same strategy when he described himself as a "free resident of this city and matriculated in the polity of San Juan [Tenochtitlan]" and "payer of royal taxes."[197] The three men, in other words, obtained licenses with no reference to the ongoing saga that pitted their community against traditional barbers. Instead, they expanded their definition of nation to claim an identity as Indigenous vassals, people from territories claimed by the crown. Like the Nahua market women of Chapter 1, they argued that they needed a license to work to pay their taxes.

Even on holidays, Lorenzo López could still be found at his stall, waiting on his customers with "scissors in hand."[198] Late in the afternoons, men from neighboring stands would take a seat inside and chat while López trimmed their beards. He risked getting fined for working on feast days, which points to the financial uncertainty experienced by hair barbers. A member of the first generation trained him and lent him money.[199] López worked in this person's blade-and-scissors shop for years to pay off his debt. By 1648 he was finally on his own, but still working every single day to feed his family.

Gonzalo Perea similarly endured recurring financial troubles. His stall at the Main Square failed to draw clients; he barely had money to eat. In 1651, he slept there for a time to save on rent. Given the circumstance, his son chose a different path, apprenticing with a weaver to secure immediate access to food and shelter.[200] Their experience reveals the precarity of the barber-and-scissors shops, especially those that were merely stands.

The community continued to face periodic attempts to enforce the twelve-license regulation. Members of the Barbers and Surgeons Guild persuaded enterprising constables to intervene based on the promise that they would collect part of the fine levied on unlicensed barbers.[201] These officials stormed into blade-and-scissors shops and barraged the proprietors with insults and threats. They demanded to see their licenses and permits. The outbursts rattled the community. Antonio Domínguez, wanting to spare his son from the troubles, apprenticed him to a hosier – a trade that promised an easier life.[202] It was clear that hair barbers needed to address the root of their problems: the 1635 ruling that limited their numbers to twelve.

One of them watched as his stall on the Main Square burned to the ground on the evening of November 16, 1658. Someone had set his business on fire, perhaps a member of the guild. Sparks jumped to neighboring stalls, the cathedral's bell ringer sounded fire, residents rushed to surround it, but the flames grew taller and "illuminated the sky."[203] The event galvanized the community. They needed to secure greater protections to survive.

### 3.7 THE RESOLUTION

By 1660, the hair-barbering community had the strength in numbers and the capital to attempt a final resolution. The ongoing hostilities were hard to bear. Juan Agustín, Pedro Asqueta, and Francisco Vélez had worked at their stalls in the Main Square for over a decade when they joined a group that led the effort.[204] They hoped to come to a mutually beneficial business arrangement. To do so, they reached out to the leaders of the Barbers and Surgeons Guild and the Brotherhood of Holy Christ. As noted, the "guild of Spanish barbers had a confraternity at Holy Trinity Church" since the sixteenth century.[205] Members of brotherhoods, according to a contemporary writer, were meant to show "charity."[206] Asian barbers asked them to be charitable with an extremely generous proposition.

The proprietors of each of the blade-and-scissors shops agreed to give a monthly contribution or "charitable" donation of four reals to the Brotherhood of Holy Christ.[207] They would also pay an additional two reals for each of their assistants. Members of this brotherhood, by comparison, only paid half-a-real per month.[208] To be clear, the hair barbers did not seek to join the "Spanish barbers' confraternity." Their contributions would simply subsidize its costs, such as the "oil for the lamps" in their chapel at Holy Trinity.[209] In return, members of the "Guild of Spanish Barbers and Surgeons" had to "renounce their case" and "never litigate against them."[210] They would be free "to exercise their trade as barbers with scissors and blades wherever they wanted" and with "no limit" on the number of "public shops."[211]

Nicolas Vega coordinated a meeting at this barbershop to discuss the proposal. In late August 1660, Martín and the other hair barbers met with twenty-eight guild members – all "master barber phlebotomists," such as Vega, and "master surgeons."[212] The deciding factor was money. Their Brotherhood of Holy Christ had "many and great expenses" associated with their Maundy Thursday procession and the burials of deceased members. The money promised to lessen their individual financial burden, so they "consented" to accept the proposed subsidy on behalf of their "art and guild." Many of the signatories were young, so perhaps the fight of the previous generations no longer seemed so pressing. Diego Benavides, for example, had only recently become a master.[213] The High Court had once "ruled in favor of the Guild of Spanish Barbers and Surgeons" by prohibiting hair barbers from "having public stores" some twenty-five years earlier, but it was time "to suspend" the fight.[214] The scissors-and-blade group brought paperwork dating to the 1620s to the meeting with guild members to explain the conflict's history. Imagine, the community had been securing copies of licenses, mandates, and court decisions for nearly forty years, guarding them as an archive of their profession.

Two weeks later at the notary's office, Martín, Asqueta, Vélez, and the rest of the group, on behalf of "all those who exercised their trade, today and in the future," met with Nicolas Vega and another barber phlebotomist, "representing all the master barbers and surgeons of the city," to finalize the agreement.[215] The agreement suggested that "Spanish barbers" had accepted that blade-and-scissors shops were a separate business. Yet the fear of competition lingered. Apart from phlebotomy, did they not provide similar services? Hair barbers did not think so, but they agreed to a caveat about location. They could open shops "anywhere they wanted," except on "the same block as a Spanish barber."[216] It was a small give for a larger victory. The arrangement met with some resistance, but they prevailed.[217] A year later, hair barbers and "master barbers and surgeons," with joined legal counsel, requested that the High Court confirm their agreement.[218] The agreement bound hair barbers "in perpetuity" to the Brotherhood of Holy Christ.[219] After decades of conflict, they hoped to finally be free to run their shops in peace. The payoff kept them in business – their very ability to pay the subsidy was a testament of their financial success. By 1670, hair barbers ran some "one hundred shops" in the city.²²⁰ Alonso Cortés Siles, from the beginning of the chapter, joined the community at this point in their history.

## 3.8 THE FIGHT WAS NOT OVER

Events on Maundy Thursday, April 4, 1697, revealed that hair barbers remained the target of ongoing hostility. Members of the Brotherhood of the Holy Cross and Maundy had worked for weeks preparing for their annual procession. They bought pitch for the torches, cleaned their vestments, prepared the banners and statue they carried through the streets, and hired trumpeters and guards to accompany them. The last preparation evinced the need for caution.

Hair barbers joined their brothers at Saint Claire Church in the morning and began their procession to the Main Square (Figure 3.2). Barber phlebotomists and barber surgeons put on the red habits of their Brotherhood of Holy Christ and met at the Church of Holy Trinity. They processed down the same street from the opposite direction, also carrying torches, banners, and a statue, and in step with their own guards. The "trumpeters played somber music."²²¹ Members of both brotherhoods met in front of the Viceroyal Palace. There was shoving and shouting. They struck each other with "clubs and crosses," some collapsing from their wounds.²²² The fight was the culmination of decades of bitterness and resentments. The writer Giovanni Francesco Gemelli Careri witnessed the scene; he heard that it was a "dispute over precedence" between men "from the Philippines" and members of the Brotherhood of Holy Christ.²²³ The "Spanish barbers" questioned the right of hair barbers to stand by their side. Their opponents reminded them that they had subsidized their brotherhood's activities since 1660.

For hair barbers, participating in the Maundy Thursday procession was an act of defiance that began when they organized their brotherhood. They named it Holy Cross and Maundy to reference the day when they showed members of the Barbers and Surgeons Guild that they belonged in Mexico City. They cared for residents in their own way, following the path of Jesus who healed the sick and washed his disciples' feet with humility on Maundy Thursday, the same day that Mary anointed his feet to express her devotion (Color Plate 7, Figure 3.4). The religious significance and metaphor of their work was lost on the members of the Brotherhood of Holy Christ, at least on April 4, 1697, when they

FIGURE 3.4 Commemorating Maundy Thursday
Source: Pedro Pardo, "María Magdalena unge los pies del señor" (siglo XVII),
photographed by Francisco Kochen. Courtesy of the Colección Museo
Vizcaínas, Colegio de San Ignacio de Loyola Vizcaínas.
The Latin on the lower left of the painting quotes chapter 12 of the Book
of John: "Mary took a pound of precious nard ointment and anointed the feet of
Jesus and wiped his feet with her hair." Hair barbers gazed at paintings such as
this one in the city's churches. They had vessels for oil like the one next to Mary
and pitchers like the one on the lower left in their blade-and-scissors shops.
A black and white version of this figure will appear in some formats.
For the color version, please refer to the plate section.

instigated the fight. They were neither charitable nor humble and cared
little for men they continued to see as unworthy competitors.

The financial agreement meant to secure the blade-and-scissors shops
remained in place. Members of the "Spanish confraternity" reorganized
in 1705, when it became the Brotherhood of Holy Christ of Healing
and "the charge of three guilds: surgeons, pharmacists, and phlebotomists."[224] This identification shows the distinction that developed
during the seventeenth century between barber phlebotomists and barber
surgeons, now considered different trades due to the licensing requirements of the Medical Board, as well as to the rise of hair barbering.
Barber phlebotomists and barber surgeons shared a history from the
sixteenth century, when "barbers and surgeons" formed their guild and

confraternity, and they continued to benefit from their exclusionary practices. Blade-and-scissors barbers did not become part of the reorganized
brotherhood, yet they continued making payments to prevent the costly
litigation that had plagued their community since their beginnings. They
had their own brotherhood to maintain a united front.

Barbers from the Philippines created an alternative path in the barbering profession, and the separation continued over the next century. By
1799, there were barbers with "blade-and-scissors" shops, "who did not
need to be examined or possess a license, so long as they abstained from
bloodletting, removing molars, applying leeches … [which] required the
approbation and permission of the Medical Board."[225] Hair barbers pioneered this distinction some 180 years earlier, when they established the
very first blade-and-scissors shops. The shops of the late eighteenth century were surely different, run by men from diverse backgrounds and
offering different services. Men from the Philippines paved the way for
them. They innovated a business that enabled people excluded by the
Barbers and Surgeons Guild to care for city residents in their own fashion.

## 3.9  CONCLUSION

The barbering profession changed over the course of the seventeenth
century, based on a growing distinction between the work of barber
phlebotomists, barber surgeons, and barbers who provided grooming
alongside noninvasive restorative services. This chapter articulates the
rise of an alternative form of barbering, spearheaded by men from the
Philippines who forged their own path.[226] They did so in the face of
systematic opposition by "Spanish barbers" who asserted sole privilege
over certain procedures, especially phlebotomy, to exclude them from the
profession. Traditional barbers who called themselves Spaniards instigated a decades-long struggle for primacy. Barbers from the Philippines,
in turn, pioneered a specialization in aesthetic and therapeutic barbering
that separated them from the ghastlier aspects of barber surgery, such as
the branding of enslaved people.

This separation included the creation of new businesses called blade-
and-scissors shops. To do so, hair barbers convinced officials at the
Viceroyal Palace and city hall charged with the crown's public health
policy that they were not a threat. Indeed, they asked to be ignored
by the Medical Tribunal. "Spanish barbers" were in line with contemporary medical practices drawn from the Greco–Roman tradition
that favored phlebotomy as a way of restoring the balance of humors.

Hair barbers promoted well-being based on a different tradition. They shared an alternative vision with Indigenous midwives and other healers who endeavored to ease the pains and sorrows that afflicted the city's residents with remedies that doctors overlooked.[227] It served their purpose that doctors did not consider their work medicine. They had their customers' acclaim. A wash and haircut, clean teeth, and a restorative drink – men left feeling better than when they walked into their shops.

Like the coachmen of Chapter 2, hair barbers sustained their neighbors and themselves. They formed a community based on their profession. They extended credit to enslaved men for self-manumission and provided jobs and guidance for those who followed in their path. They carved out spaces to protect themselves from the actions of "Spanish barbers," whose racialized attacks stemmed from a fear of competition. Hair barbers, for their part, carried on, caring for men such as silversmiths named in Chapter 4.

# 4

# Valuing the City

Francisco Salinas walked around the city with a silver plate made by a local silversmith in early January 1676. He had recently started working as a domestic worker in the household of a captain, who had promised to pay him "a salary of four pesos per month and a new set of clothes each year."[1] Salinas told the captain on his first day that "he did not need" the clothes, but he was desperate for an advance on his salary; his sister owed eight pesos in rent for their home.[2] The captain, wanting to secure the labor agreement, gave Salinas "three pesos in reals," meaning three pieces-of-eight (silver coins) minted in the city. He also handed him an "old pair of sleeves from Brittany," which was a piece of clothing made from imported fabric worn over a cotton shirt and tied to a doublet or padded jacket with strings.[3] The captain wanted Salinas to look smart in his presence. Salinas thought to pawn the sleeves to acquire the rent money, but it seemed easier to take a plate from the captain's dinnerware, which is how he came to have one that January day. Wearing the Brittany sleeves to elevate his appearance, he went to shops on Saint Francis Street to have silversmiths appraise the plate, and took it to pawn shops to see what he could get. No one offered him more than four pesos for the plate. This chapter examines the experiences of silversmiths who fostered a culture of trust around the value of silver and helped residents such as Salinas understand its worth, be it in the form of a plate or a piece-of-eight.

Mexico City was a city of silver.[4] Metal arrived almost daily from some of the richest silver deposits in the world – bars that became objects and coins that circulated around the world. Silversmiths were central actors in this production of wealth. They sustained the city by

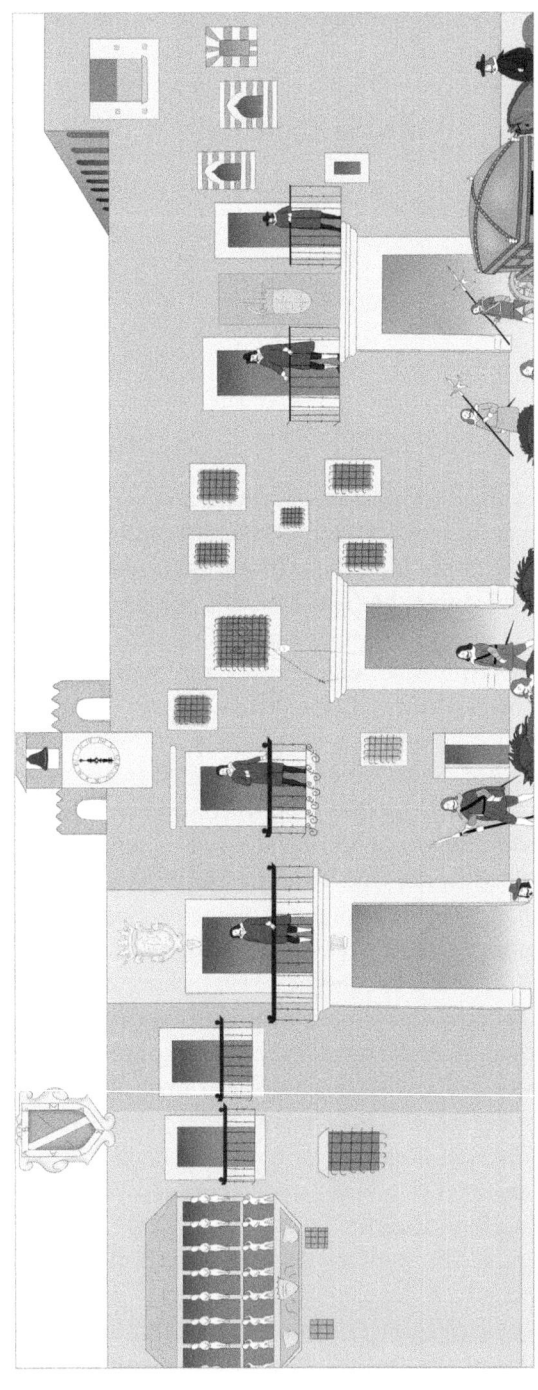

FIGURE 4.1 Fashioning silver

Source: Graphic rendering of a detail of "Biombo del Palacio de los Virreyes de México" (c.1675). Image by Matilde Grimaldi. The detail is from the upper register of the painting, which depicts the front of the Viceroyal Palace on the Main Square. The House of Coins was part of the palace complex.

valuing its most precious commodity. Value, a verb and noun, relates to people's propensity to give importance and worth to objects, and to think that some things are more useful than others. Residents valued silver. They considered that this metal was important, that it had worth, and that it was useful, specifically because it was money.[5] The Spanish crown set the face, or legal worth of coins minted in the city, which was related to their weight and purity, or fineness (metal content).[6] Silver objects were valued according to the same measures. Residents relied on silversmiths for advice on their silver property because they were weight and purity experts.

The now familiar painting mentioned in previous chapters of the Main Square and Alameda alludes to silversmiths (Color Plate 2). Note the Viceroyal Palace. Silversmiths made silverware that decorated the viceroy's dining table. They frequented the House of Coins located around the corner, named so because it contained the royal mint and foundry.[7] A graphic rendering captures the details (Figure 4.1). The figures on the balconies stand for officials who crossed the Main Square to visit shops on Saint Francis Street, claimed by silversmiths, where they commissioned silver shoe buckles to brighten their steps. The same officials received their salaries in silver coins minted feet away from their offices.

## 4.1 VISUALIZING SILVER

Silver was everywhere in the city, worn as jewelry, carried as coins, and admired in churches and people's homes as wrought silver. Women wore petticoats with silver threads.[8] Every building on Juan Gómez de Trasmonte's plan, discussed in the Introduction, had silver objects, so the work of silversmiths was omnipresent (Color Plate 1).

A graphic rendering shows the places where silversmiths spent most of their time. Their shops were on Saint Francis Street – half a mile of splendor that ran from the Main Square to the Franciscan complex (Figure 4.2). The English writer Thomas Gage remembered walking along their "beautiful street" in 1625, where he "beheld in less than an hour many millions worth" of silver, gold, and jewels.[9] The Dominican monastery had a chandelier of "exquisite workmanship," Gage wrote, with "three hundred branches wrought in silver to hold so many candles."[10] This chandelier was the kind of "curious work" made on Saint Francis Street that beautified the city. The silver "workers" Gage admired also frequented the House of Coins, "where money was daily coined," made from silver brought "upon mules" from Zacatecas.[11]

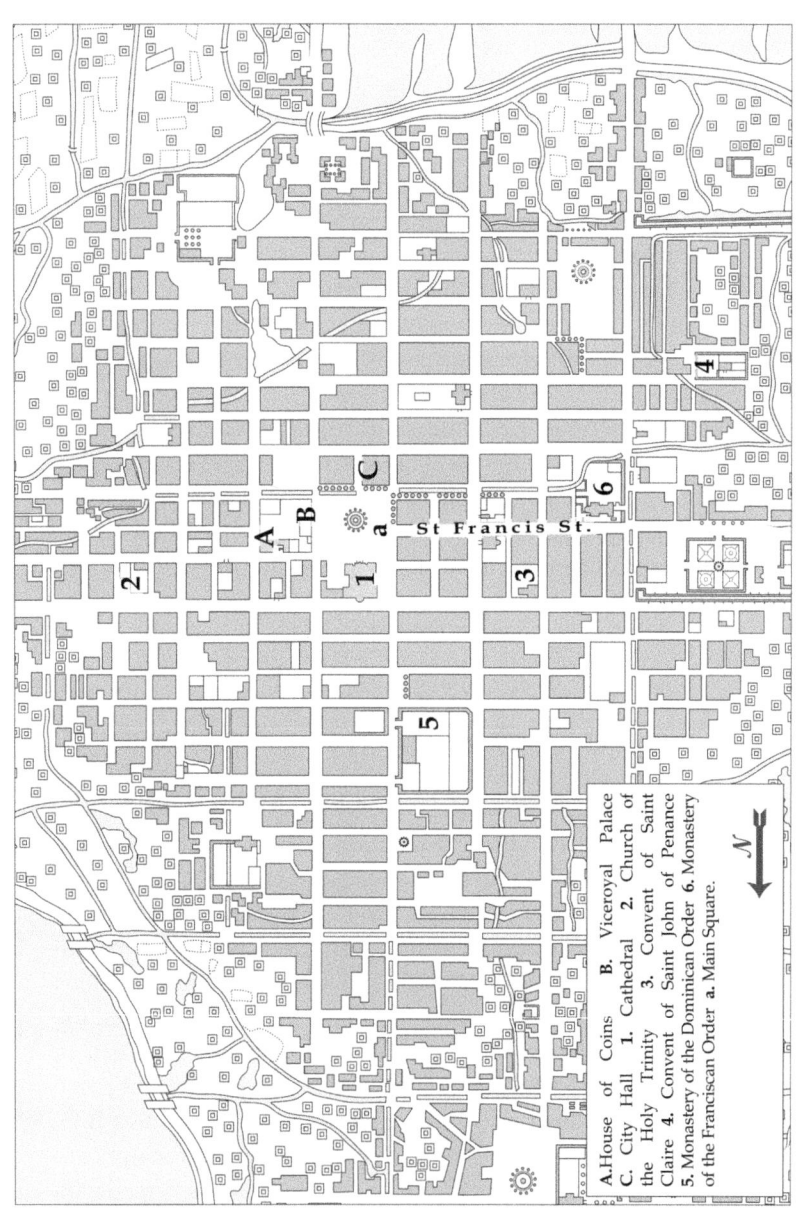

A. House of Coins   B. Viceroyal Palace
C. City Hall   1. Cathedral   2. Church of
the Holy Trinity   3. Convent of Saint
Claire   4. Convent of Saint John of Penance
5. Monastery of the Dominican Order   6. Monastery
of the Franciscan Order   a. Main Square.

FIGURE 4.2  Silvering spaces

Source: Graphic rendering of a detail of "Mexico City aus der Vogelperspektive" by Johannes Vingboons (1660), from *Atlas Blaeu – Van der Hem*. Image by Matilde Grimaldi.

The map's legend lists locations frequented by historical actors named in the chapter.

Silversmiths acquired silver from the mining regions as well, taking advantage of the same supply networks used by silver merchants and the royal treasury, and they registered their silver at the House of Coins. Holy Trinity Church was their spiritual refuge and a site for socializing with members of their brotherhood, just like the traditional barbers of Chapter 3. After 1648, silversmiths also met at the cathedral on the Main Square, where they sponsored a chapel to display their social power (Figure 4.2). The following pages examine the lives of silversmiths who occupied these spaces.

Silversmiths provided diverse services at their shops related to their ability to transform silver and to value it. They worked with residents who needed appraisals. They acted as brokers, buying and selling silver for people who invested in silver. And they made objects that held value. Silversmiths worked with molds, shaped sheet metal, and used a turn to construct their pieces, and then they hammered, chiseled, or embossed them for decoration.

A silversmith made one of the most valued "sacred objects" in the cathedral: a statue of Our Lady of the Conception in solid silver and three feet tall.[12] Gazing at the image inspired Agustín Vetancurt to compose a poem.[13]

> The silversmithery portrays thee
> in silver, Virgin, and it is good
> That in silver be portrayed should
> She who purer than silver be.

The phrasing reflects the religious belief that the Virgin Mary was pure, free of original sin, from her conception. It also reveals Vetancurt's understanding of the valuation and qualities of the precious metal. Even pure silver has infinitesimal impurities, but its relative purity was an apt metaphor. It is also too soft for silverwork, which is why the statue was 93.5 percent silver, the legal standard. Vetancurt assumed his readers had this knowledge to understand the poem. It was fitting that a statue celebrating the Virgin's purity be made of silver because the metal's value was based on its relative purity.

This chapter focuses on silversmiths who made flatware and holloware, such as the statue of the Virgin, by casting and forging silver. Their story, however, is inseparable from goldsmiths. They were all smiths, only one word in Spanish, even though they had expertise in either silver or gold and pursued three different arts or specializations: wrought metal; metal leaf; and metal thread or wire.[14] Each art had its own guild, but silversmiths and goldsmiths came together as members of the same religious brotherhood, named after the patron for metalworkers Saint Eligius, or Eloy.[15] Silversmiths allied with goldsmiths to maintain the trust of officials and residents who relied on them to value the stuff of money. This collaboration emerged in the sixteenth century, when they established a pattern of political action that made them central players in the business of valuing.

## 4.2  SIXTEENTH-CENTURY PRECEDENTS: HOW SILVERSMITHS ESTABLISHED A PATTERN OF NEEDED EXPERTISE

Andres Tapia had been working on a silver pitcher for several days at the shop of a silversmith.[16] It was June 1572. When Tapia returned from an afternoon break, he found an elderly friar talking to the shop owner about a chalice he had commissioned. Tapia, perhaps wanting to bother the friar and other clergymen in the room, started to talk about sex. The friar was furious, but the other men engaged in the discussion. Tapia had a critical point to make regarding the value of work. There are women, he said, "who are poor and have to make a living" by providing sex.[17] A "Christian man," Tapia noted, had "the obligation of satisfying his debt to a woman when he laid with her and pay her what she deserved."[18] Only one of the clerics understood Tapia's reasoning: precarious circumstances forced women to do "this work"; it was "the way of the world." Men had to pay them because they were financially responsible for their actions.[19] The cleric agreed with Tapia, but he added that such men had to do penance. Everyone else, including the friar, simply accused Tapia of being a sinner and called him a "heretic" and a "follower of Martin Luther" for denying that sex out of marriage was a sinful act. Tapia was making an economic point: people work for money. The clergymen were harping on a theological issue.

The shop owner Domingo Gómez got upset. People were speaking in raised voices and drawing the attention of passersby, so he told Tapia to leave, but everyone kept hurling accusations, drawing him back into the discussion. At that point, the friar had had enough; he held up a "handkerchief filled with reals" and "wagered against what Tapia was saying."[20] So Tapia picked up the silver pitcher at his worktable and accepted the bet; he was willing to pay the price of the object to prove that he knew more about work, value, and worth than churchmen. A customer came into the shop and tried to deescalate the situation by taking the pitcher out of his hands, but Tapia punched him in the face.

Daggers were drawn. Fortunately, shop assistants Juan and Anton, enslaved men, had the foresight and bravery to disarm and pull the brawlers apart. What had happened?

The interaction reveals that residents used silver to back their truth-claims and pay for what they valued. From the clergymen's perspective, Tapia's reasoning was an affront to Catholic doctrine. The friar bet the coins he needed to pay for his chalice because he valued the theological certainty that marriage was a sacrament. Sex was for procreation – that was the friar's truth-claim. Tapia valued sex work; he paid for it. His truth-claim was that all labor merited payment, be it sex work or his own silvering work. Tapia was willing to bet the pitcher's silver, the stuff of coins, to demonstrate his point.

The encounter illustrates how master silversmiths, such as Gómez, managed the labor in their shops. He followed a pattern that began in the 1530s and persisted throughout the seventeenth century: silversmiths relied on journeymen (such as Tapia), apprentices, and enslaved men to create silver objects.[21] Juan and Anton were able to quell the violence that afternoon because they were in Gómez's shop at their worktables. They heard the whole thing and quickly restrained their workmate to prevent a brawl. Free and enslaved men shared a similar proximity in the shops of all trades organized as guilds, as shown in Chapter 3. Master tradesmen trained free men to pass their exams and get licensed to work for a salary. Silversmiths taught enslaved men to do the same work, but they, unless manumitted, had little chance of receiving recompense for their artistry. Tapia, on the other hand, had the opportunity to become a silversmith because he was from Ciudad Real in Castile – a colonist who claimed his birth privilege to secure a position unavailable to enslaved men.

When Tapia arrived in Mexico City as a fifteen-year-old orphan back in 1552, Gabriel Villasana, an established silversmith, took him on as an apprentice and gave him a home for five years. Villasana set him up for a lucrative business. By the time of the encounter at Gómez's shop, Tapia was independent, earning a journeyman salary and, on the side, "buying and selling silver much to his benefit."[22] He had skills and knowledge valued by his fellow colonists. Indeed, Tapia appears to have felt so confident of his status and expertise that he risked losing his position in Gómez's shop during the brawl.

The event offers a glimpse of shop life and the efforts master artisans took to foster an atmosphere of trust and calm in their shops. Gómez found Tapia's behavior appalling because he was disturbing the calmness needed to make clients feel at ease and encourage them to spend money. Silversmiths worked hard to get commissions, starting when customers first entered their shops. They talked to residents to get a sense about the size, weight, and type of object they wanted. They quickly sketched out a design on paper to help their customers envision the finished product and showed them finished pieces as examples of their craftsmanship. Once a customer became more interested, the silversmith steered the conversation towards financing, which included the cost of labor and the raw material. The customer could buy the silver from the silversmith or use her own. The process required patience and tact because it involved the most valued and regulated commodity in Mexico City.

Part of gaining their customers' trust involved explaining the crown's tax policy on silver, and silversmiths' role in its implementation. They had to use taxed silver in all the objects they made. In 1525, council members had discussed the "damage" done by residents who asked silversmiths to make objects from un-taxed silver, which "defrauded his majesty of the royal fifth" (standard cut for the crown).[23] To combat such accusations, silversmiths agreed "to register" the silver residents gave them at city hall "before they made any object."[24] This practice was an early implementation of a checking process that was more firmly in place once royal treasury officials took it over.

When Gómez spoke with the friar about the silver for his chalice, he would have explained that silversmiths were obligated to present the silver intended for each object to officials at the Viceroyal Palace. Back in July 1563, Viceroy Velasco had suspended silversmiths' licenses to punish individuals who failed to report the metal they used at the royal foundry for taxation.[25] In response, members of Gómez's guild organized to convince him that "depriving them of their trade" was "dangerous and harmful for the public," because they were the ones who educated residents about the legal standard, the value of silver, and their tax obligations.[26] Velasco agreed and lifted the ban within months.

Guild members assuaged his concerns by outlining the registration process in a set of ordinances approved on October 1563; they meant "to report all the silver targeted for fabrication."[27] The ordinances detailed the steps they needed to follow.[28] First, Gómez presented his or his customer's metal to officials who "discerned if it was fived" (meaning taxed).[29] If the silver had the appropriate "marks," it was safe from taxation. If not, officials removed the king's percentage. Second, officials "weighed and registered it in a book" along with information about the "objects or jewels to be made."[30] Third, Gómez received a "registration certificate," which he had to present again when he finished the piece to have "the same officials confirm the weight" and "place a mark or symbol" that verified completion of the process.[31] The back-and-forth made it difficult for silversmiths to be accused of abiding tax evasion, and it was also supposed to protect their customers.

As Gómez would have explained to a customer such as the friar, the crown "prohibited residents and inhabitants" from "having any wrought silver in their homes" or jewels made from untaxed silver.[32] The penalty was loss of property. It behooved the friar, in other words, to have his chalice registered to protect his investment, as it would then have a mark proving he had paid the tax. Registration was a problem, however, for clients who wanted to use silver that had not been taxed. Say the friar's silver was a gift from a miner – a block of metal that did not have tax marks. In this case, royal treasury officials would have "fived" it at the first registration, meaning that he would have less silver for the chalice than if it had already been taxed.[33] The friar may not have wanted that to happen because it meant having a smaller chalice. Silversmiths and their clients discussed this conundrum, which was part of the trust-making interactions that occurred in their shops.

Silversmiths also fought to demonstrate their commitment to the legal standard. As noted, their transformative powers, the ability to melt and reinstitute precious metal, raised suspicion among councilmen. Part of the 1525 discussion about registration had been about silversmiths allegedly "adding" copper to silver to have more metal for their commissions, which meant they made things that had a greater ratio of copper to silver than allowed.[34] Silversmiths responded to these concerns by underlining their own expertise. Only they could truly determine how much silver was in any object. So, as of 1530, silversmiths annually elected a chief inspector from their ranks and had council members endorse their choice. This person had to check the workmanship of silver objects and confirm that they met the legal standard. Approved objects got stamped with a hallmark in the shape of a castle to prevent "buyers being deceived."[35] The friar would have expected to see this shape at the bottom of his chalice when he picked it up at Gómez's shop.

Tapia knew how this confirmation worked because Gabriel Villasana, the silversmith who trained him, had held this position and explained its importance in maintaining artisans' reputations. Villasana followed the steps of silversmiths who supported their trade by holding positions created to instill faith in the value of silver and commercial exchange more broadly. His peers elected him in July 1544, when he pledged "to use faithfully the office of Chief Inspector and Hallmarker to guard royal ordinances" on silver.[36] The position, by his time, carried the additional designation of Chief Hallmarker to emphasize the physicality of what these inspectors did: they marked silver. This procedure was separate from the markings done by royal treasury officials. Villasana received the city's castle hallmark and used it for the next six years to authenticate the work of his peers.[37] They would stop by his shop and wait while he inspected their pieces.

Villasana employed a simple assaying technique. He took a sharp instrument to scrape off a tiny piece of metal from the object, which left a zig-zag indentation.[38] Then, he compared its color to confirmed samples of silver, small rods with different metal contents to make sure it matched the standard.[39] Once verified, Villasana hallmarked the object. Royal officials took over the hallmarking within decades, but chief inspectors continued to check the purity of objects with the zig-zag technique. Villasana kept assiduous records, and his dutifulness garnered the attention of council members, who appointed him to serve the city in an additional capacity two years into his tenure.

In February 1546, councilmen invited Villasana to their chambers "to solemnly swear" that he would carry out the duties of Chief Inspector and Sealer of Weights and Measures.[40] The city needed him, as an "able and adequate person," to take over the position.[41] This office, created two decades earlier, was responsible for "tuning any and all measures and weights used for measurements."[42] Silversmiths had lobbied to hold this position since that time, when the focus had been on inspecting and tuning weights used to measure precious metals.[43] Villasana was thus responsible for inspecting silver objects, as well as ensuring that all weights and measures in the city complied with standards set by the crown, be it weights for precious metals or measures for wine and everything else sold in shops across the city.

The friar in 1572 could trust Gómez's weights because he knew that one of Villasana's successors had inspected them to ensure that they measured silver with the greatest precision.[44] Silversmiths and city officials continued to promote the inspection requirements. Gonzalo León, Chief Inspector and Sealer in 1581, knew that he had to "visit the shops of smiths to look at their objects and ensure they met the standard" and "tune the weights for gold and silver and everything else" according to the city's official weights.[45] The responsibilities of Chief Inspector and Sealer changed over the course of the seventeenth century. Silversmiths, however, continued to garner civic credit from city officials for doing this combined work, which subsequently enabled them to rise above suspicion and conduct their affairs more freely.[46]

Returning to trust-making conversations in the shops, silversmiths negotiated with their customers on the amount of money they charged for their workmanship. Silversmiths had contended with attempts to regulate the value of their work as early as 1527. Council members complained that they charged "excessive and exorbitant prices for their workmanship."[47] Silversmiths, on the other hand, protested that councilmen did not even know what they did in their shops. So, they compiled a list of the things and explained why a plate, for example, was not comparable to a pitcher, which took much longer to make. There was also the matter of size. Silversmiths consequently decided to set their fees according to the type and weight of the objects. The price for making plates out of one mark of silver would be one peso, and double that amount for pitchers. Silversmiths also contended that the design and level of detail had to affect the cost, which could only be determined by an "official they elected from among their peers."[48] They had to be allowed to determine their own fees for complicated pieces. Councilors heard them and agreed to approve a list of fees that matched their determinations.

City hall's effort to have maximum-set work fees applied to all artisans.[49] It correlated to their efforts to set prices for food, as discussed in Chapter 1. Notably, silversmiths explained their fees and the value of their work in a way that underlined their special knowledge of silver and measures. They were the ones who confirmed the weights used by all residents to sell their goods. It was in their purview to value their work according to the weight of the thing that carried the greatest monetary and cultural value for colonists: precious metal. They charged in silver. In time, city hall ceased focusing on max-set fees, and silversmiths, for their part, shifted their approach to negotiation. Goméz and the friar in 1572 came to an agreement over the amount he paid for the chalice. Silversmiths in the seventeenth century continued this practice, negotiating the fee alongside the price of silver to be used when customers bought it from them.

Gómez was a member of the Silversmiths and Goldsmiths Guild, which confirmed his station in the city's most profitable and prestigious trade.[50] Smiths, as noted, specialized in wrought metal, metal leaf, and metal wire. Smiths such as Gómez "worked with silver" to make objects.[51] Metal leaf workers "made bars of gold and silver for gilding, beating them down" to create metal leaf with "care, and rapid and continuous" action.[52] Notably, the colloquial phrase for coining money was beating coins because workers in the House of Coins employed the same skills.[53] Metal wire workers made "long, narrow" strings of varying widths.[54] They cast silver into thin rods and pulled them through "holes" on a plate to elongate the metal.[55] As more individuals joined the guild, artisans sought greater oversight and distinction between their specializations. Members of all guilds, as noted in Chapter 3, elected representatives from among their ranks, who wrote bylaws or modified those published by fellow artisans in Spain, and submitted them to city hall for approval and subsequently to the viceroy who confirmed them. Once ratified, guild representatives had the right to govern their members and regulate their craft and the production of their wares in accordance with these ordinances. In this fashion, artisans took part in the legislative process and had some executive powers of their own.

By the early 1570s, smiths who specialized in either silver or gold objects were already identified as a distinct group, separate from metal-leaf workers and metal-thread workers.[56] So did the other specialists. Indeed, smiths such as Gómez apparently considered that their work was superior, which caused frictions evident in an addendum to the guild's ordinances in 1598.[57] It warned metal thread workers that they were "only permitted to pull gold and silver thread," while metal leaf workers had to focus on "making sheets from beginning to end."[58] Smiths who made objects, for their part, agreed not to buy or sell either leaf or thread, which was the reserve of men trained in those arts. It was a slight concession given the scope of their work and the volume of silver handled in their shops. This confirmation, however, did not appease leaf artisans who had sought to have their own guild for over twenty years.[59] They finally succeeded in creating the Metal-Leaf Guild in 1599 that had unique ordinances detailing their training and work, which included making metal sheets of varying thicknesses.[60] Metal thread workers, by contrast, remained under the Smiths Guild for another seventy years.[61] Guild ordinances or bylaws, for clarification, were different than the previously noted ordinances related to the registration of metals.

Despite the tensions caused by artisans wanting to oversee their specialties, all smiths remained a cohesive group by virtue of belonging to the Brotherhood of Saint Eligius. They worshipped together and paid the same dues which fostered solidarities that allowed them to pursue mutually beneficial political ends, as discussed later in the chapter.

The friar gave Gómez silver coins minted in Mexico City.[62] The crown intended to open an official mint as early as 1525, having already insisted that royal appointees take control of foundries established in the aftermath of the war.[63] It was part of the implementation of the Pragmatic or Ordinances of Medina del Campo, a set of laws issued by Queen Isabel and King Ferdinand in 1497 that established new currency and dictated the workings of mints.[64] The "land had a lot of metals" and "it would serve us well," read a royal decree, "for there to be a House of Coins."[65] Having coins in circulation would "reduce the price of goods."[66] More importantly for the royal treasury, making coins would "prevent fraud and the deception" that happened at foundries where metals "were mixed below the legal standard."[67] The wording encapsulated the crown's monetary and fiscal policy. The point about prices reflected the crown's understanding that coins standardized prices because they removed the uncertainty of valuing goods in a barter economy. Exchanging a horse for a carriage, for example, could elevate the value of the horse; the two were assumed to have the same value even though a carriage was costlier to make. It was better to consider the value of a horse vis-à-vis other horses (a large one is more expensive than a small one) and set its price in coins. The seller of the horse had to trust the value of the coins he received, so the crown had to ensure they matched the legal standard so that people would not be "deceived." The decree's reference to fraud concerned this alteration, as well as tax evasion.

The solution, from the crown's perspective, was to force everyone to have their silver assayed (checked to determine its metal content) and taxed (have silver deducted), and to coin money from this same silver. The 1525 decree began a decades-long effort to build a House of Coins – a building with a royal foundry and a royal mint so that the two activities could happen in one place: the collection of taxes and the production of coins at the legal standard. It took over four decades to make this happen, starting with the creation of an interim mint in 1535.

In the meantime, two smiths who worked at the city's foundry convinced councilmen in April 1526, that they could be entrusted with assaying precious metals and making coins for the "convenience" of residents needing to "buy and sell."[68] They created nonstandard coins from "*tepuzque* gold," which was a combination of gold and copper.[69] Why them? Because smiths were the only colonists who had the skills and knowledge needed to transform metal, be it into coins or adornments. Smiths thus secured positions at the provisional foundry and mint, and subsequently at the House of Coins.

Juan de Torquemada and Vetancurt credited Viceroy Mendoza with the beginning of money-making in Mexico City – for having "founded the House of Coins in 1535."[70] The crown instructed him in May 1535 to organize a mint like those in Castile and granted 1,000 marks of silver from the royal treasury for the first run, which went into circulation via salaries and payments.[71] When Mendoza first regularized minting, workers produced silver reals in denominations of eight reals (pieces-of-eight), 4, 3, 2, 1, and a half-real, which was the least common.[72] Then, the government introduced coins made of copper "as done in Spain."[73]

According to Torquemada, Indigenous residents played a key role in determining the metal used in coins in Mexico City. They refused to accept the copper coins as payment, "disdaining" them as things without value.[74] Residents from Spain scorned them as well. Within a year, they were gone and replaced with silver coins valued at a quarter of a real. These were "very small and had little silver," so residents rejected them as well.[75] The government had no choice but to return to silver.

By the early 1570s, the House of Coins had a new home in the Viceroyal Palace complex.[76] Silversmiths with shops on Saint Francis walked across the Main Square, entered the House of Coins, and went to the office where officials registered the silver they would transform into objects. They also visited colleagues who were assayers or held other positions on the mint side. Their embrace of the registration requirement decades earlier had helped silversmiths acquire such positions. The viceroy could trust them, they suggested, because they faithfully reported all the silver they touched.

The drawing that locates the food court in Chapter 1 at the turn of the century captures the new building (Figure 4.3). The viceroyal complex is on the top register and the beginning of Saint Francis Street at the bottom. It was on the north-eastern corner of the palace complex, facing Coin Street, a name that persists today in memory of the location. The drawing shows the façade with a door and windows. Upon entering, silversmiths walked to one of the building's two patios, which had rooms all around where officials handled silver for different purposes, be it to record, tax, and assay it on the accounting side, or to mint it on the other.[77] These activities made the House of Coins an extension of the royal treasury and the responsibility of the highest officials in the city.[78] Workers minted silver on the account of the crown and for residents, who paid fees and duties to turn their silver into coins.[79] A silversmith could bring his silver to turn it into money, but silver merchants were the primary customers throughout the seventeenth century.[80]

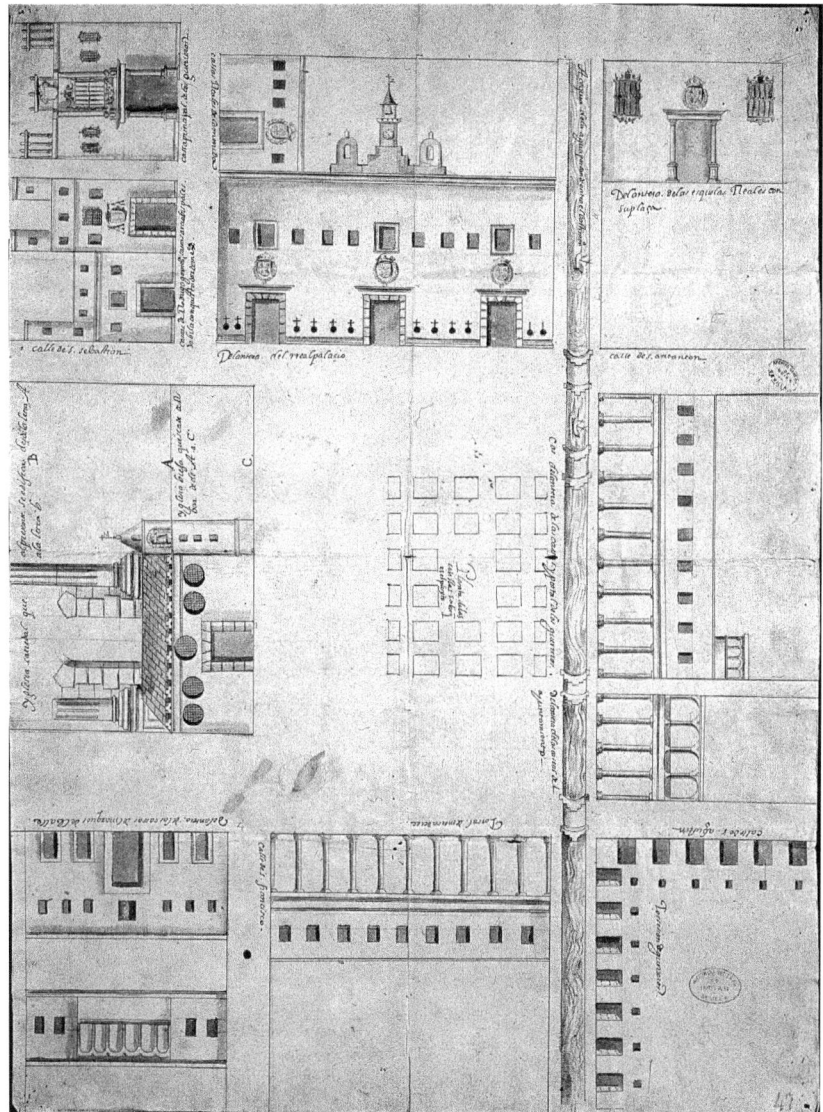

FIGURE 4.3 Silver at the Main Square
Source: "Plaza Mayor de la ciudad de México" (1596), AGI MP-México 47.
Courtesy of the Archivo General de Indias.
The label "royal" on the House of Coins emphasized that it belonged to the
Hapsburg Crown. Saint Francis Street, the dominion of silversmiths, is labeled
on the lower left.

Mint workers made coins by hand throughout the seventeenth century.[81] They melted silver into thin bars, cut them into circles, and stamped them with a hammer and die.[82] This process meant that the coins had slight differences; some had clearer marks and were more perfectly circular and even than others. A real coin from 1611 shows much wear, but nonetheless evokes the markings that testified to their legal and intrinsic value (Color Plate 8, Figure 4.4). The obverse of real coins, on the left, bear the royal coat of arms at center, flanked by the letter M, the assayer's initial (F, in this case), and denomination (face value), which is one real in this example. The M with a little circle on top or side declared their provenance – made in Mexico City.[83] The legend includes the year, name of the issuer (PHILIPPVS III), and *DEI GRATIA* (by the grace of God). The reverse bear a cross potent, with the triple-towered castle and lion devices of the Catholic Monarchs in the quadrants; the legend is HISPANIARVM ET INDIARVM REX, king of Spain and the Indies. These letters confirmed that the Hapsburg Crown backed this silver as money, which simultaneously held value as a precious metal. People believed that the mint produced high-quality coins because it was verifiable fact; they could weigh their real coins and check their purity to verify their intrinsic value.

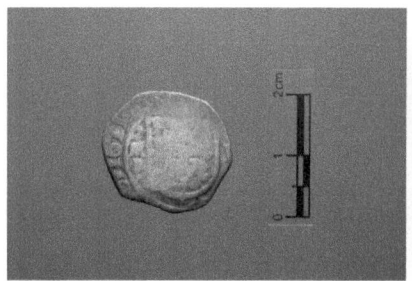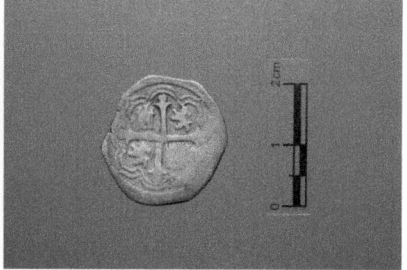

FIGURE 4.4  Silver coin
Source: "Moneda de un real" photographed by María del
Mar Gómez Talavera (Inv. 2005/84/439). Courtesy of the Museo
Arqueológico Nacional.
This coin, shown on both sides, is a rare example of an early
seventeenth-century real. It may have been clipped given the straight edge – an
illegal practice done once coins left territory under Spanish sovereignty. All
coins were irregularly shaped. The technological process that produced circular,
milled-edge coins was an eighteenth-century development.
A black and white version of this figure will appear in some formats. For the
color version, please refer to the plate section.

The crown's monetary policy changed over the course of the seventeenth century, which included new mandates that lowered the weight and metal content for silver minted in Spain.[84] These fluctuations did not apply to coins minted in Mexico City until the eighteenth century, which meant that they remained more valuable and coveted due to their intrinsic value.[85] When a silversmith based in Seville lent money to neighbors who migrated to Mexico City in 1681, he expected the amount to be paid back with "3,249 silver reals of legal fineness and weight" minted in Mexico.[86] These real coins had a higher metal content than those minted in his hometown – that is why he wanted his money back in the same coinage. Seville coins held less silver value.

The drawing from 1596 references silversmiths' creativity and the commercial activity they fostered throughout the seventeenth century (Figure 4.3). Their appropriation of Saint Francis Street started in 1580, when a councilman asked silversmiths to discuss the possibility of having them "come together on one street," and "to consider several streets" for that purpose.[87] Councilors proposed this congregation to facilitate government oversight, but smiths interpreted it differently. They did not have to move. They agreed to do so and chose Saint Francis Street because it was an opportunity to be as close as possible to the city's nexus of power and trade – the Main Square.

Whatever their specialty, artisans wanted their shops on Saint Francis Street to be in the same "place as the other" smiths.[88] Their assembly happened slowly, as more of them convinced owners to rent them spaces in buildings on that street. And to encourage them, they had Viceroy Monterrey approve their request to have landlords "give them preference in rentals on that street over other people."[89] They also formalized their presence by noting the location in their guild ordinances. This inclusion satisfied officials who assumed that smiths were simply following their directives. Smiths who made silver and gold leaf agreed to the following wording when they drew up new guild ordinances in 1598: they had "to live in their own homes and separately have their shops on Saint Francis Street."[90] Metal workers were not supposed to live and work in the same place, unlike other artisans. This restriction facilitated their move, giving them greater flexibility in the rental market because they sought out spaces that did not have to accommodate living quarters. Cristóbal Jimenez moved to Mexico City "to open a shop," and quickly apprehended where he needed to be. In 1601, he rented a space "on Saint Francis, where all the other smiths" did their business.[91] Miguel Asbister joined him five years later.[92] And so it continued, with stores opening throughout the seventeenth century, as silversmiths secured their own spaces in the buildings that lined the street.

### 4.3 VALUING AND MEASURING SILVER DURING THE 1600S–1620S: HOW SILVERSMITHS HELPED RESIDENTS INVEST IN SILVER AND UNDERSTAND MONEY

Eugenia Vázquez and her husband Pedro Ceballos traded silver. A silversmith, Ceballos advised his customers on their own investments at his shop, so he had a good eye for prospects. In July 1607, one of Ceballos's clients had him assess his silver; he had "trays, plates, pitchers, cups, drinking bowls, platters, spoons, and two bars of fived-silver."[93] Ceballos inspected, measured, and valued the pieces. The client's property weighed "305 marks and 12 ounces of silver," which, valued at "eight pesos and one *tomín*," amounted to "2,480 pesos and one tomín of common-gold."[94] Was Ceballos interested in buying it, the client asked? The silversmith considered the offer with Vázquez, a silver expert herself, and together they decided to make the purchase, promising to pay for the lot in pieces-of-eight. They meant to sell the objects at higher prices to profit on the trade.

This transaction illustrates what happened on Saint Francis Street. Apart from making objects, silversmiths participated in the most profitable trade in Mexico City and helped their customers do the same. They were the ones who determined how much a piece of silver weighed and its fineness. They also explained how to use these measures to establish the monetary value of any one silver object, be it a candlestick or a bar. Residents paid less for such objects than their official valuation, but traders needed to know this information to guide their investment decisions. Silversmiths, moreover, served as informal tax advisors by explaining the crown's complicated taxation policy.

Felipe Echagoyan published a manual, *Tables on the Order of Coins and the Value of Silver and Gold*, in 1603 to assist residents interested in buying and selling precious metals based on his experience.[95] He had been trading silver in Mexico City for more than ten years when he wrote it.[96] Residents were to buy his book, as noted in the preface, because "nearly everyone traded and carried out commerce, and those who did not were bereft and died" as paupers.[97] Trading metals promised financial gain, so people of all walks of life tried to get involved. Indeed, silversmiths relied on this promise to draw customers who sought their valuation and advising services.

To make good investments in silver residents needed to acquire monetary literacy (to know units of value used in monetary transactions and accounting), quantitative literacy (to do arithmetic), and silver literacy (to know the measures used for this metal). The manual was meant to help his readers attain this knowledge by themselves, but silversmiths well knew that the complexity of the topic meant that residents remained dependent on them to guide their financial decisions and translate the contents of manuals such as Echagoyan's.[98] Accounting units and silver measures were far easier to understand when silversmiths used physical examples at their shops than from simply reading.

Trading required keeping accounts, so Echagoyan began his work with an explanation of the units of value used in the city at the beginning of the century. The first section, "On the Value of Coins," shows the complexity residents faced. There were two types of units: metal units were coins; accounting units were imaginary or fictitious.[99] Both had a set equivalence to *maravedís*, which was the smallest unit used to value metal coins in the Spanish empire. He listed the units together to explain their values (Figure 4.5). In Echagoyan's words "most sales" in the city "were made" with reals.[100] When money changed hands, in other words, it was in the form of silver coins (metal units). In financial agreements, on the other hand, residents used accounting units. Residents used multiple units because it allowed them to quantify the value of commodities in a precise yet flexible manner.

The list combined metal and accounting units because residents thought about them together (Figure 4.5). The *escudo*, the first unit listed, was a gold coin rarely used in the city because it was minted in Spain. The next three were accounting units. The ducat was useful for residents who had business in Spain, where it was common.[101] In the city, residents were more likely to employ the next two units – the "mine-peso" and "common-silver peso" – though these disappeared within a decade of the manual's publication.[102] It was simply easier to use the unit Echagoyan listed as "tepuzque peso" (not to be confused with the coins of the 1520s), which was more commonly known as common-gold peso.[103] Officials at the royal treasury did their accounting with this unit of value. Indeed, the common-gold peso was the most common accounting unit throughout the seventeenth century, so much so that when residents spoke of "common-gold pesos" they meant silver coins.[104]

The common-gold peso had the same value as the eight-real coins that were minted in the city.[105] As Echagoyan wrote, these pesos "were worth 272 maravedís which is eight reals" (i.e., one piece-of-eight).[106]

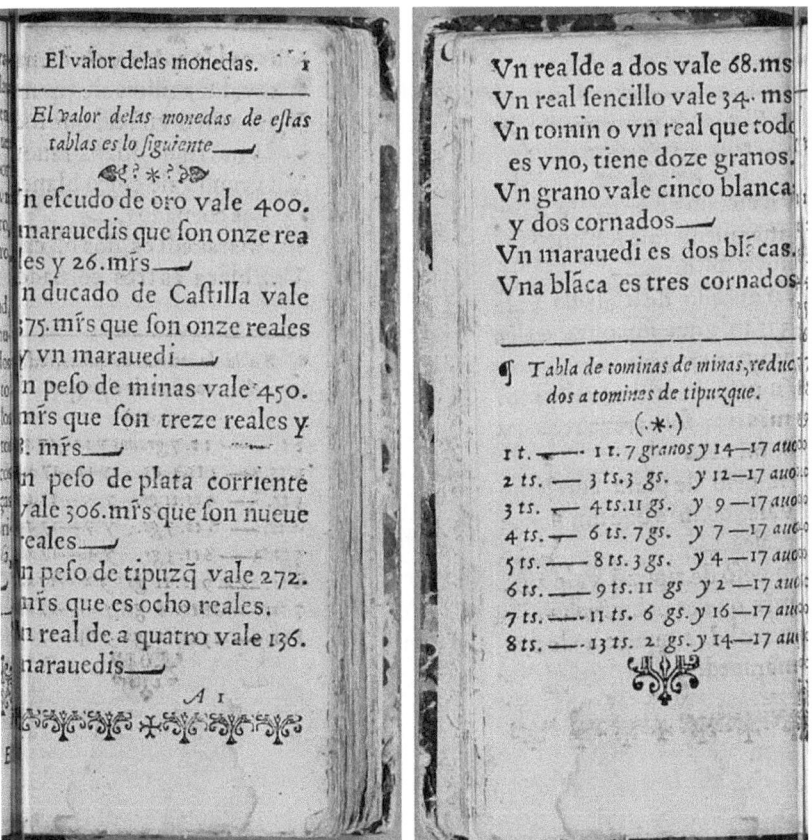

FIGURE 4.5 Units of values used in Mexico City, early 1600s
Source: Felipe Echagoyan. "El valor de las monedas de estas tablas es lo
siguiente." In *Tablas de redvciones de monedas, y del valor de todo genero
de plata y oro*, f.1–1v. México: Henrico Martinez, 1603. Courtesy of the
John Carter Brown Library, Brown University.
The manual was printed in a small size. This copy is barely six inches tall, with
tightly bound leaves.

This one-to-one equivalence encouraged residents to mentally convert
the accounting unit into the metal coins they exchanged during everyday
transactions. Two years after the manual was published, Marina Ruiz
and Antonio Fuentes had a contract drawn up confirming that her parents gave her "1,000 tepuzque pesos" as a dowry, which they received
as "1,000 pesos in silver reals" (i.e., 1,000 pieces-of-eight).[107] If the contract had noted the dowry amount in mine-pesos, they would first have
had to convert the amount to maravedís and then to reals to ascertain

the equivalence to metal units. Using accounting units other than the common-gold peso, in other words, added an extra step when it came to calculating the number of coins that would be handed over to complete a financial transaction. Due to the easy exchange, residents started using the terms interchangeably, colloquially using common-gold pesos, or simply pesos, to refer to pieces-of-eight.[108] In 1605, Alonso Delgado, a muleteer, stated that he would pay a farmer "360 common-gold pesos of eight reals."[109] He combined the accounting unit with the metal unit, indicating the slippage between the two. In Delgado's mind, common-gold pesos were pieces-of-eight.

The remaining units on Echagoyan's table were accounting or "imaginary" units (Figure 4.5). A tomín had the same value as a real (thirty-four maravedís); "they were one and the same."[110] A tomín was worth a real coin, just as a common-gold peso was worth a piece-of-eight coin.[111]

Diego Cruz wrote a letter to his mother in Granada, Spain in 1619 that illustrates how city residents thought about and calculated money. The big news was that his new wife had a dowry of "12,000 pesos in the form of a small farm" outside the city.[112] Cruz knew that his mother did not keep accounts in common-gold pesos or think about money as silver reals like he did. She used the accounting unit ducat. So, he promised to send her "200 ducats" when the farm became more profitable. She would receive this amount via a bill of exchange or possibly in real coins delivered by ship.

Echagoyan acknowledged that attaining quantitative literacy could be challenging, so he wrote his manual "as a guide for those who were not proficient in calculations."[113] All residents had to do, he wrote, was look at his tables "to understand the cost and value" of accounting and metal units.[114] The table "On tepuzque pesos reduced to maravedís," for example, had two columns: the accounting unit on the left and the fictitious unit on the right.[115] If his reader wanted to convert the value of seven common-gold (tepuzque) pesos into different units, she could simply look across the columns and see the amount equaled 1,904 maravedís. It was a simple multiplication table.

Silversmiths maintained that trading silver required silver literacy, which meant knowing the measures used for this metal. The crown used these measures to give monetary value to silver. The 1497 pragmatic, noted earlier, established the mark as the mass measure for silver, with smaller units to weigh silver with infinitesimal precision.[116] The measure for purity (fineness) was the *dineral*. Pure silver had twelve *dineros*, and a dinero contained twenty-four grains (99.9 percent silver).[117] As Echagoyan explained, however, "the purest silver" (with 288 grains) was "rarely if ever found."[118] The standard mass (*ley*) was eleven dineros and four grains of silver to twenty grains of copper (93.5 percent silver).[119] The crown established this standard, the ratio of silver to copper in metal used to make coins and other objects, because pure silver is soft and unworkable.

These two measures (for mass and purity) were the basis for the official monetary valuation: a mark of silver at the standard (with 268 grains) had a monetary value of sixty-five reals.[120] The Spanish word for money *dinero* references the measurement for purity because money was once made from standard metal. Assayers maintained the crown's standard by tuning or refining silver to this purity at the royal foundry. And silversmiths "made" objects in their shops with standard silver, which as Echagoyan noted, had the same purity as "the reals made in the House of Coins" (Figure 4.6).[121]

The section "Advice for Accounting and the Value of Silver" explained that traders used different rates to value a grain of silver at the standard than a grain of silver "for the market" (Figure 4.6).[122] The first rate was related to the official monetary valuation; a grain of standard silver "was worth 8 maravedís and a quarter."[123] This rate approximated the official monetary value of a mark: 268 grains multiplied by the rate equaled 2,211 maravedís or "65 reals and 1 maravedí."[124] A royal treasury official confirmed the valuation: "modern assayers gave this value" to each grain "to respect" the "law of the kingdom."[125] Assayers at the House of Coins ignored the extra maravedí because it amounted to a speck of a grain, which "only an angel would be able to weigh."[126]

Silversmiths benefitted from the proliferation of trading because residents needed them to measure and value their commodity. The valuation for "trading silver," as Echagoyan explained, depended on the "dineros and grains found by assayers," which was "multiplied by 8 and a third maravedís to yield the value of a mark."[127] It was a higher rate than for standard silver, as noted earlier. Echagoyan included a table in his manual listing the values of a mark with varying ratios to aid this calculation. A mark with "8 dineros and 4 grains," for example, was valued at "6 common-gold pesos."[128] To use the table, however, traders needed to determine the purity of their silver. Silver merchants relied on assayers at the House of Coins. Small-scale investors, on the other hand, went to shops, where silversmiths did the work to help them value their silver.[129] They could use Echagoyan's manual to explain their by-grain valuations to their customers.

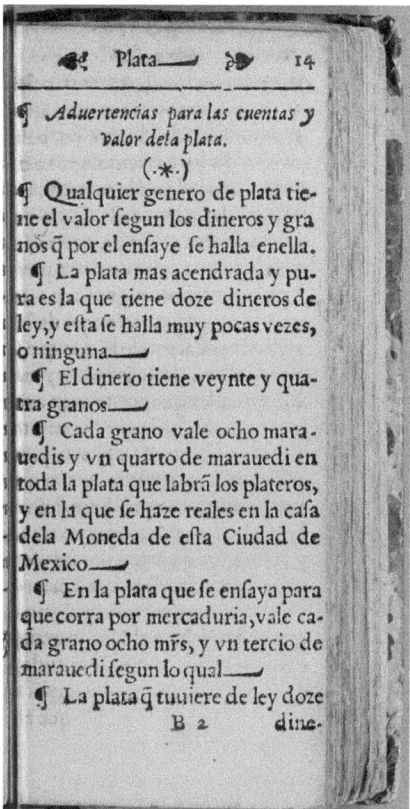

FIGURE 4.6 Valuing silver
Source: Felipe Echagoyan. "Aduertencias para las cuentas y valor de plata."
In *Tablas de redvciones de monedas, y del valor de todo genero de plata y oro*,
f.14. México: Henrico Martinez, 1603. Courtesy of the John Carter Brown
Library, Brown University.
This table is the beginning of a section of the manual that explains that res-
idents valued silver by the grain. It reads: "whatever type of silver has value
according to the dineros and grains determined in the assaying process."

Silversmiths advised residents on the tax status of their silver because
that too impacted its value in the market. As Echagoyan explained,
traders divided silver into three types: tenthed-silver; rescue-silver; and
fived-silver.[130] Their names reflected whether taxes had been paid on the
silver in question and at what rate. The crown took a one-time cut of
everything that was mined.[131] In the 1550s, the crown agreed to collect
only one-tenth of silver produced by miners in Mexico who had an official concession, and they kept that privilege throughout the seventeenth

century.[132] Officials marked their silver to designate it as silver that would only be reduced by ten percent, so tenthed-silver was silver to be tenthed.[133] In contrast, the crown required the collection of one-fifth of silver produced by miners without a concession, which was called rescue-silver. Without the official tenthed mark, it was destined to be cut by twenty percent.[134] Fived-silver or taxed-silver was the only type of silver sold as a commodity that had already experienced the deduction.

Miners were supposed to pay the extraction tax at branches of the royal treasury in mining towns called Royal Chests.[135] These had a foundry or assay office where officials weighed the silver that came in, assayed it, melted it into bars, and deducted the crown's share (a tenth or a fifth depending on the status of the miner, as well as a foundry duty of 1.5 percent).[136] The silver left the Royal Chests with hallmarks that testified it was taxed-silver (called fived-silver even if the miner paid one tenth).[137] Miners, however, did not declare all their silver. They sold it before taking it to their local Royal Chest, which meant that the person who bought it was responsible for the tax. Nonminers were levied an extraction tax of one-fifth, but in practice they ended up paying ten percent if their silver had the tenthed-silver marking; or twenty if it did not.[138] Silversmiths and their clients took this marking very seriously because it determined what they owed the crown.

Viceroy Villamanrique reported the challenges officials faced in collecting the crown's share once un-taxed silver reached Mexico City because residents traded it without declaring it. As he noted in 1592, people "were not in the practice of taking their silver to the royal treasury to pay the tax and foundry duty."[139] Instead, they sold "silver extracted by miners that had the tenthed mark" and silver that "had no mark at all."[140] It did not seem "to matter" to residents whether their silver was taxed or not when they sold it. But why would they report their property to royal treasury officials when they faced the possibility of losing up to 21.5 percent of their silver?

Faced with this quandary, viceroys tried to prevent the sale of un-taxed silver in the city, assuming vassals would declare their silver in order to be able to sell it. Viceroy Monterrey banned the "sale of tenthed-silver or rescue-silver that was not taxed" in Mexico City on pain of loss of property in 1603.[141] It was the same year Echagoyan's manual came out, so he included information to guide readers on the potential loss: a trader could see in his "Table on the Tax and Duties Paid to His Majesty for Tenthed-Silver," for example, how many grains (mass measure) officials would deduct from each mark when she took it to the House of

Coins.[142] Monterrey's successors reiterated the prohibitions in 1606, 1612, and 1617, as if making announcements would encourage resident to follow the law.[143] Whatever the residents decided, the bans pressured silversmiths to encourage compliance; declare your un-taxed silver, they told their customers, and if you do so, we can facilitate its sale.

Determining a price came next. As silversmiths explained to their customers, silver always sold for less than its monetary value. Traders did not have each piece of silver assayed to set its price according to the rates Echagoyan listed (Figure 4.6). Instead, they grouped silver by its tax-status (rescue-, tenthed-, and fived-silver), which approximated purity, and sold each type at a going market price. Rescue-silver was the cheapest. It was less pure than tenthed-silver because miners without a concession used the smelting method (they removed silver from ore with fire), which produced silver with more impurities than the more complicated amalgamation method involving mercury used by official miners.[144] Based on this knowledge, traders grouped all rescue-silver and sold it for less than tenthed-silver or amalgamated silver, which had the highest purity. A mark of taxed or fived-silver assayed at the standard (93.5% silver), as Echagoyan reiterated, "was valued at 2,211 maravedís," but traders "gave less" when they purchased it.[145] Indeed, "in sales" traders always "deducted a little or a lot of the value" of all three types of silver.[146]

Trading silver was extremely complicated due to the way it was measured, valued, taxed, and priced for sales. Silversmiths helped residents understand all these factors. They explained that the crown's monetary policy valued silver according to its weight and purity, which meant that metal units such as reals had exact measures. A silver object with the same measures as a real coin had the same value. The real was money, however, and the object was a commodity, so the latter sold for market rates. It was legal to sell taxed-silver, not tenthed- or rescue-silver, so they checked the hallmarks on their customers' silver and explained the regulations. Silversmiths provided these financial services at their shops. Yes, they created objects, but they also played a key role in the city's economy by giving residents investment advice and helping them make money from money.

\* \* \*

Silversmiths continued to claim Saint Francis Street in the decades to come. Metal artisans such as Francisco Malbaceda confirmed their preference for this space by working at their shops "on Saint Francis Street."[147] But, they also sought official approval and Viceroy Guadalcázar heard

them in 1619 when he confirmed that they all belonged on their street.
He agreed that fabrication and "all their commerce" ought to happen in
their shops.[148] Permanence required sustained political action, so silversmiths continued to remind officials that they provided important services to secure more privileges.

Silversmiths convinced Viceroy Guadalcázar in 1619 to support their
work as appraisers at the public auctions that regularly took place on
the Main Square.[149] The viceroy agreed that previous efforts to restrict
the sale of "silver jewels and objects" at these auctions had encouraged
residents to trade on their own, including pieces made from un-taxed
silver. Silversmiths proposed an alternative. If the viceroy allowed the
sale of silver at public auctions once again, they would be available on
site to determine their value based on weight and silver content, and
to check the hallmarks to confirm the silver was taxed and thus legal
to sell. Sellers would go to the auctions, silversmiths argued, because
residents would bid higher for objects if they verified what they bought.
In this manner, silversmiths expanded their reach beyond Saint Francis
Street to sales on the square.

Diego Rodríguez had "worked with gold" at his shop on Saint Francis
Street for over four years when he decided to take action against residents who were crowding him and his fellow artisans.[150] In August 1632,
Rodríguez crossed the Main Square to the Viceroyal Palace to lodge a
complaint. Tailors and barbers were "occupying rooms" that landlords
were supposed to rent to silversmiths and goldsmiths.[151] A resident had
even opened a tavern, which diminished the prestige of their location. The
viceroy had confirmed the licenses of at least four of his peers that year
to have their shops on Saint Francis after they made the deposits required of
them.[152] They all followed the ordinances, so why were officials allowing nonsmiths to do business near them? Rodríguez almost felt unsafe,
probably because thieves had assaulted him months earlier.[153] Now, he
wanted the viceroy "to designate" once again that Saint Francis Street
was "for smiths and not for other tradesmen."[154] The viceroy could not
do what Rodríguez asked because residents were free to rent or sell their
property to whomever they wanted.

The complaint, however, suggests that smiths such as Rodríguez had
a sense of ownership over these blocks based on their decades-long presence and the financial services they provided. All they could do was
continue to insist that this part of the city belonged to them. Notably,
Saint Francis Street became Silversmiths Street in the eighteenth century,
renamed in recognition of their achievement – they did indeed hold this

space. As told later in the chapter, they turned their street into an open theater for staging events that announced their stature as the wealthiest artisans-traders in Mexico City.

## 4.4 1620S–1650S: HOW SILVERSMITHS HELPED RESIDENTS PROTECT AND CONFIRM THE VALUE OF THEIR SILVER OBJECTS

Pedro Salas and Pedro Mangas were in the wine business; they had a stall at the food court on the Main Square, around the corner from Saint Francis Street.[155] They asked silversmiths who frequented their place for advice, so they knew how to value silver objects and what to look for when considering an investment. When a customer offered to sell them six silver plates in November 1623, they carefully noted that the pieces had the hallmark of the royal treasury that showed they were made from "taxed silver" and the zig-zag mark of the Chief Inspector and Sealer confirming they were "assayed at the legal standard."[156] Salas and Mangas also had a silversmith weigh the plates to calculate their value by the mark. Then, having agreed on a price with the seller, they signed a credit agreement promising to pay for their plates in reals before an appointed notary, who was charged with recording sales involving silver as per viceroyal mandate.[157] This purchase points to silversmiths' work as makers, appraisers, and educators of silver, and reveals that their legal activism influenced how residents purchased silver on the ground.

Earlier that same year, silversmiths and goldsmiths worked together to compile a set of ordinances related to the crown's tax policy and the preservation of metal standards to demonstrate their commitment to the law.[158] They followed the tradition established sixty years earlier when smiths had the viceroy confirm ordinances that outlined the steps they took to abide by royal mandates.[159] The ordinances in question were separate from their individual guild bylaws, which were amended and maintained separately.[160] These ones focused on providing evidence that they understood the responsibilities associated with handling precious metals. In their words, they "exercised their offices to serve his majesty" by helping to "augment his royal fifth."[161]

Smiths needed to recapitulate their previous agreements because officials, despite all their precautions and assurances, continued to accuse them of "maliciously" ignoring the mandates and "failing to execute them."[162] "Many people through various means defrauded" the king, officials claimed, especially on silver "made into jewelry and dinner services for their homes and to adorn themselves."[163] Residents were "gallantly" walking around the city with "silver that was not taxed or marked."[164] The estimated losses were "in the millions each year" – all from the silver "consumed by silversmiths in the city in making pieces large and small."[165] The exaggerated numbers suggest that royal treasury officials made the allegations because the crown pressed them to collect more revenue. They looked around, saw silver everywhere, and assumed it was un-taxed with the aim of collecting the fifth to meet the crown's ever-increasing demands for funds.

To what extent were the allegations that silversmiths helped residents avoid the fifth by failing to report their silver to royal treasury officials based on practice? Silversmiths emphasized that their hallmarks showed compliance. It was up to officials, they argued, to inspect residents' property if they meant to implicate them in tax evasion. Checking individual pieces of jewelry and wrought silver, however, was near impossible. Imagine a court constable stopping a merchant on the street to check if the silver buttons on his jacket had the marks of the artisan and the treasury that showed taxes had been paid. Or if he asked where the merchant had acquired the silver-thread that glittered on his jacket to ascertain if the artisan had reported his metal supply. This infringement of space and assault on private property were unlikely to happen due to the social barriers that protected wealthy residents. There was also the issue of staffing. It would have taken a corps of inspectors to investigate all the silver in people's homes. Silversmiths opined that the obstacles officials faced were not their concern. All silversmiths could do was point out that they did their part – they marked their work. It was up to royal treasury officials to do theirs.

Smiths confirmed their loyalty and attachment to procedural mandates once again in 1638 because it appeased high officials. They dared not risk losing the self-governance their predecessors had attained for their guilds, so they reiterated the checks on fraud that were already in place. The new set of Ordinances Regarding Silverwork and Goldwork simply repeated earlier statutes, going back to 1563. Members of the three guilds elected to take this political action through their brotherhood because it included all of them and added a seriousness to their commitment by linking it to religious practice. The first ordinance or stipulation, out of thirty-five, confirmed the "continuation of their confraternity and devotion to celebrate their patron Saint Eligius for the service of Our Lord."[166] Leaders of the brotherhood promised to work together for this spiritual purpose and to guarantee the "legality" of their arts.[167] To stress their joint effort, they also pointed out that they had come together on Saint Francis Street some forty years earlier to facilitate oversight.[168] Silversmiths and gold-smiths, they suggested, had long acknowledged their fiscal responsibili-ties and their joined actions evinced their trustworthiness.

The ordinances outlined the steps smiths followed when making objects out of silver or gold, detailing requirements for wrought objects, leaf, and thread. Silversmiths included a lengthy list of their products in the ordinances that pertained to their work, including washing basins, water pitchers, and cups for drinking hot chocolate. All their pieces, they suggested, received due attention. Their first step involved presenting the silver intended for each commission to royal treasury officials at the House of Coins, who "checked if it was fived and marked" and sub-jected it to that procedure if it was not.[169] Second, officials "registered in a book for this purpose" the quantity of silver involved and infor-mation about the "pieces and objects to be made."[170] On completion, silversmiths returned for another inspection, when officials weighed the objects and checked off the order as completed in the registration book. Third, they "marked" the silversmiths' works with the "hallmark they had for this purpose," which indicated that taxes had been paid and that they matched the legal standard.[171] This mark, which echoed the markings on coins, was an M with a crown set between two columns.[172] These were the same steps outlined in ordinances approved in Mexico City sixty years earlier, which, as previously noted, the crown had subse-quently applied to silversmiths all over the empire.[173]

Silversmiths, moreover, confirmed their commitment to the standard by marking their pieces "with their own marks or names."[174] These were personal hallmarks that "were registered at city hall."[175] The purpose of this requirement was to "facilitate the punishment of silversmiths who made pieces below the standard."[176] Inspectors would know who made any one object that did not comply with regulations. Nothing could be "sold, exchanged, bartered, or donated" without the marks.[177]

As an additional precaution, silversmiths confirmed their previous agreement to use silver that was tuned or adjusted to the purity stan-dard at the royal foundry for the mandated fee, rather than using the bellows, crucibles, and furnaces located in their shops to melt and tune it themselves.[178] The crown had banned silversmiths over a century ear-lier from using this equipment, which enabled them to "smelt, forge, or refine" silver (i.e., to replicate the work of the royal foundry), but they had organized to repeal it on the grounds that silversmiths needed that precise equipment to do their work.[179] They had to melt silver to pour into molds, for example, and to heat the metal to anneal their pieces.[180] Silversmiths, as such, had "bellows and other necessary gear" that permitted them to transform silver, but this equipment could only be used "to cast and forge" their pieces.[181] They embraced the requisite to use foundry-tuned silver to thwart accusations related to using nonstandard metal. Officials at the royal foundry tuned their metal to have "11 dineros and 4 grains" of silver per mark, making it worth "65 reals," and that is what they used.[182]

The Chief Inspector, moreover, assayed each piece with the simple zig-zag technique at their shops to reconfirm the standard.[183] Silversmiths did not dare sell pieces made of "false" (nonstandard) silver, but the burden of proof had to be on customers as well. So, one of the ordinances specified that residents were forbidden to purchase or "receive as payment" pieces of silver below the standard.[184] The zig-zag indentation on objects was there to help them make this determination for themselves.

Now this procedure was already in place, but it bore repeating to show that silversmiths and residents collaborated to protect the value of silver. Gonzalo Guzmán had business in Zacatecas, where he acquired tenthed-silver. He commissioned a basin from a silversmith on Saint Francis Street, who followed procedure and registered Guzmán's silver at the House of Coins in 1633. The finished piece bore a hallmark that confirmed it was "taxed-silver."[185] Royal treasury officials had weighed the original silver and collected the tax before the silversmith made the basin and subsequently stamped it. This hallmark, in turn, confirmed "the basin's value" as standard silver. Guzmán did not evade taxes precisely because the hallmark would enable him to sell his basin at a future date.

The 1638 Ordinances also addressed smiths' work as protectors of property and money. They knew of residents with "no sense of obligation" who purchased "ill-begotten silver objects" at "very low prices" and proceeded "to melt and recast" them to disguise the thefts.[186] This practice encouraged "domestics, servants, and enslaved people" to steal silver because they easily "found people who bought it" and ignored its provenance. It was for this reason that master silversmiths, "people of confidence," were the only ones who purchased silver at their shops "on Saint Francis Street."[187] They did not allow their "journeymen, apprentices, or enslaved people" to handle these sales.[188] Silversmiths, in other words, claimed that they controlled the people who worked in their shops, and that they helped other slaveowners with their vigilance. The ordinance was a promise that they would report enslaved people who dared to steal slaveowners' property.

Silversmiths also argued that they protected the currency of the land. Residents might be tempted to give them "coins and reals" to serve as the material for commissioned objects.[189] The artisans knew, however, that the crown prohibited the practice. They even cited by number the two mandates in the *Laws of Spain* on this topic, included in sections on the mints and "perjurers and falsifiers."[190] These mandates read that "no one could break, or melt, or cut any coins," and they condemned "subjects who had the audacity to melt and mix the silver of reals with another metal to make silver objects."[191] The specificity of what they cited was meant to draw attention to smiths' knowledge of all laws relating to silver and gold. Clarifying their role, silversmiths declared in the 1638 ordinance that they, men knowledgeable in the melting and fashioning of silver, would never melt their customers' coins. They preserved the king's money.

The ordinances smiths proposed in 1638 ended with a reminder of their skill as measurers. Members of their brotherhood had served as Chief Inspectors and Hallmarkers since the sixteenth century. They "adjusted the weights of the city" because they were the only profession that trained artisans in infinitesimal measurements.[192] They worked with grains of silver – miniscule amounts of metal that had value as per the crown's policy on currency. Their own measures were so finely tuned that they could distinguish the weights of "grains of wheat."[193] City officials had long acknowledged their exactitude, which is why they were appointed Chief Inspectors, charged with tuning the balances for metals, as well as inspecting weight measures for other commodities used in stores throughout the city. Their attention assured residents that they received the exact quantity of whatever they purchased. This work demonstrates that smiths played an important civic role and therefore deserved the confidence of the highest officials.

Members of the brotherhood organized the ordinances to make an argument: the city needed them. They listed every law passed in previous decades that concerned their work and outlined their responses. Indeed, some of these laws were their own creation; they were regulations smiths had passed that were subsequently adopted because they served the crown's interest. Their presentation proved convincing. The new Ordinances Regarding Silverwork and Goldwork, according to Viceroy Cadreita, "served the common good."[194] He signed them in October 1638, and the ordinances remained unchanged for over a hundred years.[195]

Diego Mota demonstrated that he adhered to the ordinances on a pair of candlesticks (Color Plate 9). A patron commissioned these objects to adorn the altar of a church chapel dedicated to Saint Anthony.[196] As per the steps of the orders, Mota registered the silver at the House of Coins and took the metal back to his shop. He shaped the stacked columns with a silversmith's lathe and embossed its floral designs. Assistants worked on different components, but the finished objects were his singular responsibility and technical achievement.[197]

Mota asserted his artistry by stamping his work with the lettering MÕTA, his personal hallmark, in a prominent place at the base (Figure 4.7). The ordinances required this identification, alongside the hallmark of "officials of the royal treasury" upon completion of the registration process.[198] The officials' mark is no longer visible underneath

FIGURE 4.7 Diego Mota's hallmark on a candlestick
Source: "Candelero de plata estilo barroco" (GCI-0142). Courtesy of the Museo Franz Mayer.
This photograph zooms in on the silversmith's hallmark MÕTA. It appears on two candlesticks, which are almost seventeen inches tall (Color Plate 9).
A black and white version of this figure will appear in some formats. For the color version, please refer to the plate section.

the candlesticks, worn down over the centuries with use. Yet it once served as an assurance to the patron that they were standard silver and proved that the silver had once been taxed, which prevented their seizure if officials were ever to inspect them. Is it possible that the candlesticks never received the treasury hallmark? Not likely. Inscribing them with his name made Mota accountable, and he would not have risked having to pay one-fifth taxes on the silver for failure to register them. More gravely than the deterrence of the fine, noncompliance could potentially lead to the loss of his shop license.

Yet, the possibility exists that silversmiths did not always comply with registration at the request of their customers. The acquisition of wrought silver points to the quandaries they faced. A resident desiring to gift her mother a pair of silver candlesticks had two options. She could visit a shop on Saint Francis Street and commission a silversmith to make them. If she did not furnish the material, the agreed-upon price included the value of the metal and fabrication fee. If she did own silver, in whatever form, she could entrust it to the artisan to make the candlesticks from that metal. When the customer picked up the order, she would pay the cost of the labor with coin money, or more likely, would have arranged for the silversmith to keep a percentage of the metal as payment.

Now, imagine what happened if the silversmith followed procedure and registered his customer's silver at the House of Coins before he made the candlesticks. If it was an object with a hallmark or a bar with foundry marks, royal officials only collected the foundry and assay fee, which, as noted, amounted to 1.5 percent of her silver. If the silver did not have the requisite marks, officials kept it to remove the royal fifth and collect the fee, which amounted to 21.5 percent of the silver. The silversmith, in this case, left with a piece of silver that weighed considerably less than the object or bar he had registered. As per the ordinances, silversmiths could only use silver that was "fived and marked by the assayer of the royal treasury."[199] The potential loss of over twenty percent explains why residents may have hesitated to comply and asked the silversmith to help them preserve all their silver. Do not register my silver, she may have asked the silversmith. Make the candlesticks in secret. And the silversmith, at that point, would have had to decide to accept the commission or not.

With the Ordinances Regarding Silverwork, silversmiths promised to make the correct and legal choice. It was their way of making evident that they did not help residents hide their silver by turning it into adornments. The artisan in the scenario above would have explained the risks to the resident and encouraged her to embrace the procedure. He would have told her that it was not simply a matter of avoiding fines and seizure of property. The hallmarks protected her investment. They confirmed that the candlesticks were standard silver and thus held a value calculated by their fineness and weight.

Silversmiths, who spoke of "old and mistreated silver," helped residents reinvent their metal.[200] The ordinances noted this work as another one of their contributions to remind officials of their fiscal interventions in such transactions. Felipa Trujillo had "two very old plates" that were no longer presentable when she had visitors, and she had lost half the top of a salt shaker, rendering it unusable.[201] Antonio Peña had transformative powers, so Trujillo gave the silversmith her objects "to make her" something new in 1646.[202] Peña inspected the plates and shaker at his shop and confirmed with Trujillo that they had been "taxed."[203] Her silver, in his able hands, would regain its luster and once again adorn her home. The object, moreover, would have his mark and the taxed hallmark to preserve its integrity in years to come. This interaction represented what Peña described as "his business," which amounted to making a living by helping residents refashion their silver and educating them about its value and the fees and taxes collected by the crown.[204] Trujillo was surely thankful for Peña's work a few years later when silversmiths' warnings came to pass.

Viceroy Alba arrived in Mexico City in June 1650 with royal orders to augment the crown's revenue, the same charge given to his predecessors.[205] Seeing silver everywhere must have confirmed his initial impression that un-taxed precious metal in private hands was an untapped source for royal income. The viceroy had been at the palace for a mere two weeks, when he commissioned the head of city hall to arrange for the inspection of residents' silver.[206] The fleet in Veracruz was waiting to leave for Spain while officials organized the delivery or "remittance of silver and gold destined for His Majesty" to the port.[207] He hoped to increase the amount of metal sent previously to signal to the king that he was quickly realizing the objective.

Residents heard of the plan from the city's criers, who announced that "everyone, regardless of their station and eminences, and all silversmiths, had to manifest all their recue silver, in the form of wrought objects or in bars, to have it taxed."[208] Viceroy Alba suspected residents were "defrauding the king," so he threatened them with "grave penalties."[209] The diarist Gregorio de Guijo hinted at the initial consternation and how easily it passed. Residents remembered other times when high officials had made similar accusations and failed to follow through with inspections to prove them. Those who understood the significance of markings and hallmarks for protecting and confirming the value of silver, looked at the ones on their objects and ignored the viceroy's pleas. Their silver was safe.

\*\*\*

They called him Cricket – a notorious thief who seemingly slipped into buildings by flying through key holes. Daring for greater spoils, he set his eyes on the troves of silver treasure held in convents. Cricket would wait until the streets cleared late at night and then, "with a lockpick, open the doors of churches to steal their silver candlesticks and lamps."[210] The sacristan of the church of the Convent of Saint Claire must have reported to the abbess that things had gone missing. The same thing happened at the Convent of Saint John of Penance. Word spread and constables were put on guard. Who was masterminding these brazen thefts, residents wondered, and where were they hiding the plunder? It all came out on January 15, 1651, when court officials "apprehended Bernardo Moreno, master silversmith, and Cricket," his accomplice, for the series of crimes.[211] The thief had a sack of silver objects taken from convents across the city, evidence of their scheme. Cricket did the stealing and Moreno the disappearing. He "melted" the silver, making it untraceable.[212] The case scandalized the city's residents, especially Moreno's fellow silversmiths. He had been working in the city for at least thirty years; why would he betray them?[213]

Silversmiths had sought to quell suspicion about their work for over a hundred years. Moreno's actions reminded residents that silversmiths could indeed melt silver, make all markings disappear, and thus transform it into a commodity. A piece of silver without hallmarks could pass as rescue-silver. The timing of the thefts was particularly damning because silversmiths were in the process of regaining the viceroy's trust. Months earlier Viceroy Alba had begun an effort to collect taxes from all the silver that "went off road," meaning it had left mining towns without being taxed.[214] He had ordered "everyone … and silversmiths to declare all their rescue-silver" to be taxed.[215] The viceroy assumed that silversmiths owned and traded un-taxed silver, and therefore ignored his predecessors' mandates, which had expressly forbidden the "sale of tenthed-silver or rescue-silver that was not taxed."[216] Silversmiths who followed the law must have resented the accusation. Yes, they traded silver, but only taxed silver with the appropriate marks. They were not thieves like Moreno.

Viceroy Alba's actions derived from the quandary faced by every new viceroy: how to stop the outflow of untaxed silver to Asia and Europe. He suspected everyone because officials at the ports reported the practice. They were supposed "to register all precious metals before embarkation,"[217] In December 1651, for instance, port officials confiscated the property of a merchant in Veracruz who had tried to hide bars of recue-silver worth 100,000 pesos in "crates filled with chocolate."[218] The viceroy could only imagine the scale, knowing that officials could not inspect every crate given the volume of shipments. The least he could do to address the problem was to mandate that all residents declare their rescue-silver in Mexico City. Yet even he must have realized that enforcement would be impossible given the number of officials required to inspect every building to find the offenders' property. It is unlikely that inspectors even visited their shops, knowing that silversmiths would never be caught with unmarked silver.

Silversmiths may have remembered the case of Moreno once again in April 1652, when bailiffs arrested two immigrants from Cadiz accused of clipping coins. They were reckless and a customer found them out – a foreman from the House of Coins, located five blocks away from the grocery store where they worked.[219] He could obviously tell that they had "pieces-of-eight" that did not weigh or look like coins made at the mint. They "had cut off silver" valued at one real.[220] One got the death penalty, and the other was exiled to Manila to work as a rower in the crown's galleys. Silversmiths reminded the viceroy at this point that they did their part to safeguard the king's money. As per their ordinances, "greed" tempted residents to destroy or debase currency.[221] Silversmiths reassured him that they would of course refuse and report anyone who asked them "to melt reals" or clippings.[222]

## 4.5 ALCHEMIZING SILVER INTO SOCIAL POWER

Silversmiths watched as masons, carpenters, and architects worked on the new cathedral year after year. Their Brotherhood of Saint Eligius and the Immaculate Conception was subsidizing the construction of an interior chapel.[223] Members gave what they could, such as Juan Falcón, who donated ten pesos at his deathbed to advance the project.[224] When their space was finally ready in 1648, they celebrated in a way that displayed their largesse to the city's residents.[225] They planned for months for the inauguration, choosing the feast day of the Immaculate Conception to honor one of their patrons. The writer Guijo, who attended the "opening of the smiths chapel" on December 8, noted the "solemn occasion."[226] The "silver statue" of Our Lady of the Conception that Vetancurt would later admire had a new home.[227] The smiths hosted a "great gathering" and the "jubilations" continued for a whole week. This event initiated a tradition meant to confirm their brotherhood's status as the most powerful and richest in the city.

Smiths from the three guilds worked together through their religious organization to gain the favor of the city's residents by financing events that included them in the splendor of silver. Silversmith José Luna donated a building to have its rental revenue pay for his brotherhood's activities.[228] Apart from the feast of the Immaculate Conception, they held sumptuous religious celebrations each year for the feast of the Nativity of the Blessed Virgin Mary in September and the feast of Saint Eligius in December.[229] Each event was an opportunity for silversmiths to alchemize silver into social power.

The festivities for the Immaculate Conception, which began at their chapel, came to encompass their street as well. An earthquake hit the city in January 1653 "with a great and sudden force."[230] Residents joined in prayer "fearing great ruin."[231] Within two days, the brotherhood had "a costly altar in the form of a castle" erected on Saint Francis Street, which drew residents who implored the Virgin for their family's safety before their "silver statue."[232] The smiths had officials close the street "to carriages and horses," which threatened the tranquility of the occasion.[233] Coachmen named in Chapter 2 drove down parallel streets for two days, and in the evenings returned to join in the communal plea for deliverance from the natural disaster.

On December 8, 1662, smiths arranged for churchmen and council members to join them at a mass in their chapel and subsequently on a procession that "left the cathedral," carrying their statue of the Lady of the Conception through the city's streets.[234] They had cleaned it for the event and added an "imperial crown with precious stones and pearls" to elevate the richness of the display.[235] Smiths walked holding quadrangular candles with four wicks to light the way; the glow had residents looking upwards towards the statue in admiration. The next day, they closed off Saint Francis Street for two blocks to host a bull run. They invited residents to join them in communal festivities to foster goodwill.

Silversmiths continued to host these events, in times of crisis and celebration, during the following decades. It was a parallel form of political action, akin to the ordinances they drew up to appease royal officials.

Viceroys witnessed the smiths' largesse year after year. Yes, their brotherhood was rich, members made money from handling silver, but they deserved this reward because they served the crown's interests and shared their wealth with neighbors.

### 4.6 VALUING FREEDOM WITH SILVER AT MID CENTURY

Francisca Reynoso entered the Viceroyal Palace in 1641 to confirm her right to alchemize silver into social power.[236] A free woman of African descent, she transformed money earned to money worn. Reynoso had silver-embellished clothing and silver chains purchased with the silver coins she made by working. She carried her wealth, keeping it safe. In showing off her belongings, Reynoso followed the steps of free and enslaved women who used silver to claim their freedom in Mexico City. Their experiences reveal that silver did indeed hold the value set by the crown and that residents gave it additional meanings and worth.

Using silver for freedom-claiming had a long legacy, based on decades of activism. Women fought for the right for self-expression since the 1590s, when city ordinances prohibited women of African descent from "wearing cloaks with silver adornments."[237] Their immediate response to sumptuary laws back then had been to obtain licenses that exempted them, which was the same political tactic employed by the market women of Chapter 1.[238] They appealed to officials at the palace for individual exemptions to challenge ordinances that sought to control their economic choices, be it purchasing silver earrings, or setting up a food stand at the central market complex. Women also ignored the ordinances. Viceroys reissued sumptuary laws because women continued to wear whatever they wanted. The prohibition from 1612 referred to these individuals, free and enslaved, who added "silver fringe" to their waistcoats and wore silver jewelry and pearls.[239] This practice continued for the remainder of the century, but it required an ongoing commitment to political action.

For women who self-purchased, silver jewelry served as a visible manumission letter that denoted their status as property owners. They wore silver every day, to church, to the market, and in their homes. Then, in early January 1644, newly appointed city bailiffs started "to bother" them.[240] They insinuated that the jewelry was stolen. They reminded women such as Juana Casilda of the nearly forgotten ordinance from decades earlier that prohibited African-descended residents from wearing silver.[241] Casilda and her friends took the matter to Viceroy Salvatierra, reminding him that they were free vassals. They had every right to "adorn" themselves with silver. He agreed and conceded to their request. Within days, city criers were announcing the new proclamation: African-descended women were "free to wear their ornaments."[242]

María Rosa understood the social and economic value of silver. A slaveowner had noted the number of silver coins he received in a bill of sale when he transferred ownership to the merchant who took her away from her family in Puebla. In 1661, Rosa was living in this person's house in Mexico City, located a block away from Saint Francis Street. She used to walk down that very street on her way to the cathedral when she accompanied the slaveowner's wife to mass. Rosa had tried to escape years earlier, and was preparing to do so again, but the circumstance of her capture and what followed complicated her plans. The slaveowner had called a traditional barber to brand her on the face with the letter S and the figure of a nail, which sounds out the word slave in Spanish.[243] How would Rosa hide her legal status when she "escaped" again?[244] More to the point, what could she do for retribution? Taking the slaveowner's silver service was one response to the harrowing violence. He valued it so much. A set commissioned from a silversmith, in the slaveowner's words, "honored his home."[245] Rosa "stole it" one plate at a time.[246] Then, she sold them, pawning them for silver coins. She meant to use the coins to purchase her freedom. Enslaved people did not value themselves as slaveowners did, but they understood the calculation. So, they participated in the silver market to get that piece of paper – a manumission letter – that confirmed they owned their own bodies.

Juana Cruz had thirty-nine pieces-of-eight. It was not safe to keep the coins at the house of the slaveowner where she lived, so Cruz asked acquaintances to introduce her to a person of confidence who might safeguard her treasure. A neighbor suggested Antonia San Diego, a free woman of African descent, and Cruz was inclined to trust her. Plus, San Diego agreed to help. She had the right to property and was relatively well-off, with "servants" working for her, so having coins in her possession was unlikely to raise suspicion.[247] In late November 1667, they all met at the neighbor's house for the arrangements. Cruz watched as San Diego counted her coins. They decided to place thirty-three pesos in a keyed wooden moneybox and the remaining six in a "green ceramic piggybank for an emergency."[248] Opening the first required an ax, while the second could simply be cracked open. The larger amount, in other words, was meant to be untouchable – her life savings. The two containers were then locked inside a wooden chest measuring about sixteen square inches. Cruz must have been heartened with the layers of protection, her coins were now in containers inside a locked chest, and she had the key. After the accounting, late in the evening, Cruz and her husband, who was also enslaved, accompanied San Diego back to her house, and she pointed out where the chest would be stored, under her bed.

María Rosa and Juana Cruz knew how much slaveowners paid at auctions; what value they listed next to people's names in inventories of their property; and what they charged enslaved people who sought to self-purchase. Slaveowners thought about enslaved people in terms of coins. They came up with prices using chilling calculations based on what buyers valued and desired in purchasing a person. They noted people's age and sex, their place of origin, what they looked like, and their overall health. All these factors, from slaveowners' perspective, influenced value. A woman's health, for example, determined if she would be able to provide reproductive labor. In 1661, a slaveowner calculated the price of a woman named Francisca Cruz based on these categories, noting it on the bill of sale: 323 pesos in silver coins. He described her as an Asian-descended person, "branded with a nail on her chin," and in her early thirties.[249] Jacinto, by contrast, witnessed as silversmith Domingo Torres negotiated with the slaveowner to reduce the amount he was asking for the sale. The buyer wanted a ten-peso discount because Jacinto was forty-four, past the age slaveowners considered to be enslaved men's most productive years.[250] Beyond the horror of bargaining for human beings, these exchanges demonstrate that enslaved people were painfully aware that slaveholders dictated prices.

Enslaved women knew that slaveowners took advantage of their desire to be free. They required more money from them for their freedom than from buyers who purchased their enslavement. In 1662, Teresa "asked and begged" the slaveowner to "grant her liberty"; he agreed when she offered to pay him 400 pesos in silver coins for the manumission letter.[251] The average price listed in bills of sale for enslaved women in their thirties at this time was 330 pesos, meaning that the slaveowner charged Teresa some seventy pesos more than he would have charged another slaveowner.[252] These figures represent a valuation based on a calculation of desperation. Slaveowners could get more silver from enslaved people because they obviously valued freedom, which was purchasable with coins.

Francisca Reynoso and Juana Casilda adorned their bodies with silver to display their freedom. María Cruz and Juana Cruz acquire silver coins to purchase their freedom. This precious metal was indeed the one thing that held the most value in Mexico City.

## 4.7 GENERATIONS OF POWER

In 1686, Cristóbal Polanco commissioned a sermon from a gifted writer and orator about Saint Eligius for the "annual celebration hosted by smiths at the cathedral."[253] This man spoke in "their language"; his words "eulogized their Saint Silversmith" and evoked "the rules of their art."[254] It gave Polanco and his fellow brothers such "joy" that they decided to have the sermon printed for wider dissemination.[255] The printing was also a gift for a patron. The smiths' brotherhood dedicated the publication to the wealthy silver miner Domingo Larrea, who would "appreciate the fineness" of the sermon and "estimate its value by the weight of their affection."[256] Writing the dedication, Polanco used the language of silver, words related to measuring its purity and value, to express the brotherhood's gratitude for "the favors" he bestowed on silversmiths. Larrea sold them silver and commissioned objects from their shops.

Polanco's role in the publication of this sermon testifies to his stature in the community of silversmiths and his savviness as an investor. Polanco was the namesake of his father, who migrated from Madrid to seek his fortune in Mexico City and raised his son to be a silversmith. He "worked in his father's shop since he was a little boy," learning the art of making objects alongside enslaved children such as Alonso because Polanco the elder, like other silversmiths, depended on the labor of enslaved people.[257] He watched his father help residents invest in silver for their mutual profit.[258] Back in 1659, for example, José Cardenas approached Polanco the elder for advice on a venture in the mining town of Tlalpujahua, some 100 miles to the northwest. Cardenas "was about the leave" when he visited Polanco's shop.[259] He was not a wealthy man but did have "a stone and adobe house" near the Alameda where he ran a store with his wife.[260] The couple had heard that they would be able to sell their merchandise for higher prices in Tlalpujahua and, more lucratively, get paid in unminted silver.

Polanco encouraged Cardenas, having conducted business in that mining town himself. Indeed, Polanco saw the trip as an opportunity to acquire silver for himself. Cardenas needed cash to cover immediate expenses, so Polanco gave him 400 pesos in reals on the condition that he would return that amount in the form of "tenthed-silver of the highest fineness."[261] The payment in silver would have a higher silver content than the coins. Cardenas was to acquire untaxed, un-assayed ingots at the "going rate of the mines of Tlalpujahua."[262] Polanco explained what marks to look for by showing him samples in his shop on Saint Francis

Street. He wanted to make sure that Cardenas knew how to identify the best metal for both of them. This interaction led to the signing of a loan agreement that protected the silversmith's interests (Cardenas used his house as collateral).

Reading such documents familiarized Polanco the younger with this aspect of the silversmithing business and prepared him for his own dealings. He applied the lesson on requiring a deposit when a neighbor borrowed some reals: never hand over silver, in any form, without getting something in return.[263] By 1685, the year before the sermon, Polanco the younger was helping residents invest in silver and trading it himself from the shop he had inherited.[264]

Polanco the younger's work as Chief Inspector and Sealer of Weights and Measures enhanced his standing in the community after the death of his father. He was already a master in the art at the age of twenty-three but nonetheless needed to earn the approbation of fellow silversmiths. They spoke kindly of "his ability" in the realm of measurements and commitment to this office, which "testified to his stature as a person."[265] Polanco was trustworthy and could thus be held accountable to confirm the silver content of wrought silver and inspect the city's metal weights. He served as inspector at the bequest of his mother, María Tolosa, who asked "for his assistance to complete his father's term" after her husband died.[266] Polanco the younger showed his fellow silversmiths that he understood their role in confirming the value of silver when he visited their shops to inspect their weights. As Polanco wrote in the dedication to the sermon years later, silversmiths "appreciated the fineness" of silver and "estimated its value by weight" – these were the activities that gave significance to their work.

Polanco's devotion to Saint Eligius stemmed from his mother's affinity for their patron. Tolosa commissioned a set of six paintings with black frames that adorned her home for many years. They depicted "the life of the glorious saint."[267] Polanco long admired and turned to them in prayer. They were the only things Tolosa described in her will, and she did so to emphasize that she had promised them to her son. It was a gesture of "grace and donation" for their shared connection to the religious figure.[268] Perhaps Polanco hung the paintings in his shop. His father had moved to the city with no money to his name. He and Tolosa established their shop with funds from her dowry. The paintings were a reminder that he was indebted to both parents for his own fortune.

Polanco remembered his father's burial at the Chapel of the Immaculate Conception in the cathedral. Following the elder's wishes, the family had arranged for his "body to be present" in this space during the mass that entrusted his "soul to God."[269] Members of the "smiths' brotherhood" joined their family for the occasion as per their custom. Silversmiths worked through their brotherhood to garner goodwill from city residents by hosting religious celebrations. For members, however, the chapel was also a spiritual home that gave them a sense of identity and belonging. Polanco's mother asked to join her husband in that space upon her passing because she identified with the work of silversmiths.[270] Tolosa was in the business of "trading silver, buying and selling all kinds of silver" to good effect; towards the end of her life, she had coins and objects valued at 25,000 common-gold pesos.[271] Polanco the younger honored her mother's wishes, arranging the burial and mass in April 1693.[272]

## 4.8 CONCLUSION

Bartolomé worked at the House of Coins in the 1660s.[273] He went through the guarded doors early in the mornings and left in the evenings to return to the slaveowner's house. Bartolomé was surrounded by silver all day long. Silversmiths brought their clients' silver to register it with mint officials and returned to have them hallmark the finished objects. Merchants delivered bars to have officials transform them into coins. Did Bartolomé sweep the floors for shards of silver and hide them? Perhaps he knew one of the enslaved artisans who worked at the shops on Saint Francis Street. They could have secretly melted the shards and fashioned a spoon for him to sell. It was all illegal, of course, but it happened. Bartolomé's perhaps-story is a reflection on value. The experiences of historical actors named in this chapter demonstrate that residents valued silver for itself and for what it could get them. Silver jewelry and flatware granted social prestige. Coins could purchase freedom.

The writer Baltazar Medina valued silver coins for another reason: they facilitated global trade.[274] The numbers underlined the scope: the House of Coins minted coins worth "4,689,740 pesos" in 1680.[275] He used the shortened version of the accounting unit common-gold peso. The United States has one basic monetary unit – the dollar – which people use to value everything, from the price of a pencil, to the cost of a ticket, to the payment due on a loan. There was no equivalent in the Spanish empire, which had accounting and metal units, including silver real coins minted in Mexico City that residents used to value and acquire everything.[276] The city, Medina explained, "drew trade from the whole globe because of its silver, which enriched all kingdoms."[277] "China and

Japan sent silk and ceramics, and India aromas and spices," while Spain shipped "velvet" and "Milan and Naples brocades, Rome engravings and the Ottomans rugs."[278] Merchants in all these countries and cities, he pointed out, sought to be paid in silver coins, which was why residents had access to these goods.[279] Medina valued luxury; Bartolomé valued something else.

Silver was the most regulated material in Mexico City because taxes on silver were the greatest source of revenue for the royal treasury, and because it could be transformed into money. Starting in the sixteenth century, silversmiths worked to convince royal officials that they could be trusted to protect the crown's interests. They kept accounts of all the silver that entered their premises. They checked the hallmarks to verify that it was taxed. They made objects to the legal standard to match the metal content of coins and thus preserved the monetary value of silver. They promised in their ordinances to report "thieves" who asked them to melt stolen silver.[280] All these measures were aimed at securing the confidence of officials who regularly expressed their suspicion that silversmiths abetted tax evasion. At the same time, officials depended on silversmiths who made themselves indispensable by becoming arbiters of value.

Silversmiths were powerful because they were the ones who valued and transformed silver. They alchemized their knowledge of silver into economic power. Their lives, as such, stand in contrast to the market women, carters, coachmen, and barbers of previous chapters who struggled to access financial opportunities. Silversmiths were working people, but their services, all related to the trading and owning of silver, garnered greater profits than feeding, transporting, or healing their neighbors.

The city shimmered with silver. People saw their reflections on the shined surface of silver candlesticks that illuminated the cathedral's chapels. They wore silver earrings that caught the light of the sun. They held silver coins in the cusp of their hands. All these objects contained the precious metal that was the stuff of silversmiths.

# Conclusion

Ana Santos freed herself in 1675.[1] She was pregnant and extremely unwell but managed to slip away on Holy Thursday late in the evening. Perhaps she wanted to deliver her child in a safe place, away from the slaveowner who had wanted a discounted price "given the risk of childbirth" at the time of sale.[2] In the last months, she had endured the inspection of a traditional barber surgeon, called by the slaveowner to look at her molars and check "if she was well and undamaged."[3] Two doctors had examined her as well. Santos kept insisting she was very sick. Doctor Osorio, chair of medicine at the University of Mexico, had explained her illness years earlier. "The principles of science" suggested that the redness and pain in her eyes "were caused by Gallic disease," meaning syphilis.[4] The "mercury treatments" did not work and her symptoms had gotten worse since the diagnosis.[5] Another doctor "took her pulse" and told the slaveowner that she merely had a cold.[6] But she was hemorrhaging, so he called Doctor Osorio to treat her once again, fearing that he would lose his investment if she did not get better. Santos heard Osorio ask the slaveowner: "Why did you not send her to my house to find out if she was healthy before the purchase?" He would have examined her and "been able to recognize as a doctor that she was sick" and thus warned him not to make the purchase.[7] The pain and weakness Santos felt and described did not matter to these men. How they treated and spoke about her body told Santos that they only valued her ability to work and reproduce. Her escape is the last action noted in the historical record; the child would not become the slaveowner's property. This harrowing but important story reveals much about people's choices and the practice of valuing in Mexico City.

Santos met barber surgeons and doctors who identified as healers. What she experienced demonstrates that men licensed by the Medical Board examined and treated enslaved people for the sake of slaveowners. Osorio confirmed that he "had been paid punctually for his visits and used various remedies" to treat her.[8] A barber phlebotomist was paid to bleed her. They all profited from the valuing of human beings as property. Hair barbers, by contrast, did not uphold slavery in this manner. They did not inspect people's teeth to gauge their health; they did not brand people. Santos fled on Holy Thursday – the most important day for their Brotherhood of the Holy Cross and Maundy, when hair barbers processed through the streets to show strength and resilience in the face of ongoing harassment from members of the Barbers and Surgeons Guild, who excluded them for having once been enslaved. Perhaps Santos saw guild members who had mistreated her in the past, for they took part in the Holy Thursday procession under their own banner. If so, she witnessed the tense dynamic between residents who had different conceptions of what it meant to care for people.

The last slaveowner to hold a bill of sale with Santos's name was Miguel Pedraza, a master silversmith. He was the one who had offered less than the asking price of 370 pesos because Santos was pregnant, but ended up paying that amount in silver coins. He had made this money by crafting silver objects and advising customers on their finances at his shop on Saint Francis Street.[9] Silversmiths were the definitive arbiters of value in Mexico City. They measured silver and determined its worth. Their work was more lucrative than selling food or being a carter because residents, especially officials, valued silversmiths' understanding of the Hapsburg Crown's monetary policy. People paid them to share that knowledge.

Residents valued other people's work. They paid people based on the value they placed on their labor. They valued the labor of enslaved people and paid slaveowners to secure it for themselves; Pedraza paid 370 common-gold pesos in reals to claim ownership over Santos. He paid a doctor to examine her, more money than he gave the barber phlebotomist who went to his house on the same day. The person who went to the market to get produce for Pedraza's meals paid vendors far less. Indigenous market women received very little for their efforts in comparison to the silversmith or Doctor Osorio, even though they provided what was arguably more essential: food. *American Metropolis* demonstrates that residents in Mexico City, a modern city, relied on people who worked very hard all their waking hours merely to survive. They also depended on people who had the opportunity to enter professions that were more lucrative. The articulation of who got to do what work and why sheds light on the long and combined history of inequality and opportunity in American cities, immigrant cities fueled by capital.

People named in the chapters valued all the time. The verb connects their experiences and underlines the activity that made them economic and political actors. They valued other people's labor and their own. They valued the goods and services they sold because valuing was part of working, part of making money. And they did so because having money made it possible for them to enjoy the privileges of freedom, to have a voice, to protect their family, and to live an easier life.

The objects they used reflected their valuations: cacao beans for the least and silver coins for the most valuable. The writer Juan de Torquemada, present in all chapters, noted this financial practice at the beginning of the seventeenth century. He explained that cacao beans were the "principal coinage" in other parts of the viceroyalty and that it had once been the case in the capital as well, when Mexica emperors backed cacao as money.[10] "But now," he added, residents "only use silver coins ... lovely, bright pieces-of-eight" – except for goods and services of low value.[11] By Torquemada's time, cacao beans had become an informal fractional unit, or money in small denominations.[12] The House of Coins rarely minted half-reals, the least valuable coin allowed for New Spain, so residents used cacao beans instead.

People bought cacao beans with silver coins to pay a market woman for apricots, a carter for a delivery, and a hair barber for a shave. They used a means of exchange with these individuals that had far less monetary value than with silversmiths, who got paid in silver. Residents also used cacao beans because they had a cultural meaning for Indigenous residents who sought to maintain their ancestral currency. Their equivalence to reals, moreover, enabled residents who might otherwise never be able to earn a salary paid in coins to get beans that they could eventually turn into silver.

Ana Santos knew market women who created the central market food complex. They cleared their stands to make room for religious observances on the Main Square during Holy Week. Back at their stands on Monday, Nahua women called out the price of their produce in cacao beans because they expected payment in the currency of their ancestors. Market women, like silversmiths, were thus involved in the valuation of money. Coined silver was money backed by the Spanish crown; cacao beans were money backed by sellers, and because residents gave them a monetary value.

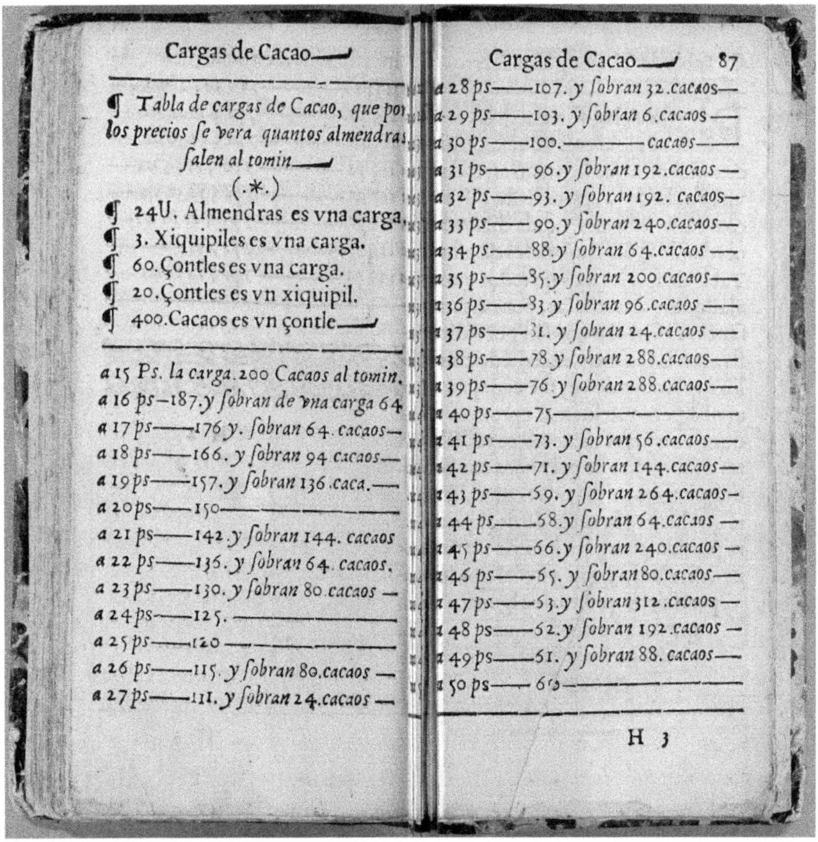

Cargas de Cacao

¶ Tabla de cargas de Cacao, que por los precios ſe vera quantos almendras ſalen al tomin

(.*.)

¶ 24U. Almendras es vna carga,
¶ 3. Xiquipiles es vna carga.
¶ 60.Çontles es vna carga.
¶ 20.Çontles es vn xiquipil.
¶ 400.Cacaos es vn çontle

a 15 Ps. la carga.200 Cacaos al tomin.
a 16 ps–187.y ſobran de vna carga 64
a 17 ps——176.y. ſobran 64. cacaos—
a 18 ps——166.y ſobran 94 cacaos—
a 19 ps——157.y ſobran 136.caca.—
a 20 ps——150
a 21 ps——142.y ſobran 144. cacaos
a 22 ps——136.y ſobran 64. cacaos.
a 23 ps——130.y ſobran 80 cacaos —
a 24 ps——125.
a 25 ps——120
a 26 ps——115. y ſobran 80.cacaos —
a 27 ps——111. y ſobran 24.cacaos —

Cargas de Cacao 87

a 28 ps——107. y ſobran 32.cacaos—
a 29 ps——103. y ſobran 6.cacaos —
a 30 ps——100. ——cacaos—
a 31 ps——96.y ſobran 192.cacaos —
a 32 ps——93. y ſobran 192. cacaos—
a 33 ps——90.y ſobran 240.cacaos—
a 34 ps——88.y ſobran 64.cacaos —
a 35 ps——85.y ſobran 200 cacaos—
a 36 ps——83 y ſobran 96.cacaos —
a 37 ps——81. y ſobran 24.cacaos —
a 38 ps——78.y ſobran 288.cacaos—
a 39 ps——76 y ſobran 288.cacaos—
a 40 ps——75
a 41 ps——73. y ſobran 56.cacaos—
a 42 ps——71. y ſobran 144.cacaos—
a 43 ps——59. y ſobran 264.cacaos-
a 44 ps——58.y ſobran 64.cacaos —
a 45 ps——66.y ſobran 240.cacaos —
a 46 ps——55. y ſobran 80.cacaos—
a 47 ps——53.y ſobran 312.cacaos —
a 48 ps——52.y ſobran 192.cacaos —
a 49 ps——51. y ſobran 88. cacaos—
a 50 ps——60

H 3

FIGURE C.1 Valuing cacao as money
Source: Felipe Echagoyan. "Tabla de cargas de Cacao, que por los precios se vera quantos almendras salen al tomin." In *Tablas de redvciones de monedas, y del valor de todo genero de plata y oro*, f.86v. México: Henrico Martinez, 1603. Courtesy of the John Carter Brown Library, Brown University. This table covers two folios. It is the only one in the manual related to this commodity. Its inclusion indicates that residents who invested in silver appreciated the value of cacao beans.

A real equaled a certain number of beans based on a ratio that varied according to the market price of cacao. Traders determined the price of a sack based on the origin and quality of the beans and by considering fluctuations related to demand and supply. This market price, in turn, determined the value of cacao beans used as money. The investor Felipe Echagoyan included a table in his 1603 manual that explains how this valuation worked (Figure C.1). It lists the prices of a sack (set at 24,000 beans) from fifteen to fifty pesos.[13] When a sack sold for fifteen pesos, 200 cacao beans equaled one real; if twenty pesos, 150 beans equaled one real, and so forth. The more expensive the sack, the more valuable the bean. A resident who wanted to buy an object worth one real, for instance, could pay the seller with 200 of the least valuable beans, or 150 of the more valuable ones. Market women confirmed this valuation when they checked the quality of beans handed to them and changed their prices accordingly.

Thomas Gage, an English visitor, gave Nahua market women two to five cacao beans when he bought "fruit" on the Main Square.[14] He understood that the number of cacao beans for any transaction depended on their market price. "In these times," he wrote, the "bigger sort" of bean is more expensive than the "lesser sort."[15] For the least valuable, "200 are worth a Spanish real."[16] The women he paid would have inspected his beans to see what "sort" they were and then told him how many he should give them to pay for the fruit. People kept using cacao beans because they were equivalent to silver coins – they were "a very small part of a real" in Gage's words – and because market women used them to value what they sold and make money.[17]

Enslaved people took advantage of cacao's value for their own ends. María Cruz lived in the house of a slaveowner and merchant.[18] He bought and sold cacao beans. Starting in the early 1630s, Cruz began to siphon beans from sacks in his storeroom, delivered by carters. The amounts were small, so the merchant failed to notice. Little by little she filled her own sack, hidden at the home of a friend. Cruz bought and sold things with beans, growing her capital. She was paying herself for the work she did for the slaveowner, with the goal of saving her earnings to self-purchase. Cruz valued her "liberty."[19] The slaveowner valued the coins he expected her to give him in return for manumission.

The Jesuit writer Bernabé Cobo was living in the city at the same time as María Cruz. He used cacao beans to buy "corn tortillas, fruits, and vegetables" at the market.[20] He gave "two or three" beans to poor people on the street. It was like "giving alms in coins," Cobo explained.[21] Cacao "served as money" because Native Americans "valued it so much."[22] Indeed, and so did residents such as Cruz, precisely because they could use it to buy and sell things they wanted, be it an apricot or their liberty.

Indigenous residents encouraged the ongoing use of cacao beans for decades to come. According to Giovanni Gemelli Careri, beans had become even more valuable by the end of the seventeenth century.[23] "In the market of Mexico," he wrote, "cacao-nuts are currency."[24] Market women valued a real at "60 or 80 beans, according as to the price of cacao runs higher or lower."[25] In 1697, he counted out the number of beans they asked for to buy "herbs."[26] The Calabrian visitor was clearly fascinated with the creation of silver coins, he visited the House of Coins, yet it was noteworthy for him that Native Americans had preserved their ancestral currency by linking it to the king's money.

Market women also continued to use cacao beans because they had to; residents did not value their work as much as other people's. They could not value their produce with silver, call out prices in reals, because no one would buy it. The ongoing use of cacao beans thus reflects the inequity people experienced in their working lives. What they earned depended in part on the value of what they sold. Wealthy residents used silver coins to pay coachmen their salaries and purchase carriages lined with Chinese silk. They valued their comfort and were thus willing to pay more money to get it. So why not food? The contrast exposes the very different economic realities that people faced when valuing their labor.

The contemporary definition of work meant "doing useful things" for the "self and the republic."[27] Economy referred to the decisions people made regarding the resources at their disposal, including the money they held in their hands. Residents worked to support themselves, to have cacao beans to purchase food and silver coins to pay rent. Their work, at the same time, sustained the city, yet the degree to which they benefitted from living there was vastly different. Doing essential work did not necessarily make their economic lives easier. Working people nevertheless tried to get something in return.

*American Metropolis* shows that having access to officials willing to support working people encouraged their political demands. They lived in a capital city, which made it possible for them to appeal directly to the most powerful officials in the Spanish empire. Torquemada made this connection: residents were able to "work to earn a living" because they lived in this "most excellent city" – the seat of government.[28] His reading of Aristotle's *Politics* influenced his thoughts on politics and economics. He cited "the philosopher" who identified the "parts" a city "needed to have" in order "to maintain" the people who lived there.[29] To his mind, Mexico had all the "qualities and conditions of an illustrious city."[30]

Torquemada wrote that the metropolis was "full of traders, workers, and artisans" who were able "to conserve" the city because officials upheld their rights and privileges, such as those who managed "city property."[31] Personalizing these claims, Bartolomé Dias, the cloth seller from the beginning of the book, convinced officials at city hall to rent him a spot on the Main Square. Torquemada lauded "magistrates who were cautious and responsive," who upheld the "justice" that "maintained the republic."[32] Dias insisted that they respond to him when he demanded justice at the General Indian Court. The stories of working people evince that residents navigated the political economy of their city, meaning that they appealed to governing officials tasked with managing the economy and influenced their decisions.

Residents, political actors, showed officials in the city's governing bodies that their work supported the city's economy. Market women, carters, coachmen, hair barbers, and silversmiths provided essential services. They convinced officials to recognize their contributions to the republic, meaning the people of Mexico City. Working people had political expectations, and they acted on them to claim parts of the city for themselves.

Officials, at the same time, valued the economic contributions of some working people over others, and they granted concessions accordingly. Carters obtained licenses to open corrals to facilitate the transport of imported and local goods; they created a profitable service that transformed the landscape of certain neighborhoods. Licenses granted to poultry vendors, in comparison, had African-descended residents traveling to faraway towns to purchase birds. The viceroy did not make it easier for them to earn a living like he did for carters. He simply allowed these men to work to secure provisions, which, according to Torquemada, was a key component of "sustaining the city."[33]

Like Torquemada, Giovanni Botero followed a philosophical tradition concerned with urban life. He outlined the purpose of cities in his widely read treatise *On the Causes of the Greatness of Cities* from 1588, which offered historical and contemporary examples of "magnificent cities," including Mexico City.[34] His ideas, evoked by intellectuals and high officials in Mexico City, had currency in local discussions regarding politics and economics throughout the seventeenth and into the eighteenth century. A city, according to Botero, was "an assembly of people" whose everyday experiences were "easier" and more "plentiful" because they lived together.[35] It was the responsibility of officials to facilitate this reality, and he offered examples. Good governors promoted "commerce"; city residents, for example, "have need for their traffic and transportation of their goods."[36] Following this idea, city hall council members organized the maintenance of the city's causeways, which made it easier for carters to do their work – to facilitate local and long-distance trade and travel. But, as told from the carters' perspective, they were the ones who pushed officials to realize the promise of governors being responsible for commerce.

Botero also noted that judges had to preserve order by enforcing laws, same as Torquemada; the "assurance of justice" enabled "trade and arts to flourish."[37] Articulating the experience of historical actors in Mexico City points to the complexity of this proposition. Residents had different experiences with justice. Ana Santos had to flee because laws that upheld slavery bound her to Miguel Pedraza, the silversmith who tried to humiliate her. City judges enforced property rights over people. As a result, Santos's life in "magnificent" Mexico was decidedly not "easier," while Pedrazas's was "more plentiful" and profitable.[38] In addition to exploiting enslaved people and profiting from their labor, he belonged to a profession that officials deemed essential and worthy of their support. Governance was oriented toward his economy.

A metropolis in the seventeenth century was the main city of a province or country, the seat of government, and a place distinguished above others by its qualities.[39] Mexico City, capital of the Viceroyalty of New Spain, was the main city in America at this time, renowned by writers who extolled its qualities. Two of them – Torquemada and Botero – shared their thoughts on the "qualities," "conditions," and "causes" that made Mexico City "great."[40] They noted that good government (a condition) supported "commerce," which was a condition and an outcome. Officials encouraged commerce – the desired quality.

Botero located Mexico City at the center of commercial activity that spanned two oceans, admiring the artisanship of Chinese goods "brought out of China to the Philippines" and from there "to Mexico," and then Seville."[41] Bartolomé Dias lived this reality; he traveled on a ship of the royal fleet organized by officials to support transpacific commerce. Dias appealed to the viceroy who recognized his role in the local market for imported goods; he valued lengths of Chinese cloth with cacao beans, he earned a living. Did he identify the same qualities as Torquemada and Botero? Did Dias think he lived in a "great" metropolis that had "good government" and "commerce"? Perhaps.

*American Metropolis* tells the history of people who made Mexico City during the seventeenth century. Botero wrote about the sheer "pleasure" of "living together in society," "delighting" in "art and theater," and simply wandering around "faire streets" to admire "gorgeous building."[42] Working people surely experienced and valued such moments. Coachmen took pleasure in playing cards; they gazed at the cathedral when they drove to the Main Square. They spent most of their time, however, working very hard to earn cacao beans and silver coins to pay for necessities. Silversmiths, in comparison, worked fewer hours and had the means to commission "art."[43]

The passing of 400 years has changed city life, yet there are echoes in the past. Residents of Mexico City and other cities today make a living in remarkably similar ways. They sell food, work in transport, encourage people to care for their bodies, and help them invest their savings. These people also experience economic disparity. Certain people's work is deemed less valuable or worthy of recompense than others. Officials recognize and support essential workers to different degrees. *American Metropolis* historizes the commonalities with a ground-up perspective of city living.

# Essay on Sources

*American Metropolis* is an archival reconstruction of the past. The governing bodies of Mexico City produced innumerable documents that testify to people's lives. Indeed, there is such an abundance of primary sources for the seventeenth century that it might seem overwhelming: legal, property, ecclesiastical, and legislative records, and the list continues. But it is not. The profusion of paperwork is inspiring because it allows scholars to access details about people, often in their own voices, such as in court records because scribes were required to write down testimonies verbatim. These materials enable a personalized rendering of history. The approach would be much more difficult, if not impossible, in other imperial settings that did not have the same bureaucratic sophistication or recognition of legal personhood as the Hapsburgs. And even within the empire, Mexico City stands apart for archival bounty from other cities, towns, and rural areas with scant presence of royal officials. This archival plenty, however, does require time, years of reading and transcribing documents to identify historical actors and piece together their experiences. Patterns emerge, showing similar trajectories or exceptional circumstances. Their stories raise historical questions and provide answers when their lives are examined together.

This essay on sources begins with archives and continues with printed primary and secondary sources to account for all the materials used in writing this history. The first section explains choices made to find historical actors and locates the documents used in archival collections in five countries. The second section describes printed primary sources that provide eyewitness accounts and contain legislative and other materials that supplement or contextualize archival discoveries. The third section provides a brief overview of the citation principles that informed the scholarly apparatus. The goal is to give an account of the book's evidentiary foundation and hopefully encourage scholars to continue writing about this place and time.

People's economic lives primarily emerge from property and contractual documents housed at the city's historic notaries archive (*Archivo General de Notarías de la ciudad de México, Acervo Histórico*, or ANM).[1] The Spanish legal system required individuals to have a notary write down and keep a copy of all transactions related to the exchange of property and services.[2] These documents, which followed strict guidelines for content and form, included bills of sale, wills and testaments, dowry agreements, promissory notes, receipts of payment, apprentice and service agreements, and rental agreements.[3] A will and testament, for example, documents the lives of coachmen Marcos and Pedro, who were part of the history told in Chapter 2.[4] An apprenticeship contract describes the barbering toolkit that Domingo Saucedo, from Chapter 3, received from a traditional barber to help him get started in the profession.[5] Notaries kept copies in volumes organized by date, so that a dowry contract, for example, comes after a bill of sale. Finding historical actors requires reading the material page by page. The archive holds 5,247 surviving volumes, associated with over 250 individual notaries, and only a small fraction of this collection has been catalogued.[6] Documents from the seventeenth century were located and transcribed on site.[7]

The second archive in importance to this history is the national archive of México, located in the capital (*Archivo General de la Nación*, or AGN).[8] The archive has nearly eighty collections with documents regarding the seventeenth century, all of which have catalogues with varying levels of detail that are available online.[9] The archive's journal publishes articles about the collections, including descriptions of the types of documents they contain and discussions of how historians have used them.[10] Archivists made these collections according to various principles; some hold documents produced by particular government bodies, such as the General Indian Court, while others relate to government projects. This history draws from eighteen of these collections, chosen because they have documents that relate to Mexico City residents.

The experiences of three historical actors show the translation from document to life story. The collection Royal Decrees – Duplicates, with documentation related to viceroyal governance in general, contains trading licenses. One granted to Manuel López, a "free man" of African descent, testifies that he made a living by selling produce, as examined in Chapter 1.[11] The collection Superior Tribunal of Justice contains legal records for cases that came before judges of first appeal, including from the municipal court. A suit filed by a creditor reveals that Pedro Salas, a wine seller, promised to pay his debt in silver coins, exemplifying the reliance on specie discussed in Chapter 4.[12] Finally, the collection Inquisition holds documentation from the Tribunal of the Holy Office, from short denunciations to full court proceedings.[13] The scribe in a trial from 1646 recorded the words of coachman Blas Loya: "I am not a thief, nor have I ever been, and I know nothing about the robberies that took place in the receptor's house."[14] He was defending himself and, in the process, left testimony of the constant antagonism experienced by African-descended men who had money to spend, as discussed in Chapter 2. Court files also contain evidence, such as a letter written by María Capacha in Granada to her son in 1618: "God put you on earth to seek a life, find it with truth … do not alter the course by marrying someone from Mexico City." She was grateful that his business was doing well but held out hope that her son would return to Spain.[15]

The seventeenth century is nearly absent in the city's archive (*Archivo Histórico de la ciudad de México*, or AHCM).[16] The law required that city hall have an archive, which kept documentation related to municipal governance, including infrastructure projects, property deeds, business permits, and ordinances, and to make them available for consultation.[17] It also kept copies of "all royal decrees, provisions, ordinances, and instructions" related to the city's "good government," and missives sent by the viceroy and other high officials related to city business.[18] A great fire, however, destroyed much of the paperwork in 1692. Fortunately, contemporaries salvaged some materials, including volumes of the minutes of council meetings called the Acts of the Council (*Actas del Cabildo*), covering 1599–1630, 1635–1643, and 1698 to 1705.[19] The acts, which record annual appointments, expenses, appeals, and other government decisions, are an invaluable source for the administration of the city.

Archives in Spain contributed documentation that offers the perspective of royal officials, as well as residents who sought favors and informed the crown about the city's affairs. The lives of working people are more difficult to find but present. The Archive of the Indies (*Archivo de Indias*, or AGI) holds materials from all territories claimed by Spanish monarchs, so its scope and the volume of materials are massive. The AGI's collections are organized by regional sections and the governing bodies that produced them, all explained and with finding aids available through the online Portal for Spanish Archives (PARES). The section

Mexico contains documents such as letters written by viceroys to the king and reports filed by the head of city hall. Councilmen wrote to Philip IV in 1633 asking him to reopen the port of Acapulco to ships from Guayaquil because they arrived with sacks of cacao beans. The city had missed the opportunity to import "20,000 loads of cacao," which meant that "residents of the city were in need of this good, used to value things, especially by poor people"; the lack of supply, moreover, "had caused prices to go up."[20] Their appeal, in other words, included an explanation of the valuation practices discussed in the Conclusion and indirectly referenced the market women of Chapter 1. The national archive of Spain (*Archivo Histórico Nacional de España*) contains materials that mainly pertain to wealthy residents. José Puente gave the crown 330,500 reals, an astronomical amount of money, to become a knight of the Order of Santiago in 1696, evincing the economic disparity between merchants such as him and a poulterer who had to go into debt to acquire turkeys valued at eight reals.[21]

Finally, various archives and libraries in England, France, and the United States contain manuscript materials about residents' economic lives, though again, mainly from the perspective of officials, as evident in the following two examples. The National Archives of the United Kingdom has correspondence that references the city's exports. An English ambassador in Spain reported to Lord Salisbury, Secretary of State, in August 1602, that silver from Mexico was "expected in the galleons in October to come to Seville," which would have included bars hallmarked at the House of Coins, discussed in Chapter 4.[22] The Newberry Library in Chicago has documentation from the High Court of Mexico; judges sent a letter to Philip IV in June 1650 supporting a plan to have slavers traffic 1,000 enslaved people because slaveowners would "benefit from their labor."[23] The reference points to the crown's orchestration of the transatlantic slave trade that brought enslaved people from sub-Saharan Africa to Mexico City, who are named in the chapters.

The notes cite documentation from the repositories mentioned above and more, using abbreviations listed in Abbreviations for Archives, Libraries, and Repositories.

Apart from manuscript materials, the book draws from seventeenth-century books, mainly legal compilations, reference books, and accounts of the city written by contemporaries. The crown ordered the printing of legal corpuses distributed to judges throughout the empire, most significantly the *Laws of the Indies*. So did viceroys. These collections are useful only as a guide because they only include summaries, so the original laws must be read whenever possible, found in archival depositories. Reference books provide insight into the ways people thought, such as the seminal dictionary by Sebastián Covarrubias and handbooks.

Eyewitness accounts appear in all chapters. Residents born in Mexico City or who lived there most of their lives published histories and chronicles and kept diaries published posthumously.[24] Visitors authored books with vivid descriptions. These contemporary tellings require caution and an awareness of the limited capacity of people's memories and writers' proneness to exaggeration. The hope here is that readers accept the author's familiarity with all types of sources and trust their use. The same, of course, can be said of archival materials.

Three contemporary historians stand out. Domingo Francisco de San Antón Muñón Chimalpahin Cuauhtlehuanitzin, born in Amaquemecan, moved to Mexico City in 1590 and kept an account of city events until the mid 1610s.[25] His annals offer an extraordinary perspective of city life at the beginning of the century, especially from the perspective of Nahua residents. Juan de Torquemada, a Franciscan friar, spent much of his life in the city; his monumental work *Monarquía indiana* is an important source for Indigenous history.[26] It includes a chapter titled "On the famous city of Mexico after Spanish settlement" that describes his adopted city, providing another eyewitness account of city life at the beginning of the century. Augustín de Vetancurt was a Franciscan friar and chronicler; a section of *Teatro Mexicano*, his magnus opus, is about his native city.[27] Torquemada and Vetancurt, whose works bookend the seventeenth century, offered descriptions and comments that introduce historical actors in all chapters. Information about other contemporary historians and writers is in the notes at first mention, as it proved useful to know their biographies when considering their work.

Two diarists offer insider perspectives for the second half of the century. Antonio de Robles, a priest, began recording his observations about everyday life when he was around twenty years old in 1667 and continued until 1703.[28] Gregorio Martín de Guijo, also a priest, worked at the cathedral and kept a diary from 1648 to 1664.[29] Both residents noted events that interested them, from crimes to natural disasters to state occasions. The writings of outsiders supplement their regular accounting of city life.

Contemporary readers traveled vicariously through the accounts of visitors from Europe, such as Thomas Gage and Giovanni Francesco Gemelli Careri, who published their musings during their lifetime. Other travelers left only manuscripts, such as Elias al-Mûsili, a Chaldean Christian priest who lived in Mexico City for some six months in 1682 and 1683 during his trip across America. Though familiar with cities in the Ottoman Empire, he could only describe it with a rhetorical question: "How can one begin to describe the churches in this city, its noble and fine edifices, its excessive wealth"? He replied, it is "something one cannot fully do."[30] Al-Mûsili's comment matched the impression of fellow visitors awed by visible signs of the city's prosperity. Their descriptions raise their own questions, such as who benefitted from this wealth, which is one of this history's central concerns.

Historians have been writing about Mexico City since it was Tenochtitlan, recording and interpreting events. Their work, dated from the nineteenth century onward, is the main secondary foundation. More specifically, this history primarily cites scholarship on seventeenth-century Mexico City, mainly in Spanish, rather than works on other places or that provide overviews of the viceroyal period.[31] The endnotes, however, do provide a guide for further reading on certain topics directly related to the book's historical actors.

To end, a final note on the writing of history. Reading an ocean of documents helps write a river that captures city life.

# List of Archives, Libraries, and Repositories

## LIST OF ARCHIVES AND LIBRARIES BY COUNTRY

### England

British Library, London
The National Archives, Kew, Richmond (TNA)

### France

*Bibliothèque nationale de France*, Paris

### Mexico

*Archivo General de la Nación*, Mexico City (AGN)
*Archivo General de Notarias de la ciudad de México*, Mexico City (ANM)
*Archivo Histórico de la ciudad de México, "Carlos de Sigüenza y Góngora"*
   (AHCM; formally *Archivo del Ex-Ayuntamiento de la ciudad de México*)
*Biblioteca Nacional de Antropología e Historia*, Mexico City (BNAH)
*Biblioteca Nacional de México, Fondo Reservado*, Mexico City (BNM)

### Spain

*Archivo General de Indias*, Seville (AGI)
*Archivo Histórico Nacional de España*, Madrid (AHNS)
*Biblioteca Nacional de España*, Madrid (BNE)

### United States

John Carter Brown Library, Brown University, Providence, RI (JCB)
Newberry Library, Chicago, IL (Newberry)

New York Public Library, New York, NY (NYPL)
Southern Methodist University Libraries, Dallas, TX

## MUSEUMS

*Museo de América,* Madrid
*Museo Arqueológico Nacional de España,* Madrid
*Museo Franz Mayer,* Mexico City
*El Museo Vizcaínas,* Mexico City

## LIST OF ARCHIVES WITH COLLECTION ABBREVIATIONS

### *Archivo General de la Nación de México* (**AGN**)

| Name of Collection (*Ramo*) | Abbreviations |
| --- | --- |
| *Bandos* | Bandos |
| *Bienes Nacionales* | BN |
| *Casa de Moneda* | Moneda |
| *Civil, Volúmenes* | Civil |
| *Cofradías y Archicofradías* | Cofradías |
| *Criminal* | Criminal |
| *General de Parte* | GP |
| *Historia* | Historia |
| *Indiferente Virreinal* | IndV |
| *Indios* | Indios |
| *Inquisición* | Inq |
| *Matrimonios* | Mat |
| *Matrimonios, Cajas* | MatC |
| *Ordenanzas* | Ord |
| *Reales Cédulas Duplicadas* | RCD |
| *Reales Cédulas Originales* | RCO |
| *Real Fisco de la Inquisición* | RFI |
| *Ríos y Acequias* | Ríos |
| *Tribunal Superior de Justicia, Colonial* | TSJ |

Materials are found in volumes and boxes, which are catalogued by files (*expedientes* or exp.) or folders (*cuadernos*). Citations list the abbreviated collection name, volume or box number, file or folder, folio number range or specific folio numbers for quotations when applicable, and year.

*Archivo General de Notarías de la ciudad de México,*
*Acervo Histórico* (**ANM**)

| Name of notary | Notary number | Abbreviation |
| --- | --- | --- |
| Nicolas de Arauz | 5 | N. Arauz |
| Álvaro de Grado | 1 | Á. Grado |
| Martín de Castro | 1 | M. Castro |
| Juan de Lerín Caballero | 11 | J. Lerín |
| Toribio Cobián | 110 | T. Cobián |
| Lorenzo de Mendoza | 378 | L. Mendoza |
| Diego de los Ríos | 557 | D. Ríos |
| Francisco de Olalde | 470 | F. Olalde |
| Francisco de Rivera | 559 | F. Rivera |
| Juan Pérez de Rivera | 497 | J. Pérez Rivera |
| Juan Pérez de Rivera Cáceres | 630 | J. P. Rivera Cáceres |
| Juan de Salas | 633 | J. Salas |

Materials are found in volumes, organized by the name of the notary and number. Citations list the notary's abbreviated name, his notary number, volume number, folio numbers, and year.

*Archivo General de Indias* (**AGI**)

| Name of Collection (*Fondos*) | Abbreviations |
| --- | --- |
| *Contaduría* | Contaduría |
| *Contratación* | Contratación |
| *Indiferente* | Ind |
| *México* | México |
| *Mapa y Planos, México* | MP-México |

Materials are found in bundles (*legajos*). Citations list the abbreviated collection name, bundle number, document number when available, folio number range when available or specific folio numbers for quotations when applicable, and year.

# Notes

INTRODUCTION

1. AGN Mat 10 e.41 f.96–97v (1629). Archival abbreviations are in the List of Archives, Libraries, and Repositories consulted.
2. The description is from Horacio Levanto, "Memorial sorbe [sic] el trato de la China con Nueua España, y estos Reynos" (Biblioteca Nacional de España, 1617), f.2. Levanto, born in Genoa, lived in Spain and Mexico City and made a fortune from transoceanic trade and other investments; he wrote to the president of the Council of the Indies expressing his opinions about transpacific trade in 1617. A study that centers Acapulco as a hub of transregional trade and uses Levanto's treaty to discuss the trade in Chinese cloth is Mariano Bonialian, "Acapulco: puerta abierta del Pacífico, válvula secreta del Atlántico," in *Relaciones intercoloniales: Nueva España y Filipinas*, ed., Jaime Olveda (Jalisco: Colegio de Jalisco, 2017), 137–138. The estimated price some ten years earlier was one and a half to two reals per *vara*, which is a linear measurement equal to .838 meters or 32.99 inches; Manuel Carrera Stampa, "The Evolution of Weights and Measures in New Spain," *Hispanic American Historical Review* 29, no. 1 (1949): 10. A real was a silver coin, one of the metal units created by the Catholic Kings in 1497; the "Ordinances on Money" are discussed in Chapter 4.
3. Entry for *tilmatli*, "Nahuatl Dictionary Online," ed., Stephanie Wood (Wired Humanities Projects, 2000).
4. The viceroyalty was a political unit of the Spanish empire, a term that describes a type of state in which a head, such as a Mexica *tlatoani* or Hapsburg king, claimed sovereignty over regions beyond their original base of territorial power. Scholars have characterized it as a polycentric monarchy to express the idea that the Spanish Hapsburgs governed an empire that consisted of distinct political units that wielded power over territories from centers such as Mexico City. For this articulation of the organization of government and the historiography it challenges, see Pedro Cardim, Tamar

Herzog, Gaetano Sabatini, and José Javier Ruiz Ibáñez, eds., *Polycentric Monarchies: How Did Early Modern Spain and Portugal Achieve and Maintain a Global Hegemony?* (Eastbourne: Sussex Academic Press, 2012). Viceroys, on behalf of Philip III, Philip IV, and Charles II, governed the territory of present-day Mexico, along with parts of the southern United States, Central America, the Caribbean Islands, and the Philippine Islands during the seventeenth century.

5. For the historiography on terrestrial routes, see Tatiana Seijas, "The Royal Road of the Interior in New Spain: Indigenous Commerce and Political Action," in *The Oxford Handbook of Borderlands of the Iberian World*, eds., Danna A. Levin Rojo, et al. (New York: Oxford University Press, 2019).

6. A study that stresses the port's centrality to hemispheric and transoceanic trade is Antonio García de León, *Tierra adentro, mar en fuera. El puerto de Veracruz y su litoral a Sotavento, 1519–1821* (México: Fondo de Cultura Económica, 2011). See also Joseph M. H. Clark, *Veracruz and the Caribbean in the Seventeenth Century* (New York: Cambridge University Press, 2023). A state of the field on ports and commerce with a bibliography is Guillermina del Valle Pavón, "Estudio introductorio," in *Contrabando y redes de Negocios: Hispanoamérica en el comercio global, 1610-1814*, ed. Guillermina del Valle Pavón (México: Instituto Mora, 2023).

7. The study of everyday life (*vida cotidiana*) in Mexico, influenced by new approaches to social history, had a fluorescence in the 1990s. A series that brings together historians, primarily based in Mexico, who participated in this historiographical turn is Pilar Gonzalbo Aizpuru, ed., *Historia de la vida cotidiana en México*, 5 vols. (México: Colegio de México, 2004–2005). Volume 2, which covers the long seventeenth century, has descriptive chapters on Mexico City.

8. People used the word "global" during the seventeenth century to describe something spherical rather than to refer to worldwide phenomenon. Used cautiously to avoid anachronisms, the word is appropriate in the historiographical context of global history, which emerged in conversation with social science concepts about globalization (mainly understood as the twentieth-century emergence of organizations that exert influence around the world or operate internationally). Early globalization refers to the historically unprecedented movement of goods and people that began in the early modern period, see, for example, Bernd Hausberger, *Historia mínima de la globalización temprana* (México: Colegio de México, 2018); Bartolomé Yun-Casalilla, *Iberian World Empires and the Globalization of Europe 1415–1668* (Singapore: Palgrave Macmillan, 2019); Mariano Bonialian, *La América española: entre el Pacífico y el Atlántico. Globalización mercantil y economía política, 1580–1840* (México: Colegio de México, 2019). See also Ryan Dominic Crewe, "Connecting the Indies: The Hispano-Asian Pacific World in Early Modern Global History," *Estudos Históricos* 30, no. 60 (2017). The Global Urban History Project is a useful resource for scholarship that connects the fields of urban and global history: www.globalurbanhistory.org. For scholarship interested in moments where global phenomenon can be seen in local stories, see, for example, Amy Stanley, "Maidservants' Tales: Narrating Domestic

and Global History in Eurasia, 1600–1900," *The American Historical Review* 121, no. 2 (2016); Jan de Vries, "Playing with Scales: The Global and the Micro, the Macro and the Nano," *Past & Present* 242, no. 1 (2019); John-Paul A. Ghobrial, "Introduction: Seeing the World like a Microhistorian," *Past & Present* 242, no. 1 (2019).

9. The English word resident relates to the Spanish words *vecino* (someone with legal residency in a municipality) and *morador* (someone presently living in a locale). A review and bibliography about the debate Herzog's work instigated regarding vecinos, defined as citizens, and community membership (*naturaleza*) is Tamar Herzog, "Early Modern Citizenship in Europe and the Americas: A Twenty Years' Conversation," *Ler História* 78 (2021). A discussion of the role of vecinos in the sixteenth century is Beatriz Rojas, "Ser vecino en Nueva España," in *Las ciudades novohispanas: Siete ensayos, historia y territorio* (México: Instituto Mora, 2016).

10. The original plan is lost but Trasmonte's contemporary, the cartographer Johannes Vingboons, reproduced several versions in Holland in subsequent years. For this provenance, see Priscilla Connolly, "¿El mapa es la ciudad? Nuevas miradas a la *Forma y Levantado de la ciudad de México 1628* de Juan Gómez de Trasmonte," *Investigaciones geográficas* 66 (2008); Priscilla Connolly and Roberto L. Mayer, "Vingboons, Trasmonte and Boot: European Cartography of Mexican Cities in the Early Seventeenth Century," *Imago Mundi* 61, no. 1 (2009). Scholars disagree on the plan's exactitude, pointing out, for example, that it leaves out certain blocks; see Connolly, 2008.

11. A biographical sketch of Trasmonte is in Martha Fernández, *Arquitectura y gobierno virreinal: los maestros mayores de la ciudad de México, siglo XVII* (México: UNAM, 1985), 77–90. See also Martha Fernández, "Relación de servicios de Juan Gómez de Trasmonte," *Anales del Instituto de Investigaciones Estéticas* 13, no. 50 (1982).

12. Other analyses of the plan include: Manuel Toussaint, Federico Gómez de Orozco, and Justino Fernández, *Planos de la ciudad de México: siglos XVI y XVII, estudio histórico, urbanístico y bibliográfico* (México: UNAM, 1938); Richard E. Boyer, "La ciudad de México en 1628: La visión de Juan Gómez de Trasmonte," *Historia Mexicana* 29, no. 3 (1980). See also Sonia Lombardo de Ruiz, Yolanda Terán Trillo, and Mario de la Torre, eds., *Atlas histórico de la ciudad de México*, 2 vols. (México: Smurfit, 1996), I: 24–25, 290–293; Richard L. Kagan and Fernando Marías, *Urban Images of the Hispanic World, 1493–1793* (New Haven: Yale University Press, 2000), 91–95, 152–155; Michael Schreffler, "The Royal Palace and the Loyal City," in *The Art of Allegiance: Visual Culture and Imperial Power in Baroque New Spain* (University Park: Pennsylvania State University Press, 2007); Roberto L. Mayer, "Trasmote y Boot. Sus vistas de tres ciudades mexicanas en el siglo XVII," *Anales del Instituto de Investigaciones Estéticas* 27, no. 87 (2012).

13. Thomas Gage resided in Mexico for five months in 1625; Thomas Gage, *The English-American his Travail by Sea and Land: Or, New Svrvey of the West-Indias* (London: R. Cotes, 1648), 55.

14. The area dimensions are from a 1637 report commissioned by city hall: "4,000 longitudinal *varas* and 2,500 in latitude"; Fernando de Cepeda and Fernando Alfonso Carrillo, "Relacion Vniversal Legitima, y verdadera del sitio en qve esta fvndada la muy noble, insigne, y muy leal Ciudad de Mexico" (México: Imprenta de Francisco Salbago, 1637), f.4. Scholars have posited measurements for the surface covered by the city of Tenochtitlan at contact that vary from 3.8 to 6.6 square miles, with a recent calculation of 3.64 square miles; see Eloy Jiménez Martínez, "En torno a la superficie de México-Tenochtitlan en 1519," *Anuario de Historia Regional y de las Fronteras* 25, no. 1 (2020). The 1637 measurements are pointedly smaller, which suggests that the engineers who measured it had a different conception of what constituted the city limits. People calculated size from different points and included different areas. A visitor in 1673 provided the same measurements as the report (4,000 by 2,500 varas); M. Josefa Arnall Juan, "El "Itinerario a Indias" (1673–1679) del P. Fr. Isidoro de la Asunción, C. D. (Manuscrito 514 de la Biblioteca Provincial y Universitaria de Barcelona)," *Boletín Americanista* 28 (1978): 209. The city grew in the intervening decades, but contemporaries repeated these official numbers.

15. The quote is from Giovanni Francesco Gemelli Careri, *A voyage round the world*, 4 vols., vol. 4 (London: Awnsham & John Churchill, 1704), 508. Gemelli Careri visited Mexico City in 1697.

16. The lacustrine complex (*cuanca lacustre*) of the Valley of Mexico had five lakes: Chalco, Texcoco, Xaltocan, Xochimilco, and Zumpango. Gage estimated that the lakes covered some 130 miles, noting one hundred "old English miles"; Gage, 1648, 43. Old English miles were longer than statute miles at a 1.3 ratio; Parliament confirmed the latter in 1593, but people continued to use the old mile until the end of the seventeenth century; see Ronald E. Zupko, *British Weights & Measures: A History From Antiquity to the Seventeenth Century* (Madison: University of Wisconsin Press, 1977).

17. Readers who know the city might imagine standing at the castle in Chapultepec Park and gazing toward the cathedral to the north-east.

18. Mexico City is located on the Trans-Mexican Volcanic Belt. Several mountain ranges surround it. The Sierra Nevada range, which has a north-south orientation, is located to the east. The range includes the stratovolcano Tláloc, likely the peak in the middle of the upper register.

19. The two-patio building with the royal foundry and mint, called *Casa de la Moneda*, was part of the viceroyal complex. A contemporary description of the palace's buildings and patios is in Isidro Sariñana y Cuenca, *Llanto del occidente en el ocaso del mas claro sol de las Españas* (México: Viuda de Bernardo Calderon, 1666), f.11v–18. Sariñama y Cuenca (c.1631–96), born in Mexico City, was a cleric and prolific writer. A fire in 1692 severely damaged the palace; a description from 1673 is in Arnall Juan, 1978, 208–209. The author's use of the name House of Coins is deliberate; other scholars writing in English have referred to this structure as the mint.

20. For the history of the Mexica, see Camilla Townsend, *Fifth Sun: A New History of the Aztecs* (New York: Oxford University Press, 2019).

21. A number of books cover the 1600s. A descriptive overview of the city's architecture and "famous" people is Francisco de la Maza, *La ciudad de México en el siglo XVII* (México: Fondo de Cultura Económica, 1985). A history that pays homage to city of the intellectual Sor Juan Inés de la Cruz is Antonio Rubial García, *Monjas, cortesanos y plebeyos: la vida cotidiana en la época de Sor Juana* (México: Taurus, 2005). A classic work that similarly celebrates the erudition of Sor Juana and Carlos de Sigüenza y Góngora and their intellectual milieux is Irving A. Leonard, *Baroque Times in Old Mexico: Seventeenth-Century Persons, Places, and Practices* (Ann Arbor: University of Michigan Press, 1966). Leonard's narrative description of the city's cultural life mentions "class, caste, race"; Ibid., ix. These categories influenced Jonathan I. Israel, *Race, Class, and Politics in Colonial Mexico, 1610–1670* (London: Oxford University Press, 1975). See also R. Douglas Cope, *The Limits of Racial Domination: Plebeian Society in Colonial Mexico City, 1660–1720* (Madison: University of Wisconsin Press, 1994). Scholars in this collection examine the city's history from varied perspectives: John F. López, ed., *A Companion to Viceregal Mexico City, 1519–1821* (Leiden: Brill, 2021). See also Sergio Miranda Pacheco, "Presentación. La ciudad, la historia y los historiadores," in *El historiador frente a la ciudad de México. Perfiles de su historia*, ed. Sergio Miranda Pacheco (México: UNAM, 2016).

22. The historiography of the city's provisioning infrastructure, cited in the chapter, has focused on the administration of the city granary (*alhóndiga*) and regulation of butcher shops, with slight attention to the purveyance of other food items; see, for example, Manuel Miño Grijalva, "La población novohispana: alimentación y recursos," in *El mundo novohispano: población, ciudades y economía, siglos XVII y XVIII* (México: Colegio de México, 2001). A 300-year overview of the history of food provision based on secondary sources is: Diego G. López Rosado, "Periodo Virreinal," in *Historia del abasto de productos alimenticios en la ciudad de México* (México: Fondo de Cultura Económica, 1988). See also Jorge Olvera Ramos, *Los mercados de la Plaza Mayor en la Ciudad de México* (México: Cal y arena, 2007).

23. The Spanish word for this concept was *derechos*.

24. Royal decree, September 23, 1552, in Vasco de Puga, *Prouisiões cedulas instruciones desu Magestad: ordenãças ... y gouernaciõ dsta nueua España* (México: Casa de Pedro Ocharte, 1563), f.142v–143.

25. There is no study to date that examines the economic value and reconstructs the combined work of people who moved goods and people in seventeenth-century Mexico City. The historiography is cited in the chapter.

26. There is no study to date that recovers the work of barbers in seventeenth-century Mexico City. The historiography is cited in the chapter.

27. Apart from art historians and numismatic experts, the historiography on silver in seventeenth-century Mexico City, cited in the chapter, has focused on silver merchants (the richest men in the capital based on their investments in silver mines and control of the Corporation of Merchants), and the impact of city-minted coins in markets in Asia and Europe.

28. ANM J. Pérez Rivera (497) 3361 f.83–84 (1617).
29. The Spanish word translated as capital is *bienes*, meaning "wealth" and "property" and "gains"; Sebastián Covarrubias Horozco, *Parte primera del tesoro de la lengva castellana, o española* (Madrid: Impresor del rey, 1674), f.96v. AGN TSJ 19 exp.656 fs.8 (1662).
30. Diego de Saavedra Fajardo, *Idea de vn principe politico cristiano* (Munich, 1643), 526. Saavedra was a diplomat.
31. The author does not accept ahistorical models that suggest societies undergo different "stages" or that they "develop" economically, in the manner of several generations of historians who conceived of economies within a Marxist framework. Mercantilism and capitalism are merely ideas about the functioning of economies rather than historical fact. As such, this study is unconcerned with the "rise of capitalism" – a topic that continues to engage the historiography. There is slight discussion in these pages about economic paradigms.
32. Entry for *trabajo*; Sebastián Covarrubias Horozco, *Parte segunda del tesoro de la lengva castellana, o española* (Madrid: Impresor del rey, 1673), f.192.
33. Entry for *tratar*; Ibid., f.195–195v.
34. Entry for *trafago*; Ibid., f.192v.
35. The word was also employed for the work of farmers, who tilled the earth to produce food. Entry for *labrar*; Ibid., f.82.
36. Entry for *trabajo*; Ibid., f.192.
37. The term working people is not an allusion to interpretations of history focused on the organization of societies by class. Labor, another word for physical work, gained distinct political meanings in the context of nineteenth-century Europe when writers such as Karl Marx posited that laborers were a social class, a working class that could exert power over property owners who belonged to the capitalist class. This conception of people being divided by class, a Marxist framework, influenced historians who looked at other parts of the world and in the more distant past to identify a phenomenon called the rise of a working-class consciousness. Cope, who wrote about the social organization of Mexico City, employed the term plebian society to refer to people of diverse ethnicities who belonged to the "lower class"; Cope, 1994, 4–7, 22.
38. ANM J. Lerín (11) 1 f.153–170 (1689).
39. The law consisted of royal legislation, but there was also common law, which drew from local customs, Roman jurisprudence, natural law (often conceived as divine law in this context), and canon law (Catholic church legislation said to be inspired by divine law). The law was also legal practice on the ground. The monarch delivered legal mandates and promulgated legislation (through the Council of the Indies) in various forms, including royal decrees (*reales cédulas*), provisions, and instructions. The monarch also empowered certain governing bodies to pass legislation. The viceroy and judges of the High Court of Mexico issued legal directives in the form of resolutions (*autos*), edicts (*bandos*), and ordinances (*ordenanzas*) for regional and local governance; accorded resolutions (*autos acordados*) were legal dictates issued by both bodies on important matters. Several compilations

of the corpus of legislation related to the monarchy's overseas possessions (termed *derecho novohispano* or *derecho indiano*) appeared in the sixteenth and seventeenth centuries, most completely with the *Laws of the Indies*; see Consejo de Indias, *Recopilacion de leyes de los reynos de las Indias*, 4 vols. (Madrid: Por Iulian de Paredes, 1681). The *Laws of the Indies* contained legislation (*leyes*) that was meant to uphold justice (*derecho*). Historians employ the term legal pluralism to describe this legal regime, which prevailed in the Spanish and other European empires; see Lauren A. Benton and Richard Jeffrey Ross, eds., *Legal Pluralism and Empires, 1500–1850* (New York: New York University Press, 2013). A classic history of this complex legislative and judicial system is Alfonso García Gallo, *Estudios de historia del Derecho Indiano* (Madrid: Instituto Nacional de Estudios Jurídicos, 1972). See also Antonio Dougnac Rodríguez, *Manual de historia del Derecho Indiano* (México: UNAM, 1994).

New legal histories have corrected an old historiographical characterization of the Spanish empire's legal system as weak and ineffective, showing just how important laws and courts were to subjects on the ground who sought justice and crucial to how the monarchy maintained power. An overview of this historiographical trajectory and new areas of research is Thomas Duve and Heikki Pihlajamäki, eds., *New Horizons in Spanish Colonial Law: Contributions to Transnational Early Modern Legal history* (Frankfurt am Main: Max Planck Institute for European Legal History, 2015).

40. See book 4, title 3, law 1 of the *Laws of the Indies*.

41. For a contemporary overview of these tribunals, see Augustín de Vetancurt, *Tratado de la ciudad de Mexico, y las grandezas que la ilustran*, 2 vols., vol. 1 (México: Doña Maria de Benavides, 1698), 28–32. See also José Luis Soberanes Fernández, *Los Tribunales de la Nueva España: Antología* (México: UNAM, 1980).

42. The four districts (*parcialidades*) were San Juan Moyotlan, San Pablo Teopan, Santa María Cuepopan, and San Sebastián Atzaqualco. In the seventeenth century, each district of San Juan Tenochtitlan constituted a community that had political representation in the Indigenous council; the districts were subdivided into neighborhoods. In the sixteenth century, each district also represented a community of Christians served by one of the four Indigenous parishes (*doctrinas*) administered by mendicant orders. Similar to city hall, the Indigenous government was concerned with infrastructure projects, public safety, and the collection of taxes, among other charges. It also served a judicial function as the court of first instance on criminal and civil matters for Indigenous residents. See Felipe Castro Gutiérrez, "El origen y conformación de los barrios de indios," in *Los indios y las ciudades de Nueva España*, ed., Felipe Castro Gutiérrez (México: UNAM, 2010); William F. Connell, *After Moctezuma: Indigenous Politics and Self-Government in Mexico City, 1524–1730* (Norman: University of Oklahoma Press, 2011).

43. The palace was the *tecpan calli*. AGN Indios 13 exp.112 f.92–92v (1640). For the history of Asian-descended people who became Indigenous vassals, see Tatiana Seijas, *Asian Slaves in Colonial Mexico: From Chinos to Indians* (New York: Cambridge University Press, 2014).

44. The tax was called *alcabala*. For the collection of this tax, see Yovana Celaya Nández, "La cesión de un derecho de la Real Hacienda: la administración del impuesto de la alcabala novohispana en el siglo XVII. Tres estudios de caso," *América Latina en la historia económica* 33, no. 1 (2010). A history of the alcabala with transcribed decrees and ordinances is Fabian de Fonseca and Carlos de Urrutia, "Alcabala," in *Historia general de real hacienda* (México: V. G. Torres, 1849).

45. Viceroys had long names and numerous titles of nobility. Viceroy Diego Roque López Pacheco Cabrera y Bobadilla was the Duke of Escalona, the Marquess of Villena, and the Count of Xiquena. He appears as Viceroy Escalona in some documentation. This book uses viceroy's short names, as they usually appear in the records. These short names referenced their last names or titles. Viceroys' full name and titles are noted at first mention. For the history of viceroys, see J. Ignacio Rubio Mañé, *Introducción al estudio de los virreyes de Nueva España, 1535–1746*, 2 vols., vol. 1 (México: Ediciones Selectas, 1955); Lewis Hanke and Celso Rodríguez, *Los virreyes españoles en América durante el gobierno de la Casa de Austria: México*, 5 vols. (Madrid: Atlas, 1976–1980).

46. AGN Indios 13 exp.112 f.92–92v (1640).

47. Vassals were appointed a legal counselor who submitted paperwork on their behalf. For the legal apparatus as it concerned Indigenous vassals, see Woodrow W. Borah, *Justice by Insurance: The General Indian Court of Colonial Mexico and the Legal Aides of the Half-Real* (Berkeley: University of California Press, 1983); Brian P. Owensby, *Empire of Law and Indian Justice in Colonial Mexico* (Stanford: Stanford University Press, 2008); Yanna Yannakakis, *Since Time Immemorial: Native Custom and Law in Colonial Mexico* (Durham: Duke University Press, 2023). For the viceroy's power as the king's highest representative, see Alejandro Cañeque, *The King's Living Image: The Culture and Politics of Viceregal Power in Colonial Mexico* (New York: Routledge, 2004).

48. AGN Indios 13 exp.112 f.92–92v (1640). Traders from the Philippines made the same request in 1640 and included the 1631 appeal.

49. Ibid.

50. The High Court (*Audiencia de México*) was the court of appeals for people who lived in Mexico City and other towns and cities in the territory under its jurisdiction. It also provided governing counsel to the viceroy. The viceroy was the president of the High Court, which consisted of: two judges (*oidores*) for civil matters; four judges (*alcaldes del crimen*) for criminal matters; two crown-appointed jurists or public prosecutors (*fiscales*) – one for civil and another for criminal matters; a bailiff or official who kept the peace at court, and other "necessary ministers and officials," such as secretaries (*secretarios*) who wrote minutes, and clerks in charge of records; see Book 2, title 15, law 3 of the *Laws of the Indies*. The court had a civil branch (*sala de lo civil*) and a criminal branch (*sala del crimen*). A history of the High Court that outlines its charges beyond its judicial function is Pilar Arregui Zamorano, *La Audiencia de México según los visitadores: siglos XVI y XVII* (México: UNAM, 1985).

51. Governing bodies in the Spanish empire had a combination of executive, judicial, and legislative powers. The aim of this triaged approach was for the crown to remain the ultimate arbiter of government. Officials working in each governing body confirmed and challenged each other's actions and decisions, and they provided the crown with lengthy reports of their doings, which was part of a system of checks and balances. Statemen worked closely, but independently. A judge of the High Court, for example, regularly reviewed city hall accounts for public works and other expenses; see book 4, title 13, law 7 of the *Laws of the Indies*. The monarchy's primary method of overseeing governing bodies was to appoint an inspector (*visitador*) to carry out an official inspection (*visita*) of a body (such as the High Court), an individual, or a region, which included interviewing people, reading documentation, and the like, and then writing a report detailing abuses of power and complaints for the Council of Indies, which was the highest governing body of the overseas empire under the Hapsburgs. A history of the Council's function and jurisdiction is Ernst Schäfer, *El Consejo Real y Supremo de las Indias. Su historia, organización y labor administrativa hasta la terminación de la Casa de Austria*, 2 vols. (Sevilla: M. Carmona, 1935). The city carried similar inspections called residencies (*residencias*) when local officials finished their terms. A classic overview of this institutional history is Clarence H. Haring, *The Spanish Empire in America* (New York: Oxford University Press, 1947).

52. The word *ayuntamiento* refers to the building or city hall and to the governing bodies within it. The term for the municipal council (*cabildo*), one part of city government, is often employed as a synonym for city hall and city government. City hall had a direct link to the crown through the Council of Indies, which received regular missives and petitions from a legal representative or general attorney (*procurador general*). A history of the political conflicts in the 1620s that strengthened direct ties between city hall and Philip IV is Gibran Bautista y Lugo, *Integrar un reino. La ciudad de México en la monarquía de España 1621–1628* (México: UNAM, 2020). See also Manuel Alvarado Morales, "El cabildo y regimiento de la ciudad de México en el siglo XVII: un ejemplo de oligarquía criolla," *Historia Mexicana* 28, no. 4 (1979).

53. The work of city government is discussed further in the chapters in relation to distinct economic activities. The head of city hall (*corregidor*), a royal appointment, presided over the members (*regidores*) of the municipal council (*cabildo*) who administered city affairs; and he oversaw municipal justice. The head of city hall (also called *alcalde mayor*), representing royal justice, and two judges (*alcaldes ordinarios*) served as the first court on civil and criminal matters for all residents except Indigenous vassals. This tribunal had jurisdiction over non-Native people living in the city and within fifteen leagues or eighty-four miles. The laws in book 4, titles 7–18 and 21 of the *Laws of the Indies* are about municipal governance; other sections cover the topic as well. A list of seventeenth-century corregidores is in: Manuel Romero de Terreros, "Los corregidores de México," *Anales del Museo de Arqueología, Historia y Etnografía* 4a, no.1 (1922). See also Aurora Flores

Olea, "Los regidores de la ciudad de México en la primera mitad del siglo XVII," *Estudios de Historia Novohispana* 3, no.3 (1970). For the historiography on corregidores in the Spanish empire, see Diego Rodríguez de Sepúlveda, "Cornerstones of Empire: Corregidores in Early Viceregal Peru" (PhD, Tulane University, 2023). For the English translation of offices, see John F. Schwaller, "*Alcalde* vs. *Mayor*: Translating the Colonial World," *The Americas* 69, no. 3 (2013).

54. AGN RCD 1 exp.98 f.96 (1548). The city's name was *Muy noble y leal ciudad de México* (without the "insigne") as of 1523.

55. The royal decree was printed in a homage to the city from 1623; see Arias de Villalobos, "Obediencia que México, cabeza de la Nueva España, dio a la Majestad Católica del rey D. Felipe de Austria … Con un discurso en verso, del estado de la misma ciudad," in *Documentos inéditos o muy raros para la historia de México*, ed., Genero García (México: Vda. de Ch. Bouret, 1907), 139–140.

56. The quote is from Gemelli Careri, 1704, 4, 528. A study of these ceremonies is Linda Curcio-Nagy, *The Great Festivals of Colonial Mexico City: Performing Power and Identity* (Albuquerque: University of New Mexico Press, 2004).

57. The city's rights were called *fueros*. A description of this ceremony is in Cristóbal Gutiérrez de Medina, *Viaje del virrey marqués de Villena* (México: Impr. Universitaria, 1947), 86. Gutiérrez de Medina (1598–1650), canon lawyer from the University of Seville, was chaplain to Viceroy Villena and lived in Mexico City during the 1640s, where he printed this homage to his patron. Careri witnessed the ceremony in 1698, when Viceroy Sarmiento "came to the triumphal arch" next to the Dominican monastery, "the gate was shut according to custom, to perform the ceremony of presenting the keys, and the tendering the oath to keep the liberties of the city"; Gemelli Careri, 1704, 4, 528. Viceroy José Sarmiento Valladares Arines de Romay was the Duke of Atrisco and the Count of Moctezuma and of Tula.

58. Pope Julius II granted ecclesiastical control, called royal patronage (*real patronato de Indias*), to Isabel of Castile and Ferdinand of Aragon over their territories in the "Indies" in the papal bull *Universalis ecclesiae regiminis* (1508). Monarchs of the Spanish Habsburg dynasty retained royal patronage, which included ecclesiastical appointments. High churchmen served at the discretion of the king, who employed them in ecclesiastical and secular capacities. The Archbishop of Mexico Francisco García Guerra, O. P., for example, served as acting viceroy (1611–1612), as did others. An analysis of another archbishop's work as representative of the crown is Gibran Bautista y Lugo, "Francisco Manso y Zúñiga (1627–1636) ¿Una corte real en el palacio arzobispal de México?," in *La Iglesia en Palacio. Los eclesiásticos en las cortes hispánicas (siglos XVI–XVII)*, ed., Rafael Valladares (Roma: Viella, 2019).

59. Iberian political theory posited that the crown's subjects in overseas territories belonged to "republics" or political communities. The foundation of a city or a town was a legal act by which settlers "formed a republic" and agreed to elect representatives (a council) to govern alongside the

monarch's appointed governor; see book 4, title 7, law 2 of the *Laws of the Indies*. Republics were governing entities, so there were as many republics as there were cities and towns. The word republic was also used in other circumstances. For the transatlantic context of republics and governance and this historiography, see Karen B. Graubart, "Introduction: Republics and the Politics of Self-Governance," in *Republics of Difference: Religious and Racial Self-governance in the Spanish Atlantic World* (New York: Oxford University Press, 2022).

60. People of Indigenous, African, and Asian descent bore a relatively higher tax burden than people who claimed Spanish ancestry. European-descended vassals mainly paid sales tax (*alcabala*) and levies on certain goods, such as wine. The varied taxes levied on Indigenous vassals in Mexico City included a uniform head tax (*tributo personal*), a cathedral-construction tax (*medio real de fábrica*), a service tax for royal expenses (*servicio real*), and a legal protection tax (*medio real de ministros*). The amount of the head tax paid by residents varied over the course of the seventeenth century. In the first decade, it amounted to 11 reals (8 for the royal treasury, 2 for the Indigenous government, 1 for city hall); see Charles Gibson, *The Aztecs under Spanish Rule: A History of the Indians of the Valley of Mexico, 1519–1810* (Stanford: Stanford University Press, 1964), 205, 391. For the sixteenth century, see José Miranda, *El tributo indígena en la Nueva España durante el siglo XVI* (México: Colegio de México, 1952). A listing of the taxes collected in the Indigenous districts in 1637 is in "Memoria de las quatro parcialidades de los naturales desta ciudad de Mexico," British Library, Add MS 13994 N.220 f.528–32. A partial transcription is in Alfonso Caso, "Los barrios antiguos de Tenochtitlan y Tlatelolco," *Memorias de la Academia Mexicana de la Historia* xv (1956): 50–59. The crown levied a tax on free people of African descent starting in the 1570s; see book 7, title 5, law one of the *Laws of the Indies*. For the history of this tax collection in the eighteenth century, see Rafael Castañeda García, "Hacia una sociología fiscal. El tributo de la población de color libre de la Nueva España, 1770–1810," *Fronteras de la Historia* 19, no. 1 (2014); Froylán de Jesús Granados Ponce, "La indispensable subsistencia de un ramo: el cobro del tributo a indios, negros y mulatos en la ciudad de México, 1780–1792" (MA, UNAM, 2017); Norah L. A. Gharala, *Taxing Blackness: Free Afromexican Tribute in Bourbon New Spain* (Tuscaloosa: University of Alabama Press, 2019). See also, Cynthia Milton and Ben Vinson III, "Counting Heads: Race and Non-Native Tribute Policy in Colonial Spanish America," *Journal of Colonialism and Colonial History* 3, no. 3 (2002); Álvaro Alcántara López, "Los otros contribuyentes: pardos y mulatos de la provincia de Acayucan, 1765–1795," in *De contribuyentes y contribuciones en la fiscalidad mexicana, siglos XVIII-XX*, ed. Yovana Celaya Nández, et al. (México: Colegio de México, 2004); Sarah Albiez-Wieck, *Taxing Difference in Peru and New Spain (16th–19th Century): Negotiating Social Differences and Belonging* (Leiden: Brill, 2022). A study of what vassalage meant to people of African descent is Herman L. Bennett, *Africans in Colonial Mexico: Absolutism, Christianity, and Afro-Creole Consciousness, 1570–1640* (Bloomington: Indiana University Press, 2003).

61. AGN Indios 13 exp.112 f.92–92v (1640).

62. Censuses, tax records, and the observations of city officials and visitors only allow for approximations of the number people in the city proper. Including the population of the surrounding lake towns, an extension of Mexico City's metropolitan space, would increase these numbers. The population figures cited are from Manuel Miño Grijalva, "Las ciudades novohispanas y su función económica, siglos xvi–xviii," in *Historia económica general de México. De la colonia a nuestros días*, ed., Sandra Kuntz Ficker (México: Colegio de México, 2010), 147–148. These conservative estimates correlate broadly to contemporary sources.

63. Estimates are based on diverse sources that only capture certain areas and segments of a city's population in any one year or decade. A comparative discussion is Stuart B. Schwartz, "Cities of Empire: Mexico and Bahia in the Sixteenth Century," *Journal of Inter-American Studies* 11, no. 4 (1969).

64. Noble David Cook, ed., *Numeración general de todas las personas de ambos sexos, edades y calidades que se ha hecho en esta ciudad de Lima, año de 1700* (Lima: COFIDE, 1985), xii.

65. A contemporary figure for Amsterdam in 1622 is 104,932; Hubert P. H. Nusteling, "La population d'Amsterdam de la fin du XVIe siècle au début du XIXe siècle. Une méthode de reconstitution," *Population* 41, no. 6 (1986): 964. An estimate for the late 1690s is 227,649; Marco H.D. van Leeuwen and James E. Oeppen, "Reconstructing the Demographic Regime of Amsterdam 1681–1920," *Economic & Social History in the Netherlands* 5 (1993): 87. The author thanks Kayo Denda for help identifying sources for this demographic comparison. Estimates for Beijing are partly based on censuses for administrative units from 1621 and 1711; Shouxian Gao, *Beijing ren kou shi* (Beijing: Zhong guo ren min da xue chu ban she, 2014), 240. The author thanks Tao Yang for identifying and translating this source.

66. AGN Mat 61 exp.73 f.288–290 (1605). People seeking to marry had to acquire a marriage license at the ecclesiastical court, where they presented witnesses who confirmed their identities and that they were single. All parties noted their name, age, occupation, ethnicity, and other distinguishing information. The *Matrimonios* collection has over 230 volumes with copies of licenses issued in Mexico City dating from 1540 to 1866, which historians have mined for ethnographic information and to discuss marriage choices.

67. For this history, see Pablo Miguel Sierra Silva, "Portuguese *Encomenderos de Negros* and the Slave Trade within Mexico, 1600–1675," *Journal of Global Slavery* 2, no. 3 (2017); Norma Angélica Castillo Palma, "La trata negrera, sus redes mercantiles portuguesas y estrategias de negocios en Nueva España durante el siglo XVII: una visión comparada," *Trashumante: Revista Americana de Historia Social* 10 (2017).

68. For the ethnonyms and archival categories of enslaved Africans sold in Mexico City, see Tatiana Seijas and Pablo Miguel Sierra Silva, "The Persistence of the Slave Market in Seventeenth-Century Central Mexico," *Slavery & Abolition* 37, no. 2 (2016).

69. For this history, see Seijas, 2014, 73–108.

70. AGN Mat 10 e.41 f.96–97v (1629).

71. A quantitative study on the pervasiveness of slavery in the capital is Seijas and Sierra Silva, 2016.

72. A discussion of categories is Ben Vinson III, *Before Mestizaje: The Frontiers of Race and Caste in Colonial Mexico* (New York: Cambridge University Press, 2018). See also Robert C. Schwaller, *Géneros de Gente in Early Colonial Mexico: Defining Racial Difference*, (Norman: University of Oklahoma Press, 2016).

73. Antonio Vázquez de Espinosa, *Compendio y descripción de las Indias Occidentales*, ed., Charles U. Clark (Washington: Smithsonian Institution, 1948), 146.

74. Torquemada noted 7,000 "Spanish residents" and 8,000 Indigenous residents in the polity of Santiago Tlatelolco; Juan de Torquemada, *Ia parte de los veynte y vn libros rituales y monarchia yndiana* (Sevilla: Matthias Clauijo, 1615), 327. The population for the polity of San Juan Tenochtitlan would have been at least four times larger than Tlatelolco's. The archbishop reported 20,000 "Spanish families" living in the city in 1629; Gil González Dávila, *Teatro eclesiastico de la primitiva iglesia de las Indias occidentales*, 2 vols., vol. 1, (Madrid: Diego Diaz de la Carrera, 1649), 60.

75. Isidro de la Asunción, a Carmelite, first visited Mexico City in 1673 and lived in the region for several years, estimated "9,000 Spanish residents, and Indians … blacks, and other nations in infinite numbers"; a partial transcription of his report is Arnall Juan, 1978, 210. A 1689 census lists 1,917 immigrants from Spain; J. Ignacio Rubio Mañé, ed., *Gente de España en la ciudad de México, año de 1689*, vol. 2a serie VII, n.1–2 (México: Boletín del Archivo General de la Nación, 1966), 13. The original census is in AGN RCD 55 f.221–275 (1689). Finally, a visitor in 1697 approximated that the city had "100,000 inhabitants … the greatest part of them blacks"; Gemelli Careri, 1704, 4, 508.

76. An explanation of the procedure is in: Francisco Fernández López, "El control de las personas: expedientes de licencias de pasajeros" in *La Casa de la Contratación. Una oficina de expedición documental para el Gobierno de las Indias (1503–1717)* (Sevilla: Universidad de Sevilla, 2018).

77. Letter, December 14, 1615, copy in British Library Add MS 13994 f.63v–64v (1615). Viceroy Diego Fernández de Córdoba was the Marquess of Guadalcázar and the Count of Posadas.

78. AGN Inq 306 exp.5 fs.15 (1619); For the history of people gaining *vecindad*; see Tamar Herzog, *Defining Nations: Immigrants and Citizens in Early Modern Spain and Spanish America* (New Haven: Yale University Press, 2003), 43–63.

79. ANM José de la Cruz (106) 721 f.136–137 (1625); AGN Mat 48, exp.68, f.195–197 (1628).

80. The historiography on the sixteenth-century demographic collapse of the Indigenous population in Central Mexico reveals chilling numbers. There were approximately 80,000 Indigenous residents (predominantly Nahuas) in Mexico City in the early 1560s (21,626 of whom were on the tax rolls); in the late 1650s, there were 6,450 heads of households or tax payers (22,575 overall, with a 1 to 3.5 ration between heads and members of their

households); see Gibson, 1964, 377–380, 460–462. See also, Susan Kellogg, "Households in Late Prehispanic and Early Colonial Mexico City: Their Structure and Its Implications for the Study of Historical Demography," *The Americas* 44, no. 4 (1988).

81. Tomás Jalpa Flores, "Migrantes y estravagantes. Indios de la periferia en la ciudad de México durante los siglos XVI–XVII," in *Los indios y las ciudades de Nueva España*, ed., Felipe Castro Gutiérrez (México: UNAM, 2010).

82. Natalia Silva Prada, "Impacto de la migración urbana en el proceso de 'separación de repúblicas.' El caso de dos parroquias indígenas de la parcialidad de San Juan Tenochtitlán, 1688–1692," *Estudios de Historia Novohispana* 24 (2001). For the sixteenth century, see Iván Rivero Hernández, *De las nubes a la laguna. Tributos y tamemes mixtecos en la ciudad de México, 1522-1560* (Zamora: Colegio de Michoacán, 2017).

83. For the exceptions that facilitated the ongoing enslavement of Native people in seventeenth-century Mexico despite the laws that abolished Indigenous slavery, see Seijas, 2014, 212–246.

84. An estimate from the early 1680s noted that the city's seven Indigenous parishes had "more than 10,000 Indians"; Baltasar de Medina, *Chronica de la Santa Provincia de San Diego de Mexico, de religiosos descalços de N.S.P.S. Francisco en la Nueva-España* (México: Juan de Ribera, 1682), f.238. Baltasar de Medina (1634–1697), born in Mexico City, was a member of the Franciscan Order (dieguino); a section of his chronicle of the order is about his native city. Fernando B. Sandoval, "Baltasar de Medina y la crónica de los dieguinos," *Historia Mexicana* 19, no. 3 (1970).

85. A study of the property transactions of Indigenous residents during the second half of the sixteenth century that led to ethnic diversification of the neighborhoods (also caused by the demographic decline of the Indigenous population due to disease) is Rebeca López Mora, "Entre dos mundos: Los indios de los barrios de la ciudad de México, 1550–1600," in *Los indios y las ciudades de Nueva España*, ed., Felipe Castro Gutiérrez (México: UNAM, 2010). An overview of the organization of space in Indigenous neighborhoods based on sixteenth- and seventeenth-century maps is Alejandro Alcántara Gallegos, "Los barrios de Tenochtitlan. Topografía, organización interna y tipología de sus predios," in *Historia de la vida cotidiana en México: Mesoamérica y los ámbitos indígenas de la Nueva España*, ed., Pablo Escalante Gonzalbo (México: Colegio de México, 2004).

86. AGN TSJ 1, exp.18 fs.28 (1600). For the neighborhood's history, see Ernesto Flores Martínez, "Tequisquiapan: Un barrio de la parcialidad de San Juan Tenochtitlan, 1570–1776" (MA, UAM, Iztapalapa, 2007).

87. The documentation for this plan to remove Indigenous people from the city center is in AGN Historia exp.1 fs.74 (1692), and partially transcribed in "Sobre los inconvenientes de vivir los indios en el centro de la ciudad," *Boletín del Archivo General de la Nación* 9, no. 1 (1938). Repeated calls to enforce the ban on Indigenous residents from the city center suggest ongoing noncompliance; see, for example, AGI México 1777 L.39 f.33–37v (1699).

88. AGN Mat 10 exp.41 f.96–97v (1629).

89. The Spanish word for free was *libre*.

90. AGN TSJ 166 exp. 5463 fs.8 (1608).
91. The Spanish word for nation was *nación*.
92. Domingo Francisco de San Antón Muñón Chimalpahin Cuauhtlehuanitzin, *Annals of His Time* (Stanford: Stanford University Press, 2006), 65.
93. The Nahua word *altepetl* means city-state or sovereign political unit.
94. There is a lengthy historiography on the two major riots, variously characterized as bread riots, presages of independence, race riots, and political protests. Officials produced copious documentation, eager to cast blame. The crown required extensive explanations for the breakdown of good government. For the infamous riot of 1692, see the bibliographies of Pilar Gonzalbo Aizpuru, "El nacimiento del miedo, 1692. Indios y españoles en la ciudad de México," *Revista de Indias* 68, no. 244 (2008); Arnaud Exbalin, "Riot in Mexico City: a Challenge to the Colonial Order?," *Urban History* 43, no. 2 (2016). A printed primary source for the event is Carlos de Sigüenza y Góngora, *Alboroto y motín de México del 8 de Junio de 1692* (México: Museo Nacional de Arqueología, Historia y Etnografía, 1932). There is a vast historiography on Carlos de Sigüenza y Góngora, a prolific scholar and official, who lived and died in his native city (1645–1700); see the bibliography and analysis of Anna H. More, *Baroque Sovereignty: Carlos de Sigüenza y Góngora and the Creole Archive of Colonial Mexico* (Philadelphia: University of Pennsylvania Press, 2013). For the 1624 riot, see Rosa Feijoo, "El tumulto de 1624," *Historia Mexicana* 14, no. 4 (1964); Gibran Bautista y Lugo, "Los indios y la rebelión de 1624 en la ciudad de México," in *Los indios y las ciudades de Nueva España*, ed. Felipe Castro Gutiérrez (México: UNAM, 2010); Angela Ballone, *The 1624 Tumult of Mexico in Perspective (c. 1620–1650): Authority and Conflict Resolution in the Iberian Atlantic* (Leiden: Brill, 2018). Government reports on the 1624 tumult are in AGI Patronato 225 R.2, the British Library (Add MS 13975), and other repositories.
95. See, for example, AGN Inq 1508 exp.3 f.17–54 (1665). Chimalpahin recorded allegations as well, including an investigation that tragically ended with the state-sanctioned murder of thirty-five people; Chimalpahin Cuauhtlehuanitzin, 2006, 155, 213–218. The historiography of this event is cited in Chapter 2.
96. Ibid., 79–81.
97. Ibid. Another Nahuatl source noted the sinking of homes in the middle of the night; "Anales de San Gregorio Acapulco, 1520–1606," in *Tlalocan*, eds., R. H. Barlow, et al. (1952), 122.
98. A description of the project from 1633 is in Bernabé Cobo, *Obras del P. Bernabé Cobo, de la Compañia de Jesus*, vol. 2 (Madrid: Atlas, 1956), 471–476. A contemporary assessment of the project (*desagüe*) is Cepeda and Carrillo, 1637. The printed report circulated widely: "Copies were given to all magistrates … and other persons of judgment that they might examine it and give their opinions"; Gemelli Careri, 1704, 4, 532. This book does not examine the hydraulics project. There is an extensive historiography on the topic, mainly written from the perspective of engineers and the history of science: see Luis González Obregón, "Reseña histórica

del desagüe del valle de México, 1449–1855," in *Memoria histórica, técnica y administrativa de las obras del desagüe del valle de México, 1449–1900* (México: Tip. de la Oficina Impresora de Estampillas, 1902); Jorge Gurría Lacroix, *El desagüe del Valle de México durante la época novohispana* (México: UNAM, 1978); Alain Mussett, *El agua en el valle de México, siglos xvi–xviii* (México: Pórtico de la ciudad de México, 1992); Vera S. Candiani, *Dreaming of Dry Land: Environmental Transformation in Colonial Mexico City* (Stanford: Stanford University Press, 2014). See also Sergio Miranda Pacheco, "Urbe inmunda: poder y prejuicios socioambientales en la urbanización y desagüe de la ciudad y valle de México en el siglo XIX," in *De olfato. Aproximaciones a los olores en la historia de México*, ed. Elodie Dupey García, et al. (México: Fondo de Cultura Económica, 2020); Elienahí Nieves Pimentel, "'Hazme la barba y harete el copete': proyectos y administración de recursos para la obra hidráulica en la cuenca de México (1524–1684)" (PhD, Instituto de Investigaciones Dr. José María Luis Mora, 2025).

99. Chimalpahin Cuauhtlehuanitzin, 2006, 187.

100. Antonio de Robles, *Diario de sucesos notables, 1665–1703*, 3 vols., vol. 3 (México: Porrúa, 1946), 49.

101. Gage, 1648, 56.

102. Visitors repeatedly noted the qualities of this local volcanic stone (*tezontli*); one described it as "easy to work with and very light, so much so that a large slab can float on water without sinking"; Vázquez de Espinosa, 1948, 146.

103. The sixteenth-century cathedral was demolished in 1626 and replaced with a grander edifice. A lengthy description of the cathedral from the 1670s is in Arnall Juan, 1978, 205–206. An overview of its construction history is in Francisco Sedano, *Noticias de México*, 2nd ed., 3 vols. (México: Secretaría de Obras y Servicios, 1974), I: 68–75. Sedano (1742–1812), a book seller, collected stories and information about his city, which were organized and printed in 1880.

104. Trasmonte was the cathedral's *maestro mayor*; he died circa 1647. Fernández, 1982 311.

105. Bernardo de Balbuena, *Grandeza mexicana* (México: Emprenta de Diego Lopez Davalos, 1604), f.64v–65. Balbuena, a poet from Valdepeñas, lived in Mexico City at the beginning of the century. His work has received wide attention from literary scholars; see, for example, Stephanie Merrim, *The Spectacular City, Mexico, and Colonial Hispanic Literary Culture* (Austin: University of Texas Press, 2010).

106. The city's gravitational pull followed Braudel's pattern of great cities being "planetary systems," drawing sellers seeking better prices for their goods, workers searching for higher wages, and people looking to get lost in busy shops; see Fernand Braudel, *La Méditerranée et le monde méditeranéen à l'époque de Philippe II*, 2nd ed., vol. 1 (Paris: A. Colin, 1966), 299.

107. Balbuena, 1604, f.76–77, 89. A history of officials involved in the transpacific trade is Nino Vallen, *Being the Heart of the World: The Pacific and the Fashioning of the Self in New Spain, 1513–1641* (New York: Cambridge University Press, 2023). See also Guillermina del Valle Pavón,

"'Se disimula y fomenta el delito': el contrabando entre México y Manila en las postrimerías del siglo XVII," in *Contrabando y redes de negocios: Hispanoamérica en el comercio global, 1610-1814*, ed. Guillermina del Valle Pavón (México: Instituto Mora, 2023).
108. AGN TSJ 195 exp.6526 fs.66 (1631).

## I FEEDING THE CITY

1. AGN TSJ 171 exp.5669 fs.4 (1625).
2. The Spanish word for the root vegetable is *camotes*. Vázquez de Espinosa, 1948, 160.
3. Gage, 1648, 59.
4. Art historical analyses of this work include Michael Schreffler, *The Art of Allegiance: Visual Culture and Imperial Power in Baroque New Spain* (University Park: Pennsylvania State University Press, 2007); Bruno de la Serna Nasser, "Apuntes sobre el Biombo del Palacio de los Virreyes: posibilidades en torno a su mecenazgo y representación," *Anales del Museo de América* 25 (2017). See also Barbara E. Mundy, "Introduction," in *The Death of Aztec Tenochtitlan. The Life of Mexico City* (Austin: University of Texas Press, 2015).
5. Scholarship that examines the commercial role of African-descended women in New Spain includes: María Elisa Velázquez Gutiérrez, *Mujeres de origen africano en la capital novohispana, siglos XVII y XVIII* (México: INAH, 2006); Pablo Miguel Sierra Silva, *Urban Slavery in Colonial Mexico: Puebla de los Ángeles, 1531-1706* (New York: Cambridge University Press, 2018); Danielle Terrazas Williams, *The Capital of Free Women: Race, Legitimacy, and Liberty in Colonial Mexico* (New Haven: Yale University Press, 2022); Sabrina Smith, "African-Descended Women: Power and Social Status in Colonial Oaxaca, 1660–1680," *The Americas* 80, no.4 (2023); Maira Cristina Córdova Aguilar, "Vida y trabajo de Cathalina de los Reyes, María Machuca, Juana Machado, Agustín García y Pedro Gonzales en la ciudad de Antequera (1649-1792)," in *Trayectorias de vida de afrodescendientes en la historia de México*, ed. Gabriela Iturralde Nieto (México: INAH, 2024).
6. Ascertaining demographic data about the city's food vendors is nearly impossible. A deep survey of documentation that mentions them by name and categorizes them by ethnicity and legal status, however, confirms the participation of residents with ties to regions around the world.
7. The quantities of beef consumed annually in the city was astonishing, with 80,000 cattle perishing in 1648 alone; see Gregorio Martín de Guijo, *Diario, 1648–1664*, 2 vols., vol. 1: 1648–1654 (México: Porrúa, 1953), 26. For meat provisioning during the eighteenth century, see Enriqueta Quiroz, *Entre el lujo y la subsistencia: mercado, abastecimiento y precios de la carne en la ciudad de México, 1750–1812* (México: Instituto Mora, 2005); "Entre el humanismo y el mercantilismo: El bien común en el abasto de carne de ciudad de México, 1708–1716," *Cuadernos de Historia* 35 (2011).

A short overview based on printed sources is William H. Dusenberry, "The Regulation of Meat Supply in Sixteenth-Century Mexico City," *Hispanic American Historical Review* 28, no. 1 (1948).

8. Overviews of the agricultural production that undergirded Tenochtitlan's urbanism include Christopher T. Morehart, "Aztec Agricultural Strategies: Intensification, Landesque Capital, and the Sociopolitics of Production," in *Oxford Handbook of the Aztecs*, eds. Deborah L. Nichols, et al. (New York: Oxford University Press, 2017); Deborah L. Nichols, "Farm to Market in the Aztec Imperial Economy," in *Rethinking the Aztec Economy*, eds., Deborah L. Nichols, et al. (Tucson: University of Arizona Press, 2017).

9. Nahuas developed two main agricultural methods for this environment. The first relied on chinampas built on the lakes and the second on terraces (*metepantli*) in the hillsides, which used rows of magueys to prevent erosion. For the latter, see Susan T. Evans, "The productivity of maguey terrace agriculture in central Mexico during the Aztec period," *Latin American Antiquity* 1, no. 2 (1990). Chinampas were plots of silt that produced harvests using a form of hydroponic agriculture. For this unique ecology, see Teresa Rojas Rabiela, *La agricultura chinampera: compilación histórica*, 2nd ed. (Chapingo: Universidad Autónoma de Chapingo, 1993); Richard M. Conway, "Rural Indians and Technological Innovation, from the Chinampas of Xochimilco and Beyond," *The Oxford Research Encyclopedia of Latin American History* (2018); *Islands in the Lake: Environment and Ethnohistory in Xochimilco, New Spain* (New York: Cambridge University Press, 2021).

10. Scholars have often observed that cities were food hubs for near and far-reaching networks; see, for example, Richard Graham, *Feeding the City: From Street Market to Liberal Reform in Salvador, Brazil, 1780–1860* (Austin: University of Texas Press, 2010), 74.

11. Legislation on food provisions is in book 4 title 18 of the *Laws of the Indies*.

12. Torquemada, 1615, 328.

13. Ibid. The Tlatelolco market (*tianguis de Tlatelolco*) was next to the Franciscan monastery of *Santiago* and the *Colegio Imperial de la Santa Cruz*. Francisco Cervantes de Salazar, *Crónica de la Nueva España* (Madrid: The Hispanic Society of America, 1914), 303. Francisco Cervantes de Salazar (c. 1514–1575) lived in Mexico City during the last twenty-five years of his life. Trained as a Latinist at the University of Salamanca, and on the faculty at the University of Mexico, he wrote a Socratic dialogue on Mexico City that discusses the qualities that make a great city; *México en 1554. Tres diálogos latinos* (México: Andrade y Morales, 1875).

14. The Saint John Market (*tianguis de San Juan*) is marked "*mercado*" on the "Map of Santa Cruz" (Uppsala University Library, Sweden, 1537–1555). Mundy locates it on the city block occupied today by the Biscaynes School (*Colegio de Vizcaínas*); Barbara E. Mundy, *The Death of Aztec Tenochtitlan*.

*The Life of Mexico City* (Austin: University of Texas Press, 2015), 84–94; "La fuente del tianguis de San Juan de México-Tenochtitlan y el segundo acueducto de Chapultepec," *Boletín de Monumentos Históricos* 32 (2014). See also Beatriz Rubio Fernández, "Los tianguis de la ciudad de México en el siglo XVI," *Anales del Museo de América* 21 (2013).

15. Torquemada, 1615, 328.
16. The *tianguis de San Hipólito* was located next to its namesake the Church of *San Hipólito*. A contemporary wrote that it was held "in sight" of the church that shares its name; Cervantes de Salazar, 1914, 303.
17. Anales de San Gregorio Acapulco, 1520–1606, 1952. In 1551, the fair, which had been operating on Wednesdays and Thursdays, was temporarily shut down, but city hall appealed that it reopen, as it benefited the "republic" for city residents to have a place where they could purchase "everything that was necessary"; March 12, 1551, Cabildo Ciudad de México, ed., *Actas de Cabildo*, vol. 6: Diciembre 1550–Diciembre 1561 (México: Municipio Libre, 1889), 15. For a discussion of goods sold at market by Indigenous residents, see James Lockhart, "Land and Living," in *The Nahuas after the Conquest: A Social and Cultural History of the Indians of Central Mexico, Sixteenth through Eighteenth Centuries* (Stanford: Stanford University Press, 1992).
18. Torquemada, 1615, 328.
19. Augustín de Vetancurt, "Tratado de la ciudad de Mexico, y las grandezas que la ilustran," in *Chronica de la Provincia del Santo Evangelio de Mexico. Quarta parte del Teatro Mexicano de los successos religiosos* (México: Doña María de Benavides, 1697), 1.
20. Ibid.
21. Ibid.
22. Ibid., 2.
23. Ibid., 3.
24. Gemelli Careri, 1704, 4, 549.
25. The town of Tacuba was covered with fruit orchards, and trees lined the thoroughfare that led directly to the city's center. ANM J. Pérez Rivera 3362 (497) f.457v–458 (1627); ANM J. P. Rivera Cáceres (630) 4368 f.155–160v, 300–306v (1652).
26. Friars planted seedlings at the Carmelite monastery in the town of Saint Angel when construction began in 1615 that grew into a "fruitful" orchard by the late 1690s with some "13,000" trees, which produced "peaches and quinces" and "several sorts of pears"; Gemelli Careri, 1704, 4, 524–525.
27. Ibid., 549.
28. A visitor in 1612 noted the colors and textures of *"zapotes colorados, chicozapotes, zapotes blancos … and zapotes negros"*; Vázquez de Espinosa, 1948, 160.
29. Based on Juan Gómez de Trasmonte's plan, the rendition depicts the city's layout in a flatter and more linear fashion than the original.
30. Vázquez de Espinosa, 1948, 146.
31. Ibid.

32. The original map has the names of these places: The Main Square is the "*plaça*"; Volador Square is "*plaçuela.*" They are next to the Viceroyal Palace "*casa real.*" Volador was also known as the *plaza de las escuelas* because it fronted the University of Mexico.

33. Deliberations about this project continued for several years due to costs; Viceroy Guadalcázar wanted two fountains with bronze fixtures, one at the Main Square and another at Volador, while city hall considered that one fountain, stone-only, sufficed; January 31, 1620; Cabildo Ciudad de México, ed., *Actas de Cabildo*, vol. 23: Mayo 1619–Diciembre 1620 (México: El Correo Español, 1906), 119–120.

34. The original map notes the locations of the markets as "*plaça de S. João*" and "*S. Ipolito.*"

35. The original map notes it as "*plaça S.tiago.*"

36. Viceroy Gaspar de Zúñiga Acevedo y Fonseca was the Count of Monterrey.

37. AGN GP 5 exp.1266 f.274v (1600). Manuel Miranda used the same phrasing to obtain a license "to sell turkeys, chickens, eggs, and other food supplies [*bastimientos*] two months later"; AGN GP 5 exp.1334 f.296 (1601).

38. AGN GP 5 exp.1266 f.274v (1600). The distance noted is five leagues. A league equaled 2.6 miles; Carrera Stampa, 1949 10.

39. AGN GP 5 exp.1266 f.274v (1600).

40. Ibid.

41. Ibid.

42. AGN Ord 1 exp.84 f.80v (1583).

43. Royal decree, March 2, 1552, in Vasco de Puga, ed., *Provisiones, cédulas, instrucciones para el gobierno de la Nueva España*, fascimilar ed. (Madrid: Cultura Hispánica, 1945), f.140v.

44. A discussion of strategies employed by vassals with mention of Mexico City is Adrian Masters, *We, the King: Creating Royal Legislation in the Sixteenth-Century Spanish New World* (Cambridge: Cambridge University Press, 2023).

45. Royal decree, May 12, 1551; reissued on January 30, 1567; codified as book 6, title 1, law 25 of the *Laws of the Indies*.

46. Royal decree, September 3, 1552, in Puga, 1945, 141.

47. Ibid.

48. Ibid.

49. Royal decree, March 2, 1552, in Puga, 1945, f.184.

50. Royal decree, April 26, 1563; codified as book 6, title 1, law 28 of the *Laws of the Indies*.

51. Royal decree, January 30, 1567; codified as book 6, title 1, law 25 of the *Laws of the Indies*.

52. Ibid.

53. Ibid.

54. Ibid.

55. Ibid.

56. The Spanish word for haggler was *regatón*. Entry for *regatón*; Covarrubias Horozco, 1673, f.157.

57. AGN Ord 1 exp.22 f.31v (1579); AGN Ord 2 exp.260 f.229 (1579). The viceroy's name was Martín Enríquez de Almanza.

58. Ibid.
59. AGN Ord 1 exp.84 f.80v (1583).
60. AGN RCD 3 exp.24 f.12–12v (1587).
61. Ibid. Viceroy Álvaro Manrique de Zúñiga was the Marquess of Villamanrique.
62. Ibid.
63. The Spanish term for retail was *por menudo*.
64. AGN RCD 3 exp.24 f.12–12v (1587).
65. Gonzalo Gómez de Cervantes, born in and resident of Mexico City, held several positions including Governor of the Province of Tlaxcala. Documents at the AGI and AGN provide glimpses of his career; see also Paul Ganster, "La familia Gómez de Cervantes: Linaje y sociedad en el México colonial," *Historia Mexicana* 31, no. 2 (1981). The author wrote a report in 1599 to the Council of Indies elaborating on the problems he identified in the local economy of his city and proposed solutions to curry royal favor. The manuscript, now at the British Library, was first published in 1944. Gonzalo Gómez de Cervantes, "Memorial de Gonzalo Gómez de Cervantes para el doctor Eugenio Salazar oidor del Real Consejo de las Indias," in *La vida económica y social de Nueva España, al finalizar el siglo XVI* (México: Antiqua librería Robredo, 1944), 99.
66. Gómez de Cervantes 1944, 100.
67. Ibid., 99, 118.
68. The Spanish word for businesses was *negocios*.
69. The payment was called *jornal* and the person *jornalero*.
70. Hapsburg law permitted enslaved people to save their earnings to self-purchase in the Roman juridical tradition of *peculium*. A discussion or self-purchase with reference to Mexico City is Chloe L. Ireton, "Purchasing Freedom: Economics of Liberty in New Spain," in *Slavery and Freedom in Black Thought in the Early Spanish Atlantic* (Cambridge: Cambridge University Press, 2024).
71. Royal decree, April 24, 1535; codified as book 4, title 9, law 22 of the *Laws of the Indies*.
72. AGN RCD 3 exp.118 f.79v (1590).
73. AGN Ord 1 exp.22 f.31v (1579); AGN Ord 2 exp.260 f.229 (1579).
74. Viceroyal order and instructions, November 27, 1574, copied in Alfonso García Gallo, ed., *Cedulario Indiano Recopilado por Diego de Encinas*, fascimile ed., 4 vols., vol. 3 (Madrid: Real Academia de la Historia, 2018), 430–431. Fonseca and Urrutia, 1849. A short overview of this tax based on printed sources is Robert S. Smith, "Sales Taxes in New Spain, 1575–1770," *Hispanic American Historical Review* 28, no. 1 (1948).
75. Viceroyal order and instructions, November 27, 1574, copied in García Gallo, 2018, 430–431.
76. Auto acordado, septiembre 23, 1588, transcribed in Juan Francisco de Montemayor de Cuenca, "Recopilacion sumaria de algunos autos acordados de la Real Audiencia ... año de 1677," in *Recopilacion sumaria de todos los autos acordados de la Real Audiencia y sala del crimen de esta Nueva España, y providencias de su superior gobierno*, ed., Eusebio Bentura Beleña (México: Felipe de Zúñiga y Ontiveros, 1787), 55.

77. The crown repeated the overall exemption in November 1591, "sales tax could not be collected from" Indigenous people, but the wording "for the time being" left an opening for the re-imposition of sales tax on things that were not fruits of the earth in the seventeenth century, despite the codification of the viceroy's order as book 8, title 13, law 19 of the *Laws of the Indies*.
78. The Spanish term for this rate and practice was *postura*.
79. See repeated entries in Cabildo Ciudad de México, ed., *Actas de Cabildo*, vol. 1: Marzo 1524–Junio 1529 (México: Municipio Libre, 1889).
80. Royal decree, April 1535, codified as book 4, title 9, law 22 of the *Laws of the Indies*.
81. January 3, 1553; Ciudad de México, 1889, 6: Diciembre 1550 - Diciembre 1561: 86.
82. Ibid.
83. Francisco del Paso y Troncoso, ed. *Epistolario de Nueva España, 1505–1818*, vol. XV (México: Porrúa, 1939), 71–73. Torquemada wrote, circa 1610, that a "true source" had "certified" that there were "7,000 Spaniards" in Mexico City and "8,000" Indigenous residents in Tenochtitlan and Tlatelolco combined; Torquemada, 1615, 327.
84. AGN Ord 2 exp.73 f.88 (1600).
85. AGN Ord 1 exp.95 f. 91 (1585).
86. AGN Ord 2 exp.119 f.125 (1602).
87. The name in Spanish was *acequia real*.
88. ANM J. Pérez Rivera (497) 3358 f.78v–81v (1606).
89. Ibid.
90. AGN Ord 1 exp.157 & 158 (1612).
91. The Spanish name for this body was *Fiel Ejecutoria*. Each January, city hall council members elected two deputies from among their ranks for the coming year's work. A discussion of some aspects of the tribunal's work is in María Luisa J. Pazos, *El Ayuntamiento de la ciudad de México en el siglo xvii: continuidad institucional y cambio social* (Sevilla: Diputación de Sevilla, 1999), 138–168. See also Ivonne Mijares, "El abasto urbano: caminos y bastimentos," in *Historia de la vida cotidiana en México: la ciudad barroca*, ed., Antonio Rubial García (México: Colegio de México, 2005). For the eighteenth century, see Mercedes Galán Lorda, "Ordenanzas del Cabildo de México sobre abastos en el siglo XVIII," *Anuario de historia del derecho español* 67 (1997); Carmen Losa Contreras, "La justicia capitular de la Nueva España en el siglo XVIII. El tribunal de fiel ejecutoría de la ciudad de México," *Cuadernos de Historia del Derecho* 5 (1998).
92. The Spanish term for this body was *mesa de propios*.
93. The Spanish word for these vendors was *mesilleros*. The orders were issued on May 5 and 14, 1609, copied in AHCM Ayuntamiento: Hacienda 2230 exp.12 f.17v–21 (1609); the May 14 order is also in AHCM Ayuntamiento: Mercados 3728 exp.1 (1609).
94. Royal decree, January 18, 1611, copied in AHCM Ayuntamiento: Hacienda 2230 exp.12 f.17v–21 (1609).
95. July 6, 1620; Ciudad de México, 1906, 23: Mayo 1619–Diciembre 1620: 182.

96. Ibid.
97. September 5, 1625; Ibid., 25: Marzo 1623–Diciembre 1625: 27.
98. Ibid.
99. The Spanish word for lean-tos was *jacal* from *xacalli* in Nahuatl.
100. AGI México 1684 (1646).
101. Viceroy Francisco Fernández de la Cueva was the Duke of Alburquerque, the Marquess of Cuéllar, and the Count of Ledesma and of Huelma.
102. Gregorio Martín de Guijo, *Diario, 1648–1664*, 2 vols., vol. 2: 1655–1664 (México: Porrúa, 1953), 112.
103. Ibid., 113.
104. Ibid.
105. Ibid.
106. April 9, 1601; Cabildo Ciudad de México, ed., *Actas de Cabildo*, vol. 14: Octubre 1599–Febrero 1602 (México: Aguilar e hijos, 1899), 236.
107. Ibid.
108. Ibid.
109. Ibid.
110. AGN Indios 9 exp.44 f.25 (1617).
111. AGN Ord 4 exp.3 f.2v–6v (1619). An abbreviated copy of the August 17, 1619 *Ordenanzas de bastimientos* is in Juan Francisco de Montemayor de Cuenca, "Recopilacion de algunos mandamientos y ordenanzas del gobierno de esta Nueva España ... año de 1677," in *Recopilacion sumaria de todos los autos acordados de la Real Audiencia y Sala del Crimen de esta Nueva España, y providencias de su superior Gobierno*, ed. Eusebio Bentura Beleña (México: Felipe de Zúñiga y Ontiveros, 1787), 5–9.
112. Clause 2, AGN Ord 4 exp.3 (1619).
113. Clause 3, AGN Ord 4 exp.3 (1619).
114. Clause 5, AGN Ord 4 exp.3 (1619).
115. Clause 4, AGN Ord 4 exp.3 (1619).
116. Clause 6, AGN Ord 4 exp.3 (1619).
117. AGN GP 5 exp.1266 f.274v (1600).
118. Clause 2, AGN Ord 4 exp.3 (1619).
119. Ibid.
120. AGN Inq 306 exp.5 fs.15 (1619).
121. Grain sold at the exchange (*alhóndiga*) and was stored at the granary or main deposit (*pósito*). Grain exchange and granary officials worked together in the same building, so the documentation often conflates them. A short overview of the grain exchange is Chester L. Guthrie, "A Seventeenth Century "Ever-Normal Granary": The *Alhóndiga* of Colonial Mexico City," *Agricultural History* 15, no. 1 (1941). An informative article that suffers from conflating sources from the late sixteenth to early nineteenth centuries is Irene Vásquez de Warman, "El pósito y la alhóndiga en la Nueva España," *Historia Mexicana* 17, no. 3 (1968). See also Pazos, 1999, 158–168.
122. City hall began overseeing grain sales in 1537, leading to the construction of a grain-measuring station (*peso de harina*) in Tacuba. The grain exchange and granary occupied different buildings near the center until they moved to refurbished spaces at city hall before 1620. The institution's

eighteenth-century incarnation is at today's *Calle Alhóndiga*; see José María Marroqui, *La ciudad de México*, 3 vols., vol. 1 (México: Tip. y lit. La Europea, 1900), 282–301.

123. The mandate that grain suppliers only sell at the grain exchange did not apply to Indigenous farmers, who retained the privilege of selling maize directly to consumers at the price of their choosing. Indigenous vassals could pay taxes (tribute) in maize (collected at the granary), and they could also sell maize at the exchange, but were not obliged to do so.

124. The Granary Section of the Laws of the Indies consists of nineteen laws; eighteen of them are based on the Ordinances for the Granary of Mexico City confirmed in 1581 by Viceroy Lorenzo Suárez de Mendoza, the 4th Count of La Coruña; see Royal confirmation, March 31, 1583, book 4, title 14 of the *Laws of the Indies*.

125. The quote is from book 4, title 14, law 1 of the *Laws of the Indies*.

126. Tenochtitlan once had a granary (*petlacalco*) that kept years-worth supplies of dried maize and seeds. It is described in book 8, chapter 18 of the *Florentine Codex*, an encyclopedia of Indigenous knowledge and a history of the Mexica compiled in the sixteenth century; see Bernardino de Sahagún, *Historia general de las cosas de Nueva España*, 3 vols., vol. 2 (México Alejandro Valdés, 1829), 306–307; Kevin Terraciano, "Introduction: An Encyclopedia of Nahua Culture, Context and Content," in *The Florentine Codex : An Encyclopedia of the Nahua World in Sixteenth-Century Mexico,* ed. Jeanette Favrot Peterson, et al. (Austin: University of Texas Press, 2019).

127. Blom argues that cities with a culture of trade, which could acquire goods and provisions from long distances, gained economic importance during the seventeenth century, in contrast to rural areas devastated by famines brought on by harvest failures associated with colder temperatures. Philipp Blom, *Nature's Mutiny: How the Little Ice Age of the Long Seventeenth Century Transformed the West and Shaped the Present* (New York: W. W. Norton, 2017).

128. Montemayor de Cuenca, 1787. Viceroy Payo Enríquez de Rivera Manrique, O.S.A. was the Archbishop of Mexico.

129. Connell argues that Indigenous leaders remained involved in the management of Indigenous markets at least until the 1640s. A case involving an Indigenous fruit importer shows that the Indigenous government controlled access to the markets; see Connell, 2011, 130–132. His findings modify Gibson, who posited that the "regulation of markets and supplies had fallen wholly to Spaniards" (meaning city hall) by the late sixteenth century; see Gibson, 1964, 395.

130. Chimalpahin Cuauhtlehuanitzin, 2006, 101.

131. Ibid.

132. Vázquez de Espinosa, 1948, 146. Tonatlan or Tomatlan was in the Indigenous district of San Sebastián Atzaqualco, located on the north-eastern part of the city.

133. For this history, see Louisa S. Hoberman, "Bureaucracy and Disaster: Mexico City and the Flood of 1629," *Journal of Latin American Studies* 6,

no. 2 (1974); Richard E. Boyer, *La gran inundación: vida y sociedad en México, 1629–1638* (México: Secretaría de Educación Pública, 1975).

134. Cepeda and Carrillo, 1637 f.1. A resident reported that the city resembled "a cadaver" after the 1629 flood, and that only "3,000" of the "7,700" great homes survived the rains; he celebrated, at the same time, that the city was not "destroyed" and had instead rebuilt more "richly" and "majestically" than before; see Medina, 1682, f.234v.

135. AGN Indios 12 exp.236 f.148 (1635).

136. For Indigenous women's legal agency, see Susan Kellogg, "From Parallel and Equivalent to Separate but Unequal: Tenochca Mexica Women, 1500–1700," in *Indian Women of Early Mexico*, ed. Susan Schroeder, et al. (Norman: University of Oklahoma Press, 1997); Lisa Sousa, "Rebellious Women," in *The Woman Who Turned Into a Jaguar, and Other Narratives of Native Women in Archives of Colonial Mexico* (Stanford: Stanford University Press, 2017).

137. Clause 3, AGN Ord 4 exp.3 (1619).

138. AGN Indios 11, exp.449 f.354 (1639).

139. Viceroy Lope Díez de Aux de Armendáriz was the Marquess of Cadreita.

140. AGN Indios 11, exp.449 f.354 (1639).

141. AGN Indios 13 exp.226 and 227 f.200–201v (1641).

142. AGN Indios 12 exp.68 f.199 (1640).

143. The couple belonged to the polity of Tlatelolco; AGN Indios 12 exp.119 f.236 (1640).

144. Guijo, 1953, 2: 114.

145. Ibid.

146. Ibid.

147. AGN Indios 29 exp.81 f.80–80v (1685).

148. Ibid.

149. Ibid.

150. Ibid.

151. Ibid.

152. For the eighteenth century, see Margarita R. Ochoa, "Doña Marcela and the *Cacicas* of Bourbon Mexico City: Family, Community, and Indigenous Rule," in *Cacicas: The Indigenous Women Leaders of Spanish America, 1492–1825*, eds., Margarita R. Ochoa, et al. (Norman: University of Oklahoma Press, 2021).

153. The markets were held at alternating locations: Mondays at San Pablo Teopan; Tuesdays at San Sebastián Atzaqualco; Wednesdays at Santa María Cuepopan; Thursdays in San Juan Moyotlan at the square of the Franciscan monastery of *San Diego de Alcalá* (across from the Church of Hippolytus); Fridays and Saturdays at the Main Square. AGN Indios 32 exp.68 f.72v–74 (1692).

154. An overview of African-descended women's work in this sector in an Atlantic context is Ana Lucia Araujo, "Women Who Fed the City," in *Humans in Shackles: An Atlantic History of Slavery* (Chicago: University of Chicago Press, 2024).

155. AGN TSJ 171 exp.5669 fs.4 (1625).

156. Viceroy Juan de Mendoza y Luna was the Marquess of Montesclaros.
157. Manuel Sánchez was "originally from the Philippine Islands"; AGN RCD 5 exp.38 f.9v (1606).
158. Ibid.
159. AGN RCD 5 exp.289 f.74 (1606).
160. Clause 2, AGN Ord 4 exp.3 (1619).
161. Viceroy García Sarmiento de Sotomayor was the Count of Salvatierra and the Marquess of Sobroso.
162. AGN RCD 35 exp.273 f.237v (1644).
163. AGN TSJ 11 exp.476 fs.2 (1644); ANM J. P. Rivera Cáceres (630) 4366 f.144–144v (1644).
164. The load cost 300 pesos. Martín paid him with property valued at that amount: eight mules and an unnamed enslaved man. Martín made easy comparisons between the value of enslaved people, animals of burden, and fruit when he calculated commodity prices. ANM J. P. Rivera Cáceres (630) 4366 f.144–144v (1644).
165. Guijo, 1953, 1: 4.
166. Ibid.
167. Ibid.
168. The Spanish word for poulterer or poultry vendor was *gallinero*. Entry for gallineros; Covarrubias Horozco, 1673, 23.
169. The hospital's name was *Hospital de la Inmaculada Concepción de Nuestra Señora y de Jesús Nazareno*; AGN GP 5 exp.1213 f.262v (1600).
170. AGN GP 5 exp.1213 f.262v (1600).
171. Ibid.
172. See, for example, AGN GP 5 exp.396 f.87v, exp.414 f.90v, and exp.446 f.95v (1599); AGN GP 5 exp.1207 f.250, exp.1266 f.265 (1600); AGN GP 5 exp.1334 f.283 (1601).
173. The scribe categorized Bañon as a free man of African descent; AGN GP 6 exp.837 f.301 (1603).
174. Ibid.
175. AGN Ord 1 exp.21 f.30v–31 (1579).
176. AGN IndV 6552 exp.58 fs.1 (1614).
177. ANM J. Pérez Rivera (497) 3357 f.67–67v (1636). The ethnonym/region designation is associated with Upper Guinea in West Africa; Seijas and Sierra Silva, 2016; Toby Green, "Beyond an Imperial Atlantic: Trajectories of Africans from Upper Guinea and West-Central Africa in the Early Atlantic World," *Past & Present* 230, no.1 (2016). For a discussion of the ethnolinguistic term Biafada in Spanish sources, see David Wheat, "Biafadas in Havana: West African Antecedents for Caribbean Social Interactions," in *The Spanish Caribbean and the Atlantic World in the Long Sixteenth Century*, eds., Ida Altman, et al. (2019).
178. ANM J. Pérez Rivera (497) 3357 f.67–67v (1636).
179. Ibid.
180. Ibid.
181. The price of hens rose to seven reals in mid November 1692. Robles noted that "they were extremely expensive," same as bread; food prices

had remained high since the bread riot in June; Antonio de Robles, *Diario de sucesos notables, 1665–1703*, 3 vols., vol. 2 (México: Porrúa, 1946), 276.

182. The scribe categorized Gutiérrez as an Asian-descended person and her unnamed father a "freed man"; ANM J. Veedor (685) 4595 f.782v–783 (1636). Domestic workers arranged personal service agreements (*escritura de servicio*), which documented the conditions of their employment.

183. Gutiérrez had "to clothe herself"; ANM J. Veedor (685) 4595 f.782v–783 (1636).

184. The scribe categorized Gracia as an African-descended person; AGN Mat 7 exp.68 f.231–233 (1634).

185. The scribe categorized Francisco as an Asian-descended person; AGN Mat 183 exp.80 fs.2 (1637).

186. ANM M. Sariñana (629) 4362 f.25v–26v (1646).

187. Ibid.

188. The phrase "as a good deed" was common in loan contracts; the documents usually noted an additional cost, which referenced the hidden interest due when the loan matured. The phrasing circumvented dictates against usury.

189. ANM M. Sariñana (629) 4362 f.25v–26v (1646).

190. Guijo, 1953, 1: 229.

191. Ibid.

192. Clause 10, AGN Ord 4 exp.3 (1619).

193. Guijo, 1953, 1: 229.

194. AGN Inq 422 exp.4 f.351–367 (1646).

195. Vetancurt, 1697, 3.

196. Ibid.

197. Residents called it the place of the food stands (*lugar de los bodegones*). December 14, 1601; Ciudad de México, 1899, 14: Octubre 1599–Febrero 1602: 332.

198. Atole is from *atolli* in Nahuatl; the Spanish word for sweet fritters is *buñuelos*.

199. Gemelli Careri, 1704, 4, 528.

200. Cervantes de Salazar, 1914, 14–15.

201. AGN Ord 1 exp.95 f.91 (1585); AGN Ord 2 exp.324 f.282 (1585).

202. ANM J. Pérez Rivera 3360 (497) f.293v (1615).

203. The Spanish word for these vessels was *pipa*.

204. A woman's dowry, for example, remained her property after marriage.

205. ANM J. Veedor (685) 4595 f.278–278v (1635).

206. The Spanish words for these snacks were *pasteles* and *empanadas*.

207. Entry for *pastel*; Covarrubias Horozco, 1673, f.135.

208. ANM J. Veedor (685) 4595 f.278–278v (1635). Esteban de Acuña lent money to at least two people in years prior, neither were formerly enslaved nor required to have a guarantor. ANM J. Pérez Rivera 3362 (497) f.356–356v (1626); ANM J. Pérez Rivera 3362BIS (497) f.300v (1633).

209. Robles, 1946, 2, 112, 255.

210. The quote is from an eyewitness account; Sigüenza y Góngora, 1932, 36.

211. AHCM Ayuntamiento: Mercados 3728 exp.2 f.19 (1693).

212. AGN Indios 32 exp.68 f.72v–74 (1692). Viceroy Gaspar Melchor Baltasar de la Cerda Silva Sandoval y Mendoza was the Count of Galve and the Lord of Salcedón and Tortola.

213. The viceroy had recently asked for an account of the boundaries of the Indigenous neighborhoods for this purpose; AGN Indios 32 exp.44 f.47–47v (1692). Documentation regarding the plans to remove Native people from the center is in AGN Historia 413 exp.1 fs.74 (1692), and partially transcribed in "Sobre los inconvenientes de vivir los indios en el centro de la ciudad," 1938.

214. For this effort, called the "extirpation of the baratillo," see Andrew Konove, "A Pernicious Commmerce," in *Black Market Capital: Urban Politics and the Shadow Economy in Mexico City* (Oakland: University of California Press, 2018).

215. AHCM Ayuntamiento: Mercados 3728 exp.2 f.19–20 (1693).

216. AGN GP 17 exp.182 f.192–192v (1696); copy in AHCM Ayuntamiento: Mercados 3728 exp.4 f.106–09 (1696).

217. AGN GP 17 exp.182 f.192–192v (1696).

218. Robles, 1946, 3, 41.

219. AGN GP 17 exp.182 f.192–192v (1696).

220. Ibid.

221. Ibid.; AGN RCO 28 exp.11 f.24 (1698).

222. Villalpando, born in Mexico City circa 1649, became one of the most celebrated and commissioned painters of his generation. Art historical analyses of this painting include: Ivan Escamilla González and Paula Mues Orts, "Espacio real, espacio pictórico y poder: *Vista de la Plaza Mayor de México* de Cristóbal de Villalpando," in *La imagen política*, ed., Cuauhtémoc Medina (México: UNAM, 2006), 177–204; Schreffler, 2007. See too: Lombardo de Ruiz, Terán Trillo, and Torre, 1996, 2: 24–25; Francisco de la Maza, *El pintor Cristóbal de Villalpando* (México: INAH, 1964), 159–176. For this painter's life and work, see Juana Gutiérrez Haces, *Cristóbal de Villalpando: ca. 1649–1714. Catálogo razonado*, (México: CONACULTA, BANAMEX, 1997).

223. Maza, 1964, 159–160.

## 2  TRANSPORTING THE CITY

1. AGI Contaduría 5422 N.34 f.18 (1640). For the fleet's journey, see Mervyn F. Lang, *Las flotas de la Nueva España (1630–1710). Despacho, azogue, comercio*, (Sevilla: Muñoz Moya, 1988), 129–131.

2. An art historical analysis of the viceroy's household is Nelly Sigaut, "Al servicio del virrey de España en el siglo XVII" in *Arte y vida cotidiana en el Mundo Hispánico. Entre lo sacro y lo profano*, ed., Paula Revenga Domínguez (Michoacán: Colegio de Michoacán, 2017).

3. The viceroy's chaplain wrote a description of the journey; Gutiérrez de Medina, 1947, 44–45. For context on viceroys' entrances, see Steven G. Flinchpaugh, "Economic Aspects of the Viceregal Entrance in Mexico City," *The Americas* 52, no. 3 (1996).

4.  The mountain range is the *Sierra Madre Oriental.*

5.  Gutiérrez de Medina, 1947, 56.

6.  For the history of coachmen in seventeenth-century Puebla, see Pablo Miguel Sierra Silva, "Life in the Big City: Mobility, Social Networks and Family," in *Urban Slavery in Colonial Mexico: Puebla de los Ángeles, 1531–1706* (New York: Cambridge University Press, 2018).

7.  Gutiérrez de Medina, 1947, 71. Otompan, Otumba in Spanish, was a city-state where Spanish soldiers and colonists retreated during the Spanish-Aztec War (1519–1521) and won a battle against Mexica soldiers, which made it symbolically significant for Hapsburg officials.

8.  Ibid., 73.

9.  Ibid., 74–75.

10.  Ibid., 79.

11.  Ibid., 84.

12.  Auto issued by High Court, August 21, 1621; Montemayor de Cuenca, 1787, 77. Several mandates regarding coaches are in: Manuel B. Trens, "Los coches en la ciudad de México," *Boletín del Archivo General de la Nación* XXV, no.4 (1954). Schreffler suggests that one of the two figures inside the carriage is meant to represent a viceroy; Schreffler, 2007, 21.

13.  Postilions guide carriages on horseback or mounted on mules, while coachmen control the animals from their seat in the vehicle. The term used in Spanish for walking drivers was *viandantes*; they worked with postilions and coachmen to guide the animals.

14.  The Spanish term for coachmen was *cocheros*. They drove carriages, called *carrozas* or coaches (*coches*). A coach was an enclosed four-wheeled vehicle for passengers drawn by horses or mules. Carriage makers (*carroceros*) made and repaired these vehicles. These artisans were sometimes called cocheros, such as Alonso López, described as a carrocero and cochero, so these individuals may have provided transport services on the side; AGN TSJ 4 exp.153 3fs (1625). A cochero was nearly always a man who drove a carriage. For the history of carriage makers, mainly for the eighteenth century, see Alvaro Recio Mir, *El arte de la carrocería en Nueva España. El gremio de la ciudad de México, sus ordenanzas y la trascendencia social del coche* (Seville: Universidad de Sevilla, 2018).

15.  One-wheeled carts were called *carretones*. Carts with two wheels and a rotating axis were called *carretas* or *chirriones*, and their drivers *chirrioneros*. This term chirrionero was also used in the sixteenth century for wagoners who traveled long distances; the term *carreteros* became more common during the seventeenth century.

16.  Chimalpahin evoked the sound of carts to describe the reverberation of an earthquake's aftershock in August 1611; Chimalpahin Cuauhtlehuanitzin, 2006, 191.

17.  The Spanish word for water carriers was *aguadores*.

18.  Torquemada, 1615, 320.

19.  Ibid.

20.  Muleteers (called *muleros* and *arrieros*) guided mule trains (*recuas*), which were a group of mules that carried goods and people or pulled transport vehicles. For the history of long-distance muleteers, see Richard E. Boyer, "Juan

Vázquez: Muleteer of Seventeenth Century Mexico," *The Americas* 37, no. 4 (1981); Bernd Hausberger, "En el camino, en busca de los arrieros novohispanos," *Historia Mexicana* 64, no. 1 (2014). For the sixteenth century, see Ivonne Mijares, "La mula en la vida cotidiana del siglo XVI," eds., Janet Long Towell, et al. (México: UNAM; INAH, 2009). For the eighteenth century, see Clara Elena Suárez Argüello, "Los arrieros novohispanos," in *Trabajo y sociedad en la historia de México: siglos XVI–XVIII*, eds., Gloria Artís, et al. (México: CIESAS, 1992); *Camino real y carrera larga: la arriería en la Nueva España durante el siglo XVIII* (México: CIESAS, 1997); José Adrián Barragán-Álvarez, "The Feet of Commerce: Mule-trains and Transportation in Eighteenth-Century New Spain" (PhD, University of Texas at Austin, 2013). Wagoners drove wagons, called *coches* and *carretas*, which were four-wheel vehicles pulled by draft animals. The common use of carros, coches, and carretas to describe vehicles involved in long-distance transportation demonstrates that different types of vehicles traveled in any one envoy.

21. The Spanish word for carrying was *acarrear*; Covarrubias Horozco, 1674, f.6.
22. The word acarrear is related to *trajinar*; 1673, f.193.
23. Torquemada, 1615, 320.
24. Ibid., 320, 328–329.
25. Vetancurt, 1697, 1.
26. Ibid. An environmental and ethnohistorical study of Indigenous canoers and their role in the commercial integration of the lakes is Richard M. Conway, "Lakes, Canoes, and the Aquatic Communities of Xochimilco and Chalco, New Spain," *Ethnohistory* 59, no. 3 (2012). See also Conway, 2021.
27. Diego de Cisneros, *Sitio, natvraleza y propriedades de la civdad de Mexico* (Mexíco: Blanco de Alcaçar, 1618), f.110.
28. Vetancurt, 1697, 1, 3.
29. An overview of officials involved in large public works is Roberto Llanas y Fernández, "Siglo XVII," in *Ingeniería en México, 400 años de historia. Obra pública en la ciudad de México* (México: UNAM, 2012).
30. Vázquez de Espinosa, 1948, 435.
31. Gemelli Careri, 1704, 4, 508.
32. The name in Spanish was *Albarradón de San Lazaro.*
33. Cepeda and Carrillo, 1637 f.4.
34. Ibid.
35. Margarita Carballal Staedtler and María Flores Hernández, "Hydraulic Features of the Mexico-Texcoco Lakes during the Postclassic Period," in *Precolumbian Water Management: Ideology, Ritual, and Power*, eds., Lisa J. Lucero, et al. (Tucson: University of Arizona Press, 2006), 164.
36. Cepeda and Carrillo, 1637 f.10.
37. AGI México 260 N.51 (1622).
38. Castro lived in the parish of Saint Catherine Martyr; AGN MatC 392A exp.11 (1612).
39. Torquemada, 1615, 329.
40. See, for example: AGN RCD 5 exp. 349 f.88v (1606); AGN Civil 1271 f.108 (1614).

41. Gage, 1648, 59. Today this route changes names as it crosses the city; staring at the *zócalo*, it is: *Calle Tacuba, Avenida Hidalgo, Avenida Puente de Alvarado, Avenida Ribera de San Cosme*, and *Calzada México-Tacuba*.

42. Cabildo Ciudad de México, ed., *Actas de Cabildo*, vol. 4: Enero 1536–Agosto 1543 (México: Municipio Libre, 1889).

43. Royal decree, August 16, 1563; codified as book 4, title 16, law 1 of the *Laws of the Indies*.

44. The crown empowered viceroys to order the construction of bridges and distribute the costs; Royal decree, July 19, 1614; reissued on February 18, 1628; codified as book 3, title 3, law 53 of the *Laws of the Indies*.

45. AGN GP 5 exp.1081f.224–224v (1600).

46. Ibid.

47. Ibid.

48. AGN Ord 1 exp.97 f.92–93v (1585).

49. August 23, 1568: Cabildo Ciudad de México, ed., *Actas de Cabildo*, vol. 7: Enero 1562–Octubre 1571 (México: 1889), 49.

50. Ibid. Council members discussed the dangers once again on November 22, 1677: Cabildo Ciudad de México, ed., *Actas de Cabildo*, vol. 8: Octubre 1571–Diciembre 1584 (México: Agular e Hijos, 1893), 306.

51. AGN Ord 1 exp.97 f.92–93v (1585).

52. Ibid.

53. Ibid.

54. Ibid.

55. November (between 8 and 15), 1591: Cabildo Ciudad de México, ed., *Actas de Cabildo*, vol. 10: Mayo 1590–Junio 1592 (México: Aguilar e hijos, 1896), 118.

56. Ibid. Council members recanted an exemption that allowed the entry of "large carts pulled by two mules or two oxen" from September 20, 1591: Ibid., 105–106.

57. Men who owned large transport businesses were called *dueños de carros*.

58. City hall had planned to construct three new dockyards at the causeways in 1568 to facilitate unloading and embarking, but one of them was still being planned in 1593; August 23, 1568: Ciudad de México, 1889, 7: Enero 1562–Octubre 1571: 49. July 30, 1593: Cabildo Ciudad de México, ed. *Actas de Cabildo*, vol. 11: Junio 1592–Diciembre 1593 (México: Aguilar e hijos, 1897), 154.

59. March 16, 1527: Ciudad de México, 1889, 1: Marzo 1524–Junio 1529: 126.

60. AGN RCD 46 exp.46 f.118–118v (1584).

61. Viceroy Pedro de Moya y Contreras was the Archbishop of Mexico.

62. High Court resolution, November 26, 1576; Montemayor de Cuenca, 1787, 8.

63. "Throwing garbage or anything else into the canals" was also prohibited; AGN Ord 2 exp.325 f.282v–283 (1585).

64. An ordinance regarding garbage from September 27, 1591 encouraged residents to report their neighbors; Juan Francisco del Barrio Lorenzot, ed., *Ordenanzas de Gremios de la Nueva España* (México: Secretaría de Gobernación, 1920), 272–273.

65. July 11, 1586; Cabildo Ciudad de México, ed., *Actas de Cabildo*, vol. 9: Enero 1585–Mayo 1590 (México: Aguilar e Hijos, 1895), 141.
66. Ibid., 142.
67. A collection of documents from 1555 to 1563 list the onerous labor demands made on Indigenous residents by the viceroy for public works. There is repeated mention, for example, of the delivery of stones called *tenayucas*; see Luis Chávez Orozco, ed., *Códice Osuna. Reproducción facsimilar de la obra* (México: Instituto Indigenista Interamericano, 1947). The term references the town of Tenayuca, once located on the shore of Lake Texcoco, near a river known for stones used in construction as late as the eighteenth century; see Joseph Antonio de Villa-señor y Sánchez, *Theatro americano. Descripcion general de los reynos, y provincias de la Nueva-España, y sus jurisdicciones,* 2 vols., vol. 1 (México: Viuda de Don J. Bernardo de Hogal, 1746), 76.
68. The *repartimiento* (meaning distribution or apportionment) was a labor draft instituted in the sixteenth century to secure Indigenous men on a rotational basis (by community) to labor in projects deemed to be in the public interest. It was reformed in the early 1600s and formally abolished in 1632 (with the exception of mining in certain areas and the hydraulics project in the Central Valley). See Gibson, 1964, 119–120, 224–236, 250–251. A study of draft-labor salaries is Sander Spanoghe, "Los salarios dentro del sistema del repartimiento forzoso en el Valle de México, 1549–1632," *Anuario de Estudios Americanos* 54, no. 1 (1997).
69. Chimalpahin Cuauhtlehuanitzin, 2006, 29.
70. It took the whole month of May in 1590, for instance, to clean the canals. Ibid., 35.
71. December 19, 1586; Ciudad de México, 1895, 9: Enero 1585–Mayo 1590: 177.
72. A study on the perception of filth and smells by the city's Indigenous residents during the sixteenth century is Barbara E. Mundy, "The Smellscape of Mexico City, 1500–1600," *Ethnohistory* 68, no. 1 (2021).
73. June 14, 1588; Ciudad de México, 1895, 9: Enero 1585–Mayo 1590: 272.
74. In addition, the ordinance gave residents with empty lots four months to build protective walls to prevent them from becoming dumps; Ibid., 285–286.
75. Ibid., 222.
76. Ibid., 349, 398.
77. November 9, 1590; Ciudad de México, 1896, 10: Mayo 1590–Junio 1592: 25.
78. November 12, 1590; Ibid.
79. Ibid., 25–26.
80. August 26, 1591; Ibid., 101–102.
81. April 10, 1592; Ibid., 170–171.
82. February 12, 1598; Cabildo Ciudad de México, ed., *Actas de Cabildo*, vol. 13: Mayo 1597–Octubre 1599 (México: Aguilar e hijos, 1898), 122–123.
83. Chimalpahin Cuauhtlehuanitzin, 2006, 61. For the epidemic, see Gibson, 1964, 449.
84. March 13, 1597; Cabildo Ciudad de México, ed., *Actas de Cabildo*, vol. 12: Enero 1594–Mayo 1597 (México: Aguilar e Hijos, 1898), 372.
85. March 13, 1597; Ibid.

86. February 12, 1598; Ciudad de México, 1898, 13: Mayo 1597–Octubre 1599: 122–123.
87. Drought and early freezes made for bad harvests in 1597, which resulted in wheat and maize shortages in 1598; the price of maize nearly doubled; Gibson, 1964, 453.
88. AGN GP 5 exp.994 f.207v (1600).
89. AGN GP 5 exp.902 f.190 (1600).
90. Three years later, Hidalgo complained once again that Indigenous workers, especially those he had hired previously, refused to work for him; AGN GP 6 exp.402 f.152 (1603).
91. The ordinances are divided into seventeen clauses or chapters; AGN Ord 1 exp.159 and exp.160 f.143v–145v (1612).
92. The Spanish word for public order was *policía*. The historiography has focused on aspects of public order related to security and law enforcement, rather than on sanitation or infrastructure. See Jorge Nacif Mina, *La policía en la historia de la ciudad de México (1524–1928)* (México: Departamento del Distrito Federal, 1986); Regina Hernández Franyuti, "Historia y significado de la palabra policía en el quehacer político de la ciudad de México, siglos XVI–XIX," *Ulúa: Revista de Historia, Sociedad y Cultura* 5 (2005); Guadalupe de la Torre Villalpando, "Bandos para el buen gobierno de la ciudad de México virreinal," *Boletín del Archivo General de la Nación* 9, no. 4 (2020). The rise of police departments in the modern sense is an eighteenth-century phenomenon; see Nicole von Germeten, *The Enlightened Patrolman: Early Law Enforcement in Mexico City* (Lincoln: University of Nebraska Press, 2022).
93. Covarrubias Horozco, 1673, f.145.
94. Covarrubias Horozco, 1674, f.47.
95. The Spanish name for this body was *Junta de Policía*. The viceroy appointed three board members, choosing a judge from the High Court, a city hall councilor, and another resident deemed knowledgeable about the city's affairs; they were supposed to meet every Wednesday afternoon. AGN Ord 1 exp.159 f.143v–145v (1612).
96. Clause 5; AGN Ord 1 exp.159 f.143v–145v (1612).
97. October 29, 1635; Cabildo Ciudad de México, ed., *Actas de Cabildo*, vol. 30: Abril 1635–Diciembre 1636 (México: Carranza y Comp., 1908), 68–69.
98. August 1, 1636; Ibid., 170, 220.
99. Gonzalo de la Cruz was categorized as an Asian-descended person in the criminal report; AGN Criminal 187 exp.19 f.289–295v (1643).
100. The three men belonged to the P'urhépecha nation (also spelled *Purépecha*); these people have also been called Tarascans (*Tarascos*). Sebastián de Abellada, Pedro Tzizi, and Juan Tarheni were from San Lucas Tiquicheo (now Tiquicheo de Nicolás Romero).
101. AGN Criminal 187 exp.19 f.289–295v (1643).
102. Ibid.
103. Andrés Pérez de las Mariñas (also spelled Marinas).
104. Viceroy Antonio Sebastián de Toledo Molina y Salazar was the Marquess of Mancera.

105. Letter from October 26, 1669; AGI México 319 [no foliation] (1669).
106. Giovanni Francesco Gemelli Careri, *Giro del mondo*, 6 vols., vol. 6: Nvova Spagna (Napoli: Guiseppe Roselli, 1699), 221.
107. Covarrubias Horozco, 1674, f.232v.
108. Clause 13; AGN Ord 1 exp.159 f.143v–145v (1612).
109. Ibid.
110. Gage, 1648, 56.
111. The average value, in property declarations from the early 1620s, of one carriage and two mules was 800 pesos; AGI México 260 N. 46, 99, 128, 149 (1622). Property records such as dowry agreements indicate a carriage alone could fetch 800 pesos or more; see, for example, ANM J. Pérez Rivera (497) 3363 f.123v (1624). The valuations for ornate carriages remained in that range throughout the century. A carriage that "had a green exterior, a deep yellow interior with bronze tacks, and silk upholstery" and came with handsome white mules, sold for 320 pesos at auction. ANM J. Pérez Rivera (497) 3362 f.426–427 (1631).
112. January 28, 1626; Cabildo Ciudad de México, ed., *Actas de Cabildo*, vol. 26: Enero 1626–Noviembre 1628 (México: El Correo Español, 1907), 214.
113. Archbishop Francisco Manso estimated there were 20,000 "familias españolas" in Mexico City prior to the 1629 flood; González Dávila, 1649, 1, f.61.
114. Clause 12; AGN Ord 1 exp.159 f.143v–145v (1612).
115. AGN BN 140 exp. 54 fs.1 (1636); the street is now called *20 de Noviembre*.
116. January 30, 1626, Ciudad de México, 1907, 26: Enero 1626–Noviembre 1628: 20–21.
117. The Ordinances for Public Order were confirmed in 1663, 1677, and 1683. The resolution from December 10, 1663 is referenced in Montemayor de Cuenca, 1787, 80–81. The 1612 Ordinances were incorporated into the Compilation of Mandates and Ordinances for Government collected for Viceroy Enríquez de Rivera in 1677; *Recopilacion sumaria de todos los autos acordados de la Real Audiencia y Sala del Crimen de esta Nueva España, y providencias de su superior Gobierno*, ed., Eusebio Bentura Beleña (México: Felipe de Zúñiga y Ontiveros, 1787), 95–99. The Ordinances for the Government of the Noble City of Mexico, approved by Viceroy Tomás Antonio Manuel Lorenzo de la Cerda y Aragón on March 27, 1683, confirmed the responsibilities of the Public Order Board, with the addition of one member from city hall; a summary is in Barrio Lorenzot, 1920, 197–198. The viceroy was the Count of Paredes and Marquess of La Laguna de Camero Viejo.
118. José María Marroqui, *La ciudad de México*, 3 vols., vol. 2 (México: Tip. y lit. La Europea, 1900), 306–321.
119. AGN RCD 3 exp.51 f.102 (1592). September 25, 1579; Ciudad de México, 1893, 8: Octubre 1571–Diciembre 1584: 401. Viceroy Luis de Velasco y Castilla was the Marquess of Salinas. His father Luis de Velasco y Ruiz de Alarcón was also Viceroy of New Spain, so the son was Viceroy Velasco II.
120. AGN Ord 1 exp.97 f.92–93v (1585).
121. The established limit was the "the bridge located between Saint Anne and Saint Catherine," which was a stone bridge that went over the Tezontle Canal; AGN Ord 1 exp.97 f.92–93v (1585).

122. AGN GP 5 exp.1096 f.232v (1600).
123. The Spanish word is *corral*. The parking corrals differed from stables (*caballerizas*) found in large homes for the pack animals of the household.
124. AGN GP 5 exp.1217 f.254v–255 (1600). The church, now called *Santa Ana Atenantitech*, began as a small chapel, an *ermita*, prior to 1555; Candy E. Ornelas Méndez, *Inventario del Archivo Parroquial de Santa Ana Atenantitech, ciudad de México* (México: ADABI, 2019), 7–9.
125. AGN GP 5 exp.1217 f.254v–255 (1600).
126. AGN GP 5 exp.1321 f.279–279v (1601).
127. Ibid.
128. AGN GP 5 exp.1355 f.289v–290 (1601).
129. AGN GP 5 exp.1431 f.313v (1601).
130. Diego Ortíz who used two-wheeled carts (*chirriones*) opened his own small corral within days of Luna; AGN GP 5 exp.1366 f.292–292v (1601).
131. AGN GP 5 exp.1318 f.278v (1601).
132. AGN Inq 284 exp.44 f.618–621v (1609). The construction of the church, now called *Parroquia de Santa Catarina Virgen y Mártir*, began in 1568, with an advocation for that saint; Candy E. Ornelas Méndez, *Inventario del Archivo Parroquial de Santa Catarina Virgen y Mártir, ciudad de México, Arquidiócesis de México* (México: ADABI, 2014), 11–15. It appears as *Santa Catharina Mártir* in seventeenth-century records.
133. AGN Inq 284 exp.44 f.618–618v (1609).
134. Ibid.
135. For the history of innkeepers and their relations with long- and short-distance transporters in another capital city, see J. A. Chartres, "The Capital's Provincial Eyes: London's Inns in the Early Eighteenth Century," *The London Journal* 3, no. 1 (1977).
136. AGN Inq 284 exp.44 f.620 (1609).
137. AGN Inq 284 exp.44 f.619–619v (1609).
138. For Nahua residents' district affiliation at this time, see Chimalpahin Cuauhtlehuanitzin, 2006, 115.
139. AGI México 260 N.13 (1622).
140. AGN RCD 5 exp.90 f.43–43v (1606).
141. AGN RCD 16 exp.272 f.139v (1620).
142. AGN TSJ 170 exp.5635 fs.17 (1624).
143. AGN Mat 98 exp.82 f.218–220 (1612).
144. One of his fellow merchants alone owed him over 28,000 pesos; AGN TSJ 170 exp.5635 fs.17 (1624).
145. AGN TSJ 169 exp.5596 fs.11 (1623).
146. AGN TSJ 330 exp.10229 fs.1 (1625).
147. October 22, 1619; Ciudad de México, 1906, 23: Mayo 1619–Diciembre 1620: 77.
148. Ibid.
149. Ibid.
150. Ibid. For city hall finances at this time, see Gibran Bautista y Lugo, "Recaudar la lealtad al rey y proteger el dinero del reino. La ciudad de México entre servicios, arbitrios y crédito, 1623-1629," in *Negociación,*

*lágrimas y maldiciones. La fiscalidad extraordinaria en la monarquía hispánica, 1620-1814*, ed. Guillermina del Valle Pavón (México: Instituto Mora, 2020).

151. November 4, 1619; Ibid., 82.

152. Ibid.

153. January 30, 1626; Ciudad de México, 1907, 26: Enero 1626–Noviembre 1628: 21–22.

154. August 6, 1635; Ciudad de México, 1908, 30: Abril 1635–Diciembre 1636: 40. The historiography of this event is in Chapter 1.

155. Cepeda and Carrillo, 1637 f.1.

156. Cobo, 1956, 2, 470.

157. August 6, 1635; Ciudad de México, 1908, 30: Abril 1635–Diciembre 1636: 40.

158. Ibid., 42.

159. Bernardo de la Cruz; AGN Ind 2306 exp.8 f.1–2 (1661).

160. AGN Inq 328 exp.45 f.309 (1619).

161. AGN Inq 328 exp.45 f.308 (1619).

162. A viceroyal ordinance from 1579, for example, instructed that people caught be castrated, pointing to the official assumption, based partly on numbers, that men were more likely to escape slaveowners than women; AGN Ord 2 exp.264 f.232–232v (1579). Archival records of people having been punished in this manner have yet to be found. It is unlikely that slaveowners pursued this allowance because the procedure on adult men had high mortality rates, risking, from slaveowners' perspective, their investment.

163. The coachman was one of thirteen enslaved people who lived in Altamirano's house; AGI México 260 exp.46 (1622); AGN TSJ 3, exp.125 (1624). When a slaveowner wrote her will and testament decades later, she listed Marcos and Pedro alongside her carriage and mules. ANM N. Arauz (5) 11 f.111v (1656).

164. Gage, 1648, 56.

165. The materials cost 90 pesos. Nicolás Patiño commissioned the vehicle from carriage maker Alonso López, who, like others, expected his clients to provide this type of decorative material; AGN TSJ 4 exp.153 3fs (1625). Another example is Alonso Gómez, a cloth merchant, who provided red cloth imported from Spain and green silk fringe to make the curtains for his carriage windows; AGN Ind 2306 exp.8 f.1–2 (1661).

166. Gage, 1648, 59.

167. AGN Historia 407 f.233 (1628).

168. AGN Inq 328 exp.45 f.307–312v (1619).

169. Royal decree, April 4, 1542; codified as book 7, title 5, law 12 of the *Laws of the Indies*. The decree banned African-descended people from the streets at night. Royal decree, November 19, 1551, reissued August 11, 1552, codified as book 7, title 5, law 15 of the *Laws of the Indies*. The decrees prohibited the use of arms except for the protection of slaveowners.

170. AGN RCD 3 exp.99 f.61v (1589).

171. AGN Ord 1 exp.164 f.146 (1612).

172. AGN Ord 1 exp.170 f.149 (1612).

173. AGN Ord 1 exp.178 f.152v (1612).

174. A primary source is a report printed in Luis Querol Roso, "Negros y mulatos de Nueva España (Historia de su alzamiento en Méjico en 1612)," *Anales de la Universidad de Valencia* 12 (1931): 141–153. See also Alfonso Reyes, "Sobre Mateo Rosas de Oquendo, poeta del siglo XVI," *Revista de Filología Española* 4, no. 4 (1917): 365–368; Chimalpahin Cuauhtlehuanitzin, 2006, 215–225. The historiography of the alleged revolt of 1612 includes: María Elena Martínez, "The Black Blood of New Spain: *Limpieza de Sangre*, Racial Violence, and Gendered Power in Early Colonial Mexico," *William and Mary Quarterly* 61, no. 3 (2004); Cristina Verónica Masferrer León, "Por las ánimas de negros bozales. Las cofradías de personas de origen africano en la ciudad de México (siglo xvii)," *Cuicuilco* 51, no.may-ago (2011); Miguel A. Valerio, "'Rebel Black Kings (and Queens)'?: Race, Colonial Psychosis, and Afro-Mexican Kings and Queens," in *Sovereign Joy: Afro-Mexican Kings and Queens, 1539–1640* (New York: Cambridge University Press, 2022). Valerio and Masferrer León discuss the events in relation to African-descended residents who established new brotherhoods and conserved existing ones after the 1612 ordinance prohibited them. For the history of African and African-descended confraternities, see Nicole von Germeten, *Black Blood Brothers: Confraternities and Social Mobility for Afro-Mexicans* (Gainesville: University Press of Florida, 2006). See also, Rafael Castañeda García and María Elisa Velázquez, "Introducción: Cofradías de "negros y mulatos" en la Nueva España," *Nuevo Mundo Mundos Nuevos* (2012); Sandra Nancy Luna García, "Espacios de convivencia y conflicto. Las cofradías de la población de origen africano en ciudad de México, siglo XVII," *Trashumante: Revista Americana de Historia Social* 10 (2017).
175. April 1, 1612; Chimalpahin Cuauhtlehuanitzin, 2006, 213.
176. Ibid., 215.
177. Querol Roso, 1931 147.
178. AGN Mat 216 exp.7 (1634).
179. AGI Contratación 5409 N.53 (1631).
180. ANM J. Pérez Rivera (497) 3357 f.73–74v (1637); AGN TSJ 174 exp.5836 (1637).
181. Rivas was from Santa Cecilia in Burgos; AGI Contratación 5358 N.3 f.23–31v (1617).
182. AGI México 74 R.3 N.59 (1622).
183. AGI Contratación 5358 N.3 f.27 (1617).
184. AGI Contratación 5422 N.34 f.17v (1640).
185. The palace description is from Arnall Juan, 1978, 208–209.
186. AGN Inq 422 exp.4 f.351–367 (1646).
187. The Spanish word for card games was *naipes*; María Angeles Cuello Martinell, "La renta de los naipes en Nueva España," *Anuario de Estudios Americanos* 22 (1965): 19–21. The historiography on this royal income and legislation focuses on the eighteenth century; see, for example, Teresa Lozano Armendares, "Los juegos de azar. ¿Una pasión novohispana? Legislación sobre juegos prohibidos en Nueva España, siglo XVIII," *Estudios de Historia Novohispana* 11 (1991).

188. AGN Inq 422 exp.4 f.351–367 (1646).
189. Royal decrees that tried to curtail gambling (*juegos de azar*) capped wagers at ten pesos. Royal decree, May 12, 1551, codified as book 7, title 2, law 1 of the *Laws of the Indies*.
190. The reunions at the merchant's carriage house came to end in 1649 when the slaveowner died; his heirs sold the property. AGN BN 56 exp.91 f.1 (1649). Fellow coachmen, players who had joined their games, likely helped Jacinto and Diego manage their changed circumstances.
191. AGN Ord 4 exp.40 f.40v (1622).
192. AGN RCD 15 exp.178 f.140–141v (1645). For the history of these bans on arms, see Robert C. Schwaller, "'For Honor and Defence': Race and the Right to Bear Arms in Early Colonial Mexico," *Colonial Latin American Historical Review* 21, no. 2 (2012).
193. AGN RCD 15 exp.178 f.140–141v (1645).
194. Ibid.
195. Ibid.
196. Blas de Loya. The documentation categorizes him as a free man of African descent; AGN Inq 422 exp.4 f.351–367 (1646). The receptor's name was Martín de Aeta.
197. AGN Inq 419 exp.50 f.447–451 (1644).
198. AGN Inq 1508 exp.3 f.29–31v (1665). The employer Juan Martín de Acosta was a wine dealer, with business that took him to silver mining cities to the north. For *Calle de la Palma*, see José María Marroqui, *La ciudad de México*, 3 vols., vol. 3 (México: Tip. y lit. La Europea, 1903), 130–133.
199. AGN Inq 1508 exp.3 f.29–31v (1665).
200. Ibid.
201. A history of these regulatory measures is Herman L. Bennett, "Policing Christians: Persons of African Descent before the Inquisition and Ecclesiastical Courts," in *Africans in Colonial Mexico: Absolutism, Christianity, and Afro-Creole Consciousness, 1570–1640* (Bloomington: Indiana University Press, 2003).
202. AGN RCD 23 exp.83 f.207–207v.
203. AGN RCD 23 exp.77 f.200–200v (1661); AGN Inq 1508 exp.3 f.54 (1665).
204. Letter from Viceroy Mancera to his successor Viceroy Pedro Nuño Colón de Portugal y Castro, October 22, 1673, printed in *Instrucciones que los vireyes de Nueva España dejaron a sus sucesores* (México: Imprenta imperial, 1867), 259. This viceroy was the Duke of Veragua, the Marquess of Jamaica, and the Count of Gelves.
205. AGN TSJ 175 exp. 5867 fs.7 (1674). Robles, 1946, I, 146.
206. The Spanish term is *cochero mayor*. Francisco de Herrera was the viceroy's chief equerry (*caballerizo mayor*), a position in the viceroyal household charged with organizing local and long-distance transportation and responsible for vehicles, animals, and facilities, including stables, corrals, and carriage houses.
207. Pedro de Alvarado was categorized as an African-descended person; AGN TSJ 175 exp. 5867 fs.7 (1674).

208. Gutiérrez de Medina, 1947, 70.
209. The mule's name in Spanish was *secretaria*.
210. Robles, 1946, 1, 147.
211. Sor Juana Inés de la Cruz, "Lamenta con todos la muerte de la Señora Marquesa de Mancera (1674)," ed. Ramón García González, *Sonetos* (Madrid: Biblioteca Virtual Miguel de Cervantes, 2006), www .cervantesvirtual.com/nd/ark:/59851/bmczc896. Leonor María del Carreto (1616–1673) invited Sor Juana Inés de la Cruz in 1664, prior to her taking monastic vows, to live in the Viceroyal Palace as her daughter's tutor; Antonio Rubial García, "Las virreinas novohispanas. Presencias y ausencias," *Estudios de Historia Novohispana* 50 (2014).
212. AGN Mat 90 exp. 120, f.282–283 (1694).
213. Decades earlier, for example, Marcos de Villega accompanied a friend to get his marriage license and returned to the same church with another coachman to arrange his own marriage; AGN Mat 89 exp.102 f.376–377 (1672); AGN Mat 122 exp.147 f.391–392 (1672). Other examples include: AGN Mat 19 exp.16 f.83–84 (1679); AGN Mat 132 exp.106 fs.2 (1682).
214. Robles, 1946, 3, 114, 129.
215. Ibid., 129.
216. Ibid.
217. Coachmen did not organize as a confraternity or religious brotherhood until the late eighteenth century; see AGN RCD 147 exp.199 f.20 (1790); David Carbajal López, "Devoción, utilidad y distinción. La reforma de las cofradías novohispanas y el culto del Santísimo Sacramento, 1750–1820," *Hispania Sacra* 68, no. 137 (2016).
218. The author thanks Amrita Chakrbarti for encouraging the link between fraternal relations and collective resistance, and for recommending Lussana's work for a comparative perspective; Sergio Lussana, *My Brother Slaves: Friendship, Masculinity, and Resistance in the Antebellum South* (Lexington: University Press of Kentucky, 2016).
219. The folding screen, titled "Biombo de la Conquista de México y Vista de la Ciudad de México" in the museum catalogue of the Franz Mayer, has paintings on both sides. For art historical analyses of this work, see the bibliography in Alberto Baena Zapatero, "Biombos mexicanos e identidad criolla," *Revista de Indias* 80, no. 280 (2020). The cityscape is very similar to a painting titled "La Mui Noble y Leal Ciudad de México" or "Plano del Conde de Moctezuma," attributed to Diego Correa on a folding screen from circa 1690 in the collection of the Museo Nacional de Historia in Mexico City: Lombardo de Ruiz, Terán Trillo, and Torre, 1996, 305–307.
220. March 27, 1653; AGI México 318 (1653). Viceroy Luis Enríquez de Guzmán was the Count of Alba de Liste and the Marquess of Villaflor.
221. AGN Ríos 1 exp.1 f.1–8 (1681). For officials' ongoing efforts to build and maintain public works, see Enriqueta Quiroz, *Economía, obras públicas y trabajadores urbanos. Ciudad de México: 1687-1807* (México: Instituto Mora, 2016).

## 3 CARING FOR THE CITY

1. AGN Inq 673 exp.37 f.315–319v (1688). The Manila Galleon fleet had three ships on this run; Robles, 1946, 2, 60–61.
2. For this history, see Tatiana Seijas, "The Rise and Fall of the Transpacific Slave Trade," in *Asian Slaves in Colonial Mexico: From Chinos to Indians* (New York: Cambridge University Press, 2014).
3. AGN Inq 673 exp.37 f.315–319v (1688).
4. Two notarized agreements from August and September 1660 lay out the conflict most clearly; see ANM F. Rivera (559) 3857 f.13v–21 (1660).
5. Guild members identified as "*maestro cirujano*" or "*maestro de barbero flemotoniano*" (*flebetamiano*) by 1660. Ibid. Surgery as a distinct specialization of academic doctors emerged in the eighteenth century.
6. Vetancurt noted that their brotherhood was in Holy Trinity Church; Vetancurt, 1697, 44.
7. Ibid., 5.
8. Vetancurt used the Spanish word *médicos* for physicians. Residents also referred to them as doctors. Ibid.
9. Ibid.
10. Ibid., 44.
11. The historiography on the Medical Board (*Protomedicato*) in Mexico has focused on its role as the regulatory body of university-trained doctors. A history of the institutionalization of the Protomedicato and the university's medical faculty during the sixteenth and seventeenth centuries is Gerardo Martínez Hernández, *La medicina en la Nueva España, siglos XVI y XVII. Consolidación de los modelos institucionales y académicos* (México: UNAM, 2014). See also John T. Lanning, *The Royal Protomedicato: The Regulation of the Medical Professions in the Spanish Empire* (Durham: Duke University Press, 1985); Francisco Fernández del Castillo and Alicia Hernández Torres, *El Tribunal del Protomedicato en la Nueva España, según el Archivo Histórico de la Facultad de Medicina* (México: UNAM, 1965). For the eighteenth century, see Luz María Hernández Sáenz, *Learning to Heal: The Medical Profession in Colonial Mexico, 1767–1831* (New York: Peter Lang, 1997).
12. The term public health or *salud publica* is not anachronistic; it was commonly employed in the seventeenth century. A short overview of public health initiatives is: Martha Eugenía Rodríguez and Ana Cecilia Rodríguez de Romo, "Asistencia médica e higiene ambiental en la ciudad de México siglos XVI–XVIII," *Gaceta Médica de México* 135, no. 2 (1999).
13. Entry for *experiencia*; Covarrubias Horozco, 1674, f.265–265v.
14. Ibid.
15. Cartographer Vingboons created an orthogonal map of Mexico City based on Juan Gómez de Trasmonte's plan; see Chapter 1 for the provenance.
16. Torquemada, 1615, 330.
17. Ibid. The *Hospital de San Hipólito* was part of the complex of the convent of the same name. A study of this institution with a chapter that covers the seventeenth century is Christina Ramos, *Bedlam in the New World: A Mexican Madhouse in the Age of Enlightenment* (Chapel Hill: University of North

Carolina Press, 2022). See also Cheryl English Martin, "The San Hipólito Hospitals of Colonial Mexico, 1566–1702" (PhD, Tulane University, 1976); Christina Ramos, "Caring for *Pobres Dementes*: Madness, Colonization, and the *Hospital de San Hipólito* in Mexico City, 1567–1700," *The Americas* 77, no. 4 (2020).

18. Torquemada, 1615, 330. The *Hospital Real San José de los Naturales* was founded in 1529 and expanded in the mid 1550s as part of the city's response to the calamitous death toll of virgin-soil epidemics. A source in Nahuatl confirms that the Indigenous government made a significant financial commitment for its expansion in 1555; see Chávez Orozco, 1947, 122–124. The royal treasury funded the enlargement as well: there needed to be "a hospital where poor Indians could be cured … and find shelter"; the 1553 royal decree is transcribed in Alfonso García Gallo, ed., *Cedulario Indiano Recopilado por Diego de Encinas*, 4 vols., vol. 1 (Madrid: Real Academia de la Historia, 2018), 219–220. The archbishopric administered this hospital, which had close ties to the university; see María Luisa Rodríguez-Sala, *El Hospital Real de los Naturales, sus administradores y sus cirujanos (1531–1764)* (México: UNAM, 2005); Antonio Zedillo Castillo, *Hospital Real de Naturales: Historia de un hospital* (México: IMSS, 1984). Bioarcheological research has revealed new data about the diseases and injuries treated at the hospital, which, as Torquemada noted, administered to people of African, Asian, European, and Native American descent; see Julie K. Wesp, "Working in the City: An Historical Bioarchaeology of Activity in Urban New Spain," *Historical Archaeology* 54, no. 1 (2020).

19. Jacinto de la Cruz; ANM D. Ríos (557) 3845 f.74 (1656). The Hospitaller Order of the Brothers of Saint John of God (*Orden Hospitalaria de San Juan de Dios*) ran the hospital from 1604 onward; the hospital was renovated during the first half of the seventeenth century, with the church dedicated in 1647; see Josefina Muriel, *Hospitales de la Nueva España. Fundaciones de los siglos XVII y XVIII*, 2 vols., vol. 2 (México: Editorial Jus, 1960), 29–38. Today, the hospital, reconstructed in the late eighteenth and late twentieth centuries, houses the Franz Mayer Museum.

20. The nuns of the Order of Saint Claire were first housed next to the Holy Trinity chapel. The new convent was built in stages between 1623 and 1662; see Josefina Muriel, *Conventos de monjas en la Nueva España* (México: Editorial Santiago, 1946), 141–165; Alan Rojas Orzechowski, "Andrés Arias Tenorio y el convento de Santa Clara de la ciudad de México: un patronazgo del siglo XVII," *Boletín de Monumentos Históricos* 21 (2011). Only part of the original convent complex survives, which is now the *Biblioteca General del Honorable Congreso de la Unión*.

21. López was born in Cuenca, Spain circa 1534 and died in 1597. For his biography, see Gerardo Martínez Hernández, "La llegada del cirujano Alonso López de Hinojosos a la Nueva España," *Revista Médica del Instituto Mexicano del Seguro Social* 49, no. 4 (2011); Germán Somolinos d'Ardois, "Vida y obra de Alonso López de Hinojosos," in *Suma y recopilación de cirugía con un arte para sangrar muy útil y provechosa* (México: Academia Nacional de Medicina, 1977). For Fuente's biography, see Martínez Hernández, 2014.

22. Alonso López de Hinojosos, *Suma y recopilación de cirugía con un arte para sangrar muy útil y provechosa*, Facsimile ed. (México: Academia Nacional de Medicina, 1977), 74.

23. January 29, 1563; Ciudad de México, 1889, 7: Enero 1562–Octubre 1571: 103.

24. The guild's sixteenth- or seventeenth-century bylaws have yet to be found in the city's archives; references in other documentation, such as contracts, provide clues on its functioning. The first mention of barbers having a guild with masters is from June 10, 1533; Cabildo Ciudad de México, ed., *Actas de Cabildo*, vol. 3: Octubre 1532–Diciembre 1535 (México: Municipio Libre, 1889), 40. They would have adopted the guild bylaws issued in a city in Spain, like locksmiths who took those of Seville and silk makers those of Granada. For summaries of ordinances of these two guilds, see Barrio Lorenzot, 1920, 44–47; 150–152.

25. The title was *barbero mayor y alcalde examinador*. Royal pragmatic, April 9, 1500; *Libro de las bulas y pragmáticas de los Reyes Católicos*, facsímil ed. (Madrid: Instituto de España, 1973), f.155v–156. The pragmatic was subsequently codified as book 3, title 17, law 1 of the *Laws of Spain*; España, *Recopilacion de las Leyes destos Reynos, hecha por mandado de la Magestad Catholica del Rey don Philippe Segundo* (Alcala de Henares: Iuan Iñiguez de Lequerica, 1581), 225v. Queen Isabel issued a similar ordinance on February 15, 1486; *Ordenanças de Seuilla* (Sevilla: Andres Grande, 1632), 239.

26. *Libro de las bulas y pragmáticas de los Reyes Católicos*, 1973, f.155v–156.

27. The "barber and phlebotomist of the king and queen" issued a *carta de examen* in February 1521 in Medina del Campo that contains the standard phrasing; it is transcribed in Luis Martín Santos, *Barberos y cirujanos de los siglos XVI y XVII* (Salamanca: Consejería de Educación y Cultura, 2000), 40–41.

28. Ibid.

29. This board was a precursor to the Protomedicato.

30. Royal pragmatic,1523; codified as book 3, title 16, law 2 of the *Laws of Spain*; España, *Recopilacion de las leyes destos reynos, hecha por mandado de la Magestad Catolica del Rey don Felipe Segundo* (Madrid: Catalina de Barrio Angulo, 1640), f.301. For this history, see María Soledad Campos Díez, *El Real Tribunal del Protomedicato castellano (siglos XIV–XIX)* (Cuenca: Ediciones de la Universidad de Castilla-La Mancha 2008), 102.

31. January 11, 1527; Ciudad de México, 1889, 1: Marzo 1524–Junio 1529: 115.

32. March 21, 1542; Ciudad de México, 1889, 4: Enero 1536–Agosto 1543: 274. Council members issued a similar pronouncement six years earlier for certain trades; artisans had to "be examined by guild leaders of their trade" and "present their titles at city hall." July 7, 1536; Ibid., 26–27.

33. April 4, 1549; Ciudad de México, 1889, 5: Septiembre 1543–Noviembre 1550: 255.

34. Ibid.

35. August 2, 1555; Ciudad de México, 1889, 6: Diciembre 1550–Diciembre 1561: 178.

36. February 27, 1548; Ciudad de México, 1889, 5: Septiembre 1543–Noviembre 1550: 210.

37. June 7, 1560; Ciudad de México, 1889, 6: Diciembre 1550–Diciembre 1561: 402–403. January 29, 1563; Ciudad de México, 1889, 7: Enero 1562–Octubre 1571: 103. May 14, 1568; Ibid., 397. February 28, 1572; Ciudad de México, 1893, 8: Octubre 1571–Diciembre 1584: 20. Appointments ceased temporarily with the arrival of Doctor Francisco Hernández, but two Chief Doctors resumed their oversight in 1577. April 15, 1577; Ibid., 282.

38. For this history, see Gerardo Martínez Hernández, "'Obedézcase pero no se cumpla': El fracaso como Protomédico de Francisco Hernández en la ciudad de México, 1571–1574," *Andamios* 19, no. 49 (2022). Doctor Francisco Hernández, a fascinating figure, lived in Mexico City from 1571 to 1577. His works, especially his writings on natural history, have received considerable scholarly attention; see Simon Varey, Rafael Chabrán, and Dora B. Weiner, eds., *Searching for the Secrets of Nature: The Life and Works of Dr. Francisco Hernández* (Stanford: Stanford University Press, 2000).

39. Royal decree, January 11, 1570; codified as book 5, title 6, law 1 of the *Laws of the Indies*.

40. Alonso López de Hinojosos, *Svmma y recopilacion de cirvgia, con vn arte para sangrar, y examen de barberos* (México: Casa Pedro Balli, 1595), f.150.

41. López de Hinojosos, 1977, 73. Somolinos comments on the works the author drew upon; Germán Somolinos d'Ardois, *El viaje del Doctor Francisco Hernandez por la Nueva España* (México: Anales del Instituto de Biología, 1952).

42. Alonso López de Hinojosos, *Svmma y recopilacion de chirvgia, con vn arte para sâgrar muy vtil y prouechoso* (México: Antonio Ricarco, 1578); 1595.

43. López de Hinojosos, 1595, f.86v–92v. The barber section is Book 2 "De la sangría artificial, el cual contiene siete capítulos" out of twelve books in the original edition; Juan López de Velasco, *Geografía y descripción universal de las Indias* (Madrid: Atlas, 1971), 95–107.

44. In this schema, humors were related to the body's four fluids, the elements, either heat and dryness or cold and wetness, and the cardinal points. Blood from the heart was associated with air, yellow bile (cholera) from the liver with fire, black bile (melancholy) from the spleen with earth, and phlegm from the brain with water. There is a vast historiography on Hippocratic-Galenic theory and its interpretation by the philosopher Avicenna, whose writings were required reading at the University of Mexico and Iberian universities; see the bibliography in Martínez Hernández, 2014.

45. López de Hinojosos, 1595, f.86v.

46. Ibid., f.89.

47. Ibid.

48. Ibid.

49. Ibid., f.92.

50. López concluded book three by suggesting that doctors adopt the practice of using leeches to draw patients' blood; this method was used in "Flanders and in all of Italy," where apothecaries sold them for this purpose. He had

found that leeches native to "this land" were not poisonous, so it would be a safe alternative and "marvelous medicine." Ibid., f.92v.

51. López de Hinojosos, 1977, 74.
52. Ibid., 73.
53. Doctor de la Fuente noted in his blurb that Doctor Bravo, an "expert in medicine and surgery," had "amended" the work, suggesting the information was correct; Ibid., 74.
54. The viceroy's full name was Martín Enríquez de Almanza.
55. López de Hinojosos, 1977, 69–70.
56. Ibid., 74.
57. An overview of this history is Michele Clouse, *Medicine, Government, and Public Health in Philip II's Spain* (Farnham: Ashgate, 2011).
58. Miguel Eugenio Muñoz, *Recopilacion de las leyes, pragmaticas reales, decretos, y acuerdos del Real Proto-Medicato* (Valencia: Viuda de Antonio Bordazar, 1751), 110. The office of *Proto Barbero* remained in place in Spain, under the jurisdiction of the Protomedicato. For this history, see Campos Díez, 2008, 38–39, 102–103.
59. January 15, 1590; Ciudad de México, 1895, 9: Enero 1585–Mayo 1590: 376.
60. January 2, 1590; Ibid., 370. January 4, 1591 (the name listed is Juan Rodríguez de Mesa, likely the same person); Ciudad de México, 1896, 10: Mayo 1590–Junio 1592: 47. January 3, 1592; Ibid., 133. January 4, 1593; Ciudad de México, 1897, 11: Junio 1592–Diciembre 1593: 58. January 10, 1594; Ciudad de México, 1898, 12: Enero 1594–Mayo 1597: 7.
61. Francisco Bravo served as Chief Doctor from 1591 to 1594. January 2, 1591; Ciudad de México, 1896, 10: Mayo 1590–Junio 1592: 46. January 3, 1592; Ibid., 132. January 4, 1593; Ciudad de México, 1897, 11: Junio 1592–Diciembre 1593: 58. January 10, 1594; Ciudad de México, 1898, 12: Enero 1594–Mayo 1597: 1898, 7.
62. López de Hinojosos, 1595, f.3v.
63. Covarrubias Horozco, 1673, 176v.
64. Lay people formed religious organizations that went by different names: confraternity (*cofradía*); ecclesiastical congregation (*congregación eclesiastica*); and brotherhood (*hermandad*). For a discussion of confraternities as corporate associations, see Manuel Carrera Stampa, *Los gremios mexicanos. La organización gremial en Nueva España, 1521–1861* (México: EDIAPSA, 1954); María Alba Pastor, "La organización corporativa de la sociedad novohispana," in *Formaciones religiosas en la América colonial*, eds., María Alba Pastor, et al. (México: UNAM, 2000), 81–140. See also, Alicia Bazarte Martínez, *Las cofradías de españoles en la ciudad de México (1526–1860)* (México: UAM, 1989); María del Pilar Martínez López-Cano, Gisela von Wobeser, and Juan Guillermo Muñoz Correa, eds., *Cofradías, capellanías y obras pías en la América colonial* (México: UNAM, 1998); Alicia Bazarte Martínez and Clara García Ayluardo, *Los costos de la salvación: las cofradías y la ciudad de México, siglos xvi al xix* (México: CIDE, 2001).
65. The Tailors Guild organized this project and got city hall to grant them land to build it. January 9, 1526; Ciudad de México, 1889, 1: Marzo 1524–Junio

1529: 71. By 1533, cobblers, blacksmiths, carpenters, barbers, silversmiths, tailors, and armorers gathered on the mornings of Corpus Christi and joined the annual procession in this order. June 19, 1533; Ciudad de México, 1889, 3: Octubre 1532–Diciembre 1535: 40.

66. The cult of San Amaro (Saint Amarus the Pilgrim) emerged in the city of Burgos, where a pilgrim from France dedicated himself to serving the poor at the Hospital of the King in the 1200s. Several legends were attached to his name in the mid sixteenth century, when Nahuas residents took an interest in his life. For this history, see Louise M. Burkhart, "The Voyage of Saint Amaro: A Spanish Legend in Nahuatl Literature," *Colonial Latin American Review* 4, no. 1 (1995).

67. The hospice closed once the city's hospitals were built. The church *Templo de la Santísima Trinidad* was completed in 1570. This church, rebuilt in 1671 and again in the 1780s, stands today at the original location on *Calle de la Santísima*.

68. Family members returned the deceased person's membership patent to indicate that the confraternity had fulfilled its material obligations.

69. The Archconfraternity of the Holy Trinity (*Santísima Trinidad*) in Mexico, founded in 1580, became an aggregate (*agregación*) or affiliate of the Archconfraternity of the Holy Trinity based in Rome to share papal indulgences. Gregory XVIII issued a papal bull on January 8, 1582 that confirmed the aggregation; AGN BN 87 exp.7 fs.2 (1582); "Summario de las gracias, e indulgencias concedidas por la santidad de Paulo Quinto, y Clemente Decimo á los Archi-Cofrades de la Santisima Trinidad de Roma, de que gozan los Archi-Cofrades de la SSma. Trinidad de Mexico, fundada en 20 de Marzo de 1580, agregada a la Archi Cofradia de Roma en el año de 1582" (México: Felipe de Zuñiga, 1781). A history of this archconfraternity is: José de Alcocer y Vera, *Excelencias de la antiquissima archicofradia de la Santissima Trinidad* (México: Juan Ruyz, 1651). The barbers' brotherhood's name appears as "*hermandad del santo cristo … en la cofradia de la santisima trinidad*" in 1660, confirming the affiliation; ANM F. Rivera (559) 3857 f.15v–21 (1660). According to the Council of Trent, indulgences (defined as the accumulated merits of Christ and the saints) could be distributed by the pope to reduce a person's punishment in purgatory. The sacrament of confession and penitence pardoned a person's sin, but did not negate sin, which could only be erased in purgatory, where the soul was purified before entrance to heaven.

70. AGN BN 87 exp.7 fs.2 (1582).

71. Scholars have differed on this point, some assuming that the brotherhoods were the guilds. This history makes a distinction because guilds had bylaws or ordinances approved by city hall and the viceroy, while confraternities had constitutions approved by the Archbishop of Mexico or the provincial of one of the religious orders.

72. The Ordinances for the Tailors Guild, for example, specified the location for elections at their "chapel in Holy Trinity"; Genaro V. Vásquez, ed., *Legislación del trabajo en los siglos xvi, xvii y xviii* (México: D.A.P.P., 1938), 84–86.

73. The town was likely Santa Ana Jilotzingo; Peter Gerhard, *A Guide to the Historical Geography of New Spain*, Rev. ed. (Norman: University of Oklahoma Press, 1993), 273.
74. The Spanish words for the stages and order were: *aprendiz*; *oficial*; *maestro*.
75. The phrasing *"examinado del arte de barberos"* appears in contracts in the early 1600s; see, for example, AGN TSJ 165 exp.5417 fs.5 (1601).
76. A notarized apprentice contract (*contrato de aprendizaje*) formalized the verbal agreement between the apprentice and master tradesman.
77. AGN TSJ 165 exp.5417 f.1 (1601).
78. Notaries made copies of the contracts for the city's archive, the apprentice, the master, and for his own records.
79. ANM J. Pérez Rivera (497) 3357 f.300-300v (1604).
80. Ibid.
81. ANM J. Pérez Rivera (497) 3358 f.95–95v (1606).
82. Ibid. Another newcomer, Antonio de Roa moved to Mexico City from Havana and arranged a similar three-year apprenticeship; the contract stipulated that he would receive "a barbering kit with tools" at completion. ANM J. Pérez Rivera (497) 3358 f.11–12 (1605).
83. ANM J. Pérez Rivera (497) 3358 f.95–95v (1606).
84. ANM J. Pérez Rivera (497) 3357 f.345v–346 (1605).
85. The apprentice Diego Sepúlveda was twelve years old; ANM J. Pérez Rivera (497) 3362 f.242v–243 (1625).
86. ANM J. Pérez Rivera (497) 3357 f.345v–346 (1605).
87. For more details about the tools of the trade, see Martín Santos, 2000, 45–46.
88. AGN TSJ 165 exp.5417 f.1 (1601).
89. Entry for *lanceta*; Covarrubias Horozco, 1673, 84v.
90. The masters Bernardino García and Juan de Angulo y Murga signed the apprentice agreements with solid handwriting. ANM J. Pérez Rivera (497) 3357 f.300-300v (1604); ANM Juan Pérez Rivera (497) 3357 f.345v–346 (1605).
91. López de Hinojosos, 1595, f.32v–35v.
92. AGN TSJ 165 exp.5417 f.4 (1601).
93. The scribe categorized Francisco as an enslaved person of Asian descent; AGN Inq 452 exp.18 f.14–15 (1602).
94. Royal pragmatic, published in 1604, codified as book 3, title 16, law 10 of the *Laws of Spain*; España, 1640, f.306.
95. AGN TSJ 330 exp.10139 fs.1 (1600).
96. López de Hinojosos, 1595, f.134.
97. The name in the minutes is Juan López, which is a typo. Diego López de Salazar appeared twenty days later to petition for his salary; January 2 and 22, 1607; Cabildo Ciudad de México, ed., *Actas de Cabildo*, vol. 16: Enero 1605–Marzo 1607 (México: Central, 1900), 436, 486. López is mentioned in: María Luisa Rodríguez-Sala, *Cinco cárceles de la ciudad de México, sus cirujanos y otros personajes: 1574–1820. ¿Miembros de un estamento profesional o de una comunidad científica?* (México: UNAM, 2009), 68, 77–78.

98. April 7 and 10, 1606; Ciudad de México, 1900, 16: Enero 1605–Marzo 1607: 266–269. The viceroy secured provisions for prisoners at the same time; AGN RCD 5 exp.48 f.9v (1606).

99. ANM J. Pérez Rivera (497) 3358 f.65v–68 (1606).

100. Originally given an annual salary of fifty pesos, López petitioned the council for a raise the following year. February 11, 1608; Cabildo Ciudad de México, ed., *Actas de Cabildo*, vol. 17: Marzo 1607–Diciembre 1610 (México: Central, 1901), 166.

101. February 25, 1621; *Actas de Cabildo*, vol. 24: Enero 1621–Febrero 1623 (México: El Correo Español, 1906), 41.

102. An analysis of his career is: Gerardo Martínez Hernández, "¿Protomédico o Protomedicato? Jerónimo de Herrera y la controversia en torno a la instauración del Tribunal del Protomedicato en la Nueva España. 1620–1622," *Historia Mexicana* 67, no. 4 (2018). Viceroy Juan de Mendoza y Luna was the Marquess of Montesclaros.

103. The 1606 appointment letter for Jerónimo de Herrera is transcribed in Ibid., 1841. AGI Escribanía 168B f.24v–27 (1606).

104. AGI Escribanía 168B f.25v (1606).

105. Ibid.

106. Juan de Barrios, *Verdadera medicina, cirvgia, y astrologia en tres libros dividida* (México: Fernando Balli, 1607), f.86.

107. January 30, 1615; Cabildo Ciudad de México, ed., *Actas de Cabildo*, vol. 20: Agosto 1614–Junio 1616 (México: A. Carranza y Comp., 1904), 98–99.

108. Ibid.

109. November 13, 1615; Ibid., 223–24.

110. For this history, see Martínez Hernández, 2014, 269–297. Herrera was Protomédico until 1628; AGN IndV 4139 exp.27 fs.2 (1628). For the new appointments, see Martínez Hernández, 2018, 1820. Viceroy Rodrigo Pacheco y Osorio de Toledo was 3rd Marquess of Cerralvo.

111. The labor arrangement was for enslaved people to work independently and give a portion of their daily earnings (*jornal*) to slaveowners and keep the rest to support themselves. The scribe categorized Francisco as an enslaved person of Asian descent; AGN IndV 4048 exp.60 fs.1 (1624).

112. Ibid.

113. Ibid.

114. Ibid. Viceroy Diego Carrillo de Mendoza y Pimentel was the 1st Marquess of Gélves.

115. AGN IndV 4048 exp.60 fs.1 (1624).

116. Ibid.

117. Ibid.

118. The group likely had majority support among guild members; ANM F. Rivera (559) 3857 f.15v–21 (1660).

119. Royal pragmatic, April 9, 1500; *Libro de las bulas y pragmáticas de los Reyes Católicos*, 1973, f.155v–156.

120. Royal pragmatic, April 9, 1500, codified as book 3, title 18, law 1 of the *Laws of Spain*; España, *Recopilacion de las leyes destos reynos, hecha por mandado de la Magestad Catholica del Rey dõ Philippe Segundo nuestro Señor* (Alcalá de Henares: Iuan Iñiguez de Lequerica, 1598), f.247.

121. AGN IndV 4048 exp.60 fs.1 (1624).
122. AGN IndV 3303 exp.8 fs.2 (1625).
123. Ibid.
124. AGN IndV 4139 exp.27 fs.2 (1628).
125. This liquor (*aguardiente de maguey*) is related to today's mezcal, a twice-distilled drink made from hearts of maguey (*Agave salmiana* and *Agave atrovirens*), which is highly intoxicating, at some 55 percent per volume. Their product was likely less potent. For the apothecary regulation, see AGN Ordenanzas 4 exp.160 f.163v (1631); printed in Montemayor de Cuenca, 1787, Part II: Recop. mandamientos, 5.
126. AGN IndV 4139 exp.27 fs.2 (1628).
127. The method was "to extract aguardiente from pulque." There were two kinds of pulque in the seventeenth century – *pulque blanco* made from fermenting the sweet water (*aguamiel*) that collects in the heart of magueys, and a more intoxicating variation, *pulque de agua* or *pulque de raíz*, from fermenting sweet water along with the root of the maguey.
128. The Spanish word for the instrument was *caña*, which referred to sugar cane, as well as the hollow stems of other plants.
129. The author thanks Gary Leo Dunbar for raising this possibility – that shops were, in his words, a kind of "safety-valve" for the city's "drinking culture."
130. Entry for *bacía*; Covarrubias Horozco, 1674, f.77.
131. Ibid., f.12.
132. López de Hinojosos, 1595, f.34.
133. Ibid., f.35.
134. ANM F. Rivera (559) 3857 f.15v–21 (1660).
135. The scribe categorized Cruz as a man of Asian descent; AGN TSJ 7 exp.256 fs.3 (1634).
136. June 22, 1635; Ciudad de México, 1908, 30: Abril 1635–Diciembre 1636: 24. Their response was translated in Homer H. Dubs and Robert S. Smith, "Chinese in Mexico City in 1635," *The Far Eastern Quarterly* 1, no. 4 (1942). These authors incorrectly assumed the barbers came from China as personal servants on the Manila Galleon, and they called for "further research."
137. Ibid., 24.
138. ANM F. Rivera (559) 3857 f.15v–21 (1660).
139. Ibid.
140. June 22, 1635; Ciudad de México, 1908, 30: Abril 1635–Diciembre 1636: 24.
141. ANM F. Rivera (559) 3857 f.15v–21 (1660).
142. June 22, 1635; Ciudad de México, 1908, 30: Abril 1635–Diciembre 1636: 24. Residents suffered from a bought of epidemics (cocoliztli and flu) in 1634; Gibson, 1964, 450.
143. June 22, 1635; Ciudad de México, 1908, 30: Abril 1635–Diciembre 1636: 24.
144. ANM F. Rivera (559) 3857 f.15v–21 (1660).
145. June 22, 1635; Ciudad de México, 1908, 30: Abril 1635–Diciembre 1636: 24.
146. Ibid.
147. Viceroyal decree, July 16, 1635; ANM F. Rivera (559) 3857 f.15v–21 (1660).

148. A group of hair barbers filed an appeal with the High Court, but the judges confirmed the original mandate on October 13, 1635. The new Viceroy Cadreita and court considered the matter closed on November 9, but another group of hair barbers initiated their own case "to repeal" the decision on December 7, 1635; ANM F. Rivera (559) 3857 f.15v–21 (1660). Viceroy Lope Díez de Aux de Armendáriz was the Marquess of Cadreita.

149. AGN RCD 18 exp.27 f.40 (1650).

150. AGN RCD 35 exp.442 f.297 (1639). The School of Saint John Lateran (*Colegio de San Juan de Letrán*), founded in the late 1540s, was a royally subsidized primary and secondary school for orphaned and abandoned boys who lived in the facility, once located on the street of the same name (today *Eje Central* between *Independencia* and *Calle Artículo* 123); see Paulino Castañeda Delgado, "El Colegio de San Juan de Letran de México (apuntes para su historia)," *Anuario de Estudios Americanos* 37 (1980).

151. AGN IndV 5509 exp.6 fs.2 (1636).

152. Domingo de Ortega similarly employed Benito de la Cruz, a free man of Asian descent, as a journeyman at his barbershop, located next to the "School for Girls"; AGN TSJ 7 exp.256 fs.3 (1634).

153. Francisco de Montoya was similarly unlikely to invalidate a four-year contract regarding Lazaro Balthazar, a ten year old who was the son of Diego Balthazar, an enslaved man of Asian descent; ANM J. Veedor (685) 4595 f.681–682 (1634). Von Mentz notes the juridical principle involved in this case, which required the enslaved father to have a written license from the slaveowner to formalize the apprentice contract of a child who was free; see Brígida von Mentz, "La 'entrega' de niños y adolescentes a un patrón: el ingreso de aprendices y sirvientes a la vida laboral en la ciudad de México en el siglo XVII," in *Trabajo, sujeción y libertad en el centro de la Nueva España* (México: CIESAS, 1999), 162.

154. ANM F. Rivera (559) 3857 f.15v–21 (1660).

155. AGN Tierras 2973 exp.53 f.116–126 (1634). For her story, see Seijas, 2014, 225–227.

156. AGN IndV 6057 exp.39 fs.1 (1642).

157. Ibid.; AGN RCD 48 exp.136 f.56v–57 (1643).

158. Jiménez was "a Native of the Philippines"; ANM J. Veedor 4595 (685) f.67v–69 (1633).

159. Jiménez was married to Isabel de San Miguel, an Indigenous woman from the town of Tlanipatlan in present-day Guerrero; they had a house in the neighborhood of Tomatlan; ANM J. Veedor 4595 (685) f.67v–69 (1633).

160. AGN IndV 2430 exp.29 fs.1 (1634).

161. The scribe categorized Domínguez as a man of Asian descent; AGN Mat 172 exp.61 fs.2 (1644).

162. The scribe categorized him as a person of Asian descent; AGN TSJ 11 exp.461 fs.10 (1642).

163. AGN TSJ 331 exp.10307 fs.6 (1632).

164. ANM J. P. Rivera Cáceres 4364 (630) f.222–223 (1642). ANM J. P. Rivera Cáceres 4364 (630) f.232–232v (1642).

165. The term was employed in the noted contracts from 1642, and at least three others in following years. ANM J. P. Rivera Cáceres 4366 (630) f. 98–98v (1644); ANM J. P. Rivera Cáceres 4366 (630) f.208v–209 (1644); ANM J. P. Rivera Cáceres 4368 (630) f.66v–67 (1651).

166. AGN TSJ 331 exp.10307 fs.6 (1632).

167. Viceroy Juan de Palafox y Mendoza, Bishop of Puebla, reformed the Medical Board and had the crown grant it increased juridical power in 1646, transforming it into a Medical Tribunal (*Real Tribunal del Protomedicato*). Afterward, the tribunal had three ranked members: the University's chair in prima (study of what makes a body healthy); the dean of the faculty of medicine; a university-affiliated doctor appointed by the viceroy. Two lawyers and a clerk supported board members in their work. For this history, see Martínez Hernández, 2014, 425–449. See also Francisco Fernández del Castillo, *La Facultad de Medicina según el archivo de la Real y Pontificia Universidad de México* (México: Consejo de Humanidades, 1953).

168. For the history of and changes to the curriculum, see Gerardo Martínez Hernández, "La repercusión de las reformas palafoxianas en la formación de los bachilleres médicos de la Real Universidad de México," in *Del aula a la ciudad. Estudios sobre la universidad y la sociedad en el México virreinal*, eds., Enrique González González, et al. (México: UNAM, 2009).

169. The appointment letter of Alonso Fernández Osorio specifies the responsibilities of Tribunal members; AGI México 186 N.34A fs.8 (1647), quoted at length in Martínez Hernández, 2014, 445–446.

170. AGN GP 8 exp.66 f.46v–47 (1641).

171. "Wearing a visible tonsure" was a sign of devotion; Stafford Poole and John F. Schwaller, eds., *The Directory for Confessors, 1585: Implementing the Catholic Reformation in New Spain* (Norman: University of Oklahoma Press, 2018), 244–247. The author thanks John F. Schwaller for guidance on the topic and the suggestion that clerics would have been regular barbershop customers.

172. AGN GP 9 exp.116 f.78 (1643).

173. Ibid.

174. AGN GP 8 exp.66 f.46v–47 (1641).

175. AGN GP 9 exp.116 f.78 (1643).

176. AGN IndV 5593 exp.47 fs.1 (1647).

177. ANM D. Ríos (557) 3844 f.19-19v (1652).

178. ANM F. Olalde 3237 (470) f.498-v (1647).

179. The Spanish terms for the credit instruments were *préstamo amigable* and *obligación de pago*. For credit instruments, see María del Pilar Martínez López-Cano, *La génesis del crédito colonial. Ciudad de México, siglo XVI*, (México: UNAM, 2001).

180. The scribe categorized Cruz as a free Asian-descended person. Cruz was a common last name among enslaved people in the city. ANM J. Veedor (685) 4596 f.162v–163 (1642).

181. See, for example, ANM F. Olalde 3237 (470) f.498-498v (1647); AGN TSJ 82 exp.2941 fs.8 (1668).

182. The scribe categorized the journeyman Thomas Lopes as a person of Asian descent; ANM D. Ríos (557) 3844 f.19-19v (1652).

183. For the legal procedure, see Juan Montero Aroca, *La herencia procesal española* (México: UNAM, 1994), 81-102.

184. ANM D. Ríos (557) 3844 f.19-19v (1652).

185. ANM D. Ríos (557) 3845 f.74 (1656); ANM J. Salas (633) 4380 f. 25v-26 (1660).

186. ANM F. Olalde (470) 3237 f.572-572v (1648).

187. The brotherhood's name appears as *"cofradia del santo Crucifixo y Labatorio de Xto N. S."*; AGN IndV 5593 exp.47 fs.1 (1647).

188. The brotherhood's name was *"cofradia del santo christo"*; ANM J. Salas (633) 4380 f.59v–60 (1659).

189. Ibid.

190. AGN IndV 5593 exp.47 fs.1 (1647).

191. Ibid.

192. Among those named in documentation was Domingo (no last name), who had "a barbershop in the stalls of the *plaza mayor*"; ANM T. Cobián 726bis (110) f.148–150 (1652).

193. ANM F. Rivera (559) 3857 f.15v-21 (1660).

194. Luis has a different interpretation of Asian barbers than what is offered in this chapter; Diego Javier Luis, "Merchants and Gunslingers," in *The First Asians in the Americas: A Transpacific History* (Cambridge: Harvard University Press, 2024).

195. Agustín and Asqueta went to the Viceroyal Palace together on February 12; AGN Indios 15 exp.29 f.20v-21 (1648); AGN Indios 15 exp.28 f.19v-20 (1648). See also AGN Indios 15 exp.62 f.44v (1648).

196. For the history of changing classifications, see chapter 5 of Seijas, 2014.

197. AGN Indios 15 exp.86 f.154v-155 (1649).

198. The scribe categorized López as an Asian-descended person. AGN IndV 2247 exp.46 f.1-3v (1650).

199. AGN TSJ 7 exp.256 fs.3 (1634).

200. ANM J. Pérez Rivera 4368 (630) f.99v-100 (1651).

201. Joseph Berenguel received a commission to shut down unlicensed shops in April 1650; AGN RCD 18 exp.27 f.40 (1650); ANM F. Rivera (559) 3857 f.15v-21 (1660). Berenguel "did not execute the mandate," which fell to Pedro de Monroy in May 1651; ANM F. Rivera (559) 3857 f.15v-21 (1660). Sebastian de la Parra similarly petitioned for a commission to "execute … the prohibition regarding" hair barbers in August 1653; AGN RCD 18 exp.507 f.249v (1653).

202. ANM L. Mendoza 2492 (378) f.171-171v (1659).

203. Guijo, 1953, 2: 1655-1664, 108-109.

204. The group included Juan de Santiago, Nicolás de Govea, Juan Bautista, Luis Trujillo, Francisco Veloz, Simón de la Cruz, Miguel de la Cruz, Pedro Govea, Francisco Rodríguez, Juan de Baeza, and Antonio del Castillo; ANM F. Rivera (559) 3857 f.15v-21 (1660).

205. Ibid.

206. Medina, 1682, f.238-238v.

207. The Spanish term was alms or *limosna*.
208. According to the 1705 constitution, members paid two reals to join, plus half a real each week, and four reals at Lent, which qualified them for funerary arrangements (fees may have been lower in the seventeenth century). If the individual died after only ten years of being a member or owed two pesos or more, the confraternity had no obligation to pay for anything; AGN IndV 1988 exp.8 fs.12 (1709); AGN BN 197 exp.11 (1710).
209. ANM F. Rivera (559) 3857 f.15v–21 (1660).
210. Ibid.
211. Ibid.
212. ANM F. Rivera (559) 3857 f.13v (1660).
213. Benavides had a barbershop on Saint Augustine Street; he married in 1655, when he was a journeyman; AGN Civil 1271 f.135-135v (1655); AGN TSJ 82 exp.2941 fs.8 (1668). Diego del Castilla was in his late twenties as well; AGN Mat 138 exp.75 f.22–24 (1682); AGN Mat 46 exp.73 f.345–348 (1699).
214. ANM F. Rivera (559) 3857 f.15v–21 (1660).
215. Ibid.
216. The contract allowed existing blade-and-scissors shops to remain at their location if a "Spanish master" subsequently moved to the same street.
217. Andres Armasola, a master barber who did not sign the agreement, tried to undermine it with a commission to shut down all but the so-called twelve licensed shops the following year; AGN GP 11 exp.70 f.69–71v (1661); AGN IndV 4472 exp.44 fs.2 (1661).
218. AGN IndV 1587 exp.16 fs.4 (1661). In 1667, another guild and brotherhood outsider, this time Viceroy Mancera's own barber phlebotomist Miguel Conde, once again tried to resurrect the twelve-license restriction; AGN GP 14 exp.40 f.38v–39v (1670). It was the last, and failed, effort.
219. ANM F. Rivera (559) 3857 f.15v–21 (1660).
220. AGN GP 14 exp.40 f.38v–39v (1670).
221. Gemelli Careri, 1699, 6: Nvova Spagna, 98–99.
222. Ibid.
223. Ibid. Gemelli Careri referred to the members of the Confraternity of Holy Cross and Maundy as "the brothers of Saint Francis" because the brotherhood was based at the Convent of Saint Claire and thus associated with the Franciscan Order.
224. The full name varied in early eighteenth-century documentation, but its primary identification was the *Cofradía del Santo Cristo de la Salud*; AGN Ind 1988 exp.8 fs.12 (1709). Another document names it the Brotherhood of Holy Christ "aggregated to the archconfraternity of the Holy Trinity and the charge of the three guilds of surgeons (*quirurgicos*), pharmacists (*pharmacopeos*), and phlebotomists (*flebotomianos*)"; AGN BN 197 exp.11 (1710). A third describes it as the "Confraternity and Brotherhood of Holy Christ, which in the charge of the three guilds, surgeons, pharmacists, and phlebotomists"; AGN Cofradías 38 (1725). Bazarte has a different interpretation of the confraternity's history than what is offered in this chapter: Bazarte Martínez, 1989; Alicia Bazarte Martínez, "Las limosnas

de las cofradías: su administración y destino," in *Cofradías, capellanías y obras pías en la América colonial*, eds., María del Pilar Martínez López-Cano, et al. (México: UNAM, 1998); "La cofradía de Cosme y Damián en el siglo xviii," *Revista fuentes humanísticas – UAM Azcapotzalco* 10 (1999); Bazarte Martínez and García Ayluardo, 2001.

225. AGN Bandos 20 exp.18 f.19 (1799). The Medical Board continued to examine barber surgeons into the nineteenth century; see Manuel Soriano, "Algunos apuntes sobre el Protomedicato," *Gaceta Médica de México* 36, no. 10 (1899): 577.

226. This chapter is partly based on sources related to 214 barber surgeons and barbers, none categorized as having African ancestry, only men of Asian, European, and Indigenous descent. Von Mentz cites the apprentice contracts of several African-descended children; Mentz, 1999. The relative absence of African and African-descended men in the barbering trade in Mexico City stands in contrast to other seventeenth-century cities in the Iberian sphere, where they did work as barbers; see, for example, Jane Landers, "The African Landscape of Seventeenth Century Cartagena and Its Hinterlands," in *The Black Urban Atlantic in the Age of Revolution*, eds., Jorge Cañizares-Esguerra, et al. (Philadelphia: University of Pennsylvania Press, 2013).

227. Scholarship on healers or *curanderos* in central Mexico has long acknowledged the unique mixing of medicinal knowledge from Mesoamerica, parts of Africa, and Iberia. Historical anthropologists have employed Inquisition sources for this line of inquiry; see Noemí Quezada, *Enfermedad y maléficio. El curandero en el México colonial* (México: UNAM, 2000); Gonzalo Aguirre Beltrán, *Medicina y magia. El proceso de aculturación en la estructura colonial* (México: Instituto Nacional Indigenista, 1963). See also Angélica Morales Sarabia, "Las enfermedades de las mujeres en la Nueva España, una taxonomía a través de las plantas emenagogas (siglo XVII)," *Nuevo Mundo Mundos Nuevos* (2016).

## 4 VALUING THE CITY

1. AGN TSJ 332 exp.10452 fs.2 (1676).
2. Ibid.
3. Ibid.
4. A history of another city of silver is Kris E. Lane, *Potosí: The Silver City that Changed the World* (Oakland: University of California Press, 2018).
5. Money is an abstraction; it is an idea related to value. People generally think about money in terms of how they use it: to make payments (medium of exchange); to measure value (index of comparison); and to store value. A classic discussion is Pierre Vilar, *A History of Gold and Money, 1450–1920* (London: NLB, 1976), 19–22. See also Georg Simmel, *The Philosophy of Money* (London: Routledge, 1978).
6. The fineness of a silver object designates the mass (weight) of the silver metal it contains vis-à-vis the object's total mass, which consists of impurities and a base metal (such as copper) or an alloy of metals.

7. The building's name was *Casa de Moneda*. A history of the mint with transcribed decrees and ordinances is: Fabian de Fonseca and Carlos de Urrutia, "Casa de Moneda," in *Historia general de real hacienda* (México: V. G. Torres, 1845). An archive-based social history of the seventeenth-century foundry and mint remains to be written. For the eighteenth century, see Felipe Castro Gutiérrez, *Historia social de la Real Casa de Moneda de México* (México: UNAM, 2012).

8. Gage, 1648, 56.

9. Ibid., 59.

10. Ibid., 56.

11. Ibid., 55–56.

12. The measurement given is one vara; Vetancurt, 1697, 18.

13. Ibid. James Woodard, a wordsmith, translated the poem: thank you.

14. The Spanish word is *plateros*.

15. A study of Mexico City's guilds, with mention of silversmiths, is Manuel Carrera Stampa, "Los gremios mexicanos. Organización gremial en Nueva España 1521–1861" (PhD, UNAM, 1954). See also the published version from the same year. A study of the smiths' guilds, based on printed sources, influenced by European historiography on feudalism and guilds, and with factual errors is George B. Martin-Veque, "The Silversmiths in Mexico: A Study in Colonial Trade Guilds" (PhD, University of Texas, Austin, 1951). A study of guilds focused on the eighteenth century is Felipe Castro Gutiérrez, *La extinción de la artesanía gremial* (México: UNAM, 1986).

16. AGN Inq 70 exp.3 fs.46 (1572).

17. AGN Inq 70 exp.3 f.61 (1572).

18. Ibid.

19. Ibid.

20. AGN Inq 70 exp.3 f.28–28v (1572).

21. In 1536, silversmith Francisco Ruiz began his business by purchasing "all the tools of his trade" and Juan, an enslaved Indigenous man who was "a silversmith," to work in his shop; ANM M. Castro (1) 33 f.495–498 (1536).

22. AGN Inq 70 exp.3 f.29 (1572).

23. June 20, 1525; Ciudad de México, 1889, 1: Marzo 1524–Junio 1529: 45.

24. Ibid.

25. The viceroy's name was Luis de Velasco y Ruiz de Alarcón. His son Luis de Velasco II also served as Viceroy of New Spain.

26. Viceroyal decree, July 6, 1563, summarized in Fonseca and Urrutia, 1845, 390–391.

27. Ordinances for Smiths (*Ordenes para batihojas y tiradores de oro y plata*), confirmed October 30, 1563, transcribed in Ibid., 391–393. Viceroy Martín Enríquez de Almanza revalidated these ordinances on November 5, 1572, noted in Fonseca and Urrutia, 1845, 393. All guilds had bylaws that outlined how they governed their members and regulated the production of their wares or services. Guilds submitted their bylaws to city hall for approval and had them confirmed by the viceroy. During the seventeenth century, council members appointed a deputy annually who was present at the elections held by each guild and recorded their membership and leadership in a Book of Elections held by the council.

28. The 1563 ordinances inspired subsequent royal decrees on the matter. The registration process was described in royal decrees from July 8, 1578; reissued on October 30, 1584, codified as book 8, title 10, law 24 of the *Laws of the Indies*. The latter decree is transcribed in full in *Historia general de real hacienda*, 6 vols., vol. 1 (México: V. G. Torres, 1845), 20.

29. The term for taxed silver is *plata quintada*. Ibid.

30. Ibid.

31. Ibid.

32. Royal decree, October 28, 1559; reissued on July 8, 1578, codified as book 8, title 10, law 47 of the *Laws of the Indies*.

33. Ibid.

34. June 20, 1525; Ciudad de México, 1889, 1: Marzo 1524–Junio 1529: 45.

35. The position in Spanish was *veedor* (or *alcalde*). March 4, 1530; Cabildo Ciudad de México, ed., *Actas de Cabildo*, vol. 2: Junio 1529–Septiembre 1532 (México: Municipio Libre, 1889), 36. Council minutes note that the silversmith who "received the most votes" from his peers got "named" Chief Inspector, whom council members subsequently approved, and who "received the city's mark and stamp." See, for example, the entry for January 24, 1533; Ibid., 3: Octubre 1532–Diciembre 1535: 16.

36. This reference in council minutes testifies to the existence of ordinances "issued in the city" by the Silversmiths and Goldsmiths Guild, which have yet to be found in the archival record. Villasana was called "*alcalde y veedor de plateros y marcador*." July 3, 1544; Ciudad de México, 1889, 5: Septiembre 1543–Noviembre 1550: 54.

37. Villasana's tenure ended on July 24, 1551; Ibid., 6: Diciembre 1550–Diciembre 1561: 27–28.

38. The Spanish word is *burilada*.

39. For more details, see Juan de Arfe y Villafañe, *Qvilatador de la plata, oro, y piedras* (Valladolid: Alonso y Diego Fernãdez de Cordoua, 1572), f.7–19v.

40. In the sixteenth century, the position was called "*fiel contraste de pesas y medidas*" or "*fiel marcador de pesas y medidas*." See, for example, February 9, 1546; Ciudad de México, 1889, 5: Septiembre 1543–Noviembre 1550: 126. The word *contraste* referred to a person who inspected weights and measures and marked them to verify their compliance. For more details, see Carrera Stampa, 1949.

41. February 9, 1546; Ciudad de México, 1889, 5: Septiembre 1543–Noviembre 1550: 126.

42. November 18, 1524; Ciudad de México, 1889, 1: Marzo 1524–Junio 1529: 23.

43. January 13 and 24, May 16, 1525; Ibid., 26, 27, 40. This requirement that residents have their weights inspected preceded a royal mandate that "justices yearly tune weights" used for "gold, silver, and pearls." A transcription of the August 17, 1535 decree is in Manuel José de Ayala, ed. *Disposiciones complementarias de las Leyes de Indias*, 3 vols., vol. 3 (Madrid: Saez hermanos, 1930), 184. In 1532, for example, the Chief Inspector and Hallmarker Francisco Toledo convinced councilmen to appoint him "to adjust and tune all weight and measures" for a salary. August 19, 1532; Ciudad de México, 1889, 2: Junio 1529–Septiembre 1532: 190.

44. The fiel contraste was silversmith Cosme de Orrantia, appointed January 1, 1571; Ciudad de México, 1889, 7: Enero 1562–Octubre 1571: 494. Viceroy Enríquez appointed Gabriel Villasana Chief Inspector on November 5, 1572; Fonseca and Urrutia, 1845, 393.

45. May 19 and 26, 1581; Ciudad de México, 1893, 8: Octubre 1571–Diciembre 1584: 495–496.

46. Silversmiths and goldsmiths held the position, such as Pedro Salcedo, who was Chief Inspector and Sealer off-and-on for over 20 years. His last appointment was on January 23, 1562; Ciudad de México, 1889, 7: Enero 1562–Octubre 1571: 19.

47. May 7, 1527; Ciudad de México, 1889, 1: Marzo 1524–Junio 1529: 130.

48. Ibid.

49. July 29, 1524; Ibid., 16.

50. The first mention of silversmiths having a guild with masters is from June 10, 1533; Ciudad de México, 1889, 3: Octubre 1532–Diciembre 1535: 40.

51. Entry for platero; Covarrubias Horozco, 1673, f.144.

52. The Spanish word for these artisans was *batihojas*. Entry for *batihojas*; Covarrubias Horozco, 1674, f.88.

53. The phrase was "*batir moneda*"; Ibid. The Spanish verb to coin is *acuñar*.

54. The Spanish word for these artisans was *tiradores*. Entry for *tira*; Covarrubias Horozco, 1673, 188.

55. "Ordenanzas de tiradores de oro y plata," confirmed on October 19, 1669; summarized in Barrio Lorenzot, 1920, 139–142.

56. Ordinances from June 1572 about the city's celebrations listed two separate guilds: silversmiths and goldsmiths, and metal leaf workers (*batihojas*); Ibid., 264–265.

57. Ordinances for Smiths, approved by Viceroy Monterrey on June 12, 1598; summarized in Ibid., 142–145. The title listed in the summary is "Ordenanzas de Batihojas," but the content reveals that it relates to all three specialties; leaf workers did not have their own guild until the following year.

58. Ibid., 143.

59. City hall considered a draft on January 8, 1580; Ciudad de México, 1893, 8: Octubre 1571–Diciembre 1584: 414.

60. The "Ordenanzas para el gremio de batihojas de panes" were approved by council members on February 19, 1599, and confirmed by Viceroy Monterrey on May 25, 1599. They are summarized in Barrio Lorenzot, 1920, 145–147. They are transcribed in Vásquez, 1938, 81–83. Viceroy Montesclaros approved the addition of several bylaws on March 3, 1607; AGN Ord 2 exp.208 f.183–184v (1607).

61. Viceroy Mancera confirmed the "Ordenanzas de tiradores de oro y plata" on October 19, 1669; summarized in Barrio Lorenzot, 1920, 139–142.

62. For a history of the mint with summaries and transcriptions of royal decrees and other laws related to its functioning, see Fonseca and Urrutia, 1845. The authors compiled this history for the viceroy in 1791. For a history of the mints in Spanish territories, see Guillermo Céspedes del Castillo, *Las casas de moneda en los reinos de Indias*, vol. 1: Las cecas indianas en 1536–1825

(Madrid: Museo Casa de la Moneda, 1996). For the laws governing this body, see book 4, title 23 of the *Laws of the Indies*.

63. For the history of these first foundries, see Román Beltrán Martínez, "Primeras casas de fundición," *Historia Mexicana* 1, no. 3 (1952).

64. The 1497 *Pragmática de Medina del Campo* was codified as the "Ordinances on Money" (*Ordenanzas que han de guardar los oficiales en la labor de la moneda sus derechos*), book 5, title 21 of the *Laws of Spain*; España, 1598, 362v–373v. The pragmatic served as the basis for policies in Spain's overseas territories. For this history, see María Teresa Muñoz Serrulla, *La moneda castellana en los reinos de Indias durante la Edad Moderna* (Madrid: Universidad Nacional de Educación a Distancia, 2015). The crown upheld a bimetallic system or standard, meaning that the government valued currency vis-à-vis gold and silver and maintained a fixed ratio between their values; see Javier de Santiago Fernández, *Política monetaria en Castilla durante el siglo XVII* (Valladolid: Junta de Castilla y León, 2000). For a comparative perspective, Desan demonstrates that the crown played a critical role in creating and enforcing England's units of account in the seventeenth century, see Christine Desan, *Making Money: Coin, Currency, and the Coming of Capitalism* (Oxford: Oxford University Press, 2014).

65. The royal decree from November 4, 1525 was included in the council minutes; Ciudad de México, 1889, 1: Marzo 1524–Junio 1529: 219.

66. Ibid.

67. Ibid.

68. April 6, 1526; Ibid., 82. The smiths were Diego Martínez and Juan Celada; their heirs had to appeal to the High Court seven years later to get paid part of the salary city hall had promised them for "their work," which points to scarcity of coin money during these decades. August 17, 1526; Ibid., 102. September 22, 1533; Ciudad de México, 1889, 3: Octubre 1532–Diciembre 1535: 53.

69. The term was *oro de tepuzque* (derived from *tepoztli*, meaning metal in Nahuatl). A study of these early coins is Iván Rivero Hernández, "El oro y los 'pesos de oro' en los inicios de Nueva España. Una propuesta de reinterpretación," *Historia Mexicana* 73, no. 2 (2023). Entry for *tepoztli*, Nahuatl Dictionary Online, 2000.

70. Vetancurt, 1697, 31.

71. Royal decree, May 21, 1535, transcribed in Fonseca and Urrutia, 1845, 111.

72. Royal decree, November 18, 1537, transcribed in García Gallo, 2018, 228–229. A 1544 decree allowed 3-real coins; see Ayala, 1930, 194.

73. Torquemada, 1615, 674. Mints in sixteenth-century Spain made coins from gold, silver, and copper; gold and silver coins were over 90 percent precious metal, with copper as an alloy. Coins that were primarily copper, with varying percentages, were called *monedas de vellón* (meaning alloy); see Javier de Santiago Fernández, "La emisión de moneda de vellón rico en el reinado de Felipe II: ¿un instrumento de financiación?" *Cuadernos de investigación histórica* 26, no. 1 (2009). The crown authorized the minting of copper coins in 1541 in Mexico City, but residents resisted their adoption; see García Gallo, 2018, 238–239.

74. Torquemada, 1615, 674. Konove shows that Torquemada's source for this information was Diego Muñoz Camargo, who wrote a history of Tlaxcala and lived in Mexico City in the mid-sixteenth century. Andrew Konove, "In Search of a Decent Coin: The Value of Small Change in Bourbon Spanish America," *Colonial Latin American Review* 30 (2022).

75. Torquemada, 1615, 674.

76. AGI México 1089 L.5 f.292v–293 (1569). Fonseca and Urrutia, 1845, 119–120; Castro Gutiérrez, 2012, 25–26. González documents that the mint moved to the palace complex in 1569; Pilar González Gutiérrez, *Creación de casas de moneda en Nueva España*, (Alcalá de Henares: Universidad de Alcalá, 1997), 90. Beltrán incorrectly dates the move to 1563; Román Beltrán Martínez, "Primeras casas de fundición," in *Historia de la ciencia y la tecnología*, ed. Elías Trabulse, et al. (México: Colegio de México, 1991), 199.

77. The organization remained the same throughout the seventeenth century. An inspection describes the activities that took place in the building's many rooms; AGN Moneda 333 exp.3 f.54–143 (1693). Silver arrived in the form of rough blocks or plates of smelted silver called ingots (*lingotes*). The secretary (*escribano*) recorded the names of owners and the amounts of silver. The assayer (*ensayador y fundidor*) checked the metal content and oversaw the foundrymen who melted and tuned or fixed (adjusted) the silver earmarked for coins to the legal metal standard. The weigher (*balanzario*) oversaw foundry workers who subtracted the royal extraction tax and the foundry and assay fee (if not already paid at a foundry in a mining town). A description of these processes is in Céspedes del Castillo, 1996, 1: Las cecas indianas, 101–146.

78. The crown mandated in 1565 that all major officials – from the mint treasurer and director to the guards – "serve him for a just quantity," and the positions went to those who paid the most money; see Fonseca and Urrutia, 1849, 2, 118. The decree was part of an empire-wide effort to secure government revenue through the sale of offices. Scholars have pointed to this policy to suggest that the mint resembled a private entity until the eighteenth century; see, for example, González Gutiérrez, 1997, 123–130.

Members of the city hall council purchased their offices as well, but the practice did not privatize this governing body, just as it did not privatize the mint. All officials who paid for their positions exerted power to benefit their private interests, but they represented the crown's interests and had responsibilities at the same time. For the historiography of this phenomenon, see Antonio Jiménez Estrella, "Poder, dinero y ventas de oficios y honores en la España del Antiguo Régimen: un estado de la cuestión," *Cuadernos de Historia Moderna* 37 (2012). See also Christoph Rosenmüller, *Corruption and Justice in Colonial Mexico, 1650–1755* (New York: Cambridge University Press, 2019).

79. The cost was calculated by weight. One mark of silver made 67 reals and the mint kept three, so that the owner received 64 reals in return. The minting charges were two reals for mint officials and one real for the crown (*señoreaje*) as a duty – three in total; see book 4, title 23, laws 7 and 8 of the *Laws of the*

*Indies*. Mint officials were supposed to hand over the royal minting charge, but they kept the 3 reals for themselves throughout the sixteenth century, citing high expenses; see González Gutiérrez, 1997, 78–79. The crown asked the viceroy to investigate in the early 1580s, which attests to the practice; AGI México 1064 L.2 f.90v (1582). In 1615, officials finally started separating out the royal minting duty, keeping only two reals as fees (instead of three) and giving one real to the royal treasury. The accounts for this royal revenue stream are in AGI Contaduría 810 N.1 (1615–1701).

80. An overview of merchant's involvement in the mint is Louisa S. Hoberman, "The Mexican Economy and Merchant Capital: Mining and the Mint," in *Mexico's Merchant Elite, 1590–1660: Silver, State, and Society* (Durham: Duke University Press, 1991). See also Guillermina del Valle Pavón, "Bases del poder de los mercaderes de plata de la ciudad de México. Redes, control del Consulado y de la Casa de Moneda a fines del siglo XVII," *Anuario de Estudios Americanos* 68, no. 2 (2011).

81. Numismatists refer to these hand-cut and borderless coins as cobs or *macuquinas*. An overview of coin-making, primarily during the eighteenth century, is in Céspedes del Castillo, 1996, 1: Las cecas indianas, 147–174.

82. The official bar cutter (*capataz*) oversaw workers who cut out the circles (*cospeles*); the official stamper or coin-fashioner (*acuñador*) oversaw workers who used a die (*cuño* or *punzón*) and a hammer to mark the silver token (heated for malleability). Next, workers washed and polished the coins (*blanquimiento*) and confirmed their legal weight. The die included the initial of the official assayer (*ensayador*), which testified to their legal metal content. The official die cutter (*tallador*) oversaw workers who made and maintained the steel dies used to stamp bars and coins at the foundry and mint.

83. The *Ordenanzas de la moneda de plata y vellon* from May 11, 1535 dictated the markings; a facsimile is in Puga, 1945, f.106–107v.

84. The Hapsburgs changed the weight, metal content, and face value of gold and silver coins minted in the Iberian kingdoms in the sixteenth and seventeenth centuries. The creation of a new piece-of-eight coin (*plata nueva*) in 1642 (for Spanish circulation only), which had a lesser weight and silver content than the same coin minted in Mexico City (*plata vieja*), had negative consequences, yet similar measures reiterated in the decades to come; see Cecilia Font de Villanueva, "Política monetaria y política fiscal en Castilla en el siglo XVII: un siglo de inestabilidades," *Revista de Historia Económica* 23, no. S1 (2005); Santiago Fernández, 2000.

85. The crown expressly mandated in 1643 that silver coins minted in Mexico City remain the same as before; see book 4, title 24, law 6 of the *Laws of the Indies*. A royal pragmatic from October 1686 again changed the weight and metal content of real coins, and modified their value, but the crown reversed course for the Mexico City mint in February 1687; see Ayala, 1930, 197–199.

86. AGN TSJ 199 exp.6777 fs.12 (1684).

87. January 15, 1580; Ciudad de México, 1893, 8: Octubre 1571–Diciembre 1584: 417.

88. AGN GP 4 exp.257 f.73 (1591).

89. Viceroyal mandate, October 17, 1597; noted in Fonseca and Urrutia, 1845, 393.
90. Ordinances for Smiths, approved by Viceroy Monterrey on June 12, 1598; summarized in Barrio Lorenzot, 1920, 142–145.
91. AGN GP 5 exp.1313 f.277 (1601).
92. AGN RCD 5 exp.33 f.7 (1606).
93. AGN TSJ 166 exp.5463 fs.8 (1608).
94. Ibid.
95. Felipe Echagoyan, *Tablas de redvciones de monedas, y del valor de todo genero de plata y oro, y del modo de hazer las cuẽtas … y de otras cosas necessarias y conuenientes para las cuentas del trato y contrato de estos Reynos* (México: Henrico Martinez, 1603). The manual also contains tables for credit transactions. His last name is also spelled Echegoyen, which is a Basque surname.
96. ANM Á. Grado (1) 66 f. 222v–223, 667v–668 (1593).
97. Echagoyan, 1603, no foliation. The preface was written by engineer, printer, and cosmographer Enrico Martínez; for this figure, see Valerie L. Mathes "Enrico Martínez of New Spain," *The Americas* 33, no. 1 (1976).
98. For these commercial manuals and merchant culture, see Elvira Vilches, "Trade, Silver, and Print Culture in the Colonial Americas," *Journal of Latin American Cultural Studies* 24, no. 3 (2015).
99. The Spanish terms were *moneda de metal* and *moneda de cuanta*. Rodríguez-Alegría has a different interpretation of these units than what is offered in this chapter; Enrique Rodríguez-Alegría, "How to Make Money," in *How to Make a New Spain: The Material Worlds of Colonial Mexico City* (New York: Oxford University Press, 2023).
100. Echagoyan, 1603, no foliation.
101. The ducat (*ducado* or *excelente de Granada*) was a gold coin that ceased to circulate in 1537 and became an accounting unit, akin to the maravedís; the *escudo* replaced it as the gold coin in circulation.
102. The Spanish terms were *peso de mina* and *peso de plata corriente*. The *peso de minas* disappeared from usage by the 1610s and only appeared as a phrase in property records that included a clause on failure of payment, which read, with slight alteration, that the creditor had the right to "send a person to collect the debt with a salary of two mine-pesos per day spent occupied in this pursuit" – an expense that was added to the amount owed.
103. The Spanish term was *peso de oro común*.
104. The fusion of units and values continued, so that the peso came to be the sole monetary unit of the Mexican Republic, represented by a coin – a peso – made of silver, in the nineteenth century.
105. This term echoed the name of coins made prior to the creation of the mint.
106. Echagoyan, 1603, f.1.
107. The groom was a silk maker; ANM J. Pérez Rivera (497) 3357 f.401–401v (1605).
108. One resident planned to use "a number of common-gold pesos" in his possession, meaning silver coins in a chest, to pay his debts; AGN BN 1175 exp.15 fs.2 (1643).

109. AGN TSJ 199 exp.6733 fs.2 (1606).
110. Echagoyan, 1603, f.1v. The word tomín derived from Arabic; Nahuas adopted it to mean money; see James Lockhart, *The Nahuas after the Conquest: A Social and Cultural History of the Indians of Central Mexico, Sixteenth through Eighteenth Centuries* (Stanford: Stanford University Press, 1992), 178–180; Nahuatl Dictionary Online, 2000.
111. Echagoyan, 1603, f.1v. A tomín was subdivided into "12 grains" for even greater numerical precision. A grain had 17 *avos*.
112. AGN Inq 306 exp.7 fs.27 (1619).
113. Echagoyan, 1603, no foliation. Another popular manual with arithmetic tables was Juan Díez, *The Sumario Compendioso of Brother Juan Díez: The Earliest Mathematical Work of the New World*, fascimile ed. (Boston: Ginn and Company, 1921).
114. Echagoyan, 1603, no foliation.
115. Ibid., f.2–2v.
116. The *marco* had 8 ounces (*onzas*): one ounce had 8 eighths (*ochavas*), so a mark had 64 eights; each eighth had 2 *adarmes*, so a mark had 128 *adarmes*; 1 adarme had 3 tomines, so a mark had 384 tomines; 1 tomín had 12 grains, so a mark had 4,608 grains. The mass measure grain should not to be confused with the accounting unit or the purity measure, which had the same name. A mark is equal to 230.05 grams in the metric system, or 8.11 ounces. The mark of gold was subdivided into different units. See Tomás Antonio Marien y Arróspide, *Tratado general de monedas, pesas, medidas y cambios de todas las naciones* (Madrid: Benito Cano, 1789), 5. The weights and measures used in Mexico City were the same as in Spain, as dictated by the crown in October 1539; a transcription is in Ayala, 1930, 184–185. The mandate was reissued; Royal decree, Dec 3, 1581; codified as book 4, title 18, law 22 of the *Laws of the Indies*.
117. Today the measure for purity is millesimal fineness. Twelve dineros would be equal to a millesimal fineness of 1000 ("fine" or "pure silver" is 99.9 percent silver and has a millesimal fineness of 999). The purity measure grain should not to be confused with the accounting unit or mass measure, which had the same name.
118. Echagoyan, 1603, 14.
119. The legal standard for silver (*ley de aleación*) in Mexico City was 930.5; it did not change until 1728 when the crown reduced it to 916.6. The legal standard for silver objects was reduced at the same time as for coins, with confirmation two years later; see AGN Bandos exp.21 f.244–245 (1730); Lawrence L. Anderson, *El arte de la platería en México 1519–1936*, 2 vols., vol. 1 (New York: Oxford University Press, 1941), 123. Sterling silver today, for comparison, is 92.5 silver; it has a minimum millesimal fineness of 925.
120. "Ordinances on Coins," law 5, "Que pone el valor del marco de plata"; España, 1598, 363v.
121. Echagoyan, 1603, 14.
122. Ibid.
123. Ibid.

124. Ibid., 15v–16.
125. AGI México 27 N.74 [anejo 8] (1609).
126. Ibid.
127. Echagoyan, 1603, 16.
128. Ibid., 18.
129. Their techniques varied depending on scale and purpose. Smiths had books at their disposal that summarized technical knowledge and best practices, such as Jerónimo Bezerra, *Breve relacion del ensaye de plata y oro* (México: Francisco Rodriguez Lupercio, 1671).
130. The terms in Spanish are: *plata del diezmo*; *plata del rescate*; *plata quintada*. Echagoyan, 1603, 16.
131. This tax was also called right of extraction (*derecho de extracción*). For the laws governing the taxation of natural resources, see book 8, title 10 of the *Laws of the Indies*.
132. For this history, see Jaime J. Lacueva Muñoz, *La plata del rey y de sus vasallos: minería y metalurgia en México (siglos XVI y XVII)* (Madrid: CSIC, 2010). See also AGN RCD 1 exp.120v–121v (1556); AGN RCD 47 exp.300 f.193 (1571); AGN RCD 47 exp.354 f.234 (1572).
133. The Spanish term for the mark used for tenthed-silver was *marca del diezmo*. Miners with concessions had contracts with the crown to purchase mercury for the amalgamation process; officials marked their silver to ensure that they paid for their mercury with silver. AGN GP 2 exp.1024 f.229 (1580).
134. The crown mandated that nonofficial miners stamp their rescue-silver with their own mark and "take it to an assay office … to pay one-fifth"; royal decree, May 17, 1557; reissued on November 14, 1562; codified as book 4, title 22, law 7 of the *Laws of the Indies*.
135. The Spanish term was *cajas reales*, named after the containers that held the crown's silver.
136. A description of these processes is in Céspedes del Castillo, 1996, 1: Las cecas indianas, 101–146. See also Peter J. Bakewell, *Silver Mining and Society in Colonial Mexico: Zacatecas, 1546–1700* (London: Cambridge University Press, 1971), 181. The foundry and assay fee or duty (*razón de la fundición, ensayador, y marcador*) paid for the foundry's operating costs. The crown charged "1.5 percent"; Royal decree, June 5, 1552; reissued on August 14, 1619; codified as book 4, title 22, law 13 of the *Laws of the Indies*.
137. The markings included the weight of the piece, a stamp for the royal tax, and another stamp confirming the payment made for the foundry and assay process.
138. Lacueva Muñoz, 2010.
139. AGI México 22 N.158 f.4–4v (1592).
140. Ibid.
141. Viceroy Monterrey issued this ban on September 17, 1603, copied in: "Testimony of ordinances," May 18, 1651; AGI México 37 N.4 fs.8 (1651).
142. Echagoyan, 1603, 44v–45.
143. AGN Ord 1 exp.166 f.146v–148 (1612). The ordinances from September 1603 and April 1606 are noted in AGN Ord 3 exp.30 f.33–36 (1616); AGN

Ord 3 exp.48 f.54v–58 (1617). The ordinance issued on April 10, 1606 is noted in Montemayor de Cuenca, 1787, 90–91. Viceroy Guadalcázar revoked the 1616 prohibition, but reinstated it eight months later. AGN Ord 3 exp.30 f.33–36 (1616); AGN Ord 3 exp.48 f.54v–58 (1617).

144. There is a vast historiography on smelting and amalgamation – the two refining methods used in Mexico during the sixteenth and seventeenth centuries; see the bibliography of Saúl Guerrero, *Silver by Fire, Silver by Mercury: A Chemical History of Silver Refining in New Spain and Mexico, 16th to 19th Centuries* (Leiden: Brill, 2017).

145. Echagoyan, 1603, 16v–17.

146. Ibid., 16v.

147. ANM J. Pérez Rivera (497) 3360 f.678–684v (1616).

148. AGN Ord 2 exp.28 f.27–29 (1619).

149. Ibid.

150. AGN Mat 64 exp.22 f.82–85v (1628); AGN Mat 29 exp.65 f.160–161 (1631).

151. Diego Rodríguez del Puerto was a goldsmith; AGN GP 7 exp.331 f.222 (1632).

152. AGN GP 7 exp.150 f.110 (1632); AGN GP 7 exp.156 f.113 (1632); AGN GP 7 exp.292 f.189v (1632); AGN GP 7 exp.318 f.213v (1632).

153. AGN GP 7 exp.173 f.121v (1632).

154. AGN GP 7 exp.331 f.222 (1632).

155. AGN TSJ 170 exp.5626 fs.12 (1624).

156. AGN TSJ 170 exp.5626 f.2 (1624).

157. AGN Ord 3 exp.23 and 24 f.25v–27v (1616).

158. The 1623 ordinances have yet to be found in the archive. They are referenced in the ordinances approved by Viceroy Cadreita in 1638; see AGN RCD 58 f.122–137, cuaderno 3 (1638), transcribed in Anderson, 1941, 1, 435–449.

159. "Órdenes para batihojas y tiradores de oro y plata," October 30, 1563, transcribed in Fonseca and Urrutia, 1845, 391–393.

160. Members of the metal leaf workers guild, for example, added bylaws to their guild ordinances in 1607; AGN Ord 2 exp.208 f.183–184v (1607).

161. Anderson, 1941, 1, 435.

162. Ibid.

163. Ibid., 438.

164. Ibid.

165. Ibid.

166. Ordinance 1; Ibid., 436.

167. Ibid.

168. Ordinance 26; Ibid., 445.

169. Ordinance 8; Ibid., 439–440.

170. Ibid., 439.

171. Ibid.

172. Illustrated examples are in Cristina Esteras Martín, *Marcas de platería hispanoamericana. Siglos XVI–XX* (Madrid: Ediciones Tuero, 1992), 13–27. See also Anderson, 1941, 1, 281–367.

173. Silversmiths implemented the registration process in 1563, which formed a basis for the registration requirement decreed on July 8, 1578 and October 30, 1584; these decrees were codified as book 8, title 10, law 24 of the *Laws of the Indies.*
174. Ordinance 17; Anderson, 1941, 1, 442.
175. Ibid.
176. Ibid.
177. Ibid.
178. A royal decree from 1528 prohibited silversmiths from having "bellows, or a furnace, or crucibles, or any smelting equipment" in their homes or workshops; see García Gallo, 2018, 242.
179. Royal decrees, November 9, 1526 and August 21, 1528, transcribed in Ibid., 241–242.
180. To anneal means to heat a metal object and then cool it slowly to strengthen its structure.
181. Ordinance 21; Anderson, 1941, 1, 444.
182. Ordinance 23; Ibid., 445.
183. Ordinance 29; Ibid., 447.
184. Ordinance 25; Ibid., 445.
185. AGN TSJ 7 exp.236 f.11–11v (1633).
186. Ordinance 28; Anderson, 1941, 1, 446.
187. Ordinance 28; Ibid.
188. Ordinance 28; Ibid.
189. Ordinance 31; Ibid., 448.
190. Book 5, title 21, law 67 and book 8, title 17, law 6 of the *Laws of Spain.*
191. España, 1598, I: f.371v, II: f.216v.
192. Ordinance 33; Anderson, 1941, 1, 448.
193. Ordinance 33; Ibid.
194. Ordinance 36; Ibid., 449.
195. The next set of "Ordinances for the Noble Art," approved by the viceroy on July 2, 1746, contained the same thirty-five orders, with the addition of two more related to the training and licensing of individuals; see AGN Moneda 1059 (1746). A summary of these ordinances is in Vásquez, 1938, 135–150.
196. The design dates the candlesticks to circa 1640. An inscription at their base reads "S. ANTo D La MEda," which suggests their provenance. For more details, see Cristina Esteras Martín, "Candaleros, numero de catálogo 32," in *El arte de la platería mexicana, 500 años,* ed. Lucía García-Noriega y Nieto (México: Centro Cultural Arte Contemporáneo, 1989); "El oro y la plata americanos, del valor ecónomico a la expresión artística," in *El oro y la plata de las Indias en la época de los Austrias,* ed. Concepción Lopezosa Aparicio (Madrid: Fundación ICO, 1999), 412. See also Cristina Esteras Martín, "Candeleros," in *La platería del Museo Franz Mayer. Obras escogidas, siglos XVI–XIX* (México: Museo Franz Mayer, 1992).
197. A summary of the tools and techniques used by silversmiths is in Artemio de Valle-Arizpe, *Notas de platería* (México: Editorial Polis, 1941), 251–256.
198. Ordinances 8 and 17; Anderson, 1941, 1, 439–440, 442.

199. Ordinance 24; Ibid., 445.
200. Ordinance 28; Ibid., 446.
201. AGN BN 56 exp.19 fs.4 (1648).
202. Ibid.
203. Ibid.
204. Ibid.
205. For the fleet's journey, see Lang, 1988, 151–153.
206. This order appears to be the first for Mexico City. Viceroy Salvatierra had previously mandated residents in Zacatecas to manifest their silver objects for inspection before officials at the local royal treasury branch; AGN RCD 49 exp.459 f.372–372v (1643).
207. AGN RCD 14 exp.784 f.494 (1650).
208. Guijo, 1953, 1: 1648–1654, 112.
209. Ibid.
210. Ibid., 147.
211. Ibid.
212. Ibid.
213. Moreno was a *maestro platero de masonería*. Silversmith Antonio Peña, for example, had trusted him to acquire four marks of rescue-silver on his behalf only three years earlier; AGN BN 56 exp.19 fs.4 (1648). In 1619, Moreno lived on the "street that went from the convent of Saint Lawrence to the hermitage of Saint Martin"; AGN TSJ 170 exp.5621 fs.7 (1624).
214. The Spanish term for this practice was *descaminar*. The viceroy had expressed orders from the crown to deal with this problem; AGN RCO 3 exp.100 f.175–176 (1650). The viceroy issued a set of ordinances on May 18, 1651, confirming previous prohibitions and implementing new ones that targeted activity in mining towns; AGI México 37 N.4 fs.8 (1651).
215. The decree was proclaimed on July 13, 1650; Guijo, 1953, 1: 1648–1654, 112.
216. Testimony of ordinances, May 18, 1651; AGI México 37 N.4 fs.8 (1651).
217. AGN RCD 14 exp.786 f.496 (1650).
218. Guijo, 1953, 1: 186–187. A study on individual shipments is Carmen Heredia Moreno, "Plata labrada en las flotas de Nueva España," in *El sueño de El Dorado. Estudios sobre la plata iberoamericana, siglos XVI–XIX*, ed. Jesús Paniagua Pérez, et al. (León: Universidad de León, 2012).
219. Guijo, 1953, 1: 196.
220. Ibid., 194.
221. Ordinance 31; Anderson, 1941, 1, 448.
222. Ibid.
223. The confraternity's name was *Hermandad de San Eligio y de Nuestra Señora de la Concepción*; AGN BN 845 exp.2bis (1691).
224. AGN BN 1175 exp.15 fs.1 (1644).
225. For the chapel's construction, see Manuel Toussaint, *La Catedral de México y el sagrario metropolitano: su historia, su tesoro, su arte* (México: Porrúa, 1973), 143–144.
226. Guijo, 1953, 1: 24.
227. Ibid.
228. The building was valued at over 6,700 pesos; AGN BN 913 exp.83 fs.2 (1667).

229. For the celebration of the Immaculate Conception in Mexico City, including smiths' participation, see Francisco Montes González, "'Donde seda y oro, hizo maridaje artificioso': el esplendor de la orfebrería novohispana en el juramento concepcionista de la Real Universidad de México," in *Ophir en las Indias: estudios sobre la plata americana: siglos XVI–XIX,* ed. Jesús Paniagua Pérez, et al. (León: Universidad de León, 2010); Beatriz Aracil, "Festejando la Inmaculada Concepción: Arte y literatura en algunas relaciones de fiestas del siglo XVII novohispano," *Fuentes Humanísticas* 55, no. II (2017).
230. Guijo, 1953, 1: 205.
231. Ibid.
232. Ibid., 206–207.
233. Ibid.
234. Ibid., 2: 1655–1664: 183.
235. Ibid.
236. AGN GP 8 exp.103 f.67v (1641). A study that examines women's empowerment and self-adornment in another capital city is Tamara J. Walker, *Exquisite Slaves: Race, Clothing, and Status in Colonial Lima* (Cambridge: Cambridge University Press, 2017).
237. AGN RCD 3 exp.181 f.156 (1598). City ordinances followed an empire-wide decree that prohibited women from wearing "gold, silk, or pearls" except if married to a "Spaniard"; Royal decree, February 11, 1571, codified as book 7, title 5, law 28 of the *Laws of the Indies.*
238. AGN RCD 3 exp.185 f.160v (1598).
239. Ordinances issued by the viceroy and confirmed by the High Court, April 14, 1612, transcribed in Vásquez, 1938, 100–101.
240. AGN RCD 48 exp.247 f.160v–161 (1644).
241. AGN RCD 48 exp.248 f.161 (1644).
242. AGN RCD 48 exp.247 f.160v–161 (1644).
243. Entry for *esclavo*; Covarrubias Horozco, 1674, 246–246v.
244. AGN IndV 2306 exp.8 fs.2 (1661).
245. Ibid.
246. Ibid.
247. AGN TSJ 195 exp.6548 fs.7 (1667).
248. Ibid.
249. ANM T. Cobián (110) 731 f.270–270v (1661).
250. The reduced price was 250 pesos. Ibid.
251. ANM T. Cobián (110) 732 f.105v–106v (1662).
252. These numbers are based on a database of over 3,000 bills of sale from the city's notary archive.
253. Juan Martínez de la Parra, *Sermon Panegirico, elogio sacro de San Eligio Obispo de Noyons, abogado y patron de los plateros* (México: Doña Maria de Benavides, 1686). Martínez (1653–1701), a member of the Society of Jesus, lived in Mexico City for nearly thirty years.
254. Ibid.
255. Ibid.
256. Ibid.

257. AGN TSJ 19 exp.656 fs.8 (1662); ANM N. Arauz (5) 12 f.15–18v (1657).

258. AGN TSJ 19 exp.656 fs.8 (1662).

259. AGN TSJ 17 exp.602 fs.4 (1660).

260. Ibid.

261. Ibid.

262. Ibid.

263. AGN TSJ 332 exp.10433 fs.2 (1664).

264. A register of smiths from November 10, 1685 lists Polanco; AGI Ind 1700 (1696), transcribed in José Torre Revello, *El gremio de plateros en las Indias occidentales* (Buenos Aires: Imprenta de la Universidad, 1932), xxviii–xxix. The report was part of an investigation that forced these shop owners to pay sales tax (through the guild), after decades of noncompliance.

265. AGN TSJ 19 exp.656 fs.8 (1662).

266. ANM J. Lerín (11) 1 f.153–170 (1689). Polanco the elder bid for the position in the 1650s, which as noted, was leased by the city for a set term after 1620. In 1647, a silversmith paid 182 pesos for this position, which enabled him to collect the fees paid for the work of inspecting wrought silver objects and tuning metal measures; Certification, November 13, 1646, AGI México 1684 (1647).

267. ANM J. Lerín (11) 1 f.153–170 (1689).

268. Ibid.

269. AGN TSJ 19 exp.656 fs.8 (1662).

270. ANM J. Lerín (11) 1 f.153–170 (1689).

271. Ibid.

272. AGN Civil 336 exp.5 (1693).

273. AGN Mat 139 exp.49 fs.3 (1665).

274. For this history, see Bernd Hausberger, "La distribución transcontinental de la plata americana en la globalización temprana," in *Historia económica del peso mexicano: Del mercado global a la gestión política de la moneda,* ed. Bernd Hausberger, et al. (México: Colegio de México, 2023); Mariano Bonialian and Bernd Hausberger, "Consideraciones sobre el comercio y el papel de la plata hispanoamericana en la temprana globalización, siglos XVI–XIX," *Historia Mexicana* 68, no. 1 (2018).

275. Medina, 1682, f.234. Data on the city's mintage (the number of coins issued) post 1690 is in John Jay TePaske, "New World Mintage: México, Santo Domingo, Lima, and Potosí," in *A New World of Gold and Silver,* ed., Kendall W. Brown (Leiden: Brill, 2010).

276. Scholarship on the "chronic scarcity" of specie during the seventeenth century is based on official reports, rather than sustained quantitative analysis of local property records. Scholars emphasize the exportation of silver coins minted in the city and correlate it to an absence of coins in local circulation. A study that challenges the historiographical assumption that the local economy in Mexico City suffered from a shortage of coins in the late seventeenth and early eighteenth centuries is Enriqueta Quiroz "La moneda menuda en la circulación monetaria de la ciudad de México, siglo XVIII," *Mexican Studies/Estudios Mexicanos* 22, no. 2 (2006). For the

eighteenth, see also Antonio Ibarra, "Mercado colonial, plata y moneda en el siglo XVIII Novohispano. Comentarios para un diálogo con Ruggiero Romano, a propósito de su nuevo libro," *Historia Mexicana* 49, no.2 (1999). People living elsewhere in Mexico during the seventeenth century, such as in mining towns, by contrast, did indeed have coin shortages; see Bakewell, 1971, 211.

277. Medina, 1682, f.234v.

278. Ibid.

279. Pieces-of-eight were accepted as currency, for example, in Istanbul; Şevket Pamuk, "In the Absence of Domestic Currency: Debased European Coinage in the Seventeenth-Century Ottoman Empire," *The Journal of Economic History* 57, no. 2 (1997).

280. Ordinance 28; Anderson, 1941, 1, 446.

## CONCLUSION

1. The scribe categorized Ana de los Santos as a woman of African descent and described her as "white." AGN TSJ 88 exp.3132 fs.41 (1675–1676).

2. AGN TSJ 88 exp.3132 f.10v (1675).

3. AGN TSJ 88 exp.3132 f.32 (1675).

4. AGN TSJ 88 exp.3132 f.26v (1675).

5. Ibid. For the medicines used in Mexico City, including mercury for syphilis, see Paula S. DeVos, *Compound Remedies: Galenic Pharmacy from the Ancient Mediterranean to New Spain* (Pittsburgh: University of Pittsburgh Press, 2021).

6. AGN TSJ 88 exp.3132 f.31v–32 (1675).

7. AGN TSJ 88 exp.3132 f.26v (1675).

8. Ibid.

9. AGN RCD 30 exp.961 f.275v (1682). A resident, for example, trusted Pedraza to manage a 3,000-pesos investment; AGN Capellanías 272 exp.117 f.143–144 (1694).

10. Torquemada, 1615, 360. An overview of cacao as money in the sixteenth century is José Luis de Rojas, "El cacao," in *La moneda indígena y sus usos en la Nueva España en el siglo XVI* (México: CIESAS, 1998). An outdated understanding of money maintained that advanced states had coin money (true money) that permitted real trade – a mark of so-called civilization; lesser states did not have money (because they did not have coins), so they could only barter.

11. Torquemada, 1615, 674.

12. Fractional units have a lesser value than a main unit, which was the real, a metal unit, in the case of Mexico City. Like silver, cacao was a commodity with intrinsic value. Cacao, therefore, was not fiduciary money such as paper bills, which have no inherent value.

13. A load (*carga*) equaled 24,000 cacao beans; Echagoyan, 1603, 86v–87.

14. Gage, 1648, 51, 59.

15. Ibid., 51.
16. Ibid.
17. Ibid.
18. The scribe categorized María de la Cruz as an enslaved woman of African descent; AGN IndV 803 exp.17 fs.4 (1637).
19. AGN IndV 803 exp.17 fs.4 (1637).
20. Cobo, 1956, 2, 258–259.
21. Ibid.
22. Ibid.
23. The chronicler noted a ratio of 60 to 80 beans per real, less than the valuation recorded half a century earlier, when it was 200 beans per real or more; Gemelli Careri, 1704, 4, 509.
24. Ibid.
25. Ibid.
26. Ibid.
27. Entry for *trabajo*; Sebastián Covarrubias Horozco, *Tesoro de la lengva castellana, o española* (Madrid: Impresor del Rey, 1611), 2a: 50.
28. Torquemada, 1615, 328, 331.
29. Ibid., 330.
30. Ibid., 331.
31. Ibid., 330–331.
32. Ibid.
33. Ibid., 330.
34. First published in Rome in 1588, *Delle cause della grandezza delle città* was quickly translated into Spanish (Madrid, 1593), English (London 1606), and other languages; it circulated widely along with Botero's other key work *The Reason of State*. Various scholars have connected Botero to political and literary culture in Mexico City, including Osvaldo F. Pardo, "Giovanni Botero and Bernardo de Balbuena: Art and Economy in *La grandeza mexicana*," *Journal of Latin American Cultural Studies* 10, no. 1 (2001); Alejandro Cañeque, "Theater of Power: Writing and Representing the Auto de Fe in Colonial Mexico," *The Americas* 52, no. 3 (1996).
35. Giovanni Botero, *A Treatise, Concerning the Causes of the Magnificencie and Greatnes of Cities* (London: Printed by T. P., 1606), 2, 9. The author checked the original Italian; all Botero quotes are from the first English translation to maintain contemporary phrasing.
36. Ibid., 13.
37. Ibid., 2, 45, 97–98.
38. Ibid., 2, 9.
39. Entry for metropolis, "Oxford English Dictionary" (Oxford: Oxford University Press, 2023).
40. Torquemada and Botero both used the words in quotations.
41. Botero, 1606, 56.
42. Ibid., 9.
43. Ibid.

ESSAY ON SOURCES

1. A short overview of its history is Pilar Gonzalbo Aizpuru, "El Archivo General de Notarías de la ciudad de México," *Historia Mexicana* 35, no. 4 (1986).

2. For the implementation of this practice, see Ivonne Mijares, *Escribanos y escrituras públicas en el siglo XVI: el caso de la ciudad de México* (México: UNAM, 1997).

3. Scribes learned their trade through apprenticeships and by reading manuals that contained sample forms with details for exceptions. Yrolo included examples of some 150 documents used in Mexico City at the turn of the century, including a "sale of slave," a "declaration made by someone by which he says that so many pesos he sent to Castile belong to someone else," a "bill of lading for a mule train," and a "power of attorney to place a son in an apprenticeship"; Nicolás de Yrolo Calar, *La política de escrituras: estudio preliminar, indices, glosario y apéndices*, eds., María del Pilar Martínez López-Cano, et al. (México: UNAM, 1996), 33–216.

4. ANM N. Arauz (5) 11 f.111v (1656).

5. ANM J. Pérez Rivera (497) 3357 f.345v–346 (1605).

6. The author did not use these catalogues. A catalogue of the volumes of two notaries from the seventeenth century, first issued as a CD, is now online. *Catálogo de protocolos del Archivo General de Notarías de la ciudad de México*, Edición en disco compacto ed., IV vols., vol. II: Juan Pérez de Rivera, escribano público (1582–1631), Juan Pérez de Rivera, escribano de provincia (1611–1617) y Juan Pérez de Rivera Cáceres, escribano público (1632–1651) (México: UNAM, 2005); "Catálogo de Protocolos del Archivo General de Notárias de la ciudad de México, Colección Siglo XVII. En línea," eds., Ivonne Mijares, et al. (México: UNAM, 2016). The third volume on CD also contains notaries from the seventeenth century. *Catálogo de protocolos del Archivo General de Notarías de la ciudad de México*, Edición en disco compacto ed., IV vols., vol. III: Diferentes escribanos reales de los siglos XVI y XVII (México: UNAM, 2005). See also, Ivonne Mijares, *Catálogo de protocolos del Archivo General de Notarías de la ciudad de México: introducción* (México: UNAM, 2002). Catalogues for other notaries that only identify documents related to art are: Guillermina Ramírez Montes, *Catáogos de documentos de arte en el Archivo de Notarías de la ciudad de México* (México: UNAM, 1990); Guillermina Ramírez Montes and Guillermino Luckie, *Catálogos de documentos de arte, Archivo de Notarías de la ciudad de México: protocolos I* (México: UNAM, 1993); Silvia Bravo Sandoval and Raquel Pineda Mendoza, *Catálogos de documentos de arte, Archivo de Notarías de la ciudad de México: protocolos II* (México: UNAM, 1996); Edén Mario Zárate Sánchez, *Catálogos de documentos de arte, Archivo de Notarías de la ciudad de México: protocolos III* (México: UNAM, 2004); Raquel Pineda Mendoza and Edén Mario Zárate Sánchez, *Catálogos de documentos de arte, Archivo de Notarías de la ciudad de México: protocolos IV* (México: UNAM, 2005); Raquel Pineda Mendoza, *Catálogos de documentos de arte, Archivo de Notarías de la ciudad de México: protocolos V* (México: UNAM, 2015).

7. The archive has an online catalogue that proved helpful for documentation from the sixteenth century: "Catálogo de Protocolos del Archivo General de Notárias de la ciudad de México, Fondo Siglo XVI. En línea," eds., Ivonne Mijares, et al. (México: UNAM, 2014).

8. A book that reflects on archival theory and historians' use of documentation from the AGN and other archives is Zeb Tortorici, *Sins against Nature: Sex and Archives in Colonial New Spain* (Durham: Duke University Press, 2018).

9. A bibliographic tool is Archivo General de la Nación, *Fuentes primarias para la traza urbana de la ciudad de México en la época colonial: catálogo documental,* 2 vols. (México: Secretaría de Gobernación, 2000).

10. The journal is the *Boletín del Archivo General de la Nación,* published since 1930.

11. AGN RCD 5 exp.289 (1606).

12. AGN TSJ 170 exp.5626 fs.12 (1624).

13. A classic work that explains this collection is Solange Alberro, *Inquisición y sociedad en México, 1571–1700* (México: Fondo de Cultura Económica, 1988). Another foundational monograph is Martin A. Nesvig, *Ideology and Inquisition: The World of the Censors in Early Mexico* (New Haven: Yale University Press, 2009).

14. AGN Inq 422 exp.4 f.351–67 (1646).

15. AGN Inq 306 exp.7 fs.27 (1619).

16. A history and guide is Lina Odena Güemes, *Archivo Histórico del Distrito Federal: guía general* (México: Gobierno del Distrito Federal: Verdehalago, 2000). See also Manuel Carrera Stampa, "El Archivo del ex Ayuntamiento de México," *Historia Mexicana* 12, no.4 (1963).

17. Royal decree, May 26, 1573; Royal decree, May 1, 1586; codified as book 4, title 9, laws 16 and 20 of the *Laws of the Indies.*

18. Royal decree, June 15, 1628; February 27, 1575; codified as book 4, title 9, law 18 and 19 of the *Laws of the Indies.*

19. Only volumes 14–27, 30–33, and 38 survive for the seventeenth century, covering the months and years: October 1599 to August 1630; April 1635 to December 1643; January 1698 to December 1705. These volumes were edited and printed from 1899 to 1911 and are available online. The first two decades have printed catalogues, see María Isabel Monroy Padilla, ed., *Guía de las Actas de Cabildo de la ciudad de México: Años 1601–1610, siglo XVII* (México: Universidad Iberoamericana, 1987); *Guía de las Actas de Cabildo de la ciudad de México: Años 1611–1620, siglo XVII* (México: Universidad Iberoamericana, 1988).

20. AGI México 1684 f.10Ar–10Av (1633).

21. AHNS Ordenes Militares 5875 (1696).

22. TNA, SP 94/8 (1602).

23. Newberry, New Vault Ayer MS 1139 f.19 (1651).

24. A bibliographic tool for identifying printed sources is Francisco de Solano, *Las voces de la ciudad: México a través de sus impresos (1539–1821),* (Madrid: CSIC, 1994).

25. For his life and work, see chapter 4 of Camilla Townsend, *Annals of Native America: How the Nahuas of Colonial Mexico Kept Their History Alive* (New York: Oxford University Press, 2017).
26. For his life and influences, see José Alcina Franch, "Fray Juan de Torquemada (¿1564?-1624)," *Revista de Indias* 29, no. 1 (1969); Miguel León-Portilla, "New Light on the Sources of Torquemada's *Monarchia Indiana*," *The Americas* 35, no. 3 (1979).
27. For his life and works, see John F. Schwaller, "Fr. Agustín de Vetancurt: The 'Via crucis en mexicano,'" *The Americas* 74, no. 119–137 (2017).
28. Robles's manuscript was held in the library of the Padres del Oratorio de México and subsequently in the *Biblioteca Nacional* but is no longer available; the first edition was Antonio de Robles, *Diario de algunas cosas notables que han sucedido en esta Nueva España*, ed., Manuel Orozco y Berra, vols. II & III (México: J. R. Navarro, 1853–1854).
29. Guijo's diary was held at the Real Universidad and subsequently in the national library, but is no longer available; the first edition was Gregorio Martín de Guijo, *Diario de sucesos notables. Comprende los años de 1648 a 1664*, ed., Manuel Orozco y Berra, vol. I (México: J. R. Navarro, 1853).
30. Caesar E. Farah, ed., *An Arab's Journey to Colonial Spanish America: The Travels of Elias al-Mûsili in the Seventeenth Century* (New York: Syracuse University Press, 2003), 81.
31. A bibliography of secondary and primary sources is María Dolores Morales Martínez, María Amparo Ros Torres, and Esteban Sánchez de Tagle, eds., *Ciudad de México, época colonial. Bibliografía* (México: INAH, 1993). Books and collections with long periodizations include Serge Gruzinski, *La ciudad de México: una historia* (México: Fondo de Cultura Económica, 2004); José Luis Soberanes Fernández and Manuel Andreu Gálvez, eds., *500 años de historia de la ciudad de México. Estudio histórico-jurídico con motivo del quinto centenario de la fundación de la ciudad de México* (Pamplona: Ediciones Universidad de Navarra, 2021). A meditation on modernity and urban living is Mauricio Tenorio-Trillo, *I Speak of the City: Mexico City at the Turn of the Twentieth Century* (Chicago: University of Chicago Press, 2012).

# Bibliography

## PRINTED PRIMARY SOURCES

Alcocer y Vera, José de. *Excelencias de la antiquissima archicofradia de la Santissima Trinidad*. México: Juan Ruyz, 1651.

"Anales de San Gregorio Acapulco, 1520–1606." *Tlalocan* III (1952): 103–141.

Arfe y Villafañe, Juan de. *Qvilatador de la plata, oro, y piedras*. Valladolid: Alonso y Diego Fernādez de Cordoua, 1572.

Arnall Juan, M. Josefa. "El 'Itinerario a Indias' (1673–1679) del P. Fr. Isidoro de la Asunción, C.D. (Manuscrito 514 de la Biblioteca Provincial y Universitaria de Barcelona)." *Boletín Americanista* 28 (1978): 197–252.

Ayala, Manuel José de, ed. *Disposiciones complementarias de las Leyes de Indias*. 3 vols. Vol. 3. Madrid: Saez hermanos, 1930.

Balbuena, Bernardo de. *Grandeza mexicana*. México: Emprenta de Diego Lopez Davalos, 1604.

Barrio Lorenzot, Juan Francisco del, ed. *Ordenanzas de Gremios de la Nueva España*, ed., Genaro Estrada. México: Secretaría de Gobernación, 1920.

Barrios, Juan de. *Verdadera medicina, cirvgia, y astrologia en tres libros dividida*. México: Fernando Balli, 1607.

Bezerra, Jerónimo. *Breve relacion del ensaye de plata y oro*. México: Francisco Rodriguez Lupercio, 1671.

Botero, Giovanni. *A Treatise, Concerning the Causes of the Magnificencie and Greatnes of Cities*. Translated by Robert Peterson. London: Printed by T. P., 1606. Rome, 1588.

Cepeda, Fernando de, and Fernando Alfonso Carrillo. *Relacion Vniversal Legitima, y verdadera del sitio en qve esta fvndada la muy noble, insigne, y muy leal Ciudad de Mexico*. México: Imprenta de Francisco Salbago, 1637.

Cervantes de Salazar, Francisco. *México en 1554. Tres diálogos latinos*. México: Andrade y Morales, 1875. *Ludouici Viuis Valentini exercitationem, aliquot Dialogi*, 1554.

Cervantes de Salazar, Francisco. *Crónica de la Nueva España*. Madrid: The Hispanic Society of America, 1914.

Chávez Orozco, Luis, ed., *Códice Osuna. Reproducción facsimilar de la obra*. México: Instituto Indigenista Interamericano, 1947.

Chimalpahin Cuauhtlehuanitzin, Domingo Francisco de San Antón Muñón. *Annals of His Time*. Translated by James Lockhart, Susan Schroeder and Doris Namala. Stanford: Stanford University Press, 2006.

Cisneros, Diego de. *Sitio, natvraleza y propriedades de la civdad de Mexico*. Mexíco: Blanco de Alcaçar, 1618.

Ciudad de México, Cabildo, ed., *Actas de Cabildo*. Vol. 1: Marzo 1524–Junio 1529. México: Municipio Libre, 1889.

Ciudad de México, Cabildo, ed. *Actas de Cabildo*. Vol. 2: Junio 1529–Septiembre 1532. México: Municipio Libre, 1889.

Ciudad de México, Cabildo, ed., *Actas de Cabildo*. Vol. 3: Octubre 1532–Diciembre 1535. México: Municipio Libre, 1889.

Ciudad de México, Cabildo, ed. *Actas de Cabildo*. Vol. 4: Enero 1536–Agosto 1543. México: Municipio Libre, 1889.

Ciudad de México, Cabildo, ed., *Actas de Cabildo*. Vol. 5: Septiembre 1543–Noviembre 1550. México: Municipio Libre, 1889.

Ciudad de México, Cabildo, ed., *Actas de Cabildo*. Vol. 6: Diciembre 1550–Diciembre 1561. México: Municipio Libre, 1889.

Ciudad de México, Cabildo, ed. *Actas de Cabildo*. Vol. 7: Enero 1562–Octubre 1571, México: Municipio Libre, 1889.

Ciudad de México, Cabildo, ed., *Actas de Cabildo*. Vol. 8: Octubre 1571–Diciembre 1584, México: Agular e Hijos, 1893.

Ciudad de México, Cabildo, ed., *Actas de Cabildo*. Vol. 9: Enero 1585–Mayo 1590. México: Aguilar e Hijos, 1895.

Ciudad de México, Cabildo, ed., *Actas de Cabildo*. Vol. 10: Mayo 1590–Junio 1592. México: Aguilar e hijos, 1896.

Ciudad de México, Cabildo, ed., *Actas de Cabildo*. Vol. 11: Junio 1592–Diciembre 1593. México: Aguilar e hijos, 1897.

Ciudad de México, Cabildo, ed., *Actas de Cabildo*. Vol. 12: Enero 1594–Mayo 1597. México: Aguilar e Hijos, 1898.

Ciudad de México, Cabildo, ed., *Actas de Cabildo*. Vol. 13: Mayo 1597–Octubre 1599. México: Aguilar e hijos, 1898.

Ciudad de México, Cabildo, ed., *Actas de Cabildo*. Vol. 14: Octubre 1599–Febrero 1602. México: Aguilar e hijos, 1899.

Ciudad de México, Cabildo, ed., *Actas de Cabildo*. Vol. 16: Enero 1605–Marzo 1607. México: Central, 1900.

Ciudad de México, Cabildo, ed. *Actas de Cabildo*. Vol. 17: Marzo 1607–Diciembre 1610 México: Central, 1901.

Ciudad de México, Cabildo, ed. *Actas de Cabildo*. Vol. 20: Agosto 1614–Junio 1616. México: A. Carranza y Comp., 1904.

Ciudad de México, Cabildo, ed., *Actas de Cabildo*. Vol. 23: Mayo 1619–Diciembre 1620. México: El Correo Español, 1906.

Ciudad de México, Cabildo, ed., *Actas de Cabildo*. Vol. 24: Enero 1621–Febrero 1623. México: El Correo Español, 1906.

Ciudad de México, Cabildo, ed., *Actas de Cabildo.* Vol. 25: Marzo 1623–Diciembre 1625. México: El Correo Español, 1906.

Ciudad de México, Cabildo, ed., *Actas de Cabildo.* Vol. 26: Enero 1626–Noviembre 1628. México: El Correo Español, 1907.

Ciudad de México, Cabildo, ed., *Actas de Cabildo.* Vol. 30: Abril 1635–Diciembre 1636. México: Carranza y Comp., 1908.

Cobo, Bernabé. *Obras del P. Bernabé Cobo, de la Compañia de Jesus.* Vol. 2, Madrid: Atlas, 1956.

Covarrubias Horozco, Sebastián. *Tesoro de la lengua castellana, o española.* Madrid: Impresor del Rey, 1611.

Covarrubias Horozco, Sebastián. *Parte primera del tesoro de la lengua castellana, o española.* Madrid: Melchor Sanchez, 1674. 1611.

Covarrubias Horozco, Sebastián. *Parte segunda del tesoro de la lengua castellana, o española.* Madrid: Melchor Sanchez, 1673. 1611.

Echagoyan, Felipe. *Tablas de redvciones de monedas, y del valor de todo genero de plata y oro, y del modo de hazer las cuẽtas ... y de otras cosas necessarias y conuenientes para las cuentas del trato y contrato de estos Reynos.* México: Henrico Martinez, 1603.

España. *Recopilacion de las Leyes destos Reynos, hecha por mandado de la Magestad Catholica del Rey don Philippe Segundo.* Alcalá de Henares: Iuan Iñiguez de Lequerica, 1581. 1567.

España. *Recopilacion de las leyes destos reynos, hecha por mandado de la Magestad Catholica del Rey dõ Philippe Segundo nuestro Señor.* Alcalá de Henares: Iuan Iñiguez de Lequerica, 1598.

España. *Recopilacion de las leyes destos reynos, hecha por mandado de la Magestad Catolica del Rey don Felipe Segundo.* Madrid: Catalina de Barrio Angulo, 1640.

Farah, Caesar E., ed. *An Arab's Journey to Colonial Spanish America: The Travels of Elias al-Mûsili in the Seventeenth Century.* New York: Syracuse University Press, 2003.

Fonseca, Fabian de, and Carlos de Urrutia. *Historia general de real hacienda.* 6 vols. Vol. 1, México: V. G. Torres, 1845. Manuscript 1791.

Fonseca, Fabian de, and Carlos de Urrutia. *Historia general de real hacienda.* 6 vols. Vol. 2, México: V. G. Torres, 1849. Manuscript 1791.

Gage, Thomas. *The English-American His Travail by Sea and Land: Or, New Svrvey of the West-Indias.* London: R. Cotes, 1648.

García Gallo, Alfonso, ed. *Cedulario Indiano Recopilado por Diego de Encinas.* fascimile ed. 4 vols. Madrid: Real Academia de la Historia, 2018.

Gemelli Careri, Giovanni Francesco. *Giro del mondo.* 6 vols. Vol. 6: Nvova Spagna, Napoli: Giuseppe Roselli, 1699.

Gemelli Careri, Giovanni Francesco. *A voyage round the world.* 4 vols. Vol. 4, London: Awnsham & John Churchill, 1704.

General de la Nación, Archivo. *Fuentes primarias para la traza urbana de la ciudad de México en la época colonial: catálogo documental.* 2 vols. México: Secretaría de Gobernación, 2000.

González Dávila, Gil. *Teatro eclesiastico de la primitiva iglesia de las Indias occidentales.* 2 vols. Vol. 1, Madrid: Diego Diaz de la Carrera, 1649.

Gómez de Cervantes, Gonzalo. "Memorial de Gonzalo Gómez de Cervantes para el doctor Eugenio Salazar oidor del Real Consejo de las Indias." In *La vida económica y social de Nueva España, al finalizar el siglo XVI*, edited by Alberto María Carreño, 75–199. México: Antiqua librería Robredo, 1944.

Guijo, Gregorio Martín de. *Diario de sucesos notables. Comprende los años de 1648 a 1664.* Documentos para la historia de Méjico, 1a serie. Edited by Manuel Orozco y Berra, Vol. I, México: J. R. Navarro, 1853.

Guijo, Gregorio Martín de. *Diario, 1648–1664.* 2 vols. Vol. 2: 1655–1664, México: Porrúa, 1953.

Guijo, Gregorio Martín de. *Diario, 1648–1664.* 2 vols. Vol. 1: 1648–1654, México: Porrúa, 1953.

Gutiérrez de Medina, Cristóbal. *Viaje del virrey marqués de Villena.* México: Impr. Universitaria, 1947. *Viage de tierra, y mar, feliz por mar y tierra, que hizo el excellentissimo señor Marqves de Villena mi señor*, 1640.

Indias, Consejo de. *Recopilacion de leyes de los reynos de las Indias.* 4 vols. Madrid: Por Iulian de Paredes, 1681.

*Instrucciones que los vireyes de Nueva España dejaron a sus sucesores.* México: Imprenta imperial, 1867.

Levanto, Horacio. "Memorial sorbe [sic] el trato de la China con Nueua España, y estos Reynos." Biblioteca Nacional de España, 1617.

*Libro de las bulas y pragmáticas de los Reyes Católicos.* facsímil ed. Madrid: Instituto de España, 1973. 1503.

López de Hinojosos, Alonso. *Suma y recopilación de cirugía con un arte para sangrar muy útil y provechosa.* Facsimile ed. México: Academia Nacional de Medicina, 1977. 1578.

López de Hinojosos, Alonso. *Svmma y recopilacion de chirvgia, con vn arte para sãgrar muy vtil y prouechoso.* México: Antonio Ricarco, 1578.

López de Hinojosos, Alonso. *Svmma y recopilacion de cirvgia, con vn arte para sangrar, y examen de barberos.* México: Casa Pedro Balli, 1595. 1578.

López de Velasco, Juan. *Geografía y descripción universal de las Indias.* Madrid: Atlas, 1971.

"Map of Santa Cruz." Uppsala University Library, Sweden, 1537–1555.

Marien y Arróspide, Tomás Antonio. *Tratado general de monedas, pesas, medidas y cambios de todas las naciones.* Madrid: Benito Cano, 1789.

Martínez de la Parra, Juan. *Sermon Panegirico, elogio sacro de San Eligio Obispo de Noyons, abogado y patron de los plateros.* México: Doña Maria de Benavides, 1686.

Medina, Baltasar de. *Chronica de la Santa Provincia de San Diego de Mexico, de religiosos descalços de N.S.P.S. Francisco en la Nueva-España.* México: Juan de Ribera, 1682.

Montemayor de Cuenca, Juan Francisco de. "Recopilacion de algunos mandamientos y ordenanzas del gobierno de esta Nueva España ... año de 1677." In *Recopilacion sumaria de todos los autos acordados de la Real Audiencia y Sala del Crimen de esta Nueva España, y providencias de su superior Gobierno*, edited by Eusebio Bentura Beleña, 1–114. México: Felipe de Zúñiga y Ontiveros, 1787.

Montemayor de Cuenca, Juan Francisco de. "Recopilacion sumaria de algunos autos acordados de la Real Audiencia ... año de 1677." In *Recopilacion sumaria de todos los autos acordados de la Real Audiencia y sala del crimen de esta Nueva España, y providencias de su superior gobierno*, edited by Eusebio Bentura Beleña, 1–100. México: Felipe de Zúñiga y Ontiveros, 1787.

Muñoz, Miguel Eugenio. *Recopilacion de las leyes, pragmaticas reales, decretos, y acuerdos del Real Proto-Medicato*. Valencia: Viuda de Antonio Bordazar, 1751.

O'Gorman, Edmundo. "Sobre los inconvenientes de vivir los indios en el centro de la ciudad." *Boletín del Archivo General de la Nación* 9, no.1 (1938): 1–34.

*Ordenanças de Seuilla*. Sevilla: Andres Grande, 1632.

Paso y Troncoso, Francisco del, ed. *Epistolario de Nueva España, 1505–1818.* 6 vols. Vol. XV. México: Porrúa, 1939.

Puga, Vasco de. *Prouisiões cedulas instruciones desu Magestad: ordenãças ... y gouernaciõ dsta nueua España*. México: Casa de Pedro Ocharte, 1563.

Puga, Vasco de, ed. *Provisiones, cédulas, instrucciones para el gobierno de la Nueva España*. fascimilar ed. Madrid: Cultura Hispánica, 1945.

Ramírez de Santillana, Juana Inés (Sor Juan Inés de la Cruz), "Lamenta con todos la muerte de la Señora Marquesa de Mancera (1674)." In *Sonetos*, edited by Ramón García González. Madrid: Biblioteca Virtual Miguel de Cervantes, 2006. www.cervantesvirtual.com/nd/ark:/59851/bmczc896.

Robles, Antonio de. *Diario de algunas cosas notables que han sucedido en esta Nueva España*. Documentos para la historia de Méjico, 1a serie. Edited by Manuel Orozco y Berra, Vol. II & III, México: J. R. Navarro, 1853–1854.

Robles, Antonio de. *Diario de sucesos notables, 1665–1703.* 3 vols. México: Porrúa, 1946.

Rubio Mañé, J. Ignacio, ed. *Gente de España en la ciudad de México, año de 1689*. Vol. 2a serie, VII, n.1–2. México: Boletín del Archivo General de la Nación, 1966.

Saavedra Fajardo, Diego de. *Idea de vn principe politico cristiano*. Munich, 1643.

Sahagún, Bernardino de. *Historia general de las cosas de Nueva España.* 3 vols. Vol. 2, México Alejandro Valdés, 1829.

Sariñana y Cuenca, Isidro. *Llanto del occidente en el ocaso del mas claro sol de las Españas*. México: Viuda de Bernardo Calderon, 1666.

Sigüenza y Góngora, Carlos de. *Alboroto y motín de México del 8 de junio de 1692*. México: Museo Nacional de Arqueología, Historia y Etnografía, 1932.

*Summario de las gracias, e indulgencias concedidas por la santidad de Paulo Quinto, y Clemente Decimo á los Archi-Cofrades de la Santisima Trinidad de Roma, de que gozan los Archi-Cofrades de la SSma. Trinidad de Mexico, fundada en 20 de Marzo de 1580, agregada a la Archi Cofradia de Roma en el año de 1582*. México: Felipe de Zuñiga, 1781.

Torquemada, Juan de. *Ia parte de los veynte y vn libros rituales y monarchia yndiana*. Sevilla: Matthias Clauijo, 1615.

Torre Villalpando, Guadalupe de la. "Bandos para el buen gobierno de la ciudad de México virreinal." *Boletín del Archivo General de la Nación* 9, no.4 (2020): 43–59.

Vetancurt, Augustín de. "Tratado de la ciudad de Mexico, y las grandezas que la ilustran." In *Chronica de la Provincia del Santo Evangelio de Mexico. Quarta parte del Teatro Mexicano de los successos religiosos*, 1–45. México: Doña María de Benavides, 1697.

Vetancurt, Augustín de. "Tratado de la ciudad de Mexico, y las grandezas que la ilustran." In *Teatro Mexicano. Descripcion breve de los svcessos exemplares, historicos, politicos, militares, y religiosos del nuevo mundo.* 2 vols. Vol. 1, México: Doña Maria de Benavides, 1698.

Vázquez de Espinosa, Antonio. *Compendio y descripción de las Indias Occidentales.* Edited by Charles U. Clark. Washington: Smithsonian Institution, 1948. Manuscript c.1629.

Villa-señor y Sánchez, Joseph Antonio de. *Theatro americano. Descripcion general de los reynos, y provincias de la Nueva-España, y sus jurisdicciones.* 2 vols. Vol. 1, México: Viuda de Don J. Bernardo de Hogal, 1746.

Villalobos, Arias de. "Obediencia que México, cabeza de la Nueva España, dio a la Majestad Católica del rey D. Felipe de Austria … Con un discurso en verso, del estado de la misma ciudad." In *Documentos íneditos o muy raros para la historia de México*, edited by Genero García, 106–280. México: Vda. de Ch. Bouret, 1907.

Yrolo Calar, Nicolás de. *La política de escrituras: estudio preliminar, indices, glosario y apéndices.* Edited by María del Pilar Martínez López-Cano, Ivonne Mijares and Javier Sanchiz Ruiz. México: UNAM, 1996. México, 1605.

## SECONDARY SOURCES

Aguirre Beltrán, Gonzalo. *Medicina y magia. El proceso de aculturación en la estructura colonial.* México: Instituto Nacional Indigenista, 1963.

Alba Pastor, María. "La organización corporativa de la sociedad novohispana." In *Formaciones religiosas en la América colonial*, edited by María Alba Pastor and Alicia Mayer, 81–140. México: UNAM, 2000.

Alberro, Solange. *Inquisición y sociedad en México, 1571–1700.* México: Fondo de Cultura Económica, 1988.

Albiez-Wieck, Sarah. *Taxing Difference in Peru and New Spain (16th–19th Century): Negotiating Social Differences and Belonging.* Leiden: Brill, 2022.

Alcántara Gallegos, Alejandro. "Los barrios de Tenochtitlan. Topografía, organización interna y tipología de sus predios." In *Historia de la vida cotidiana en México: Mesoamérica y los ámbitos indígenas de la Nueva España*, edited by Pablo Escalante Gonzalbo, 167–198. México: Colegio de México, 2004.

Alcántara López, Álvaro. "Los otros contribuyentes: pardos y mulatos de la provincia de Acayucan, 1765–1795." In *De contribuyentes y contribuciones en la fiscalidad mexicana, siglos XVIII–XX*, edited by Yovana Celaya Nández and Graciela Márquez Colín, 55–104. México: Colegio de México, 2004.

Alcina Franch, José. "Fray Juan de Torquemada (¿1564?–1624)." *Revista de Indias* 29, no.1 (1969): 31–50.

Alvarado Morales, Manuel. "El cabildo y regimiento de la ciudad de México en el siglo XVII: Un ejemplo de oligarquía criolla." *Historia Mexicana* 28, no.4 (1979): 489–514.

Anderson, Lawrence L. *El arte de la platería en México 1519–1936*. 2 vols. Vol. 1, New York: Oxford University Press, 1941.

Aracil, Beatriz. "Festejando la Inmaculada Concepción: Arte y literatura en algunas relaciones de fiestas del siglo XVII novohispano." *Fuentes Humanísticas* 55, no.2 (2017): 181–197.

Araujo, Ana Lucia. "Women Who Fed the City." In *Humans in Shackles: An Atlantic History of Slavery*, 236–260. Chicago: University of Chicago Press, 2024.

Arregui Zamorano, Pilar. *La Audiencia de México según los visitadores: siglos XVI y XVII*. México: UNAM, 1985.

Baena Zapatero, Alberto. "Biombos mexicanos e identidad criolla." *Revista de Indias* 80, no.280 (2020): 651–686.

Bakewell, Peter J. *Silver Mining and Society in Colonial Mexico: Zacatecas, 1546–1700*. London: Cambridge University Press, 1971.

Ballone, Angela. *The 1624 Tumult of Mexico in Perspective (c. 1620–1650): Authority and Conflict Resolution in the Iberian Atlantic*. Leiden: Brill, 2018.

Barragán-Álvarez, José Adrián. "The Feet of Commerce: Mule-trains and Transportation in Eighteenth-Century New Spain." Dissertation, University of Texas at Austin, 2013.

Bautista y Lugo, Gibran. "Los indios y la rebelión de 1624 en la ciudad de México." In *Los indios y las ciudades de Nueva España*, edited by Felipe Castro Gutiérrez, 197–216. México: UNAM, 2010.

Bautista y Lugo, Gibran. "Francisco Manso y Zúñiga (1627–1636) ¿Una corte real en el palacio arzobispal de México?" In *La Iglesia en Palacio. Los eclesiásticos en las cortes hispánicas (siglos XVI-XVII)*, edited by Rafael Valladares, 111–131. Roma: Viella, 2019.

Bautista y Lugo, Gibran. "Recaudar la lealtad al rey y proteger el dinero del reino. La ciudad de México entre servicios, arbitrios y crédito, 1623–1629." In *Negociación, lágrimas y maldiciones. La fiscalidad extraordinaria en la monarquía hispánica, 1620–1814*, edited by Guillermina del Valle Pavón, 75–106. México: Instituto Mora, 2020.

Bautista y Lugo, Gibran. *Integrar un reino. La ciudad de México en la monarquía de España 1621–1628*. México: UNAM, 2020.

Bazarte Martínez, Alicia. *Las cofradías de españoles en la ciudad de México (1526–1860)*. México: UAM, 1989.

Bazarte Martínez, Alicia. "Las limosnas de las cofradías: su administración y destino." In *Cofradías, capellanías y obras pías en la América colonial*, edited by María del Pilar Martínez López-Cano, Gisela von Wobeser and Juan Guillermo Muñoz Correa, 65–74. México: UNAM, 1998.

Bazarte Martínez, Alicia. "La cofradía de Cosme y Damián en el siglo xviii." *Revista fuentes humanísticas – UAM Azcapotzalco* 10 (1999): 47–57.

Bazarte Martínez, Alicia, and Clara García Ayluardo. *Los costos de la salvación: las cofradías y la ciudad de México, siglos xvi al xix*. México: CIDE, 2001.

Beltrán Martínez, Román. "Primeras casas de fundición." *Historia Mexicana* 1, no.3 (1952): 372–394.

Beltrán Martínez, Román. "Primeras casas de fundición." In *Historia de la ciencia y la tecnología*, edited by Elías Trabulse and Germán Somolinos d'Ardois, 180–202. México: Colegio de México, 1991.

Bennett, Herman L. *Africans in Colonial Mexico: Absolutism, Christianity, and Afro-Creole Consciousness, 1570–1640*. Bloomington: Indiana University Press, 2003.

Benton, Lauren A., and Richard Jeffrey Ross, eds. *Legal Pluralism and Empires, 1500–1850*. New York: New York University Press, 2013.

Blom, Philipp. *Nature's Mutiny: How the Little Ice Age of the Long Seventeenth Century Transformed the West and Shaped the Present*. New York: W. W. Norton, 2017.

Bonialian, Mariano. *El Pacífico hispanoamericano: política y comercio asiático en el imperio español, 1680–1784. La centralidad de lo marginal*. México: Colegio de México, 2012.

Bonialian, Mariano. "Acapulco: puerta abierta del Pacífico, válvula secreta del Atlántico." In *Relaciones intercoloniales: Nueva España y Filipinas*, edited by Jaime Olveda, 127–146. Jalisco: Colegio de Jalisco, 2017.

Bonialian, Mariano. *La América española: entre el Pacífico y el Atlántico. Globalización mercantil y economía política, 1580–1840*. México: Colegio de México, 2019.

Bonialian, Mariano, and Bernd Hausberger. "Consideraciones sobre el comercio y el papel de la plata hispanoamericana en la temprana globalización, siglos XVI–XIX." *Historia Mexicana* 68, no.1 (2018): 197–244.

Borah, Woodrow W. *Justice by Insurance: The General Indian Court of Colonial Mexico and the Legal Aides of the Half-Real*. Berkeley: University of California Press, 1983.

Boyer, Richard E. *La gran inundación: vida y sociedad en México, 1629–1638*. México: Secretaría de Educación Pública, 1975.

Boyer, Richard E. "La ciudad de México en 1628: La visión de Juan Gómez de Trasmonte." *Historia Mexicana* 29, no.3 (1980): 447–471.

Boyer, Richard E. "Juan Vázquez: Muleteer of Seventeenth Century Mexico." *The Americas* 37, no.4 (1981): 421–443.

Braudel, Fernand. *La Méditerranée et le monde méditéranéen à l'époque de Philippe II*. 2nd ed. Vol. 1, Paris: A. Colin, 1966.

Bravo Sandoval, Silvia, and Raquel Pineda Mendoza. *Catálogos de documentos de arte, Archivo de Notarías de la ciudad de México: protocolos II*. México: UNAM, 1996.

Burkhart, Louise M. "The Voyage of Saint Amaro: A Spanish Legend in Nahuatl Literature." *Colonial Latin American Review* 4, no.1 (1995): 29–57.

Campos Díez, María Soledad. *El Real Tribunal del Protomedicato castellano (siglos XIV–XIX)*. Cuenca: Ediciones de la Universidad de Castilla-La Mancha, 2008.

Candiani, Vera S. *Dreaming of Dry Land: Environmental Transformation in Colonial Mexico City*. Stanford: Stanford University Press, 2014.

Cañeque, Alejandro. "Theater of Power: Writing and Representing the Auto de Fe in Colonial Mexico." *The Americas* 52, no.3 (1996): 321–343.

Cañeque, Alejandro. *The King's Living Image: The Culture and Politics of Viceregal Power in Colonial Mexico*. New York: Routledge, 2004.

Carbajal López, David. "Devoción, utilidad y distinción. La reforma de las cofradías novohispanas y el culto del Santísimo Sacramento, 1750–1820." *Hispania Sacra* 68, no.137 (2016): 377–389.

Carballal Staedtler, Margarita, and María Flores Hernández. "Hydraulic Features of the Mexico-Texcoco Lakes during the Postclassic Period." In *Precolumbian Water Management: Ideology, Ritual, and Power*, edited by Lisa J. Lucero and Barbara W. Fash, 155–170. Tucson: University of Arizona Press, 2006.

Cardim, Pedro, Tamar Herzog, Gaetano Sabatini, and José Javier Ruiz Ibáñez, eds. *Polycentric Monarchies: How Did Early Modern Spain and Portugal Achieve and Maintain a Global Hegemony?* Eastbourne: Sussex Academic Press, 2012.

Carrera Stampa, Manuel. "Planos de la ciudad de México en 1715, hecho por Nicolás de Fer." *Boletín de la Sociedad Mexicana de Geografía y Estadística* LXV, no.2–3 (1948): 413–433.

Carrera Stampa, Manuel. "The Evolution of Weights and Measures in New Spain." *Hispanic American Historical Review* 29, no.1 (1949): 2–24.

Carrera Stampa, Manuel. *Los gremios mexicanos. La organización gremial en Nueva España, 1521–1861*. México: EDIAPSA, 1954.

Carrera Stampa, Manuel. "Los gremios mexicanos. Organización gremial en Nueva España 1521–1861." Dissertation, UNAM, 1954.

Carrera Stampa, Manuel. "El Archivo del ex Ayuntamiento de México." *Historia Mexicana* 12, no.4 (1963): 621–632.

Caso, Alfonso. "Los barrios antiguos de Tenochtitlan y Tlatelolco." *Memorias de la Academia Mexicana de la Historia* xv (1956): 7–63.

Castañeda Delgado, Paulino. "El Colegio de San Juan de Letran de México (apuntes para su historia)." *Anuario de Estudios Americanos* 37 (1980): 69–126.

Castañeda García, Rafael. "Hacia una sociología fiscal. El tributo de la población de color libre de la Nueva España, 1770–1810." *Fronteras de la Historia* 19, no.1 (2014): 152–173.

Castañeda García, Rafael, and María Elisa Velázquez. "Introducción: Cofradías de "negros y mulatos" en la Nueva España." *Nuevo Mundo Mundos Nuevos* (2012). http://journals.openedition.org/nuevomundo/64475.

Castañeda García, Rafael, and Juan Carlos Ruiz Guadalajara, eds. *Africanos y afrodescendientes en la América hispánica septentrional. Espacios de convivencia, sociabilidad y conflicto*. 2 vols. San Luis Potosí: Colegio de San Luis, 2020.

Castillo Palma, Norma Angélica. "La trata negrera, sus redes mercantiles portuguesas y estrategias de negocios en Nueva España durante el siglo XVII: una visión comparada." *Trashumante: Revista Americana de Historia Social* 10 (2017): 126–147.

Castro Gutiérrez, Felipe. *La extinción de la artesanía gremial*. México: UNAM, 1986.

Castro Gutiérrez, Felipe. "El origen y conformación de los barrios de indios." In *Los indios y las ciudades de Nueva España*, edited by Felipe Castro Gutiérrez, 106–122. México: UNAM, 2010.

Castro Gutiérrez, Felipe. *Historia social de la Real Casa de Moneda de México*. México: UNAM, 2012.

*Catálogo de protocolos del Archivo General de Notarías de la ciudad de México.* Edición en disco compacto. IV vols. Vol. II: Juan Pérez de Rivera, escribano público (1582–1631), Juan Pérez de Rivera, escribano de provincia (1611–1617) y Juan Pérez de Rivera Cáceres, escribano público (1632–1651), México: UNAM, 2005.

*Catálogo de protocolos del Archivo General de Notarías de la ciudad de México.* Edición en disco compacto. IV vols. Vol. III: Diferentes escribanos reales de los siglos XVI y XVII, México: UNAM, 2005.

*Catálogo de Protocolos del Archivo General de Notárias de la ciudad de México, Colección Siglo XVII. En línea.* edited by Ivonne Mijares and Seminario de documentación e historia novohispana. México: UNAM, 2016. http://cpagncmxvii.historicas.unam.mx/catalogo.jsp

*Catálogo de Protocolos del Archivo General de Notárias de la ciudad de México, Fondo Siglo XVI. En línea.* edited by Ivonne Mijares and Seminario de documentación e historia novohispana. México: UNAM, 2014. http://cpagncmxvi.historicas.unam.mx/catalogo.jsp

Celaya Nández, Yovana. "La cesión de un derecho de la Real Hacienda: la administración del impuesto de la alcabala novohispana en el siglo XVII. Tres estudios de caso." *América Latina en la historia económica* 33, no.1 (2010): 91–125.

Céspedes del Castillo, Guillermo. *Las casas de moneda en los reinos de Indias.* Vol. 1: Las cecas indianas en 1536–1825. Madrid: Museo Casa de la Moneda, 1996.

Chartres, J. A. "The Capital's Provincial Eyes: London's Inns in the Early Eighteenth Century." *The London Journal* 3, no.1 (1977): 24–39.

Clark, Joseph M. H. *Veracruz and the Caribbean in the Seventeenth Century.* New York: Cambridge University Press, 2023.

Clouse, Michele. *Medicine, Government, and Public Health in Philip II's Spain.* Farnham: Ashgate, 2011.

Connell, William F. *After Moctezuma: Indigenous Politics and Self-Government in Mexico City, 1524—1730.* Norman: University of Oklahoma Press, 2011.

Connolly, Priscilla. "¿El mapa es la ciudad? Nuevas miradas a la Forma y Levantado de la ciudad de México 1628 de Juan Gómez de Trasmonte." *Investigaciones geográficas* 66 (2008): 116–134.

Connolly, Priscilla, and Roberto L. Mayer. "Vingboons, Trasmonte and Boot: European Cartography of Mexican Cities in the Early Seventeenth Century." *Imago Mundi* 61, no.1 (2009): 47–66.

Conway, Richard M. "Lakes, Canoes, and the Aquatic Communities of Xochimilco and Chalco, New Spain." *Ethnohistory* 59, no.3 (2012): 541–568.

Conway, Richard M. "Rural Indians and Technological Innovation, From the Chinampas of Xochimilco and Beyond." *The Oxford Research Encyclopedia of Latin American History* (2018). https://doi.org/10.1093/acrefore/9780199366439.013.530.

Conway, Richard M. *Islands in the Lake: Environment and Ethnohistory in Xochimilco, New Spain.* New York: Cambridge University Press, 2021.

Cook, Noble David, ed. *Numeración general de todas las personas de ambos sexos, edades y calidades que se ha hecho en esta ciudad de Lima, año de 1700.* Lima: COFIDE, 1985.

Cope, R. Douglas. *The Limits of Racial Domination: Plebeian Society in Colonial Mexico City, 1660–1720.* Madison: University of Wisconsin Press, 1994.

Córdova Aguilar, Maira Cristina. "Vida y trabajo de Cathalina de los Reyes, María Machuca, Juana Machado, Agustín García y Pedro Gonzales en la ciudad de Antequera (1649–1792)." In *Trayectorias de vida de afrodescendientes en la historia de México,* edited by Gabriela Iturralde Nieto, 69–107. México: INAH, 2024.

Crewe, Ryan Dominic. "Connecting the Indies: The Hispano-Asian Pacific World in Early Modern Global History." *Estudos Históricos* 30, no.60 (2017): 17–34.

Cuello Martinell, María Angeles. "La renta de los naipes en Nueva España." *Anuario de Estudios Americanos* 22 (1965): 231–335.

Curcio-Nagy, Linda. *The Great Festivals of Colonial Mexico City: Performing Power and Identity.* Albuquerque: University of New Mexico Press, 2004.

Desan, Christine. *Making Money: Coin, Currency, and the Coming of Capitalism.* Oxford: Oxford University Press, 2014.

DeVos, Paula S. *Compound Remedies: Galenic Pharmacy from the Ancient Mediterranean to New Spain.* Pittsburgh: University of Pittsburgh Press, 2021.

Dougnac Rodríguez, Antonio. *Manual de historia del Derecho Indiano.* México: UNAM, 1994.

Dubs, Homer H., and Robert S. Smith. "Chinese in Mexico City in 1635." *The Far Eastern Quarterly* 1, no.4 (1942): 387–389.

Dusenberry, William H. "The Regulation of Meat Supply in Sixteenth-Century Mexico City." *Hispanic American Historical Review* 28, no.1 (1948): 38–52.

Duve, Thomas, and Heikki Pihlajamäki, eds. *New Horizons in Spanish Colonial Law: Contributions to Transnational Early Modern Legal History.* Frankfurt am Main: Max Planck Institute for European Legal History, 2015.

Escamilla González, Ivan, and Paula Mues Orts. "Espacio real, espacio pictórico y poder: *Vista de la Plaza Mayor de México* de Cristóbal de Villalpando." In *La imagen política,* edited by Cuauhtémoc Medina, 177–204. México: UNAM, 2006.

Esteras Martín, Cristina. "Candaleros, numero de catálogo 32." In *El arte de la platería mexicana, 500 años,* edited by Lucía García-Noriega y Nieto, 190–191. México: Centro Cultural Arte Contemporáneo, 1989.

Esteras Martín, Cristina. *Marcas de platería hispanoamericana. Siglos XVI–XX.* Madrid: Ediciones Tuero, 1992.

Esteras Martín, Cristina. "Candeleros." In *La platería del Museo Franz Mayer. Obras escogidas, siglos XVI–XIX,* 94–95. México: Museo Franz Mayer, 1992.

Esteras Martín, Cristina. "El oro y la plata americanos, del valor ecónomico a la expresión artística." In *El oro y la plata de las Indias en la época de los Austrias,* edited by Concepción Lopezosa Aparicio, 392–423. Madrid: Fundación ICO, 1999.

Evans, Susan T. "The Productivity of Maguey Terrace Agriculture in Central Mexico during the Aztec Period." *Latin American Antiquity* 1, no.2 (1990): 117–132.

Exbalin, Arnaud. "Riot in Mexico City: A Challenge to the Colonial Order?" *Urban History* 43, no.2 (2016): 215–231.

Feijoo, Rosa. "El tumulto de 1624." *Historia Mexicana* 14, no.4 (1964): 656–679.

Fernández del Castillo, Francisco. *La Facultad de Medicina según el archivo de la Real y Pontificia Universidad de México.* México: Consejo de Humanidades, 1953.

Fernández del Castillo, Francisco, and Alicia Hernández Torres. *El Tribunal del Protomedicato en la Nueva España, según el Archivo Histórico de la Facultad de Medicina.* México: UNAM, 1965.

Fernández López, Francisco. "El control de las personas: expedientes de licencias de pasajeros." In *La Casa de la Contratación. Una oficina de expedición documental para el Gobierno de las Indias (1503–1717),* 175–212. Sevilla: Universidad de Sevilla, 2018.

Fernández, Martha. "Relación de servicios de Juan Gómez de Trasmonte." *Anales del Instituto de Investigaciones Estéticas* 13, no.50 (1982): 329–336.

Fernández, Martha. *Arquitectura y gobierno virreinal: los maestros mayores de la ciudad de México, siglo XVII.* México: UNAM, 1985.

Flinchpaugh, Steven G. "Economic Aspects of the Viceregal Entrance in Mexico City." *The Americas* 52, no.3 (1996): 345–365.

Flores Martínez, Ernesto. "Tequisquiapan: Un barrio de la parcialidad de San Juan Tenochtitlan, 1570–1776." MA thesis, UAM Iztapalapa, 2007.

Flores Olea, Aurora. "Los regidores de la ciudad de México en la primera mitad del siglo XVII." *Estudios de Historia Novohispana* 3 (1970): 1–24.

Font de Villanueva, Cecilia. "Política monetaria y política fiscal en Castilla en el siglo XVII: un siglo de inestabilidades." *Revista de Historia Económica* 23, no.S1 (2005): 329–347.

Ganster, Paul. "La familia Gómez de Cervantes: Linaje y sociedad en el México colonial." *Historia Mexicana* 31, no.2 (1981): 197–232.

Gao, Shouxian. *Beijing ren kou shi.* Beijing: Zhong guo ren min da xue chu ban she, 2014.

García de León, Antonio. *Tierra adentro, mar en fuera. El puerto de Veracruz y su litoral a Sotavento, 1519–1821.* México: Fondo de Cultura Económica, 2011.

García Gallo, Alfonso. *Estudios de historia del Derecho Indiano.* Madrid: Instituto Nacional de Estudios Jurídicos, 1972.

Gerhard, Peter. *A Guide to the Historical Geography of New Spain.* Rev. ed. Norman: University of Oklahoma Press, 1993.

Germeten, Nicole von. *Black Blood Brothers: Confraternities and Social Mobility for Afro-Mexicans.* Gainesville: University Press of Florida, 2006.

Germeten, Nicole von. *The Enlightened Patrolman: Early Law Enforcement in Mexico City.* Lincoln: University of Nebraska Press, 2022.

Gharala, Norah L. A. *Taxing Blackness: Free Afromexican Tribute in Bourbon New Spain.* Tuscaloosa: University of Alabama Press, 2019.

Ghobrial, John-Paul A. "Introduction: Seeing the World Like a Microhistorian." *Past & Present* 242, no.1 (2019): 1–22.

Gibson, Charles. *The Aztecs Under Spanish Rule: A History of the Indians of the Valley of Mexico, 1519–1810*. Stanford: Stanford University Press, 1964.

Gonzalbo Aizpuru, Pilar. "El Archivo General de Notarías de la ciudad de México." *Historia Mexicana* 35, no.4 (1986): 675–688.

Gonzalbo Aizpuru, Pilar, ed. *Historia de la vida cotidiana en México*. 5 vols. México: Colegio de México, 2004–05.

Gonzalbo Aizpuru, Pilar. "El nacimiento del miedo, 1692. Indios y españoles en la ciudad de México." *Revista de Indias* 68, no.244 (2008): 9–34.

González, Francisco Montes. "'Donde seda y oro, hizo maridaje artificioso': el esplendor de la orfebrería novohispana en el juramento concepcionista de la Real Universidad de México." In *Ophir en las Indias: estudios sobre la plata americana: siglos XVI–XIX*, edited by Jesús Paniagua Pérez and Nuria Salazar Simarro, 259–268. León: Universidad de León, 2010.

González Gutiérrez, Pilar. *Creación de casas de moneda en Nueva España*. Alcalá de Henares: Universidad de Alcalá, 1997.

González Obregón, Luis, ed. "Reseña histórica del desagüe del valle de México, 1449–1855." In *Memoria histórica, técnica y administrativa de las obras del desagüe del valle de México, 1449–1900*, 29–272. México: Tip. de la Oficina Impresora de Estampillas, 1902.

Graham, Richard. *Feeding the City: From Street Market to Liberal Reform in Salvador, Brazil, 1780–1860*. Austin: University of Texas Press, 2010.

Granados Ponce, Froylán de Jesús. "La indispensable subsistencia de un ramo: el cobro del tributo a indios, negros y mulatos en la ciudad de México, 1780–1792." MA Thesis, UNAM, 2017.

Graubart, Karen B. "Introduction: Republics and the Politics of Self-Governance." In *Republics of Difference: Religious and Racial Self-Governance in the Spanish Atlantic World*, 1–17. New York: Oxford University Press, 2022.

Green, Toby. "Beyond an Imperial Atlantic: Trajectories of Africans from Upper Guinea and West-Central Africa in the Early Atlantic World." *Past & Present* 230, no.1 (2016): 91–122.

Gruzinski, Serge. *La ciudad de México: una historia*. Translated by Paula López Caballero. México: Fondo de Cultura Económica, 2004. 1996.

Guerrero, Saúl. *Silver by Fire, Silver by Mercury: A Chemical History of Silver Refining in New Spain and Mexico, 16th to 19th Centuries*. Leiden: Brill, 2017.

Gurría Lacroix, Jorge. *El desagüe del Valle de México durante la época novohispana*. México: UNAM, 1978.

Guthrie, Chester L. "A Seventeenth Century 'Ever-Normal Granary': The *Alhóndiga* of Colonial Mexico City." *Agricultural History* 15, no.1 (1941): 37–43.

Gutiérrez Haces, Juana. *Cristóbal de Villalpando: ca. 1649–1714. Catálogo razonado*. México: CONACULTA, BANAMEX, 1997.

Hanke, Lewis, and Celso Rodríguez. *Los virreyes españoles en América durante el gobierno de la Casa de Austria: México*. 5 vols. Madrid: Atlas, 1976–1980.

Haring, Clarence H. *The Spanish Empire in America*. New York: Oxford University Press, 1947.

Hausberger, Bernd. "En el camino, en busca de los arrieros novohispanos." *Historia Mexicana* 64, no.1 (2014): 65–104.

Hausberger, Bernd. *Historia mínima de la globalización temprana.* México: Colegio de México, 2018.

Hausberger, Bernd. "La distribución transcontinental de la plata americana en la globalización temprana." In *Historia económica del peso mexicano: Del mercado global a la gestión política de la moneda,* edited by Bernd Hausberger and Antonio Ibarra, 31–72. México: Colegio de México, 2023.

Heredia Moreno, Carmen. "Plata labrada en las flotas de Nueva España." In *El sueño de El Dorado. Estudios sobre la plata iberoamericana, siglos XVI–XIX,* edited by Jesús Paniagua Pérez, Nuria Salazar Simarro and Moisés Gámez, 219–234. León: Universidad de León, 2012.

Hernández Franyuti, Regina. "Historia y significado de la palabra policía en el quehacer político de la ciudad de México, siglos XVI–XIX." *Ulúa: Revista de Historia, Sociedad y Cultura* 5 (2005): 9–34.

Hernández Sáenz, Luz María. *Learning to Heal: The Medical Profession in Colonial Mexico, 1767–1831.* New York: Peter Lang, 1997.

Herzog, Tamar. *Defining Nations: Immigrants and Citizens in Early Modern Spain and Spanish America.* New Haven: Yale University Press, 2003.

Herzog, Tamar. "Early Modern Citizenship in Europe and the Americas: A Twenty Years' Conversation." *Ler História* 78 (2021): 225–237.

Hoberman, Louisa S. "Bureaucracy and Disaster: Mexico City and the Flood of 1629." *Journal of Latin American Studies* 6, no.2 (1974): 211–230.

Hoberman, Louisa S. "The Mexican Economy and Merchant Capital: Mining and The Mint." In *Mexico's Merchant Elite, 1590–1660: Silver, State, and Society,* 71–93. Durham: Duke University Press, 1991.

Ibarra, Antonio. "Mercado colonial, plata y moneda en el siglo XVIII Novohispano. Comentarios para un diálogo con Ruggiero Romano, a propósito de su nuevo libro." *Historia Mexicana* 49, no.2 (1999): 279–308.

Ireton, Chloe L. "Purchasing Freedom: Economics of Liberty in New Spain." In *Slavery and Freedom in Black Thought in the Early Spanish Atlantic,* 117–150. Cambridge: Cambridge University Press, 2024.

Israel, Jonathan I. *Race, Class, and Politics in Colonial Mexico, 1610–1670.* London: Oxford University Press, 1975.

Jalpa Flores, Tomás. "Migrantes y estravagantes. Indios de la periferia en la ciudad de México durante los siglos XVI–XVII." In *Los indios y las ciudades de Nueva España,* edited by Felipe Castro Gutiérrez, 79–104. México: UNAM, 2010.

Jiménez Estrella, Antonio. "Poder, dinero y ventas de oficios y honores en la España del Antiguo Régimen: un estado de la cuestión." *Cuadernos de Historia Moderna* 37 (2012): 259–272.

Jiménez Martínez, Eloy. "En torno a la superficie de México-Tenochtitlan en 1519." *Anuario de Historia Regional y de las Fronteras* 25, no.1 (2020): 15–45.

Kagan, Richard L., and Fernando Marías. *Urban Images of the Hispanic World, 1493–1793.* New Haven: Yale University Press, 2000.

Kellogg, Susan. "Households in Late Prehispanic and Early Colonial Mexico City: Their Structure and Its Implications for the Study of Historical Demography." *The Americas* 44, no.4 (1988): 483–494.

Kellogg, Susan. "From Parallel and Equivalent to Separate but Unequal: Tenochca Mexica Women, 1500–1700." In *Indian Women of Early Mexico*, edited by Susan Schroeder, Stephanie G. Wood and Robert S. Haskett, 123–143. Norman: University of Oklahoma Press, 1997.

Konove, Andrew. "A Pernicious Commmerce." In *Black Market Capital: Urban Politics and the Shadow Economy in Mexico City*, 15–35. Oakland: University of California Press, 2018.

Konove, Andrew. "In Search of a Decent Coin: The Value of Small Change in Bourbon Spanish America." *Colonial Latin American Review* 30 (2022): 589–610.

Lacueva Muñoz, Jaime J. *La plata del rey y de sus vasallos: minería y metalurgia en México (siglos XVI y XVII)*. Madrid: CSIC, 2010.

Landers, Jane. "The African Landscape of Seventeenth Century Cartagena and Its Hinterlands." In *The Black Urban Atlantic in the Age of Revolution*, edited by Jorge Cañizares-Esguerra, Matt D. Childs and James Sidbury, 147–162. Philadelphia: University of Pennsylvania Press, 2013.

Lane, Kris E. *Potosí: The Silver City That Changed the World*. Oakland: University of California Press, 2018.

Lang, Mervyn F. *Las flotas de la Nueva España (1630–1710). Despacho, azogue, comercio*. Sevilla: Muñoz Moya, 1988.

Lanning, John T. *The Royal Protomedicato: The Regulation of the Medical Professions in the Spanish Empire*. Durham: Duke University Press, 1985.

Leeuwen, Marco H.D. van, and James E. Oeppen. "Reconstructing the Demographic Regime of Amsterdam 1681–1920." *Economic & Social History in the Netherlands* 5 (1993): 61–102.

León-Portilla, Miguel. "New Light on the Sources of Torquemada's *Monarchia Indiana*." *The Americas* 35, no.3 (1979): 287–316.

Leonard, Irving A. *Baroque Times in Old Mexico: Seventeenth-Century Persons, Places, and Practices*. Ann Arbor: University of Michigan Press, 1966. 1959.

Llanas y Fernández, Roberto. "Siglo XVII." In *Ingeniería en México, 400 años de historia. Obra pública en la ciudad de México*, 109–187. México: UNAM, 2012.

Lockhart, James. *The Nahuas after the Conquest: A Social and Cultural History of the Indians of Central Mexico, Sixteenth through Eighteenth Centuries*. Stanford: Stanford University Press, 1992.

Lombardo de Ruiz, Sonia, Yolanda Terán Trillo, and Mario de la Torre, eds. *Atlas histórico de la ciudad de México*. 2 vols. México: Smurfit, 1996.

López, John F., ed. *A Companion to Viceregal Mexico City, 1519–1821*. Leiden: Brill, 2021.

López Mora, Rebeca. "Entre dos mundos: Los indios de los barrios de la ciudad de México, 1550–1600." In *Los indios y las ciudades de Nueva España*, edited by Felipe Castro Gutiérrez, 57–77. México: UNAM, 2010.

López Rosado, Diego G. "Periodo Virreinal." In *Historia del abasto de productos alimenticios en la ciudad de México*, 53–149. México: Fondo de Cultura Económica, 1988.

Lorda, Mercedes Galán. "Ordenanzas del Cabildo de México sobre abastos en el siglo XVIII." *Anuario de historia del derecho español* 67 (1997): 1315–1338.

Losa Contreras, Carmen. "La justicia capitular de la Nueva España en el siglo XVIII. El tribunal de fiel ejecutoría de la ciudad de México." *Cuadernos de Historia del Derecho* 5 (1998): 127–208.

Lozano Armendares, Teresa. "Los juegos de azar. ¿Una pasión novohispana? Legislación sobre juegos prohibidos en Nueva España, siglo XVIII." *Estudios de Historia Novohispana* 11 (1991): 155–181.

Luis, Diego Javier. "Merchants and Gunslingers." In *The First Asians in the Americas: A Transpacific History*, 107–139. Cambridge: Harvard University Press, 2024.

Luna García, Sandra Nancy. "Espacios de convivencia y conflicto. Las cofradías de la población de origen africano en ciudad de México, siglo XVII." *Trashumante: Revista Americana de Historia Social* 10 (2017): 32–52.

Lussana, Sergio. *My Brother Slaves: Friendship, Masculinity, and Resistance in the Antebellum South.* Lexington: University Press of Kentucky, 2016.

Marroqui, José María. *La ciudad de México.* 3 vols. Vol. 1, México: Tip. y lit. La Europea, 1900.

Marroqui, José María. *La ciudad de México.* 3 vols. Vol. 2, México: Tip. y lit. La Europea, 1900.

Marroqui, José María. *La ciudad de México.* 3 vols. Vol. 3, México: Tip. y lit. La Europea, 1903.

Martin, Cheryl English. "The San Hipólito Hospitals of Colonial Mexico, 1566–1702." Dissertation, Tulane University, 1976.

Martín Santos, Luis. *Barberos y cirujanos de los siglos XVI y XVII.* Salamanca: Consejería de Educación y Cultura, 2000.

Martin-Veque, George B. "The Silversmiths in Mexico: A Study in Colonial Trade Guilds." Dissertation, University of Texas, Austin, 1951.

Martínez, María Elena. "The Black Blood of New Spain: *Limpieza de Sangre*, Racial Violence, and Gendered Power in Early Colonial Mexico." *William and Mary Quarterly* 61, no.3 (2004): 479–520.

Martínez Hernández, Gerardo. "La repercusión de las reformas palafoxianas en la formación de los bachilleres médicos de la Real Universidad de México." In *Del aula a la ciudad. Estudios sobre la universidad y la sociedad en el México virreinal*, edited by Enrique González González, Mónica Hidalgo Pego and Adriana Álvarez Sánchez, 87–106. México: UNAM, 2009.

Martínez Hernández, Gerardo. "La llegada del cirujano Alonso López de Hinojosos a la Nueva España." *Revista Médica del Instituto Mexicano del Seguro Social* 49, no.4 (2011): 459–463.

Martínez Hernández, Gerardo. "¿Protomédico o Protomedicato? Jerónimo de Herrera y la controversia en torno a la instauración del Tribunal del Protomedicato en la Nueva España. 1620–1622." *Historia Mexicana* 67, no.4 (2018): 1811–1872.

Martínez Hernández, Gerardo. "'Obedézcase pero no se cumpla': El fracaso como Protomédico de Francisco Hernández en la ciudad de México, 1571–1574." *Andamios* 19, no.49 (2022): 417–440.

Martínez Hernández, Gerardo. *La medicina en la Nueva España, siglos XVI y XVII. Consolidación de los modelos institucionales y académicos.* México: UNAM, 2014.

Martínez López-Cano, María del Pilar. *La génesis del crédito colonial. Ciudad de México, siglo XVI*. México: UNAM, 2001.

Martínez López-Cano, María del Pilar, Gisela von Wobeser, and Juan Guillermo Muñoz Correa, eds. *Cofradías, capellanías y obras pías en la América colonial*. México: UNAM, 1998.

Masferrer León, Cristina Verónica. "Por las ánimas de negros bozales. Las cofradías de personas de origen africano en la ciudad de México (siglo xvii)." *Cuicuilco* 51, no.mayo (2011): 83–102.

Masters, Adrian. *We, the King: Creating Royal Legislation in the Sixteenth-Century Spanish New World*. Cambridge: Cambridge University Press, 2023.

Mathes, Valerie L. "Enrico Martínez of New Spain." *The Americas* 33, no.1 (1976): 62–71.

Mayer, Roberto L. "Trasmote y Boot. Sus vistas de tres ciudades mexicanas en el siglo XVII." *Anales del Instituto de Investigaciones Estéticas* 27, no.87 (2012): 177–198.

Maza, Francisco de la. *El pintor Cristóbal de Villalpando*. México: INAH, 1964.

Maza, Francisco de la. *La ciudad de México en el siglo XVII*. México: Fondo de Cultura Económica, 1985. 1968.

Mentz, Brígida von. "La 'entrega' de niños y adolescentes a un patrón: el ingreso de aprendices y sirvientes a la vida laboral en la ciudad de México en el siglo XVII." In *Trabajo, sujeción y libertad en el centro de la Nueva España*, 111–171. México: CIESAS, 1999.

Merrim, Stephanie. *The Spectacular City, Mexico, and Colonial Hispanic Literary Culture*. Austin: University of Texas Press, 2010.

Mijares, Ivonne. *Escribanos y escrituras públicas en el siglo XVI: el caso de la ciudad de México*. México: UNAM, 1997.

Mijares, Ivonne. *Catálogo de protocolos del Archivo General de Notarías de la ciudad de México: introducción*. México: UNAM, 2002.

Mijares, Ivonne. "El abasto urbano: caminos y bastimentos." In *Historia de la vida cotidiana en México: la ciudad barroca*, edited by Antonio Rubial García, 109–140. México: Colegio de México, 2005.

Mijares, Ivonne. "La mula en la vida cotidiana del siglo XVI." In *Caminos y mercados de México*. Edited by Janet Long Towell and Amalia Attolini Lecón, 291–310. México: UNAM; INAH, 2009.

Milton, Cynthia, and Ben Vinson III. "Counting Heads: Race and Non-Native Tribute Policy in Colonial Spanish America." *Journal of Colonialism and Colonial History* 3, no. 3 (2002).

Miño Grijalva, Manuel. "Las ciudades novohispanas y su función económica, siglos xvi–xviii." In *Historia económica general de México. De la colonia a nuestros días*, edited by Sandra Kuntz Ficker, 143–170. México: Colegio de México, 2010.

Miño Grijalva, Manuel. "La población novohispana: alimentación y recursos." In *El mundo novohispano: población, ciudades y economía, siglos XVII y XVIII*, 270–331. México: Colegio de México, 2001.

Miranda, José. *El tributo indígena en la Nueva España durante el siglo XVI*. México: Colegio de México, 1952.

Miranda Pacheco, Sergio. "Presentación. La ciudad, la historia y los historiadores." In *El historiador frente a la ciudad de México. Perfiles de su historia*, edited by Sergio Miranda Pacheco, 7–14. México: UNAM, 2016.

Miranda Pacheco, Sergio. "Urbe inmunda: poder y prejuicios socioambientales en la urbanización y desagüe de la ciudad y valle de México en el siglo XIX." In *De olfato. Aproximaciones a los olores en la historia de México*, edited by Elodie Dupey García and Guadalupe Pinzón Ríos, 193–249. México: Fondo de Cultura Económica, 2020.

Monroy Padilla, María Isabel, ed. *Guía de las Actas de Cabildo de la Ciudad de México: Años 1601–1610, siglo XVII*. México: Universidad Iberoamericana, 1987.

Monroy Padilla, María Isabel, ed. *Guía de las Actas de Cabildo de la Ciudad de México: Años 1611–1620, siglo XVII*. México: Universidad Iberoamericana, 1988.

Montero Aroca, Juan. *La herencia procesal española*. México: UNAM, 1994.

Morales Martínez, María Dolores, María Amparo Ros Torres, and Esteban Sánchez de Tagle, eds. *Ciudad de México, época colonial. Bibliografía*. México: INAH, 1993.

Morales Sarabia, Angélica. "Las enfermedades de las mujeres en la Nueva España, una taxonomía a través de las plantas emenagogas (siglo XVII)." *Nuevo Mundo Mundos Nuevos* (2016). http://journals.openedition.org/nuevomundo/69565.

More, Anna H. *Baroque Sovereignty: Carlos de Sigüenza y Góngora and the Creole Archive of Colonial Mexico*. Philadelphia: University of Pennsylvania Press, 2013.

Morehart, Christopher T. "Aztec Agricultural Strategies: Intensification, Landesque Capital, and the Sociopolitics of Production." In *Oxford Handbook of the Aztecs*, edited by Deborah L. Nichols and Enrique Rodríguez-Alegría, 263–280. New York: Oxford University Press, 2017.

Mundy, Barbara E. "La fuente del tianguis de San Juan de México-Tenochtitlan y el segundo acueducto de Chapultepec." *Boletín de Monumentos Históricos* 32 (2014): 9–25.

Mundy, Barbara E. *The Death of Aztec Tenochtitlan. The Life of Mexico City*. Austin: University of Texas Press, 2015.

Mundy, Barbara E. "The Smellscape of Mexico City, 1500–1600." *Ethnohistory* 68, no.1 (2021): 77–101.

Muñoz Serrulla, María Teresa. *La moneda castellana en los reinos de Indias durante la Edad Moderna*. Madrid: Universidad Nacional de Educación a Distancia, 2015.

Muriel, Josefina. *Conventos de monjas en la Nueva España*. México: Editorial Santiago, 1946.

Muriel, Josefina. *Hospitales de la Nueva España. Fundaciones de los siglos XVII y XVIII*. 2 vols. Vol. 2, México: Editorial Jus, 1960.

Mussett, Alain. *El agua en el valle de México, siglos xvi-xviii*. México: Pórtico de la ciudad de México, 1992.

Nacif Mina, Jorge. *La policía en la historia de la ciudad de México (1524–1928)*. México: Departamento del Distrito Federal, 1986.

*Nahuatl Dictionary Online.* edited by Stephanie Wood. Wired Humanities Projects, 2000. https://nahuatl.wired-humanities.org.

Nesvig, Martin A. *Ideology and Inquisition: The World of the Censors in Early Mexico.* New Haven: Yale University Press, 2009.

Nichols, Deborah L. "Farm to Market in the Aztec Imperial Economy." In *Rethinking the Aztec Economy*, edited by Deborah L. Nichols, Frances F. Berdan and Michael E. Smith, 19–43. Tucson: University of Arizona Press, 2017.

Nieves Pimentel, Elienahí. "'Hazme la barba y harete el copete': proyectos y administración de recursos para la obra hidráulica en la cuenca de México (1524–1684)." Dissertation, Instituto de Investigaciones Dr. José María Luis Mora, 2025.

Nusteling, Hubert P. H. "La population d'Amsterdam de la fin du XVIe siècle au début du XIXe siècle. Une méthode de reconstitution." *Population* 41, no.6 (1986): 961–977.

Ochoa, Margarita R. "Doña Marcela and the Cacicas of Bourbon Mexico City: Family, Community, and Indigenous Rule." In *Cacicas: The Indigenous Women Leaders of Spanish America, 1492–1825*, edited by Margarita R. Ochoa and Sara V. Guengerich. Norman: University of Oklahoma Press, 2021.

Odena Güemes, Lina. *Archivo Histórico del Distrito Federal: guía general.* México: Verdehalago, 2000.

Olvera Ramos, Jorge. *Los mercados de la Plaza Mayor en la ciudad de México.* México: Cal y arena, 2007.

Ornelas Méndez, Candy E. *Inventario del Archivo Parroquial de Santa Catarina Virgen y Mártir, ciudad de México, Arquidiócesis de México.* México: ADABI, 2014.

Ornelas Méndez, Candy E. *Inventario del Archivo Parroquial de Santa Ana Atenantitech, ciudad de México.* México: ADABI, 2019.

Owensby, Brian P. *Empire of Law and Indian Justice in Colonial Mexico.* Stanford: Stanford University Press, 2008.

*Oxford English Dictionary.* Oxford: Oxford University Press, 2023. www.oed.com.

Pamuk, Şevket. "In the Absence of Domestic Currency: Debased European Coinage in the Seventeenth-Century Ottoman Empire." *The Journal of Economic History* 57, no.2 (1997): 345–366.

Pardo, Osvaldo F. "Giovanni Botero and Bernardo de Balbuena: Art and Economy in *La grandeza mexicana*." *Journal of Latin American Cultural Studies* 10, no.1 (2001): 103–117.

Pazos Pazos, María Luisa J. *El Ayuntamiento de la ciudad de México en el siglo xvii: continuidad institucional y cambio social.* Sevilla: Diputación de Sevilla, 1999.

Pineda Mendoza, Raquel, and Edén Mario Zárate Sánchez. *Catálogos de documentos de arte, Archivo de Notarías de la ciudad de México: protocolos IV.* México: UNAM, 2005.

Pineda Mendoza, Raquel. *Catálogos de documentos de arte, Archivo de Notarías de la ciudad de México: protocolos V.* México: UNAM, 2015.

Poole, Stafford, and John F. Schwaller, eds. *The Directory for Confessors, 1585: Implementing the Catholic Reformation in New Spain*. Norman: University of Oklahoma Press, 2018.

Querol Roso, Luis. "Negros y mulatos de Nueva España (Historia de su alzamiento en Méjico en 1612)." *Anales de la Universidad de Valencia* 12 (1931): 121–165.

Quezada, Noemí. *Enfermedad y maléficio. El curandero en el México colonial*. México: UNAM, 2000.

Quiroz, Enriqueta. *Entre el lujo y la subsistencia: mercado, abastecimiento y precios de la carne en la ciudad de México, 1750–1812*. México: Instituto Mora, 2005.

Quiroz, Enriqueta. "La moneda menuda en la circulación monetaria de la ciudad de México, siglo XVIII." *Mexican Studies/Estudios Mexicanos* 22, no.2 (2006): 219–249.

Quiroz, Enriqueta. "Entre el humanismo y el mercantilismo: El bien común en el abasto de carne de ciudad de México, 1708–1716." *Cuadernos de Historia* 35 (2011): 35–59.

Quiroz, Enriqueta. *Economía, obras públicas y trabajadores urbanos. Ciudad de México: 1687–1807*. México: Instituto Mora, 2016.

Ramírez Montes, Guillermina. *Catáogos de documentos de arte en el Archivo de Notarías de la ciudad de México*. México: UNAM, 1990.

Ramírez Montes, Guillermina, and Guillermino Luckie. *Catálogos de documentos de arte, Archivo de Notarías de la ciudad de México: protocolos I*. México: UNAM, 1993.

Ramos, Christina. "Caring for *Pobres Dementes*: Madness, Colonization, and the *Hospital de San Hipólito* in Mexico City, 1567–1700." *The Americas* 77, no.4 (2020): 539–571.

Ramos, Christina. *Bedlam in the New World: A Mexican Madhouse in the Age of Enlightenment*. Chapel Hill: University of North Carolina Press, 2022.

Recio Mir, Alvaro. *El arte de la carrocería en Nueva España. El gremio de la ciudad de México, sus ordenanzas y la trascendencia social del coche*. Seville: Universidad de Sevilla, 2018.

Restall, Matthew. *When Montezuma Met Cortés: The True Story of the Meeting That Changed History*. New York: ECCO, 2018.

Reyes, Alfonso. "Sobre Mateo Rosas de Oquendo, poeta del siglo XVI." *Revista de Filología Española* 4, no.4 (1917): 341–370.

Rivero Hernández, Iván. *De las nubes a la laguna. Tributos y tamemes mixtecos en la ciudad de México, 1522–1560*. Zamora: Colegio de Michoacán, 2017.

Rivero Hernández, Iván. "El oro y los "pesos de oro" en los inicios de Nueva España. Una propuesta de reinterpretación." *Historia Mexicana* 73, no.2 (2023): 543–588.

Rodríguez-Alegría, Enrique. "How to Make Money." In *How to Make a New Spain: The Material Worlds of Colonial Mexico City*, 24–52. New York: Oxford University Press, 2023.

Rodríguez-Sala, María Luisa. *El Hospital Real de los Naturales, sus administradores y sus cirujanos (1531–1764)*. México: UNAM, 2005.

Rodríguez-Sala, María Luisa. *Cinco cárceles de la ciudad de México, sus cirujanos y otros personajes: 1574–1820, ¿Miembros de un estamento profesional o de una comunidad científica?* México: UNAM, 2009.

Rodríguez, Martha Eugenía, and Ana Cecilia Rodríguez de Romo. "Asistencia médica e higiene ambiental en la ciudad de México siglos XVI–XVIII." *Gaceta Médica de México* 135, no.2 (1999): 189–198.

Rodríguez de Sepúlveda, Diego. "Cornerstones of Empire: Corregidores in Early Viceregal Peru." Dissertation, Tulane University, 2023.

Rojas, Beatriz. "Ser vecino en Nueva España." In *Las ciudades novohispanas: Siete ensayos, historia y territorio.* México: Instituto Mora, 2016.

Rojas, José Luis de. "El cacao." In *La moneda indígena y sus usos en la Nueva España en el siglo XVI*, 127–187. México: CIESAS, 1998.

Rojas Orzechowski, Alan. "Andrés Arias Tenorio y el convento de Santa Clara de la ciudad de México: un patronazgo del siglo XVII." *Boletín de Monumentos Históricos* 21 (2011): 5–17.

Rojas Rabiela, Teresa. *La agricultura chinampera: compilación histórica.* 2nd ed. Chapingo: Universidad Autónoma de Chapingo, 1993.

Romero de Terreros, Manuel. "Los corregidores de México." *Anales del Museo de Arqueología, Historia y Etnografía* 4a, no.1 (1922): 84–92.

Rosenmüller, Christoph. *Corruption and Justice in Colonial Mexico, 1650–1755.* New York: Cambridge University Press, 2019.

Rubial García, Antonio. *Monjas, cortesanos y plebeyos: la vida cotidiana en la época de Sor Juana.* México: Taurus, 2005.

Rubial García, Antonio. "Las virreinas novohispanas. Presencias y ausencias." *Estudios de Historia Novohispana* 50 (2014): 3–44.

Rubio Fernández, Beatriz. "Los tianguis de la ciudad de México en el siglo XVI." *Anales del Museo de América* 21 (2013): 160–173.

Rubio Mañé, J. Ignacio, ed. *Introducción al estudio de los virreyes de Nueva España, 1535–1746.* 2 vols. Vol. 1, México: Ediciones Selectas, 1955.

Sandoval, Fernando B. "Baltasar de Medina y la crónica de los dieguinos." *Historia Mexicana* 19, no.3 (1970): 319–346.

Santiago Fernández, Javier de. *Política monetaria en Castilla durante el siglo XVII.* Valladolid: Junta de Castilla y León, 2000.

Santiago Fernández, Javier de. "La emisión de moneda de vellón rico en el reinado de Felipe II: ¿un instrumento de financiación?" *Cuadernos de investigación histórica* 26, no.1 (2009): 193–211.

Schäfer, Ernst. *El Consejo Real y Supremo de las Indias. Su historia, organización y labor administrativa hasta la terminación de la Casa de Austria.* 2 vols. Sevilla: M. Carmona, 1935.

Schreffler, Michael. *The Art of Allegiance: Visual Culture and Imperial Power in Baroque New Spain.* University Park: Pennsylvania State University Press, 2007.

Schwaller, John F. "*Alcalde* vs. *Mayor*: Translating the Colonial World." *The Americas* 69, no.3 (2013): 391–400.

Schwaller, John F. "Fr. Agustín de Vetancurt: The 'Via crucis en mexicano.'" *The Americas* 74, no.2 (2017): 119–137.

Schwaller, Robert C. "'For Honor and Defence': Race and the Right to Bear Arms in Early Colonial Mexico." *Colonial Latin American Historical Review* 21, no.2 (2012): 239–266.

Schwaller, Robert C. *Géneros de Gente in Early Colonial Mexico: Defining Racial Difference*. Norman: University of Oklahoma Press, 2016.

Schwartz, Stuart B. "Cities of Empire: Mexico and Bahia in the Sixteenth Century." *Journal of Inter-American Studies* 11, no.4 (1969): 616–637.

Sedano, Francisco. *Noticias de México*. 2nd ed. 3 vols. México: Secretaría de Obras y Servicios, 1974. 1880.

Seijas, Tatiana. *Asian Slaves in Colonial Mexico: From Chinos to Indians*. New York: Cambridge University Press, 2014.

Seijas, Tatiana. "Inns, Mules, and Hardtack for the Voyage: The Local Economy of the Manila Galleon in Mexico." *Colonial Latin American Review* 25, no.1 (2016): 56–76.

Seijas, Tatiana. "The Royal Road of the Interior in New Spain: Indigenous Commerce and Political Action." In *The Oxford Handbook of Borderlands of the Iberian World*, edited by Danna A. Levin Rojo and Cynthia Radding. New York: Oxford University Press, 2019.

Seijas, Tatiana, and Pablo Miguel Sierra Silva. "The Persistence of the Slave Market in Seventeenth-Century Central Mexico." *Slavery & Abolition: A Journal of Slave and Post-Slave Studies* 37, no.2 (2016): 307–333.

Seijas, Tatiana, and Dana Velasco Murillo. "Introduction." *Colonial Latin American Review* 30, no.4 (2021): 485–497. A new mining and minting history for the Americas.

Serna Nasser, Bruno de la. "Apuntes sobre el Biombo del Palacio de los Virreyes: posibilidades en torno a su mecenazgo y representación." *Anales del Museo de América* 25 (2017): 162–177.

Sierra Silva, Pablo Miguel. *Urban Slavery in Colonial Mexico: Puebla de los Ángeles, 1531–1706*. New York: Cambridge University Press, 2018.

Sierra Silva, Pablo Miguel. "Portuguese *Encomenderos de Negros* and the Slave Trade within Mexico, 1600–1675." *Journal of Global Slavery* 2, no.3 (2017): 221–247.

Sigaut, Nelly. "Al servicio del virrey de España en el siglo XVII." In *Arte y vida cotidiana en el Mundo Hispánico. Entre lo sacro y lo profano*, edited by Paula Revenga Domínguez, 223–242. Michoacán: Colegio de Michoacán, 2017.

Silva Prada, Natalia. "Impacto de la migración urbana en el proceso de 'separación de repúblicas.' El caso de dos parroquias indígenas de la parcialidad de San Juan Tenochtitlán, 1688–1692." *Estudios de Historia Novohispana* 24 (2001): 77–109.

Simmel, Georg. *The Philosophy of Money*. London: Routledge, 1978. 1907.

Smith, Robert S. "Sales Taxes in New Spain, 1575–1770." *Hispanic American Historical Review* 28, no.1 (1948): 2–37.

Smith, Sabrina. "African-Descended Women: Power and Social Status in Colonial Oaxaca, 1660–1680." *The Americas* 80, no.4 (2023): 569–598.

Soberanes Fernández, José Luis. *Los Tribunales de la Nueva España: Antología*. México: UNAM, 1980.

Soberanes Fernández, José Luis, and Manuel Andreu Gálvez, eds. *500 años de historia de la ciudad de México. Estudio histórico-jurídico con motivo del quinto centenario de la fundación de la ciudad de México.* Pamplona: Ediciones Universidad de Navarra, 2021.

Solano, Francisco de. *Las voces de la ciudad: México a través de sus impresos (1539–1821).* Madrid: CSIC, 1994.

Somolinos d'Ardois, Germán. *El viaje del Doctor Francisco Hernandez por la Nueva España.* México: Anales del Instituto de Biología, 1952.

Somolinos d'Ardois, Germán. "Vida y obra de Alonso López de Hinojosos." In *Suma y recopilación de cirugía con un arte para sangrar muy útil y provechosa,* 1–46. México: Academia Nacional de Medicina, 1977.

Soriano, Manuel. "Algunos apuntes sobre el Protomedicato." *Gaceta Médica de México* 36, no.10 (1899): 563–589.

Sousa, Lisa. "Rebellious Women." In *The Woman Who Turned Into a Jaguar, and Other Narratives of Native Women in Archives of Colonial Mexico,* 262–295. Stanford: Stanford University Press, 2017.

Spanoghe, Sander. "Los salarios dentro del sistema del repartimiento forzoso en el Valle de México, 1549–1632." *Anuario de Estudios Americanos* 54, no.1 (1997): 43–64.

Stanley, Amy. "Maidservants' Tales: Narrating Domestic and Global History in Eurasia, 1600–1900." *The American Historical Review* 121, no.2 (2016): 437–460.

Suárez Argüello, Clara Elena. "Los arrieros novohispanos." In *Trabajo y sociedad en la historia de México: siglos XVI–XVIII,* edited by Gloria Artís, Brígida Von Mentz, Luz María Mohar Betancourt, Beatriz Scharrer Tamm and Clara Elena Suárez Argüello, 75–145. México: CIESAS, 1992.

Suárez Argüello, Clara Elena. *Camino real y carrera larga: la arriería en la Nueva España durante el siglo XVIII.* México: CIESAS, 1997.

Tenorio-Trillo, Mauricio. *I Speak of the City: Mexico City at the Turn of the Twentieth Century.* Chicago: University of Chicago Press, 2012.

TePaske, John Jay. "New World Mintage: México, Santo Domingo, Lima, and Potosí." In *A New World of Gold and Silver,* edited by Kendall W. Brown, 213–259. Leiden: Brill, 2010.

Terraciano, Kevin. "Introduction: An Encyclopedia of Nahua Culture, Context and Content." In *The Florentine Codex: An Encyclopedia of the Nahua World in Sixteenth-Century Mexico,* edited by Jeanette Favrot Peterson and Kevin Terraciano, 1–18. Austin: University of Texas Press, 2019.

Terrazas Williams, Danielle. *The Capital of Free Women: Race, Legitimacy, and Liberty in Colonial Mexico.* New Haven: Yale University Press, 2022.

Torre Revello, José. *El gremio de plateros en las Indias occidentales.* Buenos Aires: Imprenta de la Universidad, 1932.

Tortorici, Zeb. *Sins against Nature: Sex and Archives in Colonial New Spain.* Durham: Duke University Press, 2018.

Toussaint, Manuel. *La Catedral de México y el sagrario metropolitano: su historia, su tesoro, su arte.* México: Porrúa, 1973.

Toussaint, Manuel, Federico Gómez de Orozco, and Justino Fernández. *Planos de la ciudad de México: siglos XVI y XVII, estudio histórico, urbanístico y bibliográfico*. México: UNAM, 1938.

Townsend, Camilla. *Annals of Native America: How the Nahuas of Colonial Mexico Kept their History Alive*. New York: Oxford University Press, 2017.

Townsend, Camilla. *Fifth Sun: A New History of the Aztecs*. New York: Oxford University Press, 2019.

Trens, Manuel B. "Los coches en la ciudad de México." *Boletín del Archivo General de la Nación* 25, no.4 (1954): 538–587.

Valerio, Miguel A. "'Rebel Black Kings (and Queens)'?: Race, Colonial Psychosis, and Afro-Mexican Kings and Queens." In *Sovereign Joy: Afro-Mexican Kings and Queens, 1539–1640*, 80–125. New York: Cambridge University Press, 2022.

Valle Pavón, Guillermina del. "Disputa entre los consulados de Cádiz y México por los mercados de Nueva España, fines del siglo XVII y primeras décadas del siglo XVIII." *Trocadero* 21–22 (2010): 265–282.

Valle Pavón, Guillermina del. "Bases del poder de los mercaderes de plata de la ciudad de México. Redes, control del Consulado y de la Casa de Moneda a fines del siglo XVII." *Anuario de Estudios Americanos* 68, no.2 (2011): 565–598.

Valle Pavón, Guillermina del, ed. *Contrabando y redes de negocios: Hispanoamérica en el comercio global, 1610–1814*. México: Instituto Mora, 2023.

Valle-Arizpe, Artemio de. *Notas de platería*. México: Editorial Polis, 1941.

Vallen, Nino. *Being the Heart of the World: The Pacific and the Fashioning of the Self in New Spain, 1513–1641*. New York: Cambridge University Press, 2023.

Varey, Simon, Rafael Chabrán, and Dora B. Weiner, eds. *Searching for the Secrets of Nature: The Life and Works of Dr. Francisco Hernández*. Stanford: Stanford University Press, 2000.

Vásquez de Warman, Irene. "El pósito y la alhóndiga en la Nueva España." *Historia Mexicana* 17, no.3 (1968): 395–426.

Vásquez, Genaro V., ed. *Legislación del trabajo en los siglos xvi, xvii y xviii*. México: D.A.P.P., 1938.

Velasco Murillo, Dana. *Urban Indians in a Silver City: Zacatecas, Mexico, 1546–1810*. Stanford: Stanford University Press, 2016.

Velázquez Gutiérrez, María Elisa. *Mujeres de origen africano en la capital novohispana, siglos XVII y XVIII*. México: INAH, 2006.

Vilar, Pierre. *A History of Gold and Money, 1450–1920*. London: NLB, 1976. 1972.

Vilches, Elvira. "Trade, Silver, and Print Culture in the Colonial Americas." *Journal of Latin American Cultural Studies* 24, no.3 (2015): 315–334.

Vinson III, Ben. *Before Mestizaje: The Frontiers of Race and Caste in Colonial Mexico*. New York: Cambridge University Press, 2018.

Vries, Jan de. "Playing with Scales: The Global and the Micro, the Macro and the Nano." *Past & Present* 242, no.1 (2019): 23–36.

Walker, Tamara J. *Exquisite Slaves: Race, Clothing, and Status in Colonial Lima*. Cambridge: Cambridge University Press, 2017.

Wesp, Julie K. "Working in the City: An Historical Bioarchaeology of Activity in Urban New Spain." *Historical Archaeology* 54, no.1 (2020): 92–109.

Wheat, David. "Biafadas in Havana: West African Antecedents for Caribbean Social Interactions." In *The Spanish Caribbean and the Atlantic World in the Long Sixteenth Century*, edited by Ida Altman and David Wheat, 163–186, Lincoln: University of Nebraska, 2019.

Yannakakis, Yanna. *Since Time Immemorial: Native Custom and Law in Colonial Mexico*. Durham: Duke University Press, 2023.

Yun-Casalilla, Bartolomé. *Iberian World Empires and the Globalization of Europe 1415–1668*. Singapore: Palgrave Macmillan, 2019.

Zárate Sánchez, Edén Mario. *Catálogos de documentos de arte, Archivo de Notarías de la ciudad de México: protocolos III*. México: UNAM, 2004.

Zedillo Castillo, Antonio. *Hospital Real de Naturales: Historia de un hospital*. México: IMSS, 1984.

Zupko, Ronald E. *British Weights & Measures: A History from Antiquity to the Seventeenth Century*. Madison: University of Wisconsin Press, 1977.

# Index

Page numbers in *italics* refer to figures, and page numbers followed by 'n' refer to endnotes.

Printed by Integrated Books International,
United States of America